OiL PAN REMOVA

PG 81

CHILTON'S Repair and Tune-Up Guide

Ford Vans

1966–77

ILLUSTRATED

Prepared by the

Automotive Editorial Department

Chilton Book Company

Chilton Way

Radnor, Pa. 19089

215–687-8200

president and chief executive officer **WILLIAM A. BARBOUR;** executive vice president **RICHARD H. GROVES;** vice president and general manager **JOHN P. KUSHNERICK;** managing editor **KERRY A. FREEMAN, S.A.E.;** senior editor **RICHARD J. RIVELE;** editor **ROBERT J. BROWN**

CHILTON BOOK COMPANY　　　　RADNOR, PENNSYLVANIA

Copyright © 1977 by Chilton Book Company
All rights reserved
Published in Radnor, Pa., by Chilton Book Company
and simultaneously in Ontario, Canada,
by Thomas Nelson & Sons, Ltd.

Manufactured in the United States of America

67890   65432109

Chilton's Repair & Tune-Up Guide: Ford Vans 1966–77
ISBN 0-8019-6585-3 pbk.

Library of Congress Catalog Card No. 76-57320

SAFETY NOTICE

Proper service and repair procedures are vital to the safe, reliable operation of all motor vehicles, as well as the personal safety of those performing repairs. This book outlines procedures for servicing and repairing vehicles using safe, effective methods. The procedures contain many NOTES, CAUTIONS and WARNINGS which should be followed along with standard safety procedures to eliminate the possibility of personal injury or improper service which could damage the vehicle or compromise its safety.

It is important to note that repair procedures and techniques, tools and parts for servicing motor vehicles, as well as the skill and experience of the individual performing the work vary widely. It is not possible to anticipate all of the conceivable ways or conditions under which vehicles may be serviced, or to provide cautions as to all of the possible hazards that may result. Standard and accepted safety precautions and equipment should be used when handling toxic or flammable fluids, and safety goggles or other protection should be used during cutting, grinding, chiseling, prying, or any other process that can cause material removal or projectiles.

Some procedures require the use of tools specially designed for a specific purpose. Before substituting another tool or procedure, you must be completely satisfied that neither your personal safety, nor the performance of the vehicle will be endangered.

Contents

Chapter 1

General Information, Lubrication, and Maintenance

Introduction

The first Ford Van vehicles, the Falcon Club Wagon and the Econoline Van and Pickup, were introduced in 1961.

This book covers all 1966 through 1977 models. There are Club Wagons, the windowed passenger models, and Econolines, the work and play vans. There are Econoline Display Vans with windows on the curb side and rear, and Window Vans with the same glass arrangement as Club Wagons. There are also cab-only cutaway vans, supplied to motor home and specialty manufacturers. Engines covered are the 170, 240, and 300 cubic inch sixes and the 302, 351, and 460 V8s. The 170 was last used in 1970, and the 240 and 302 were dropped after 1974.

The most significant change in van design since their innovation was brought out by Ford in mid-1975 with the distinctive, longer-nosed, body-on-frame construction van which gives marked improvements in durability, load capacity, handling, safety, comfort, and serviceability.

Serial Number Identification

VEHICLE

The vehicle identification plate is located on the lock face panel of the left front door. There are three lines of information on the plate, which consists of arrangements of letters and numbers.

The first line from the top is the warranty number, which is a code that identifies the series of vehicle, the engine, the assembly plant, and the numerical sequence in which the vehicle was built.

The second line of numbers contains codes that identify the wheelbase (in.), color, model code, trim code, body type

Vehicle Identification Chart

Code Letter	Assembly Plant	Code Letter	Assembly Plant
C	Ontario	N	Norfolk
D	Dallas	P	Twin Cities
E	Mawah	R	San Jose
H	Lorain	S	(Pilot Plant) Allen Park
K	Kansas City	U	Louisville
L	Michigan Truck	V	Kentucky Truck

Assembly plant codes

1

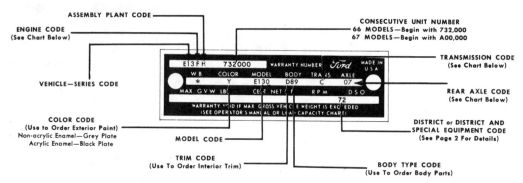

The vehicle identification plate for 1966–67 Falcon Club Wagon and Econoline

ENGINE CODES

CODE	CYL.	C.I.D.	CARB. VENTURI
A	6	240	1V
F	6	170	1V

*—NOT SHOWN ON FALCON CLUB WAGON AND ECONOLINE

TRANSMISSION CODES

CODE	TRANSMISSION TYPE
C	3-Speed Manual
G	H.D. Cruise-O-Matic

REAR AXLE CODES

REGULAR	RATIO	RATING	LOCKING
01	3.50:1	2300 lb.	—
02	4.00:1	2300 lb.	—
07	3.00:1	3050 lb.	A7
11	3.50:1	3050 lb.	B1
12	4.11:1	3050 lb.	B2
13	4.57:1	3050 lb.	B3

Engine, transmission, and rear axle codes for 1966–67 Falcon Club Wagon and Econoline

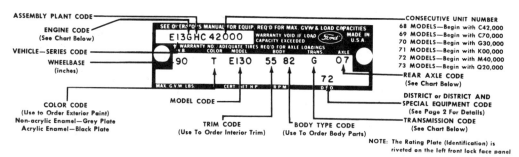

The vehicle identification plate for 1968–77 Econolines and Club Wagons

NOTE: The Rating Plate (Identification) is riveted on the left front lock face panel

ENGINE CODES

CODE	CYL.	CID	CARB. VENTURI	CODE	CYL.	CID	CARB. VENTURI
A	6	240 (68-73)	1V	G	8	302 (69-73)	2V
F	6	170 (68-70)	1V	N	8	289 (68)	2V
B	6	300 (73)	1V	1*	6	240 (73)	1V

*1973 Low Compression Engine.

TRANSMISSION CODES

CODE	TRANSMISSION TYPE
C	3-Speed Manual Shift
G	3-Speed Cruise-O-Matic

REAR AXLE CODES

REGULAR CODES	RATIO	RATING	LOCKING CODES	REGULAR CODES	RATIO	RATING	LOCKING CODES
07 (68-71)	3.00:1	3050 lb.	—	31 (68-71)	3.54:1	4800 lb.	C1 (68-71)
10	3.25:1	3050 lb.	—	33 (68-71)	3.73:1	4800 lb.	C3 (68-71)
11	3.50:1	3050 lb.	—	35 (68-71)	4.10:1	4800 lb.	C5 (68-71)
12 (72-73)	3.70:1	3050 lb.	—	36 (68-71)	4.56:1	4800 lb.	C6 (68-71)
12 (68-70)	4.11:1	3050 lb.	—	71 (71-73)	3.54:1	5050 lb.	—
13 (68-70)	4.57:1	3050 lb.	—	72 (71-73)	3.73:1	5050 lb.	—
17	3.25:1	3300 lb.	—	73 (71-73)	4.10:1	5050 lb.	—
08	3.50:1	3300 lb.	—	74 (68-71)	4.56:1	5050 lb.	—
05	4.11:1	3300 lb.	—	—	3.54:1	5050 lb.	G1 (71-73)
06 (68-71)	4.57:1	3300 lb.	—	—	3.73:1	5050 lb.	G2 (1971)
09 (72-73)	3.70:1	3300 lb.	—	—	4.10:1	5050 lb.	G3 (71-73)

Engine (1968–74), transmission and rear axle (1968–77) codes code, transmission code and the rear axle code.

The third line gives the maximum gross vehicle weight (GVW) in lbs., the certified net horsepower @ rpm (thru 1972), and the D.S.O. number, which is the district to which the vehicle was delivered and if applicable, the sequential number of that particular vehicle having specially-ordered, factory-installed equipment.

E	Econoline	
	Basic Series	
	100 Series	
E-11	E-100 Club Wagon	
E-12	E-100 Custom Club Wagon	
E-13	E-100 Chateau Wagon	
E-14	E-100 Regular Van	
E-15	E-100 Window Van	
E-16	E-100 Display Van	
	200 Series	
E-21	E-200 Club Wagon	
E-22	E-200 Custom Club Wagon	
E-23	E-200 Chateau Wagon	
E-24	E-200 Regular Van	
E-25	E-200 Window Van	
E-26	E-200 Display Van	
	Bus Models	
E-27	E-200 Standard	
E-28	E-200 Custom	
E-29	E-200 Chateau	
E-30	Camper	
	300 Series	
E-31	E-300 Club Wagon	
E-32	E-300 Custom Club Wagon	
E-33	E-300 Chateau Wagon	
E-34	E-300 Regular Van	
E-35	E-300 Window Van	
E-36	E-300 Display Van	
	Bus Models	
E-37	E-300 Standard	
E-38	E-300 Custom	
E-39	Chateau	

1968–74 Model codes

ENGINE

The engine identification tag identifies the cubic inch displacement of the engine, the model year, the year and month in which the engine was built, where it was built and the change level number. The change level is usually the number one (1), unless there are parts on the engine that will not be completely in-

E	Econoline	
	100 Series	
E-01	E-100 Club Wagon 5 Passenger	
E-02	E-100 Club Wagon 8 Passenger	
E-04	E-100 Cargo Van	
E-05	E-100 Window Van	
E-06	E-100 Display Van	
	150 Series	
E-11	E-150 Club Wagon 5 Passenger	
E-12	E-150 Club Wagon 8 Passenger	
E-14	E-150 Cargo Van	
E-15	E-150 Window Van	
E-16	E-150 Display Van	
	250 Series	
E-21	E-250 Club Wagon 5 Passenger	
E-22	E-250 Club Wagon 8 Passenger	
E-23	E-250 Club Wagon 12 Passenger	
E-24	E-250 Cargo Van	
E-25	E-250 Window Van	
E-26	E-250 Display Van	
E-27	E-250 Cutaway	
E-28	E-250 Cutaway (Parcel)	
	350 Series	
E-34	E-350 Cargo Van	
E-35	E-350 Window Van	
E-36	E-350 Display Van	
E-37	E-350 Cutaway	
E-38	E-350 Cutaway (Parcel)	

1974–77 model codes

B	300-1V	6
H	351-2V	8
A	460-4V	8

1974–77 engine codes

terchangeable and will require minor modification.

The engine identification tag is located under the ignition coil attaching bolt.

TRANSMISSION

The transmission identification number is located on a metal tag or plate attached to the case or it is stamped directly on the transmission case.

Routine Maintenance

See the Maintenance Intervals Chart for the recommended intervals for the operations in this section.

AIR CLEANER

An oil bath air cleaner was standard equipment on all engines in 1966 and 1967. The oil bath unit was optional on some later models. All 1968 and later engines came equipped with a paper element type air cleaner.

The procedure for cleaning an oil bath air cleaner and refilling the reservoir is as follows:

1. Unlock and open the engine compartment cover.
2. Remove the carburetor-to-air cleaner retaining wing nut. On a closed crankcase ventilation equipped engine, loosen the hose clamp at the air cleaner body and disconnect the hose. On the 240 and 300 six engine, remove the bolts securing the air cleaner body to the support brackets.
3. Remove the air cleaner assembly from the engine. Be careful not to spill the oil out of the air cleaner.
4. Remove the cover and drain the oil from the reservoir. Wash all of the air cleaner parts in a suitable cleaning solvent. Dry all of the parts with compressed air, or allow them to air dry.
5. Inspect the gasket between the oil reservoir chamber and the air cleaner body. Replace the gasket as necessary.
6. Saturate the filter element with clean engine oil.
7. Fill the oil reservoir to the full mark with engine oil. Use SAE 30 above 32°F and SAE 20 for lower temperatures.
8. Replace the air cleaner assembly on the carburetor and tighten the wing nut.

NOTE: *Check the air filter more often if the vehicle is operated under severe dusty conditions and replace or clean it as necessary.*

The procedure for replacing the paper air cleaner element is as follows:

1. Unlock and open the engine compartment cover.
2. Remove the wing nut holding the air cleaner assembly to the top of the carburetor.
3. Disconnect the crankcase ventilation hose at the air cleaner and remove the entire air cleaner assembly from the carburetor.
4. Remove and discard the old filter element, and inspect the condition of the air cleaner mounting gasket. Replace the gasket as necessary.

5. Install the air cleaner body on the carburetor so that the word FRONT faces toward the front of the vehicle.
6. Place the new filter element in the air cleaner body and install the cover and tighten the wing nut. If the word TOP appears on the element, make sure that the side the word appears on is facing up when the element is in place.
7. Connect the crankcase ventilation hose to the air cleaner.

PCV VALVE

Check the PCV valve to see if it is free and not gummed up, stuck or blocked. To check the valve, remove it from the engine and work the valve by sticking a screwdriver in the crankcase side of the valve. It should move. It is possible to clean the PCV valve by soaking it in a solvent and blowing it out with compressed air. This can restore the valve to some level of operating order. This should be used only as an emergency measure. Otherwise the valve should be replaced.

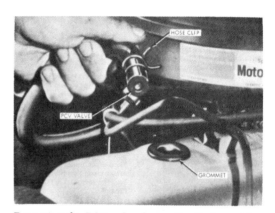

Removing the PCV valve from a 6 cylinder engine

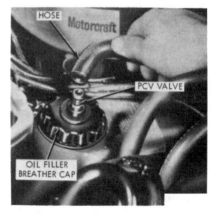

Removing the PCV valve from a V8 engine

FLUID LEVEL CHECKS

Engine Oil

Check the engine oil level every time you fill the gas tank. The oil level should be above the ADD mark and not above the FULL mark on the dipstick. Make sure that the dipstick is inserted into the crankcase as far as possible and that the vehicle is resting on level ground.

NOTE: *Don't check the level immediately after stopping the engine; wait a few minutes to let the oil drain back into the pan.*

Transmission

MANUAL

Before checking the lubricant level in the transmission, make sure that the vehicle is on level ground. Remove the fill plug from the right-side of the transmission. Remove the plug slowly when it starts to reach the end of the threads on the plug. Hold the plug up against the hole and move it away slowly. This is so as to minimize the loss of lubricant through the fill hole. The level of the lubricant should be up to the bottom of the fill hole. If lubricant is not present at the bottom of the fill hole, add SAE 90 or 80 transmission lube until it reaches the proper level. A suction gun is used to fill a manual transmission with lubricant.

AUTOMATIC TRANSMISSION

The fluid level in an automatic transmission is checked when the transmission is at operating temperatures. If the vehicle has been sitting and is cold, drive it at highway speeds for at least 20 minutes to warm the transmission.

1. With the transmission in Park, the engine running at idle speed, the foot brakes applied and the vehicle resting on level ground, move the transmission gear selector through each of the gear positions, including Reverse, allowing time for the transmission to engage. Return the shift selector to the Park position and apply the parking brake. Do not turn the engine off; leave it running at idle speed.

2. Clean all dirt from around the transmission dipstick cap and the end of the filler tube.

3. Pull the dipstick out of the tube, wipe it off with a clean cloth, and push it back into the tube all the way, making sure that it seats completely.

4. Pull the dipstick out of the tube again and read the level of the fluid on the stick. The level should be between the ADD mark and the FULL mark. If fluid must be added, add enough fluid through the tube to raise the level up to between the ADD and FULL marks. Do not overfill the transmission because this will cause foaming, loss of fluid through the vent, and malfunctioning of the transmission. Use type F transmission fluid (Ford Spec. ESW-M2C33-F) in all C4 and C6 transmissions through 1976. Use the new type fluid (Ford Spec. ESP-M2C138-CJ) in 1977 C6 transmissions.

Brake Master Cylinder

The master cylinder is located under the floor pan on the right (driver's) side on 1966 and 1967 models. It is accessible by removing the attaching screws holding an access plate to the floor and removing the plate.

On 1968 and later model Ford vans, the brake master cylinder is located under the hood on the driver's side.

Before removing the master cylinder reservoir cap, make sure that the vehicle is resting on level ground and clean all dirt away from the top of the master cylinder. Pry off the retaining clip or unscrew the cap. The brake fluid level should be within ¼ in. of the top of the reservoir on both single and dual type master cylinders.

If the level of the brake fluid is less than half the volume of the reservoir, it is advised that you check the brake hydraulic system for leaks. Leaks most commonly occur at the wheel cylinder.

On some 1968 and later models there is a rubber diaphragm in the top of the master cylinder cap. As the fluid level drops in the reservoir due to normal brake shoe wear or leakage, the diaphragm takes up the space. This is to prevent the loss of brake fluid out the vented cap and con-

o ○ADD ▷◀━━▶○ DONT ADD IF BETWEEN ARROWS   CHECK WHEN HOT & IDLING IN PARK

Automatic transmission dipstick

tamination by dirt. After filling the master cylinder to the proper level with brake fluid, but before replacing the cap, fold the rubber diaphragm up into the cap, then replace the cap on the reservoir and snap the retaining clip into place.

When replacing the screw-on cap on pre-1968 models, make sure that the gasket is in good condition and properly in place on the cap. If it is cracked or damaged in any way, it should be replaced.

Coolant

The coolant level should be maintained at 2 in. below the bottom of the radiator filler neck when the engine is cold and 1 in. below the bottom of the filler neck when the engine is hot.

For best protection against freezing and overheating, maintain an approximate 50% water and 50% antifreeze mixture in the cooling system.

Avoid using water that is known to have a high alkaline content or is very hard, except in emergency cases. Drain and flush the cooling system as soon as possible after using such water.

CAUTION: *Cover the radiator cap with a thick cloth before removing it from a radiator in a vehicle that is hot. Turn the cap counterclockwise slowly until pressure can be heard escaping. Allow all pressure to escape from the radiator before completely removing the radiator cap.*

Rear Axle

Clean the area around the fill plug before removing the plug. The lubricant level should be maintained to the bottom of the fill hole with the vehicle level. If lubricant does not appear at the hole when the plug is removed, additional lubricant should be added. Use hypoid gear lubricant SAE 80 or 90.

NOTE: *Limited-slip rear axles require that a special additive be used along with the hypoid lubricant. If it isn't used, the result will be noise and rough operation.*

Steering Gear

The steering gear is located under the floor, on the left-side at the end of the steering shaft.

The procedure for checking and add-

ing lubricant to pre-1969 models is as follows:

1. Remove the floor mat and the steering gear access plate.
2. Remove the steering gear housing filler plug.
3. With a clean punch break the bubble which will be formed so that you can read the true lubricant level.
4. Slowly turn the steering wheel to the left stop. If the lubricant rises within the filler plug hole as the wheel turns, there is sufficient lubricant in the gear. Skip Steps 5 through 7 and proceed with Step 8. If the lubricant does not rise in the hole, perform the following Steps.
5. Turn the steering gear to the right stop in order to position the sector shaft teeth away from the filler plug hole.
6. Remove the cover-to-housing (top) retaining bolt.
7. Fill the gear through the filler plug hole until lubricant comes out of the cover bolt hole. Install the cover retaining bolt.
8. Install the filler plug, the steering gear access plate, and the floor mat.

The procedure for checking and adding lubricant to 1969–74 models is as follows:

1. Remove the steering gear housing filler plug.
2. With a clean punch or similar instrument, clean out or push the loose lubricant into the filler plug hole.
3. Turn the steering wheel to the left. Then turn the steering wheel slowly to the right until the linkage reaches the stop. Lubricant should rise in the filler plug hole. If lubricant does not rise in the filler plug hole, add to the supply.

The location of the steering gear does not allow any clearance for the removal of a cover bolt to create a vent. To prevent air from being trapped and forming pockets in the housing while lubricant is being added, it is suggested that a curved length of 1/4 in. tubing be adapted to the end of the grease gun being used. This tube should be inserted into the filler hole and extend down toward the bottom of the housing cavity. By this method, the lower housing cavity will fill first and as lubricant is added, air will be expelled upward and out the fill hole.

To add lubricant, turn the steering wheel to the extreme left to position the ball nut away from the filler plug hole and fill the steering gear by the method described above until the lubricant rises in the filler plug hole.

NOTE: *The steering gear on 1975–77 models is permanently lubricated. No service is required unless solid grease (not an oily film) is escaping.*

Power Steering Reservoir

Position the vehicle on level ground. Run the engine until the fluid is at normal operating temperature. Turn the steering wheel all the way to the left and right several times. Position the wheels in the straight-ahead position, then shut off the engine. Check the fluid level on the dipstick which is attached to the reservoir cap. The level should be between the ADD and FULL marks on the dipstick, and at the FULL-HOT line on later models. Add fluid accordingly. Do not overfill. Use power steering fluid.

WHEEL BEARINGS

Packing and Adjustment

Before handling the bearings there are a few things that you should remember to do and try to avoid.

DO the following:

1. Remove all outside dirt from the housing before exposing the bearing.

2. Treat a used bearing as gently as you would a new one.

3. Work with clean tools in clean surroundings.

4. Use clean, dry canvas gloves, or at least clean, dry hands.

5. Clean solvents and flushing fluids are a must.

6. Use clean paper when laying out the bearings to dry.

7. Protect disassembled bearings from rust and dirt. Cover them up.

8. Use clean rags to wipe bearings.

9. Keep the bearing in oil-proof paper when they are to be stored or are not in use.

10. Clean the inside of the housing before replacing the bearing.

Do NOT do the following:

1. Don't work in dirty surroundings.

2. Don't use dirty, chipped, or damaged tools.

3. Try not to work on wooden work benches or use wooden mallets.

4. Don't handle bearings with dirty or moist hands.

5. Do not use gasoline for cleaning; use a safe solvent.

6. Do not spin-dry bearings with compressed air. They will be damaged.

7. Do not spin unclean bearings.

8. Avoid using cotton waste or dirty cloths to wipe bearings.

9. Try not to scratch or nick bearing surfaces.

10. Do not allow the bearing to come in contact with dirt or rust at any time.

FRONT

To remove the wheel bearings from the front hubs:

1. Jack the van up until the wheel to be serviced is off the ground and can spin freely. It is easier to check all the bearings at the same time. If the equipment needed is available, raise the front end of the van so that both front wheels are off the ground. Use jackstands or suitable blocks to support the vehicle. Make sure that the van is completely stable before proceeding any further.

2. Remove the lug nuts and remove the wheel/tire assembly from the hub. It is possible to remove the hub assembly from the spindle with the wheel/tire assembly still attached, but the added weight makes handling of the entire assembly a little clumsy which could result in possible damage to the bearings or spindle. Remove the caliper assembly on disc brakes. See Chapter 9 for details.

3. Remove the grease cap with a screwdriver or pliers.

Removing the grease cap

4. Remove the cotter pin and discard it. Cotter pins should never be reused.

5. Remove the nut lock, adjusting nut, and washer from the spindle.

6. Wiggle the hub so that the outer

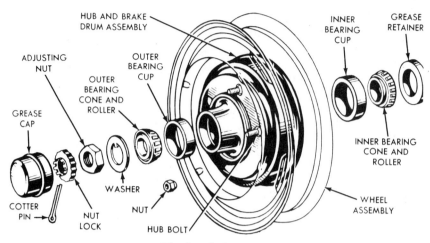

HUB AND BRAKE DRUM ASSEMBLY

INNER BEARING CUP

GREASE RETAINER

ADJUSTING NUT

OUTER BEARING CUP

OUTER BEARING CONE AND ROLLER

GREASE CAP

INNER BEARING CONE AND ROLLER

COTTER PIN

NUT LOCK

WASHER

NUT

HUB BOLT

WHEEL ASSEMBLY

The front hub assembly

wheel bearing comes loose and can be removed. Remove the outer bearing.

7. Remove the hub from the spindle and place it on a work surface, supported by two blocks of wood under the brake drum.

NOTE: *If the drum brake hub will not come off easily, back off the brake shoe adjustment screw so that the shoes do not contact the brake drum.*

8. Place a block of wood or drift pin through the spindle hole and tap out the inner grease seal. Tap lightly so not to damage the bearing. When the seal falls out, so will the inner bearing. Discard the seal.

Perform the above procedures to all the wheels that are going to be serviced.

9. Place all of the bearings, nuts, nut locks, washers and grease caps in a container of solvent. Use a light soft brush to thoroughly clean each part. Make sure that every bit of dirt and grease is rinsed off, then place each cleaned part on an absorbent cloth or paper and allow them to dry completely.

10. Clean the inside of the hub, including the bearing races, and the spindle. Remove all traces of old lubricant from these components.

11. Inspect the bearings for pitting, flat spots, rust, and rough areas. Check the races in the hub and the spindle for the same defects and rub them clean with a cloth that has been soaked in solvent. If the races show hairline cracks or worn shiny areas, they must be replaced. The races are installed in the hub with a press fit and are removed by driving them out

with a suitable punch or drift. Place the new races squarely onto the hub and place a block of wood over them. Drive the race into place with a hammer, striking the block of wood. Never hit the race with any metal object.

Replacement seals, bearings, and other required parts can be bought at an auto parts store. The old parts should be taken along to be compared with the replacement parts to ensure a perfect match.

12. Pack the wheel bearings with grease. There are special devices made for the specific purpose of greasing bearings, but if one is not available, pack the wheel bearings by hand. Put a large dab of grease in the palm of your hand and push the bearing through it with a sliding motion. The grease must be forced through the side of the bearing and in between each roller. Continue until the grease begins to ooze out the other side and through the gaps between the rollers; the bearing must be completely packed with grease.

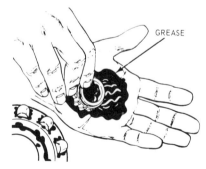

GREASE

Packing the wheel bearings with grease by hand

NOTE: *Sodium based grease is not compatible with lithium based grease. Be careful not to mix the two types. The best way to prevent this is to completely clean all of the old grease from the hub and spindle before installing any new grease.*

13. Turn the hub assembly over so that the inner side faces up, making sure that the race and inner area are clean, and drop the inner wheel bearing into place. Using a hammer and a block of wood, tap the new grease seal in place. Never hit the seal with the hammer directly. Move the block of wood around the circumference until it is properly seated.

Installing the grease seal

14. Slide the hub assembly onto the spindle and push it as far as it will go, making sure that it has completely covered the brake shoes. Keep the hub centered on the spindle to prevent damage to the grease seal and the spindle threads.

15. Place the outer wheel bearing in place over the spindle. Press it in until it is snug. Place the washer on the spindle after the bearing. Screw on the spindle nut and turn it down until a slight binding is felt.

16. With a torque wrench, tighten the nut to 17–25 ft lbs to seat the bearings. Install the nut lock over the nut so that the cotter pin hole in the spindle is aligned with a slot in the nut lock. Back off the adjusting nut and the nut lock two slots of the nut lock and install the cotter pin.

17. Bend the longer of the two ends opposite the looped end out and over the end of the spindle. Trim both ends of the cotter pin just enough so that the grease cap will fit, leaving the bent end shaped over the end of the spindle.

18. Install the grease cap and the wheel/tire assembly. The wheel should

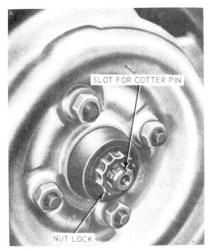

Nut lock installed so that a slot is aligned with cotter pin hole

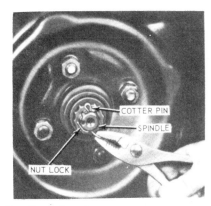

Bending the cotter pin

rotate freely with no noise or noticeable end-play.

19. Adjust the brakes.

REAR

Only the heavy-duty full-floating rear axles require periodic wheel bearing maintenance service. These axles are the Dana (Spicer) 60, 61, and 70 models and can be identified by the large bearing hub protruding through the center of the wheel.

Rear wheel bearing service is not required on any of the semi-floating, lighter-duty, rear axles, unless the axle shafts or bearings are removed. See Chapter 7 for these procedures.

1. Set the parking brake and loosen the axle shaft bolts.

2. Raise the rear wheels off the floor and support the axle housing. Release the parking brake.

3. Remove the axle shaft bolts and

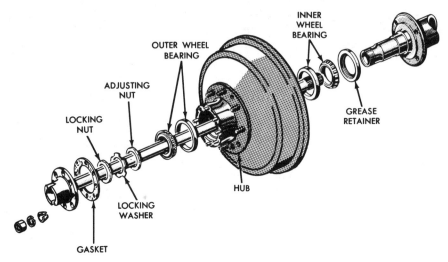

Full-floating rear axle bearings through 1974—this early model retains the axle shaft flange with stud nuts and tapered dowels instead of bolts.

lockwashers. If there are studs with tapered dowels instead of bolts, strike the axle shaft flange in the center to loosen them. Remove the axle shaft and gasket.

4. Pry out the locking wedge from inside the adjusting nut with a screwdriver on 1975–77 models.

5. Remove the locknut, locking washer, and wheel bearing adjusting nut. The locknut and locking washer are used only on models through 1974.

6. Support the wheel so that all load is taken off the bearings. Remove the outer bearing cone and pull the wheel, tire, and hub assembly straight out. One

way this can be done is to rest the tire on a greased board.

7. Clean the axle housing spindle.

8. Use a brass drift to drive the inner bearing cone and seal out of the hub. Clean out the hub. If the bearing cups need replacement, drive them out with the brass drift. Make sure that the new cups are seated squarely by making sure that a .015 in. feeler gauge will not enter beneath the cup.

9. Clean and pack the bearings with grease as described for front wheel bearings. Place the inner bearing in the hub and carefully force in a new seal.

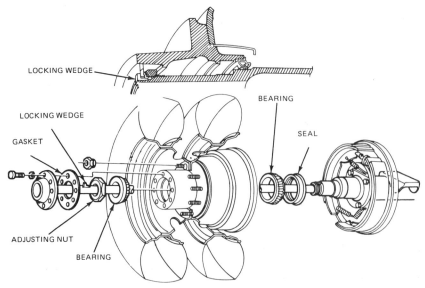

1975–77 full-floating rear axle bearings

10. Tape the spindle threads to prevent damage. Slide the wheel, tire, and hub assembly straight on.

11. Remove the tape and install the outer wheel bearing and adjusting nut. Let the wheel and tire assembly rest on the bearings.

12. Rotate the wheel and tighten the adjusting nut to 50–80 ft lbs. for models through 1974, and to 120–140 ft lbs. for 1975–77.

13. On models through 1974, back the adjusting nut off ⅜ turn. Install a new locking washer coated with axle lube, smooth side out. Install the locknut and tighten it to 90–110 ft lbs.

14. On 1975–77 models, back the adjusting nut off ⅛ to ¼ turn.

15. The wheel assembly should rotate freely; end play should be .001–.010 in. measured with a dial indicator.

16. On 1975–77 models, position the locking wedge in the keyway slot. It must not be bottomed against the shoulder of the nut by about ¼ in. and must not be pressed into a previously cut groove in the nylon retainer.

17. On models through 1974, bend two locking washer tabs in over the adjusting nut, and two tabs out over the locknut.

18. Replace the axle shaft with a new gasket and new lockwashers and retaining bolts, tightened to 40–50 ft lbs.

TIRES AND WHEELS

Ford does not give recommended tire pressures, as such, for all vans. They were issued for models through 1972 with factory-installed tire sizes. They do give very specific load limits for factory-installed tire sizes at specific pressures. The pressure must be adjusted according to the expected maximum load. Make sure not to exceed the maximum pressure marked on the sidewall. Pressures should be checked before driving, since pressure can increase as much as 6 psi due to heat. It is a good idea to have an accurate gauge and to check pressures weekly. Not all gauges on service station pumps are to be trusted. In general, truck-type tires require higher pressures and flotation or car-type tires, lower pressures.

When replacing tires, give some thought to these points, especially if you are switching to larger tires or to another profile series (50, 60, 70, 78):

1. All four tires should be of the same construction type. Radial, bias, or bias-belted tires should not be mixed.

2. The wheels must be the correct width for the tire. Tire dealers have charts of tire and rim compatibility. A mismatch can cause sloppy handling and rapid tread wear. The old rule of thumb is that the tread width should match the rim width (inside bead to inside bead) within an inch. For radial tires, the rim width should be 80% or less of the tire (not tread) width.

3. The height (mounted diameter) of the new tires can greatly change speedometer accuracy, engine speed at a given road speed, fuel mileage, acceleration, and ground clearance. Speedometer drive gears are available to correct the speedometer. Tire manufacturers furnish full measurement specifications.

NOTE: *Dimensions of tires marked the same size may vary significantly, even among tires from the same manufacturer.*

4. The spare tire should be useable, at least for low speed operation, with the new tires.

5. There shouldn't be any body interference when loaded, on bumps, or in turning.

The best way to keep out of major trouble with these points is to stick to tire and wheel sizes available as factory options. Measure carefully if you go outside these sizes; otherwise identical models may vary considerably, even from side to side.

Tire Rotation

Tire rotation is recommended to obtain maximum tire wear. The pattern you use depends on personal preference, the type of tires, and whether you have a useable spare. Radial tires should not be cross-switched; they last longer if their direction of rotation is not changed. Truck type tires sometimes have directional tread indicated by arrows on the sidewalls; the arrow shows the direction of rotation. They will wear rapidly if reversed. Studded snow tires will lose their studs if their direction of rotation is reversed.

NOTE: *Mark the wheel position or direction of rotation on radial or studded tires before removing them for storage.*

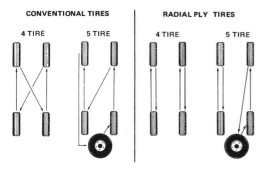

Tire rotation patterns—the radial tire pattern may also be used for bias or bias-belted tires.

CAUTION: *Avoid overtightening the lug nuts or the brake disc or drum may be permanently distorted. Alloy wheels can also be cracked by overtightening. Use of a torque wrench is highly recommended. Tighten the lug nuts in a criss-cross pattern. Recommended torques are:*

1966–77	5 lug		90 ft lbs.
1968–73	8 lug		135 ft lbs.
1974–77	8 lug	E-250	90 ft lbs.
		E-300, 350	135 ft lbs
		E-300, 350 dual wheels	210 ft lbs.

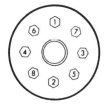

8 LUG WHEEL   5 LUG WHEEL

Lug nut torque sequences

FUEL FILTER

The inline filter is of one-piece construction and cannot be cleaned.

1. Unlock and remove the engine compartment cover. Remove the air cleaner.

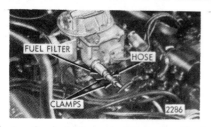

Replacing the fuel filter on a V8 engine. Replacement on a six is similar

2. Loosen the retaining clamp securing the fuel inlet hose to the fuel filter.

3. Unscrew the fuel filter from the carburetor and discard the gasket. Disconnect the fuel filter from the hose and discard the retaining clamp.

4. Install a new clamp on the inlet hose and connect the hose to the filter. Place a new gasket on the new fuel filter and screw the filter into the carburetor inlet port. Tighten the filter.

5. Position the fuel line hose clamp and tighten the clamp securely.

6. Start the engine and check for fuel leaks.

7. Install the air cleaner. Close and lock the engine compartment cover.

BATTERY

Check the fluid level in the battery about once a month and more often in hot and dry weather. The level should be at the bottom of the filler hole. Electrolyte should at least cover the plates.

Tap water can be used to fill the battery, except in areas where the water is known to have a high mineral or alkali content. Use distilled water in these areas.

Corrosion or accumulated dry battery acid can be removed from the terminals with a solution of baking soda or ammonia and water. After cleaning the terminals, flush them with water and coat the terminals with grease to help prevent corrosion. Another trick is to cut a three inch circle of felt with a hole in the middle large enough to fit the felt over the battery terminal. Soak the felt in oil and fasten the cable to the terminal with the felt in place. This also helps to retard corrosion.

Keep in mind that in cold weather the efficiency of the battery is reduced. If you add water to the battery during freezing weather, drive the vehicle for several miles to mix the water with the battery electrolyte.

Pushing, Towing, and Jump Starting

To push start your vehicle, (manual transmission only) follow the procedures below:

Check to make sure that the bumpers of both vehicles are aligned so that neither will be damaged. Be sure that all electrical system components are turned off (headlights, heater blower, etc.). Turn on the ignition switch. Place the shift lever in Third gear and push in the clutch pedal. Have the driver of the other vehicle push your vehicle at a gentle but steadily increased rate of speed. At about 15 mph, signal the driver of the pushing vehicle to fall back, slightly depress the accelerator pedal, and release the clutch pedal slowly. The engine should start.

When you are doing the pushing, make sure that the two bumpers match so that you won't damage the vehicle you are to push. Another good idea is to put an old tire between the two vehicles.

Whenever you are towing another vehicle, make sure that the tow chain or rope is sufficiently long and strong, and that it is securely attached to both vehicles. Attach the chain at a point on the frame or as close to it as possible. Once again, go slowly and tell the other driver to do the same. Warn the other driver not to allow too much slack in the line when he gains traction or can move under his own power. Otherwise, he may run over the tow line and damage both vehicles.

If your vehicle has to be towed by a tow truck, it can be towed forward with the driveshaft connected no faster than 30 mph and no farther than 15 miles. Otherwise, disconnect the driveshaft and tie it up. If your vehicle has to be towed backward, make sure that the steering wheel is secured in the straight-ahead position.

Jacking and Hoisting

It is very important to be careful about running the engine on vehicles equipped with limited-slip differentials, while the vehicle is up on a jack. If the drive train is engaged, power is transmitted to the wheel with the best traction and the vehicle will drive itself off the jack.

Jack up the front of all 1966–67 models and 1974–77 E-250 and 350 models under the outer end of the axle. Jack up all other twin I-beam models under the axle radius arm within 3 in. of the sloped

section. Jack up the rear of the van under the axle housing. Be sure to block the diagonally opposite wheel. Place jackstands under the vehicle at the points mentioned or directly under the frame when you are going to work under the vehicle.

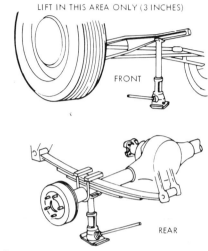

Jacking points

When raising the vehicle on a hoist, position the front end adapters under the center of the lower suspension arm or the spring supports as near to the wheels as practical. The rear hoist adapters should be placed under the spring mounting pads or the rear axle housing. Be careful not to touch the rear shock absorber mounting brackets.

E-250, 300 front jacking point

Lubrication

See the Maintenance Intervals Chart for the recommended intervals for the operations in this section.

*FUEL AND OIL
RECOMMENDATIONS*

All engines through 1973 are designed to operate on regular grade leaded gasoline. 1974–77 models may use unleaded, low-lead, or regular gasoline. 1975–77 models with a catalytic converter must use unleaded fuel only. If your engine pings or knocks, use a higher octane fuel or retard the ignition timing of the engine, but not more than three degrees from the setting required for normal operation. This is only recommended for an emergency situation until you can get some higher octane fuel. A little knocking at low speeds is acceptable, but continued knock at high speeds is damaging to the engine.

Many factors help to determine the proper oil. The question of viscosity revolves around the anticipated ambient temperatures to be encountered. The recommended viscosities for various temperatures are listed here. They are broken down into multiviscosities and single viscosities. Multiviscosity oils are recommended because of their wider range of acceptable temperatures and driving conditions. SE rated oil must be used.

Consistent Temperature (°F)	Multi-Viscosity Oil	Single Viscosity Oil
below +32	5W-30	——
−10 to +90	10W-30	——
−10 to over +90	10W-40	——
−10 to +32	——	10W *
+10 to +60	——	20W-20
+32 to +90	——	30
over +60	——	40

* Use the next higher viscosity for sustained driving or speeds over 60 mph.

NOTE: *Always use detergent oil. Detergent oil does not clean or loosen deposits, it merely prevents or inhibits the formation of deposits.*

LUBRICANT CHANGES

Engine Oil

The oil should be changed more frequently if the vehicle is being operated in very dusty areas. Before draining the oil, make sure that the engine is at operating temperature. Hot oil will hold more impurities in suspension and will flow better, allowing the removal of more oil and dirt. To get the engine hot enough, drive the vehicle for 15 minutes at expressway speeds or the equivalent in city driving.

Drain the oil into a suitable receptacle. After the drain plug is loosened, unscrew the plug with your fingers, using a rag to shield your fingers from the heat. Push in on the plug as you unscrew it so that you can feel when all of the screw threads are out of the hole. You can then remove the plug quickly with the minimum amount of oil running down your arm and you will also have the plug in your hand and not in the bottom of a pan of hot oil. Be careful of the oil. If it is at operating temperatures, it is hot enough to burn you.

Engine Oil Filter

The manufacturer recommends that the oil filter be changed at every other oil change on most models. However, if the vehicle is subjected to severe operating conditions, change the filter every time the engine oil is changed. The following would be considered "severe operating conditions":

1. Extended periods of idling or low-speed operation such as off-road or door-to-door delivery service.

2. Towing trailers over 2,000 lbs gross loaded weight for long distances.

3. When the ambient temperature remains below + 10°F for 60 days or more and most trips are less than 10 miles.

4. In severe dust conditions.

The oil filter is located on the left-side of all engines installed in Ford vans. To remove the filter after draining the oil, you may need an oil filter wrench since the filter may have been fitted too tightly and the heat from the engine may have made it even tighter. A filter wrench can be obtained at an auto parts store and is well worth the investment, since it will save you a lot of grief.

NOTE: *To remove the oil filter with power steering and a V8 engine through 1974, it is necessary to have the wheels in the straight-ahead position. After unscrewing the filter, place it at a horizontal position and allow the oil to drain. Next, slide the filter rearward to remove it from the vehicle. Some effort may be required to slide the oil filter between the engine crossmember and the power steering hoses. On 1973 and 1974 models, the front wheels must be in a full right turn position (against the stops) in order to remove the filter. Follow the procedure outlined above.*

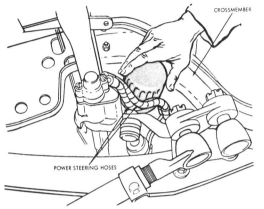

Removing the oil filter through 1974 with V8 and power steering

Loosen the filter with a filter wrench. With a rag wrapped around the filter, unscrew the filter from the boss on the side of the engine. Be careful of the hot oil that will run down the side of the filter. Make sure that you have a pan under the filter before you start to remove it from the engine, should some of the hot oil happen to get on you, you will have a place to dump the filter in a hurry. Wipe the base of the mounting boss with a clean, dry cloth. When you install the new filter, smear a small amount of oil on the gasket with your finger, just enough to coat the entire surface where it comes in contact with the mounting plate. When you tighten the filter, rotate it only a half-turn after it comes in contact with the mounting boss.

Manual Transmission

Remove the drain plug which is located at the bottom of the transmission. If there is no drain plug, remove the lower extension housing to case bolt. Allow all the lubricant to run out before replacing the plug. Refill the transmission with SAE 80 or 90 lubricant. See the "Capacities" chart.

If you are experiencing hard shifting and the weather is very cold, use a lighter viscosity lubricant in the transmission. If you don't have a pressure gun to install the oil, use a suction gun.

Automatic Transmission

Aside from checking and adding fluid in order to maintain the proper level, there are no factory recommendations regarding the replacement of the automatic transmission fluid, except for severe service.

The transmission is filled at the factory with a high quality fluid that both transmits power and lubricates and will last a long time. In most cases, the need to change the fluid in the automatic transmission will never arise under normal use. But since this is a truck and possibly will be subjected to more severe operating conditions than a conventional vehicle, the fluid may have to be replaced. Also, an internal leak in the radiator could develop and contaminate the fluid, necessitating fluid replacement.

The extra load of operating the vehicle with a heavy load, towing a heavy trailer, etc., causes the transmission to create more heat due to increased friction. This extra heat is transferred to the transmission fluid and, if the fluid is allowed to become too hot, it will change its chemical composition or become scorched. When this occurs, valve bodies become clogged and the transmission doesn't operate as efficiently as it should. Serious damage to the transmission can result.

You can tell if the transmission fluid is scorched by noting a distinctive "burned" smell and discoloration. Scorched transmission fluid is dark brown or black as opposed to its normal bright, clear red color. Since transmission fluid "cooks" in stages, it may develop forms of sludge or varnish. Pull the dipstick out and place the end on a tissue or paper towel. Particles of sludge can be seen more easily this way. If any of the above conditions do exist, the transmission fluid should be completely drained, the filtering screens cleaned, the transmission inspected for possible damage and new fluid installed.

C4

This transmission is used on all 1966–74 models and the 1975–77 E-100 and 150 sixes.

1. Disconnect the fluid filler tube from the transmission pan to drain the fluid.

2. When the fluid has stopped draining from the transmission, remove and thoroughly clean the pan and the screen. Discard the pan gasket.

3. Place a new gasket on the pan and install the pan on the transmission.

4. Connect the filler tube to the pan and tighten the fitting securely.

5. Add three quarts of type F fluid to the transmission through the dipstick tube.

6. Check the fluid level. With the transmission at room temperatures (70°F to 95°F) and the engine idling, the level should be between the middle and top holes on the dipstick. If the fluid level is below the middle hole, add enough fluid through the filler tube to raise the level to between the middle hole and the ADD mark. Please note that this check is only for when the transmission is at room temperatures. See the "Fluid Level Checks" Section for checking the transmission when it is at operating temperatures.

7. Replace the dipstick.

C6

This transmission is used on all 1975–77 models except the E-100 and 150 sixes.

1. Place a drain pan under the transmission. Loosen the pan bolts and pull one corner down to start the fluid draining. Remove and empty the pan.

2. When all the fluid has drained from the transmission, remove and clean the pan and screen. Make sure not to leave any solvent residue or lint from rags in the pan.

3. Install the pan with a new gasket and tighten the bolts in a criss-cross pattern.

4. Add three quarts of fluid through the dipstick tube. Use type F fluid for models through 1976; use the new type fluid (Ford Spec. ESP-M2C138-CJ) in 1977 C6 transmissions. The level should be at or below the ADD mark.

5. Check the fluid level as soon as the transmission reaches operating temperature for the first time. Make sure that the level is between ADD and FULL.

Rear Axle

On axles with a rear differential cover, loosen the bolts to let the lubricant drain out. On axles without a rear differential cover, the lubricant will have to be removed with a suction gun through the filler opening. Use the suction gun or a service station filler hose to fill the housing with SAE 80 or 90 hypoid gear oil to the filler plug hole level.

NOTE: *Limited-slip rear axles require that a special additive be used along with the hypoid lubricant. If it isn't used, the result will be noise and rough operation.*

CHASSIS GREASING

The lubrication chart indicates where the grease fittings are located on Ford vans and other level checks that should be made at the time of a chassis grease job.

Capacities

Year	Engine No. Cyl Displacement (Cu In.)	Engine Crankcase (qts) Add 1 Qt For New Filter	TRANSMISSION (pts) (Total Capacity)		Drive Axle (pts) Integral/ Removeable Carrier °	Gasoline Tank (gals) Std/Opt or Long Wheelbase	COOLING SYSTEM		
			Man-ual	Auto-matic C4/C6			Without Heater	With Heater	With A/C Or HD Cooling
1966	6-170	3.5	3.5	14	2.5/5	14	9	10	——
	6-240	4	3.5	16	2.5/5	14	11	12	——

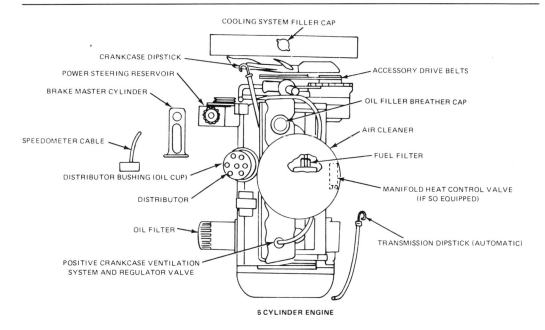

COOLING SYSTEM FILLER CAP

CRANKCASE DIPSTICK

POWER STEERING RESERVOIR

BRAKE MASTER CYLINDER

SPEEDOMETER CABLE

DISTRIBUTOR BUSHING (OIL CUP)

DISTRIBUTOR

OIL FILTER

POSITIVE CRANKCASE VENTILATION
SYSTEM AND REGULATOR VALVE

ACCESSORY DRIVE BELTS

OIL FILLER BREATHER CAP

AIR CLEANER

FUEL FILTER

MANIFOLD HEAT CONTROL VALVE
(IF SO EQUIPPED)

TRANSMISSION DIPSTICK (AUTOMATIC)

6 CYLINDER ENGINE

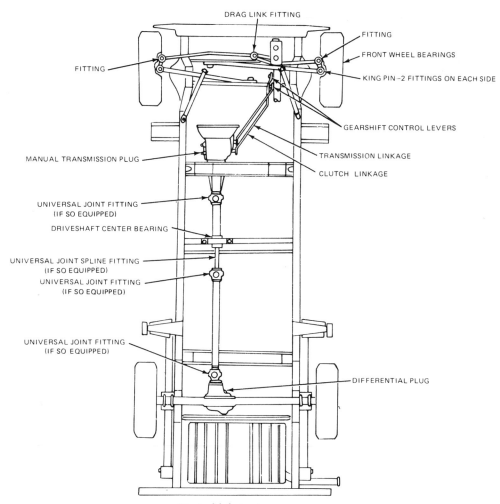

DRAG LINK FITTING

FITTING

FRONT WHEEL BEARINGS

KING PIN –2 FITTINGS ON EACH SIDE

FITTING

GEARSHIFT CONTROL LEVERS

TRANSMISSION LINKAGE

CLUTCH LINKAGE

MANUAL TRANSMISSION PLUG

UNIVERSAL JOINT FITTING
(IF SO EQUIPPED)

DRIVESHAFT CENTER BEARING

UNIVERSAL JOINT SPLINE FITTING
(IF SO EQUIPPED)

UNIVERSAL JOINT FITTING
(IF SO EQUIPPED)

UNIVERSAL JOINT FITTING
(IF SO EQUIPPED)

DIFFERENTIAL PLUG

Typical lubrication points

Capacities (cont.)

Year	Engine No. Cyl Displacement (Cu In.)	Engine Crankcase (qts) Add 1 Qt For New Filter	TRANSMISSION (pts) (Total Capacity) Man-ual	Auto-matic C4/C6	Drive Axle (pts) Integral/ Removeable Carrier °	Gasoline Tank (gals) Std/Opt or Long Wheelbase	COOLING SYSTEM Without Heater	With Heater	With A/C Or HD Cooling
1967	6-170	3.5	3.5	16	2.5/5	14	9	10	——
	6-240	4	3.5	21	2.5/5	14	11	12	——
1968	6-170	3.5	3.5	——	6/5	15/24	9	10	——
	6-240	4	3.5	20.5	6/5	15/24	11	12	16.3
	8-302	4	3.5	20.5	6/5	15/24	15.3	16.3	——
1969	6-170	3.5	3.5	20.5	6/5	24	——	9.1	——
	6-240	4	3.5	20.5	6/5	24	——	14.4	16.6
	8-302	4	3.5	20.5	6/5	24	——	15.2	17.5
1970	6-170	3.5	3.5	——	6	24/21 Cal	——	9.3	9.3
	6-240	4	3.5	20.5	6	24/21 Cal	——	14.5	16.8
	8-302	5	3.5	20.5	6	24/21 Cal	——	15.3	17.5
1971	6-240	4	3.5	20.5	6	21	——	14.5	16.8
	8-302	5	3.5	20.5	6	21	——	15.3	17.5
1972	6-240	4	3.5	20.5	6	20.3/23.3	——	14.5	16.8
	8-302	5	3.5	20.5	6	20.3/23.3	——	15.3	17.5
1973–74	6-240	4	4	20.5	6	20.3/23	——	14	14.5
	6-300	4	4	20.5	6	20.3/23	——	14.5	16.3
	8-302	6	4	20.5	6	20.3/23	——	15.3	17.5
1975	6-300	5	4	20.5/24.5	6/6.5	18/22.1/18 aux	——	14.5	16.6
	8-351	5	4	24.5	6/6.5	18/22.1/18 aux	——	20	24
	8-460	5	——	24.5	6/6.5	18/22.1/18 aux	——	28	28
1976	6-300	5	3.5	20/24.5	6/6.5	18/22.1/24.6/ 18 aux	——	14.5	14.5
	8-351	5	3.5	24.5	6/6.5	18/22.1/24.6/ 18 aux	——	20	24

Capacities (cont.)

Year	Engine No. Cyl Displacement (Cu In.)	Engine Crankcase (qts) Add 1 Qt For New Filter	TRANSMISSION (pts) (Total Capacity)		Drive Axle (pts) Integral/ Removeable Carrier °	Gasoline Tank (gals) Std/Opt or Long Wheelbase	COOLING SYSTEM		
			Man-ual	Auto-matic C4/C6			Without Heater	With Heater	With A/C Or HD Cooling
	8-460	5	——	2.45	6/6.5	18/22.1/24.6/ 18 aux	——	28	28
1977	6-300	5	3.5	20/24.5	5.5/6	18/22.1/24.6/ 18 aux	——	14.5	14.5
	8-351	5	3.5	24.5	5.5/6	18/22.1/24.6/ 18 aux	——	17	20
	8-460	5	——	24.5	5.5/6	18/22.1/24.6/ 18 aux	——	28	28

° Integral carrier axles have a removeable rear differential cover.

Maintenance Intervals Chart

(Read in thousands of miles or months, whichever comes first) #

Item	'66–'72	'73	'74 E-100, 200	'74 E-300	'75 E-100	'75–'76 E-150, 250, 350	'75–'76 E-350, GVW over 10,000	'77* E-100	'77* E-150, 250, 350
Replace air cleaner paper element	12	12	24	12	30U/24L	30	12	30AB/24C	30
Clean oil bath air cleaner	6	8	—	—	—	—	4	6C	6
Replace PCV valve	12	12	24	12	30U/24L	30	16	36A/48B/24C	30L
Change coolant	24 mo	24 mo	24 mo	24 mo	24 mo	24 mo	24 mo	36 mo/45	36 mo/42
Pack and adjust wheel bearings①	24	24	24	24	20U/24L	20	20	30	30
Rotate tires	6	as needed	as needed	as needed	as needed	as needed	as needed	as needed	as needed
Change fuel filter	12	12	12	12	15U	15	12	12	12
Change engine oil	6	4	6	4	5U/6L	5	4	7.5AB/6C	6
Change engine oil filter	6	8	12	4	10U/12L	10	4	15AB/12C	12
Change automatic transmission fluid, severe service only	—	—	—	—	20U/24L	25	20	22.5AB/18C	18
Adjust automatic transmission bands	18	18	12	12	15U/12L	15	15	22.5AB/18C	18
Change rear axle lubricant, full-floating axles only	—	—	24	24	—	25	25	—	24
Grease chassis	6	6	6	6	5U/6L	5	5	7.5AB/6C	6

* Check the underhood emission control specifications sticker to find whether maintenance schedule A, B, or C applies.
U Vehicles restricted to unleaded fuel L Vehicles not restricted to unleaded fuel ① Rear wheel bearings also with full-floating rear axle
Minimum intervals for a van driven the average 12,000 miles per year under ideal conditions. Halve service intervals for severe use such as trailer towing or off-road driving.

Chapter 2

Tune-Up and Troubleshooting

Tune-Up Procedures

SPARK PLUGS

Spark plugs ignite the air and fuel mixture in the cylinder as the piston reaches the top of the compression stroke. The controlled explosion that results forces the piston down, turning the crankshaft and the rest of the drive train.

The average life of a spark plug is 12,000–15,000 miles (more with unleaded fuel, but this is dependent on a number of factors: the mechanical condition of the engine; the type of fuel; driving conditions; and the driver himself.

When you remove the spark plugs, check their condition. They are a good indicator of the condition of the engine. It is a good idea to remove the spark plugs at regular intervals, such as every 3,000 or 4,000 miles, so that you can keep an eye on the mechanical state of the engine.

A small deposit of light tan or gray material on a spark plug that has been used for any period of time is considered normal. Any other color, or abnormal amounts of deposits, indicate that there is something amiss in the engine.

The gap between the center electrode and the side or ground electrode can be expected to increase not more than 0.001 in. for every 1,000 miles under normal conditions.

When, and if, a plug fouls and begins to misfire, you will have to investigate, correct the cause of the fouling and either clean or replace the plug.

There are several reasons why a spark plug will foul and you can learn which reason is at fault by just looking at the plug. A few of the most common reasons for plug fouling and a description of fouled plug appearance, is listed in the "Troubleshooting" Section, which also offers solutions to fouling causes.

Removal

1. Number the spark plug wires so that the correct firing order is maintained.

2. Remove the wire from the end of the spark plug by grasping the wire by the rubber boot. If the boot sticks to the plug, remove it by twisting and pulling at the same time. Do not pull the wire itself or you will most certainly damage the delicate carbon core.

3. Use a spark plug socket to loosen all of the plugs about two turns.

4. If compressed air is available, blow off the area around the spark plug holes. Otherwise, use a rag or brush to clean the area. Be careful not to allow any foreign matter to drop into the spark plug holes.

Tune-Up Specifications

Year	Engine No.Cyl Displacement (cu in.)	Spark Plugs		Distributor		Ignition Timing (deg)		Intake Valve Opens (deg)	Fuel Pump Pressure (psi)	Compression Pressure (psi)	Idle Speed (rpm)		Valve Clearance (in.) ▲	
		Original Type	Gap (in.)	Point Dwell (deg)	Point Gap (in.)	Manual Trans	Auto Trans				Manual Trans	Auto Trans	Intake	Exhaust
1966–67	6-170	BF82	0.034	40	0.025	4B①	8B①②	9B	4-6	155–195	625	625	Hydraulic	
	6-240	BTF42	0.034	40	0.025	6B①	10B①	12B	4-6	150–200	625	550	Hydraulic	
1968–69	6-170	BF82	0.034	37	0.027	6B	—	9B	4-6	150–200	700③	—	Hydraulic	
	6-240	BTF42	0.034	37	0.027	6B	6B	12B	4-6	150–200	600④	500	Hydraulic	
	8-302	BTF31	0.030	27	0.021	6B	6B	16B	4-6	130–170	625	550	Hydraulic	
1970–71	6-170	BF82	0.034	38	0.027	6B	6B	9B	4-6	⑤	775	775	Hydraulic	
	6-240	BTF42	0.034	38	0.027	6B	6B	12B	4-6	⑤	850/500⑥	575/500⑥	Hydraulic	
	8-302	BTF31	0.030	27⑧	0.021⑦	6B	6B	16B	4-6	⑤	800/500⑥	600/500⑥	Hydraulic	

1972	6-240	BF42	0.034	38	0.027	6B	6B	N.A.	4–6	⑤	850/500⑥	600/500⑥	Hydraulic
	8-302	BF42	0.034	28	0.017	6B	6B	N.A.	4–6	⑤	800/500⑥	600/500⑥	Hydraulic
1973	6-240	BRF42	0.034	36	0.027	6B	6B	N.A.	4–6	⑤	850	650	Hydraulic
	6-300	BRF31	0.034	36	0.027	10B	10B	N.A.	4–6	⑤	600	550	Hydraulic
	8-302	BRF42	0.034	28	0.017	6B	6B	N.A.	4–6	⑤	850	650	Hydraulic
1974	6-240	BRF42	0.034	36	0.027	6B	6B	N.A.	4–6	⑤	850	650	Hydraulic
	6-300	BRF42	0.034	36	0.027	10B	10B	N.A.	4–6	⑤	650	550	Hydraulic
	8-302	BRF42	0.034⑩	28	0.017	⑨	⑨	N.A.	4–6	⑤	⑨	⑨	Hydraulic
1975–77	All	See Underhood Specifications Sticker											

① TDC with Thermactor
② 10° B in 1967
③ 750 in 1969
④ 775 in 1969 with solenoid energized; 500 with solenoid de-energized
⑤ Compare highest and lowest readings. The lowest reading must be within 75% of the highest.
⑥ Higher idle speed—solenoid energized; lower idle speed—solenoid de-energized

⑦ 0.017 in. for E-300
⑧ 29° for E-300
⑨ Set to specifications shown on engine compartment sticker
⑩ 0.052–0.056 in. in California
▲ Operating clearance is zero (with lifter plunger in its normal operating position); collapsed lifter clearance is 0.10 in. for all engines
N.A. Not available

NOTE: *The underhood specifications sticker often reflects tune-up specification changes made in production. Sticker figures must be used if they disagree with those in this chart.*

23

Distributor Wiring Sequences and Firing Orders

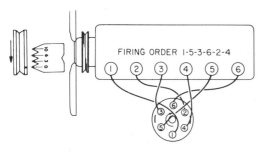

Distributor wiring and firing order for the 170, 240 and 300 sixes

5. Remove the plugs by unscrewing them the rest of the way out of the engine.

Inspection

Check the plugs for deposits and wear. If they are going to be replaced, clean the plugs thoroughly. Remember that any kind of deposit will decrease the efficiency of the plug. Plugs can be cleaned on a spark plug cleaning machine, which can be found in service stations or you can do an acceptable job of cleaning with a stiff brush.

Check the spark plug gap before reinstalling the plugs. The ground electrode must be parallel to the center electrode and the specified size wire gauge should pass through the gap with a slight drag. If the electrodes are worn, it is possible to file them level.

Installation

1. Insert the plugs in the spark plug holes and tighten them hand-tight. Take care not to cross-thread them.

2. Tighten the plugs.

3. Install the spark plug wires on the plugs. Make sure that each wire is firmly connected to each plug.

BREAKER POINTS

NOTE: *None of the discussion on breaker points applies to the solid-state, or electronic, ignition system on some 1974 and all 1975–77 models.*

The points function as a circuit breaker for the primary circuit of the ignition system. The ignition coil must boost the 12 volts of electrical pressure supplied by the battery to as much as 25,000 volts in order to fire the spark plugs. To do this,

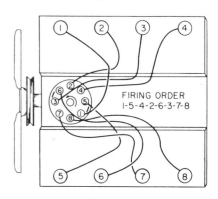

Distributor wiring and firing order for the 302 and 460 V8s

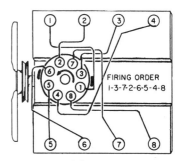

Distributor wiring and firing order for the 351 V8

the coil depends on the points and the condenser to make a clean break in the primary ciccuit.

The coil has both primary and secondary circuits. When the ignition is turned on, the battery supplies voltage through the coil and on to the points. The points are connected to ground, completing the primary circuit. As the current passes through the coil, a magnetic field is created in the iron center core of the coil. As the cam in the distributor turns, the points open and the primary circuit is interrupted. The magnetic field in the primary circuit of the coil collapses and cuts through the secondary circuit windings around the iron core. Because of the scientific phenomenon called "electromagnetic induction," the battery voltage is at this point increased to a level sufficient to fire the spark plugs.

When the points open, the electrical charge in the primary circuit jumps the gap created between the two open contacts of the points. If this electrical charge were not transferred elsewhere, the metal contacts of the points would melt and the gap between the points would start to change rapidly. If this gap is not maintained, the points will not break the primary circuit. If the primary circuit is not broken, the secondary circuit will not have enough voltage to fire the spark plugs.

The function of the condenser is to absorb excessive voltage from the points when they open and thus prevent the points from becoming pitted or burned.

There are two ways to check the breaker point gap: It can be done with a feeler gauge or a dwell meter. Either way you set the points, you are basically adjusting the amount of time that the points remain open. The time is measured in degrees of distributor rotation. When you measure the gap between the breaker points with a feeler gauge, you are setting the maximum amount the points will open when the rubbing block on the points is on a high point of the distributor cam. When you adjust the points with a dwell meter, you are adjusting the number of degrees that the points will remain closed before they start to open as a high point of the distributor cam approaches the rubbing block of the points.

When you replace a set of points, always replace the condenser at the same time.

When you change the point gap or dwell, you will also have changed the ignition timing. So, if the point gap or dwell is changed, the ignition timing must be adjusted also. Changing the ignition timing, however, does not affect the dwell of the breaker points.

Replacement of the Breaker Points and Condenser

1. Remove the coil high-tension wire from top of the distributor cap. Remove the distributor cap from the distributor and place it out of the way. Remove the rotor from the distributor shaft.

2. Loosen the screw which holds the condenser lead to the body of the breaker points and remove the condenser lead from the points.

3. Remove the screw which holds and grounds the condenser to the distributor body. Remove the condenser from the distributor and discard it.

4. Remove the points assembly attaching screws and adjustment lock-

screws. A screwdriver with a holding mechanism will come in handy here so that you don't drop a screw into the distributor and have to remove the entire distributor to retrieve it.

5. Remove the points by lifting them straight up and off the locating dowel on the plate. Wipe off the cam and apply new cam lubricant. Discard the old set of points.

6. Slip the new set of points onto the locating dowel and install the screws that hold the assembly onto the plate. Do not tighten them all the way.

7. Attach the new condenser to the plate with the ground screw.

8. Attach the condenser lead to the points at the proper place.

9. Apply a small amount of cam lubricant to the shaft where the rubbing block of the points touches.

Adjustment of the Breaker Points with a Feeler Gauge

1. If the contact points of the assembly are not parallel, bend the stationary contact so that they make contact across the entire surface of the contacts. Bend only the stationary bracket part of the point assembly; not the moveable contact.

2. Turn the engine until the rubbing block of the points is on one of the high points of the distributor cam. You can do this by either turning the ignition switch to the start position and releasing it quickly ("bumping" the engine) or by using a wrench on the bolt which holds the crankshaft pulley to the crankshaft.

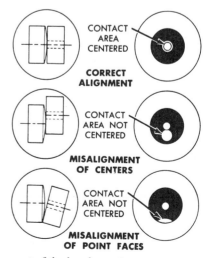

Alignment of the breaker point contacts

3. Place the correct size feeler gauge between the contacts. Make sure that it is parallel with the contact surfaces.

4. With your free hand, insert a screwdriver into the notch provided for adjustment or into the eccentric adjusting screw, then twist the screwdriver to either increase or decrease the gap to the proper setting.

5. Tighten the adjustment lockscrew and recheck the contact gap to make sure that it didn't change when the lockscrew was tightened.

6. Replace the rotor and distributor cap, and the high-tension wire that connects the top of the distributor and the coil. Make sure that the rotor is firmly seated all the way onto the distributor shaft and that the tab of the rotor is aligned with the notch in the shaft. Align the tab in the base of the distributor cap with the notch in the distributor body. Make sure that the cap is firmly seated on the distributor and that the retainer clips are in place. Make sure that the end of the high-tension wire is firmly placed in the top of the distributor and the coil.

Adjustment of the Breaker Points with a Dwell Meter

1. Adjust the points with a feeler gauge as described above.

2. Connect the dwell meter to the ignition circuit according to the manufacturer's instructions. One lead of the meter is connected to a ground and the other lead is to be connected to the distributor post on the coil. An adapter is usually provided for this purpose.

3. If the dwell meter has a set line on it, adjust the meter to zero the indicator.

4. Start the engine.

NOTE: *Be careful when working on any vehicle while the engine is running. Make sure that the transmission is in Neutral or Park and that the parking brake is applied. Keep hands, clothing, tools, and the wires of the test instruments clear of the rotating fan blades.*

5. Observe the reading on the dwell meter. If the reading is within the specified range, turn off the engine and remove the dwell meter.

6. If the reading is above the specified range, the breaker point gap is too small.

If the reading is below the specified range, the gap is too large. In either case, the engine must be stopped and the gap adjusted in the manner previously covered. After making the adjustment, start the engine and check the reading on the dwell meter. When the correct reading is obtained, disconnect the dwell meter.

7. Check the adjustment of the ignition timing.

IGNITION TIMING

Ignition timing is the measurement, in degrees of crankshaft rotation, of the point at which the spark plugs fire in each of the cylinders. It is measured in degrees before or after Top Dead Center (TDC) of the compression stroke. Ignition timing is controlled by turning the distributor body in the engine.

Ideally, the air/fuel mixture in the cylinder will be ignited by the spark plug just as the piston passes TDC of the compression stroke. If this happens, the piston will be beginning the power stroke just as the compressed and ignited air/fuel mixture starts to expand. The expansion of the air/fuel mixture then forces the piston down on the power stroke and turns the crankshaft.

Because it takes a fraction of a second for the spark plug to ignite the mixture in the cylinder, the spark plug must fire a little before the piston reaches TDC. Otherwise, the mixture will not be completely ignited as the piston passes TDC and the full power of the explosion will not be used by the engine.

The timing measurement is given in degrees of crankshaft rotation before the piston reaches TDC (BTDC). If the setting for the ignition timing is 5° BTDC, each spark plug must fire 5° before each piston reaches TDC. This only holds true, however, when the engine is at idle speed.

As the engine speed increases, the pistons go faster. The spark plugs have to ignite the fuel even sooner if it is to be completely ignited when the piston reaches TDC. To do this, the distributor has a means to advance the timing of the spark as the engine speed increases. This is accomplished by centrifugal weights within the distributor and a vacuum diaphragm mounted on the side of the distributor. It is necessary to disconnect the vacuum lines from the diaphragm when the ignition timing is being set.

If the ignition is set too far advanced (BTDC), the ignition and expansion of the fuel in the cylinder will occur too soon and tend to force the piston down while it is still traveling up. This causes engine ping. If the ignition spark is set too far retarded after TDC (ATDC), the piston will have already passed TDC and started on its way down when the fuel is ignited. This will cause the piston to be forced down for only a portion of its travel. This will result in poor engine performance and lack of power.

The timing is best checked with a timing light. This device is connected in series with the No. 1 spark plug. The current that fires the spark plug also causes the timing light to flash.

There is a notch on the crankshaft pulley on all engines, except the late model 302 cu in. V8. A scale of degrees of crankshaft rotation is attached to the engine block in such a position that the notch will pass close by the scale. On the late model 302 cu in. V8 engines, the scale is located on the crankshaft pulley and a pointer is attached to the engine block so that the scale will pass close by. When the engine is running, the timing light is aimed at the mark on the crankshaft pulley and the scale.

Ignition Timing Adjustment

1. Locate the timing marks on the crankshaft pulley and the front of the engine. On some sixes, the marks are on the flywheel.

2. Clean the timing marks so that you can see them.

3. Mark the timing marks with a piece of chalk or with paint. Color the mark on the scale that will indicate the correct timing when it is aligned with the mark on the pulley or the pointer. It is also helpful to mark the notch in the pulley or the tip of the pointer with a small dab of color.

4. Attach a tachometer to the engine.

5. Attach a timing light according to the manufacturer's instructions. If the timing light has three wires, one is attached to the No. 1 spark plug with an adapter. The other wires are connected to the battery. The red wire goes to the positive side of the battery and the black wire

is connected to the negative terminal of the battery.

6. Disconnect the vacuum line to the distributor at the distributor and plug the vacuum line. A golf tee does a fine job.

7. Check to make sure that all of the wires clear the fan and then start the engine.

8. Adjust the idle to the correct setting.

9. Aim the timing light at the timing marks. If the marks that you put on the flywheel or pulley and the engine are aligned when the light flashes, the timing is correct. Turn off the engine and remove the tachometer and the timing light. If the marks are not in alignment, proceed with the following steps.

10. Turn off the engine.

11. Loosen the distributor lockbolt just enough so that the distributor can be turned with a little effort.

12. Start the engine. Keep the wires of the timing light clear of the fan.

13. With the timing light aimed at the pulley and the marks on the engine, turn the distributor in the direction of rotor rotation to retard the spark, and in the opposite direction of rotor rotation to ad-

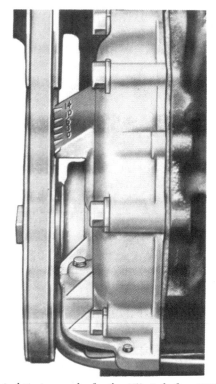

Typical timing marks for the 170 six before 1968

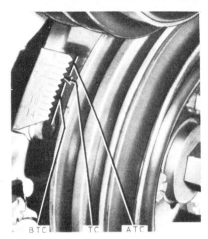

Timing marks for 1968 and later sixes

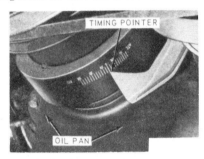

Timing marks for the 302 V8

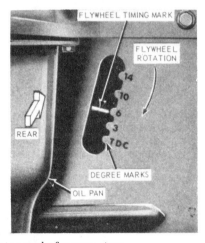

Timing marks for some sixes

vance the spark. Align the marks on the pulley and the engine with the flashes of the timing light.

14. When the marks are aligned, tighten the distributor lockbolt and recheck the timing with the timing light to make sure that the distributor did not move when you tightened the lockbolt.

15. Turn off the engine and remove the timing light.

VALVE LASH

Valve adjustment determines how far the valves enter the cylinder and how long they stay open and closed.

If the valve clearance is too large, part of the lift of the camshaft will be used in removing the excessive clearance. Consequently, the valve will not be opening as far as it should. This condition has two effects: the valve train components will emit a tapping sound as they take up the excessive clearance and the engine will perform poorly because the valves don't open fully and allow the proper amount of gases to flow into and out of the engine.

If the valve clearance is too small, the intake valve and the exhaust valves will open too far and they will not fully seat on the cylinder head when they close. When a valve seats itself on the cylinder head, it does two things: it seals the combustion chamber so that none of the gases in the cylinder escape and it cools itself by transferring some of the heat it absorbs from the combustion in the cylinder to the cylinder head and to the engine's cooling system. If the valve clearance is too small, the engine will run poorly because of the gases escaping from the combustion chamber. The valves will also become overheated and will warp, since they cannot transfer heat unless they are touching the valve seat in the cylinder head.

NOTE: *While all valve adjustments must be made as accurately as possible, it is better to have the valve adjustment slightly loose than slightly tight as a burned valve may result from overly tight adjustments.*

Adjustment

170 Cu In. 6 Cylinder (Solid Lifters)

1. Start the engine and let it run until it has reached operating temperature.

2. Remove the valve cover and gasket.

3. With the engine idling, adjust the valve lash using a step-type feeler gauge. This type of feeler gauge is sometimes more commonly known as a "go-no go" type feeler gauge. The proper clearance is reached when the smaller step on the gauge blade will pass through the gap

while the larger step on the same blade will not pass through the gap.

Pass the proper size gauge blade between the valve stem and the rocker arm. If the clearance is correct, move on to the next valve. If the clearance is in need of adjustment, turn the adjusting screw on the opposite end of the rocker arm with a wrench until the proper clearance is reached. Turn the screw clockwise to decrease the clearance and counterclockwise to increase the clearance. Use this procedure for all of the valves.

4. After all of the valves have been adjusted, replace the valve cover gasket and cover. If the gasket is made of rubber, and is not torn, squashed or otherwise damaged it can be used again. If the gasket is cork, it is advised that the gasket be replaced.

5. Tighten the valve cover retaining bolts to 3–5 ft lbs.

302 Cu In. V8

Some early models of the 302 cu in. V8 are equipped with adjustable rockers whereas the later models are equipped with positive stop type rocker mounting studs. Positive stop equipped rockers are adjusted by turning the adjusting nut down until it stops. You can identify a positive stop mounting stud by determining whether or not the shank portion of the stud that is exposed just above the cylinder head is the same diameter as the threaded portion at the top of the stud, to which the rocker arm retaining nut attaches. If the shank portion is larger than the threaded area, it is a positive stop mounting stud. Use the procedure given below for adjusting the valve lash on positive stop type mounting stud equipped vehicles.

There are two different procedures for adjusting the valves on the V8 engines. One is a preferred procedure and one is an alternate procedure. The preferred procedure is recommended, but the alternate procedure may be used.

NOTE: *These procedures are not tune-up procedures, but rebuild procedures to be performed only after valve train reassembly.*

Preferred Procedure through 1969

1. Position the piston(s) on TDC of the compression stroke, using the timing mark on the crankshaft pulley as a reference for starting with the No. 1 cylinder. You can tell if a piston is coming up on its compression stroke by removing the spark plug of the cylinder you are working on and placing your thumb over the hole while the engine is cranked over. Air will try to force its way past your thumb when the piston comes up on the compression stroke. Make sure that the high-tension coil wire leading to the distributor is removed before cranking the engine. Remove the valve covers.

2. Starting with No. 1 cylinder, and the piston in the position as mentioned above, apply pressure to slowly bleed down the valve lifter until the plunger is completely bottomed.

3. While holding the valve lifter in the fully collapsed position, check the available clearance between the rocker arm and the valve stem tip. Use a feeler gauge.

4. If the clearance is not within the specified amount, rotate the rocker arm stud nut clockwise to decrease the clearance and counterclockwise to increase the clearance. Normally, one turn of the rocker arm stud nut will vary the clearnance by 0.066 in. Check the break-away torque of each stud nut with a torque wrench, turning it counterclockwise. It should be anywhere from 4.5 to 15 ft lbs. Replace the nut and/or the stud as necessary.

5. When both valves for the No. 1 cylinder have been adjusted, proceed on to the other valves, following the firing order sequence 1–5–4–2–6–3–7–8.

Checking the valve clearance on either the 240, 300 six or the 302 V8

6. Replace the valve covers and gaskets.

Alternate Procedure through 1969

Follow Step 1 of the preferred procedure given above, but instead of collapsing the lifter as in Step 2, loosen the rocker retaining nut until there is end-play present in the pushrod; then tighten the nut to remove all pushrod-to-rocker arm clearance. When the pushrod-to-rocker arm clearance has been eliminated, tighten the stud nut an additional ¾ turn to place the lifter plunger in the desired operating range.

Adjusting the valve clearance on either the 240, 300 six or the 302 V8

Repeat this procedure for all of the cylinders, using the firing order sequence as a guide. It takes ¼ turn of the crankshaft to bring the next piston in the firing order sequence up to TDC at the end of its compression stroke.

Positive Stop Type Mounting Stud from 1970

1. Crank the engine until No. 1 cylinder is at TDC of the compression stroke and the timing pointer is aligned with the TDC mark on the crankshaft damper.
2. Scribe a mark on the damper at this point. This is mark A.
3. Scribe three additional marks on the damper; one at 90° from TDC (mark B), one at 180° (mark C), and the other one at 270° of rotation from TDC (¾ turn from TDC). The mark at 270° is mark D.
4. With the timing pointer aligned with Mark A on the damper, tighten the following valves until the nuts contact the rocker shoulder, then torque them to 18–20 ft lbs: No. 1, intake and exhaust.

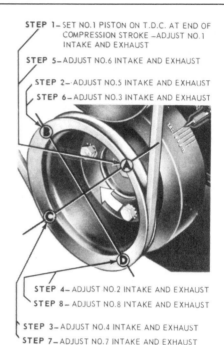

STEP 1– SET NO.1 PISTON ON T.D.C. AT END OF COMPRESSION STROKE –ADJUST NO.1 INTAKE AND EXHAUST

STEP 5–ADJUST NO.6 INTAKE AND EXHAUST

STEP 2– ADJUST NO.5 INTAKE AND EXHAUST

STEP 6–ADJUST NO.3 INTAKE AND EXHAUST

STEP 4– ADJUST NO.2 INTAKE AND EXHAUST

STEP 8– ADJUST NO.8 INTAKE AND EXHAUST

STEP 3– ADJUST NO.4 INTAKE AND EXHAUST

STEP 7– ADJUST NO.7 INTAKE AND EXHAUST

Placement of marks on the crankshaft pulley for adjusting the valves on a 302 V8

5. Rotate the crankshaft 90° to mark B and tighten the following valves: No. 5 intake and exhaust.
6. Rotate the crankshaft 90° to align mark C with the timing pointer and tighten the following valves: No. 4 intake and exhaust.
7. Rotate the crankshaft another 90° to mark D and adjust valves No. 2 intake and exhaust.
8. Continue in this manner (turning the crankshaft ¼ turn at a time) until all of the valves are adjusted in the firing order; 1–5–4–2–6–3–7–8.

240 AND 300 CU IN. SIXES

NOTE: *These are not tune-up service procedures, but rebuild procedures to be done only after valve train reassembly.*

Preferred Procedure

1. Disconnect the brown lead (I terminal) and the red and blue lead (S terminal) at the starter relay. Install an auxiliary starter switch between the battery and the S terminals of the starter relay. Crank the engine with the ignition switch in the Off position.
2. Make two chalk marks on the crankshaft damper. Space the marks about 120°

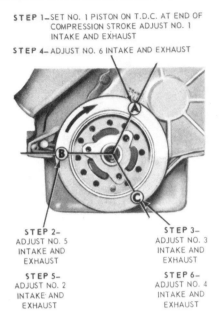

STEP 1—SET NO. 1 PISTON ON T.D.C. AT END OF COMPRESSION STROKE ADJUST NO. 1 INTAKE AND EXHAUST

STEP 4—ADJUST NO. 6 INTAKE AND EXHAUST

STEP 2—
ADJUST NO. 5
INTAKE AND
EXHAUST

STEP 3—
ADJUST NO. 3
INTAKE AND
EXHAUST

STEP 5—
ADJUST NO. 2
INTAKE AND
EXHAUST

STEP 6—
ADJUST NO. 4
INTAKE AND
EXHAUST

Placement of marks on the crankshaft pulley for adjusting the valves on a 240, 300 six

apart so that with the TDC timing mark, the damper is divided into 3 equal parts of 120° each (each segment representing ⅓ of the distance around the damper's circumference).

3. Rotate the crankshaft until the No. 1 piston is on TDC at the top of the compression stroke.

4. With the No. 1 piston on TDC at the top of the compression stroke, adjust the intake and exhaust valve clearance for the No. 1 cylinder. Loosen the rocker arm stud nut until there is end-play in the pushrod; then tighten the nut to just remove all the pushrod-to-rocker arm clearance. This may be determined by rotating and/or moving the pushrod with your fingers as the stud nut is tightened. When the pushrod-to-rocker arm clearance has been eliminated, tighten the stud nut an additional 1 turn to place the hydraulic lifter plunger in the desired operating range.

5. Repeat this procedure for the remaining set of valves, turning the crankshaft with an auxiliary starter switch ⅓ of a turn at a time, in the direction of rotation, while adjusting the valves in the firing order sequence, 1–5–3–6–2–4.

This procedure requires 2 complete turns of the crankshaft.

6. Operate the engine and check for rough idling or noisy lifters. Valve clearance set too tight will cause rough idle, and clearance set too loose will cause noisy lifters.

Alternate Procedure

1. Follow Steps 1, 2, and 3 in the "Preferred procedure," above.

2. Position the pistons on TDC of the compression stroke. Apply pressure to slowly bleed down the valve lifter until the plunger is completely bottomed. While holding the valve lifter in the fully collapsed position, check the available clearance between the rocker arm and valve stem tip. If the clearance is not within specifications, rotate the rocker arm stud nut clockwise to decrease the clearance and counterclockwise to increase the clearance.

3. Repeat this procedure for all remaining valves.

351, 460 Cu In. V8s

These engines require no preliminary valve adjustment after valve train reassembly.

CARBURETOR

This Section contains only tune-up adjustment procedures for carburetors. Descriptions, adjustments and overhaul procedures for carburetors can be found in the "Fuel System" Section (Chapter 4) of this book.

When the engine in your van is running, the air/fuel mixture from the carburetor is being drawn into the engine by a partial vacuum created by the downward movement of the pistons on the intake stroke. The amount of air/fuel mixture that enters the engine is controlled by the throttle plate(s) in the bottom of the carburetor. When the engine is not running, the throttle plates are closed, completely blocking off the air/fuel passage(s) at the bottom of the carburetor. The throttle plates are connected by the throttle linkage to the accelerator pedal in the passenger compartment. When you depress the pedal, you open the throttle plates in the carburetor to admit more air/fuel mixture to the engine.

The idle adjusting screw contacts a lever (throttle lever) on the outside of the carburetor. When the screw is turned, it opens or closes the throttle plates of the carburetor, raising or lowering the idle speed of the engine. This screw is called the curb idle adjusting screw.

Idle Speed Adjustment

1. Start the engine and run it until it reaches operating temperature.
2. If it hasn't already been done, check and adjust the ignition timing. After you have set the timing, turn off the engine.
3. Attach a tachometer to the engine.
4. Turn the headlights on high beam through 1973, or as specified on the underhood specifications sticker for later models.
5. On vans with manual transmissions, engage the parking brake and place the transmission in Neutral; vehicles equipped with automatic transmission, engage the parking brake, and place the gear selector in Drive. Block the wheels.

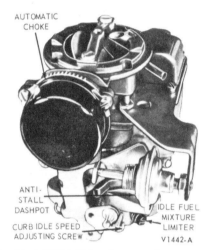

Carter Model YF 1-bbl carburetor adjustments

Carter Model YF 1-bbl carburetor equipped with a solenoid

6. Make sure that the choke plate is in the fully open position.
7. Adjust the engine curb idle rpm to the proper specifications. The tachometer reading must be taken with the carburetor air cleaner in place. If it is impossible to make the adjustment with the air cleaner in position, remove it and make the adjustment. Then replace the air cleaner and check the tachometer for the proper rpm reading.

On carburetors equipped with a solenoid throttle positioner, loosen the jam nut on the solenoid at the bracket and rotate the solenoid in or out to obtain the specified curb idle rpm. Some late models have an adjusting screw. Disconnect the solenoid lead wire at the connector, set the automatic transmission in Neutral, then adjust the carburetor throttle stop screw to obtain the lower specified speed or 500 rpm. Connect the solenoid lead wire and open the throttle slightly by hand. The solenoid plunger will follow the throttle lever and remain in the fully extended position as long as the ignition is on and the solenoid energized.

Idle Mixture Adjustment

In 1968, limiter caps were installed on the idle mixture screws to prevent incorrect adjustment. A satisfactory adjustment should be obtainable within the range of the limiter caps.

The idle mixture screws are adjusted by turning them in and out until the fastest and smoothest idle is obtained. On models not equipped with limiter caps, start the adjustment procedure with the adjustment screw seated LIGHTLY. Then turn the screw out 1 to 1–½ turns as a starting point.

NOTE: *Always favor a slightly rich mixture over a slightly lean mixture.*

If a satisfactory idle cannot be obtained within the range of the limiter caps, it is possible to remove the caps to obtain a better idle. This should be done only as a last resort.

NOTE: *The exhaust must be checked with an exhaust gas analyzer if the limiter caps are removed and the carburetor adjusted without them.*

Check the following as being possible causes for not obtaining a satisfactory idle before removing the limiter caps:

1. Vacuum leaks

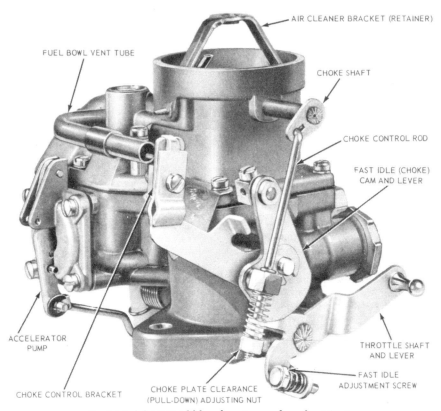

Ford Model 1100 1-bbl carburetor used on the 170 six

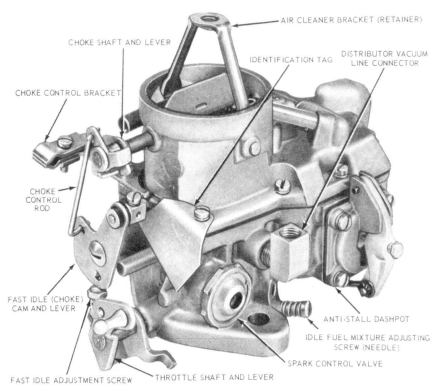

Ford Model 1100 1-bbl carburetor used on the 240 six

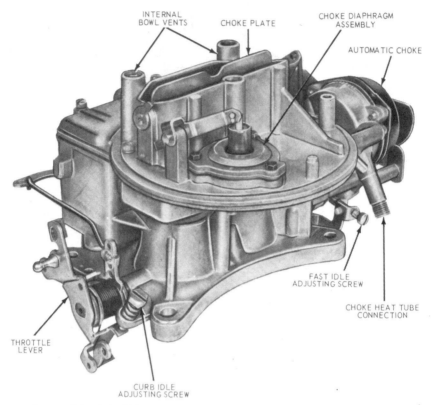

Autolite Model 2100 2-bbl carburetor—view shows the curb idle adjustment screws

2. Ignition system wiring continuity
3. Spark plugs
4. Distributor breaker points dwell
5. Ignition timing
6. Fuel level and fuel bowl vent
7. Crankcase ventilation system
8. Engine compression

Remove the plastic limiter caps by cutting them with a pair of side cutter pliers and a knife. After the cut is made, pry the limiter apart and remove it. Adjust the carburetor to the best idle and maximum engine rpm.

There are service limiter caps available for replacement of the factory caps. They are installed by pushing them straight on with either your thumb or a ³/₈ in. drive socket wrench extension. Position the caps so that they are in the maximum counterclockwise positions, up against the stop of the carburetor body. This places the adjusting screw in the maximum allowable outward, or rich mixture, setting.

NOTE: *The factory recommended pro-*

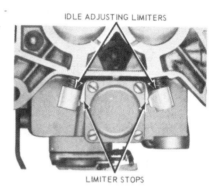

Autolite Model 2100 2-bbl carburetor—bottom view showing the idle mixture screws with limiter caps

cedure for adjusting the idle mixture on 1975–77 models requires the addition of an artificial mixture enrichment substance (propane) to the air intake. This requires special tools not generally available. The previous procedure is specifically recommended by the factory only for models through 1974.

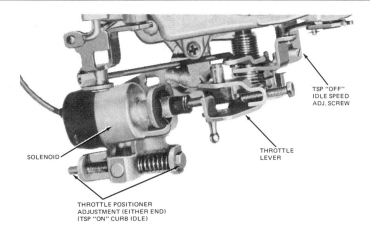

TSP "OFF"
IDLE SPEED
ADJ. SCREW

THROTTLE
LEVER

SOLENOID

THROTTLE POSITIONER
ADJUSTMENT (EITHER END)
(TSP "ON" CURB IDLE)

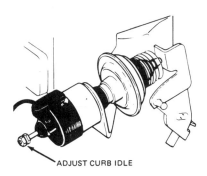

ADJUST CURB IDLE

Adjustment for two types of throttle solenoids

FORD MOTOR COMPANY			
ENGINE EXHAUST EMISSION CONTROL INFORMATION			

ENGINE FAMILY 300
ENGINE DISPLACEMENT 300 CID
SPARK PLUG BRF-42 GAP .042-.046

VALVE LASH	HYD — NOT ADJ	DISTRIBUTOR POINTS GAP NONE DWELL NONE	
TRANSMISSION/GEAR	AUTO/NEUT	AUTO/DRIVE	MAN/NEUT
IGNITION TIMING	10' BTDC		
TIMING RPM	700		
CHOKE SETTING	NONE		
FAST IDLE RPM	HIGH CAM		
	KICK DOWN	1500	
CURB IDLE RPM	A/C		
	NON A/C		600
TSP OFF RPM	A/C		
	NON A/C		

MAKE ALL ADJUSTMENTS WITH ENGINE AT NORMAL OPER-
ATING TEMPERATURE. A C AND HEADLIGHTS OFF CONSULT
SERVICE PUBLICATIONS FOR ADDITIONAL INSTRUCTIONS ON
THE FOLLOWING PROCEDURES

IGNITION TIMING — ADJUST WITH HOSES DISCONNECTED
AND PLUGGED AT THE DISTRIBUTOR. THROTTLE SOLENOID
POSITIONER DISCONNECTED (IF SO EQUIPPED) AND TRANS-
MISSION IN NEUTRAL

CURB IDLE — ADJUST WITH ALL VACUUM HOSES CON-
NECTED AIR CLEANER IN POSITION AND THROTTLE SOLE-
NOID POSITIONER ENERGIZED (IF SO EQUIPPED) WHENEVER
THE CURB IDLE IS RESET. CHECK AND ADJUST THE DECEL
THROTTLE CONTROL SYSTEM (IF SO EQUIPPED) PER H D
MAINTENANCE PROCEDURES

IDLE MIXTURE — PRESET AT THE FACTORY DO NOT REMOVE
THE LIMITER CAPS EXCEPT IN ACCORDANCE WITH SERVICE
PUBLICATIONS.

NON-CATALYST

THIS ENGINE CONFORMS TO U.S. ENVIRONMENTAL PROTECTION AGENCY
REGULATIONS APPLICABLE TO 1977 MODEL YEAR GASOLINE-
FUELED HEAVY DUTY ENGINES.   D7TE-9C485-ALA   **7-154**

Engine Tune-Up

Engine tune-up is a procedure performed to restore engine performance, deteriorated due to normal wear and loss of adjustment. The three major areas considered in a routine tune-up are compression, ignition, and carburetion, although valve adjustment may be included.

A tune-up is performed in three steps: *analysis*, in which it is determined whether normal wear is responsible for performance loss, and which parts require replacement or service; *parts replacement or service*; and *adjustment*, in which engine adjustments are returned to original specifications. Since the advent of emission control equipment, precision adjustment has become increasingly critical, in order to maintain pollutant emission levels.

Analysis

The procedures below are used to indicate where adjustments, parts service or replacement are necessary within the realm of a normal tune-up. If, following these tests, all systems appear to be functioning properly, proceed to the Troubleshooting Section for further diagnosis.

—Remove all spark plugs, noting the cylinder in which they were installed. Remove the air cleaner, and position the throttle and choke in the full open position. Disconnect the coil high tension lead from the coil and the distributor cap. Insert a compression gauge into the spark plug port of each cylinder, in succession, and crank the engine with

Maxi. Press. Lbs. Sq. In.	Min. Press. Lbs. Sq. In.	Max. Press. Lbs. Sq. In.	Min. Press. Lbs. Sq. In.
134	101	188	141
136	102	190	142
138	104	192	144
140	105	194	145
142	107	196	147
146	110	198	148
148	111	200	150
150	113	202	151
152	114	204	153
154	115	206	154
156	117	208	156
158	118	210	157
160	120	212	158
162	121	214	160
164	123	216	162
166	124	218	163
168	126	220	165
170	127	222	166
172	129	224	168
174	131	226	169
176	132	228	171
178	133	230	172
180	135	232	174
182	136	234	175
184	138	236	177
186	140	238	178

Compression pressure limits
ⓒ Buick Div. G.M. Corp.)

the starter to obtain the highest possible reading. Record the readings, and compare the highest to the lowest on the compression pressure limit chart. If the difference exceeds the limits on the chart, or if all readings are excessively low, proceed to a wet compression check (see Troubleshooting Section).

—Evaluate the spark plugs according to the spark plug chart

in the Troubleshooting Section, and proceed as indicated in the chart.

—Remove the distributor cap, and inspect it inside and out for cracks and/or carbon tracks, and inside for excessive wear or burning of the rotor contacts. If any of these faults are evident, the cap must be replaced.

—Check the breaker points for burning, pitting or wear, and the contact heel resting on the distributor cam for excessive wear. If defects are noted, replace the entire breaker point set.

—Remove and inspect the rotor. If the contacts are burned or worn, or if the rotor is excessively loose on the distributor shaft (where applicable), the rotor must be replaced.

—Inspect the spark plug leads and the coil high tension lead for cracks or brittleness. If any of the wires appear defective, the entire set should be replaced.

—Check the air filter to ensure that it is functioning properly.

Parts Replacement and Service

The determination of whether to replace or service parts is at the mechanic's discretion; however, it is suggested that any parts in questionable condition be replaced rather than reused.

—Clean and regap, or replace, the spark plugs as needed. Lightly coat the threads with engine oil and install the plugs. CAUTION: *Do not over-torque taper-seat spark plugs, or plugs being installed in aluminum cylinder heads.*

—If the distributor cap is to be reused, clean the inside with a dry rag, and remove corrosion from the rotor contact points with fine emery cloth. Remove the spark plug wires one by one, and clean the wire ends and the inside of the towers. If the boots are loose, they should be replaced.

If the cap is to be replaced, transfer the wires one by one, cleaning the wire ends and replacing the boots if necessary.

—If the original points are to remain in service, clean them lightly with emery cloth, lubricate the contact heel with grease specifically designed for this purpose. Rotate the crankshaft until the heel rests on a high point of the distributor cam, and adjust the point gap to specifications.

When replacing the points, remove the original points and condenser, and wipe out the inside of the distributor housing with a clean, dry rag. Lightly lubricate the contact heel and pivot point, and install the points and condenser. Rotate the crankshaft until the heel rests on a high point of the distributor cam, and adjust the point gap to specifications. NOTE: *Always replace the condenser when changing the points.*

—If the rotor is to be reused, clean the contacts with solvent. Do not alter the spring tension of the rotor center contact. Install the rotor and the distributor cap.

—Replace the coil high tension lead and/or the spark plug leads as necessary.

—Clean the carburetor using a spray solvent (e.g., Gumout Spray). Remove the varnish from the throttle bores, and clean the linkage. Disconnect and plug the fuel line, and run the engine until it runs out of fuel. Partially fill the float chamber with solvent, and reconnect the fuel line. In extreme cases, the jets can be pressure flushed by inserting a rubber plug into the float vent, running the spray nozzle through it, and spraying the solvent until it squirts out of the venturi fuel dump.

—Clean and tighten all wiring connections in the primary electrical circuit.

Additional Services

The following services *should* be performed in conjunction with a routine tune-up to ensure efficient performance.

—Inspect the battery and fill to the proper level with distilled water. Remove the cable clamps, clean clamps and posts thoroughly, coat the posts lightly with petroleum jelly, reinstall and tighten.

—Inspect all belts, replace and/or adjust as necessary.

—Test the PCV valve (if so equipped), and clean or replace as indicated. Clean all crankcase ventilation hoses, or replace if cracked or hardened.

—Adjust the valves (if necessary) to manufacturer's specifications.

Adjustments

—Connect a dwell-tachometer between the distributor primary lead and ground. Remove the distributor cap and rotor (unless equipped with Delco externally adjustable distributor). With the ignition off, crank the engine with a remote starter switch and measure the point dwell angle. Adjust the dwell angle to specifications. NOTE: *Increasing the gap decreases the dwell angle and* *vice-versa.* Install the rotor and distributor cap.

—Connect a timing light according to the manufacturer's specifications. Identify the proper timing marks with chalk or paint. NOTE: *Luminescent (day-glo) paint is excellent for this purpose.* Start the engine, and run it until it reaches operating temperature. Disconnect and plug any distributor vacuum lines, and adjust idle to the speed required to adjust timing, according to specifications. Loosen the distributor clamp and adjust timing to specifications by rotating the distributor in the engine. NOTE: *To advance timing, rotate distributor opposite normal direction of rotor rotation, and vice-versa.*

—Synchronize the throttles and mixture of multiple carburetors (if so equipped) according to procedures given in the individual car sections.

—Adjust the idle speed, mixture, and idle quality, as specified in the car sections. Final idle adjustments should be made with the air cleaner installed. CAUTION: *Due to strict emission control requirements on 1969 and later models, special test equipment (CO meter, SUN Tester) may be necessary to properly adjust idle mixture to specifications.*

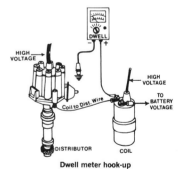

Dwell meter hook-up

Trouble-shooting

The following section is designed to aid in the rapid diagnosis of engine problems. The systematic format is used to diagnose problems ranging from engine starting difficulties to the need for engine overhaul. It is assumed that the user is equipped with basic hand tools and test equipment (tach-dwell meter, timing light, voltmeter, and ohmmeter).

Troubleshooting is divided into two sections. The first, *General Diagnosis*, is used to locate the problem area. In the second, *Specific Diagnosis*, the problem is systematically evaluated.

General Diagnosis

PROBLEM: Symptom	Begin diagnosis at Section Two, Number ———
Engine won't start:	
Starter doesn't turn	1.1, 2.1
Starter turns, engine doesn't	2.1
Starter turns engine very slowly	1.1, 2.4
Starter turns engine normally	3.1, 4.1
Starter turns engine very quickly	6.1
Engine fires intermittently	4.1
Engine fires consistently	5.1, 6.1
Engine runs poorly:	
Hard starting	3.1, 4.1, 5.1, 8.1
Rough idle	4.1, 5.1, 8.1
Stalling	3.1, 4.1, 5.1, 8.1
Engine dies at high speeds	4.1, 5.1
Hesitation (on acceleration from standing stop)	5.1, 8.1
Poor pickup	4.1, 5.1, 8.1
Lack of power	3.1, 4.1, 5.1, 8.1
Backfire through the carburetor	4.1, 8.1, 9.1
Backfire through the exhaust	4.1, 8.1, 9.1
Blue exhaust gases	6.1, 7.1
Black exhaust gases	5.1
Running on (after the ignition is shut off)	3.1, 8.1
Susceptible to moisture	4.1
Engine misfires under load	4.1, 7.1, 8.4, 9.1
Engine misfires at speed	4.1, 8.4
Engine misfires at idle	3.1, 4.1, 5.1, 7.1, 8.4

PROBLEM: Symptom	Probable Cause
Engine noises: ①	
Metallic grind while starting	Starter drive not engaging completely
Constant grind or rumble	*Starter drive not releasing, worn main bearings
Constant knock	Worn connecting rod bearings
Knock under load	Fuel octane too low, worn connecting rod bearings
Double knock	Loose piston pin
Metallic tap	*Collapsed or sticky valve lifter, excessive valve clearance, excessive end play in a rotating shaft
Scrape	*Fan belt contacting a stationary surface
Tick while starting	S.U. electric fuel pump (normal), starter brushes
Constant tick	*Generator brushes, shreaded fan belt
Squeal	*Improperly tensioned fan belt
Hiss or roar	*Steam escaping through a leak in the cooling system or the radiator overflow vent
Whistle	*Vacuum leak
Wheeze	Loose or cracked spark plug

①—It is extremely difficult to evaluate vehicle noises. While the above are general definitions of engine noises, those starred (*) should be considered as possibly originating elsewhere in the car. To aid diagnosis, the following list considers other potential sources of these sounds.

Metallic grind:
Throwout bearing; transmission gears, bearings, or synchronizers; differential bearings, gears; something metallic in contact with brake drum or disc.

Metallic tap:
U-joints; fan-to-radiator (or shroud) contact.

Scrape:
Brake shoe or pad dragging; tire to body contact; suspension contacting undercarriage or exhaust; something non-metallic contacting brake shoe or drum.

Tick:
Transmission gears; differential gears; lack of radio suppression; resonant vibration of body panels; windshield wiper motor or transmission; heater motor and blower.

Squeal:
Brake shoe or pad not fully releasing; tires (excessive wear, uneven wear, improper inflation); front or rear wheel alignment (most commonly due to improper toe-in).

Hiss or whistle:
Wind leaks (body or window); heater motor and blower fan.

Roar:
Wheel bearings; wind leaks (body and window).

Specific Diagnosis

This section is arranged so that following each test, instructions are given to proceed to another, until a problem is diagnosed.

INDEX

Group		Topic
1	*	Battery
2	*	Cranking system
3	*	Primary electrical system
4	*	Secondary electrical system
5	*	Fuel system
6	*	Engine compression
7	**	Engine vacuum
8	**	Secondary electrical system
9	**	Valve train
10	**	Exhaust system
11	**	Cooling system
12	**	Engine lubrication

*—The engine need not be running.
**—The engine must be running.

SAMPLE SECTION

Test and Procedure	Results and Indications	Proceed to
4.1—Check for spark: Hold each spark plug wire approximately ¼″ from ground with gloves or a heavy, dry rag. Crank the engine and observe the spark.	→ If no spark is evident:	→ 4.2
	→ If spark is good in some cases:	→ 4.3
	→ If spark is good in all cases:	→ 4.6

DIAGNOSIS

1.1—Inspect the battery visually for case condition (corrosion, cracks) and water level.	If case is cracked, replace battery:	1.4
	If the case is intact, remove corrosion with a solution of baking soda and water (CAUTION: *do not get the solution into the battery*), and fill with water:	1.2
1.2—Check the battery cable connections: Insert a screwdriver between the battery post and the cable clamp. Turn the headlights on high beam, and observe them as the screwdriver is gently twisted to ensure good metal to metal contact.	If the lights brighten, remove and clean the clamp and post; coat the post with petroleum jelly, install and tighten the clamp:	1.4
	If no improvement is noted:	1.3

Testing battery cable connections using a screwdriver

1.3—Test the state of charge of the battery using an individual cell tester or hydrometer.

Spec. Grav. Reading	Charged Condition
1.260-1.280	Fully Charged
1.230-1.250	Three Quarter Charged
1.200-1.220	One Half Charged
1.170-1.190	One Quarter Charged
1.140-1.160	Just About Flat
1.110-1.130	All The Way Down

State of battery charge

Electrolyte temperature (°F)	Specific gravity correction	
+ 120	+ 016	
	+ 012	
+ 100	+ 008	ADD to reading
	+ 004	
+ 80	no correction	
	− 004	
+ 60	− 008	
	− 012	
+ 40	− 016	
	− 020	
+ 20	− 024	SUBTRACT from reading
	− 028	
0	− 032	
	− 036	
− 20	− 040	

The effect of temperature on the specific gravity of battery electrolyte

If indicated, charge the battery. NOTE: *If no obvious reason exists for the low state of charge (i.e., battery age, prolonged storage), the charging system should be tested:*   1.4

Test and Procedure	*Results and Indications*	*Proceed to*
1.4—Visually inspect battery cables for cracking, bad connection to ground, or bad connection to starter.	If necessary, tighten connections or replace the cables:	2.1

Tests in Group 2 are performed with coil high tension lead disconnected to prevent accidental starting.

Test and Procedure	*Results and Indications*	*Proceed to*
2.1—Test the starter motor and solenoid: Connect a jumper from the battery post of the solenoid (or relay) to the starter post of the solenoid (or relay).	If starter turns the engine normally:	2.2
	If the starter buzzes, or turns the engine very slowly:	2.4
	If no response, replace the solenoid (or relay).	3.1
	If the starter turns, but the engine doesn't, ensure that the flywheel ring gear is intact. If the gear is undamaged, replace the starter drive.	3.1
2.2—Determine whether ignition override switches are functioning properly (clutch start switch, neutral safety switch), by connecting a jumper across the switch(es), and turning the ignition switch to "start".	If starter operates, adjust or replace switch:	3.1
	If the starter doesn't operate:	2.3
2.3—Check the ignition switch "start" position: Connect a 12V test lamp between the starter post of the solenoid (or relay) and ground. Turn the ignition switch to the "start" position, and jiggle the key.	If the lamp doesn't light when the switch is turned, check the ignition switch for loose connections, cracked insulation, or broken wires. Repair or replace as necessary:	3.1
	If the lamp flickers when the key is jiggled, replace the ignition switch.	3.3

Checking the ignition switch "start" position

Test and Procedure	*Results and Indications*	*Proceed to*
2.4—Remove and bench test the starter, according to specifications in the car section.	If the starter does not meet specifications, repair or replace as needed:	3.1
	If the starter is operating properly:	2.5
2.5—Determine whether the engine can turn freely: Remove the spark plugs, and check for water in the cylinders. Check for water on the dipstick, or oil in the radiator. Attempt to turn the engine using an 18″ flex drive and socket on the crankshaft pulley nut or bolt.	If the engine will turn freely only with the spark plugs out, and hydrostatic lock (water in the cylinders) is ruled out, check valve timing:	9.2
	If engine will not turn freely, and it is known that the clutch and transmission are free, the engine must be disassembled for further evaluation:	Next Chapter

Tests and Procedures	Results and Indications	Proceed to
3.1—Check the ignition switch "on" position: Connect a jumper wire between the distributor side of the coil and ground, and a 12V test lamp between the switch side of the coil and ground. Remove the high tension lead from the coil. Turn the ignition switch on and jiggle the key.	If the lamp lights:	3.2
	If the lamp flickers when the key is jiggled, replace the ignition switch:	3.3
	If the lamp doesn't light, check for loose or open connections. If none are found, remove the ignition switch and check for continuity. If the switch is faulty, replace it:	3.3

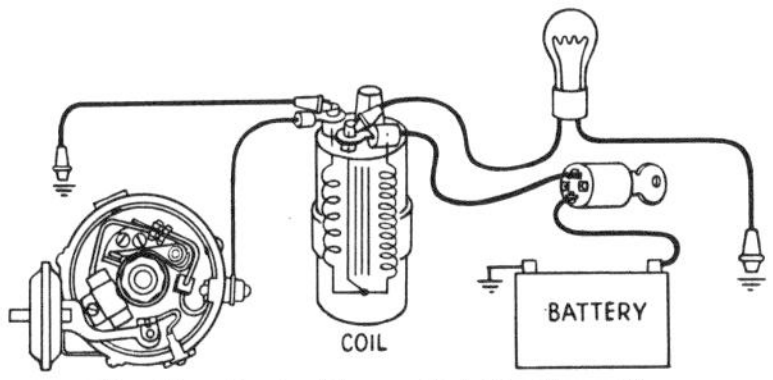

Checking the ignition switch "on" position

3.2—Check the ballast resistor or resistance wire for an open circuit, using an ohmmeter.	Replace the resistor or the resistance wire if the resistance is zero.	3.3
3.3—Visually inspect the breaker points for burning, pitting, or excessive wear. Gray coloring of the point contact surfaces is normal. Rotate the crankshaft until the contact heel rests on a high point of the distributor cam, and adjust the point gap to specifications.	If the breaker points are intact, clean the contact surfaces with fine emery cloth, and adjust the point gap to specifications. If pitted or worn, replace the points and condenser, and adjust the gap to specifications:	3.4
	NOTE: *Always lubricate the distributor cam according to manufacturer's recommendations when servicing the breaker points.*	
3.4—Connect a dwell meter between the distributor primary lead and ground. Crank the engine and observe the point dwell angle.	If necessary, adjust the point dwell angle: NOTE: *Increasing the point gap decreases the dwell angle, and vice-versa.*	3.6
	If dwell meter shows little or no reading:	3.5

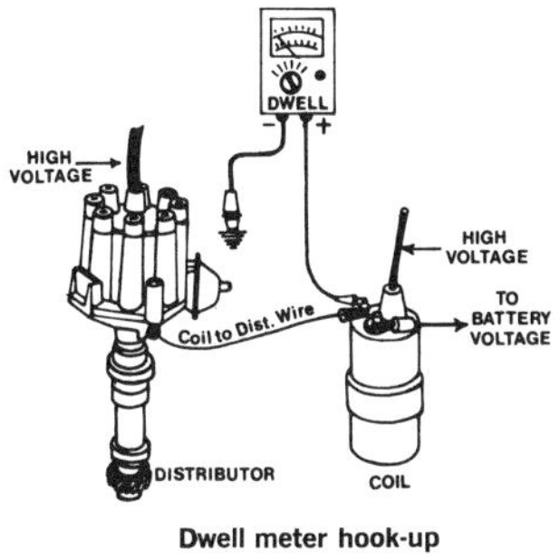

Dwell meter hook-up

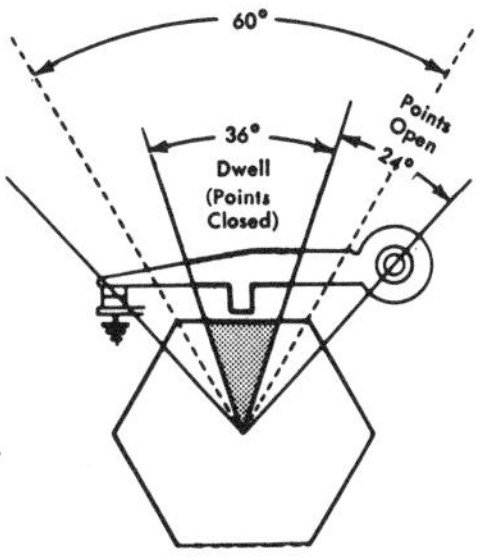

Dwell angle

3.5—Check the condenser for short: Connect an ohmmeter across the condenser body and the pigtail lead.	If any reading other than infinite resistance is noted, replace the condenser:	3.6

Checking the condenser for short

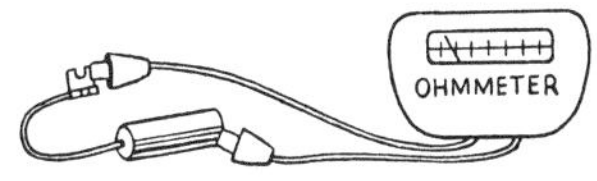

Test and Procedure	Results and Indications	Proceed to
3.6—Test the coil primary resistance: Connect an ohmmeter across the coil primary terminals, and read the resistance on the low scale. Note whether an external ballast resistor or resistance wire is utilized.	Coils utilizing ballast resistors or resistance wires should have approximately 1.0Ω resistance; coils with internal resistors should have approximately 4.0Ω resistance. If values far from the above are noted, replace the coil:	4.1
Testing the coil primary resistance		
4.1—Check for spark: Hold each spark plug wire approximately $\frac{1}{4}''$ from ground with gloves or a heavy, dry rag. Crank the engine, and observe the spark.	If no spark is evident:	4.2
	If spark is good in some cylinders:	4.3
	If spark is good in all cylinders:	4.6
4.2—Check for spark at the coil high tension lead: Remove the coil high tension lead from the distributor and position it approximately $\frac{1}{4}''$ from ground. Crank the engine and observe spark. CAUTION: *This test should not be performed on cars equipped with transistorized ignition.*	If the spark is good and consistent:	4.3
	If the spark is good but intermittent, test the primary electrical system starting at 3.3:	3.3
	If the spark is weak or non-existent, replace the coil high tension lead, clean and tighten all connections and retest. If no improvement is noted:	4.4
4.3—Visually inspect the distributor cap and rotor for burned or corroded contacts, cracks, carbon tracks, or moisture. Also check the fit of the rotor on the distributor shaft (where applicable).	If moisture is present, dry thoroughly, and retest per 4.1:	4.1
	If burned or excessively corroded contacts, cracks, or carbon tracks are noted, replace the defective part(s) and retest per 4.1:	4.1
	If the rotor and cap appear intact, or are only slightly corroded, clean the contacts thoroughly (including the cap towers and spark plug wire ends) and retest per 4.1: If the spark is good in all cases: If the spark is poor in all cases:	4.6 4.5
4.4—Check the coil secondary resistance: Connect an ohmmeter across the distributor side of the coil and the coil tower. Read the resistance on the high scale of the ohmmeter.	The resistance of a satisfactory coil should be between $4K\Omega$ and $10K\Omega$. If the resistance is considerably higher (i.e., $40K\Omega$) replace the coil, and retest per 4.1: NOTE: *This does not apply to high performance coils.*	4.1
Testing the coil secondary resistance		

Test and Procedure	Results and Indications	Proceed to
4.5—Visually inspect the spark plug wires for cracking or brittleness. Ensure that no two wires are positioned so as to cause induction firing (adjacent and parallel). Remove each wire, one by one, and check resistance with an ohmmeter.	Replace any cracked or brittle wires. If any of the wires are defective, replace the entire set. Replace any wires with excessive resistance (over 8000Ω per foot for suppression wire), and separate any wires that might cause induction firing.	4.6
4.6—Remove the spark plugs, noting the cylinders from which they were removed, and evaluate according to the chart below.	See below.	See below.

	Condition	Cause	Remedy	Proceed to
	Electrodes eroded, light brown deposits.	Normal wear. Normal wear is indicated by approximately .001″ wear per 1000 miles.	Clean and regap the spark plug if wear is not excessive: Replace the spark plug if excessively worn:	4.7
	Carbon fouling (black, dry, fluffy deposits).	If present on one or two plugs:		
		Faulty high tension lead(s).	Test the high tension leads:	4.5
		Burnt or sticking valve(s).	Check the valve train: (Clean and regap the plugs in either case.)	9.1
		If present on most or all plugs: Overly rich fuel mixture, due to restricted air filter, improper carburetor adjustment, improper choke or heat riser adjustment or operation.	Check the fuel system:	5.1
	Oil fouling (wet black deposits)	Worn engine components. NOTE: *Oil fouling may occur in new or recently rebuilt engines until broken in.*	Check engine vacuum and compression: Replace with new spark plug	6.1
	Lead fouling (gray, black, tan, or yellow deposits, which appear glazed or cinder-like).	Combustion by-products.	Clean and regap the plugs: (Use plugs of a different heat range if the problem recurs.)	4.7

	Condition	Cause	Remedy	Proceed to
	Gap bridging (deposits lodged between the electrodes).	Incomplete combustion, or transfer of deposits from the combustion chamber.	Replace the spark plugs:	4.7
	Overheating (burnt electrodes, and extremely white insulator with small black spots).	Ignition timing advanced too far.	Adjust timing to specifications:	8.2
		Overly lean fuel mixture.	Check the fuel system:	5.1
		Spark plugs not seated properly.	Clean spark plug seat and install a new gasket washer: (Replace the spark plugs in all cases.)	4.7
	Fused spot deposits on the insulator.	Combustion chamber blow-by.	Clean and regap the spark plugs:	4.7
	Pre-ignition (melted or severely burned electrodes, blistered or cracked insulators, or metallic deposits on the insulator).	Incorrect spark plug heat range.	Replace with plugs of the proper heat range:	4.7
		Ignition timing advanced too far.	Adjust timing to specifications:	8.2
		Spark plugs not being cooled efficiently.	Clean the spark plug seat, and check the cooling system:	11.1
		Fuel mixture too lean.	Check the fuel system:	5.1
		Poor compression.	Check compression:	6.1
		Fuel grade too low.	Use higher octane fuel:	4.7

Test and Procedure	Results and Indications	Proceed to
4.7—Determine the static ignition timing: Using the flywheel or crankshaft pulley timing marks as a guide, locate top dead center on the *compression* stroke of the No. 1 cylinder. Remove the distributor cap.	Adjust the distributor so that the rotor points toward the No. 1 tower in the distributor cap, and the points are just opening:	4.8
4.8—Check coil polarity: Connect a voltmeter negative lead to the coil high tension lead, and the positive lead to ground (NOTE: *reverse the hook-up for positive ground cars*). Crank the engine momentarily. Checking coil polarity	If the voltmeter reads up-scale, the polarity is correct: If the voltmeter reads down-scale, reverse the coil polarity (switch the primary leads):	5.1 5.1

Test and Procedure	*Results and Indications*	*Proceed to*
5.1—Determine that the air filter is functioning efficiently: Hold paper elements up to a strong light, and attempt to see light through the filter.	Clean permanent air filters in gasoline (or manufacturer's recommendation), and allow to dry. Replace paper elements through which light cannot be seen:	5.2
5.2—Determine whether a flooding condition exists: Flooding is identified by a strong gasoline odor, and excessive gasoline present in the throttle bore(s) of the carburetor.	If flooding is not evident:	5.3
	If flooding is evident, permit the gasoline to dry for a few moments and restart. If flooding doesn't recur:	5.6
	If flooding is persistant:	5.5
5.3—Check that fuel is reaching the carburetor: Detach the fuel line at the carburetor inlet. Hold the end of the line in a cup (not styrofoam), and crank the engine.	If fuel flows smoothly:	5.6
	If fuel doesn't flow (NOTE: *Make sure that there is fuel in the tank*), or flows erratically:	5.4
5.4—Test the fuel pump: Disconnect all fuel lines from the fuel pump. Hold a finger over the input fitting, crank the engine (with electric pump, turn the ignition or pump on); and feel for suction.	If suction is evident, blow out the fuel line to the tank with low pressure compressed air until bubbling is heard from the fuel filler neck. Also blow out the carburetor fuel line (both ends disconnected):	5.6
	If no suction is evident, replace or repair the fuel pump:	5.6
	NOTE: *Repeated oil fouling of the spark plugs, or a no-start condition, could be the result of a ruptured vacuum booster pump diaphragm, through which oil or gasoline is being drawn into the intake manifold (where applicable).*	
5.5—Check the needle and seat: Tap the carburetor in the area of the needle and seat.	If flooding stops, a gasoline additive (e.g., Gumout) will often cure the problem:	5.6
	If flooding continues, check the fuel pump for excessive pressure at the carburetor (according to specifications). If the pressure is normal, the needle and seat must be removed and checked, and/or the float level adjusted:	5.6
5.6—Test the accelerator pump by looking into the throttle bores while operating the throttle.	If the accelerator pump appears to be operating normally:	5.7
	If the accelerator pump is not operating, the pump must be reconditioned. Where possible, service the pump with the carburetor(s) installed on the engine. If necessary, remove the carburetor. Prior to removal:	5.7
5.7—Determine whether the carburetor main fuel system is functioning: Spray a commercial starting fluid into the carburetor while attempting to start the engine.	If the engine starts, runs for a few seconds, and dies:	5.8
	If the engine doesn't start:	6.1

Test and Procedures	*Results and Indications*	*Proceed to*
5.8—Uncommon fuel system malfunctions: See below:	If the problem is solved:	6.1
	If the problem remains, remove and recondition the carburetor.	

Condition	*Indication*	*Test*	*Usual Weather Conditions*	*Remedy*
Vapor lock	Car will not restart shortly after running.	Cool the components of the fuel system until the engine starts.	Hot to very hot	Ensure that the exhaust manifold heat control valve is operating. Check with the vehicle manufacturer for the recommended solution to vapor lock on the model in question.
Carburetor icing	Car will not idle, stalls at low speeds.	Visually inspect the throttle plate area of the throttle bores for frost.	High humidity, 32-40° F.	Ensure that the exhaust manifold heat control valve is operating, and that the intake manifold heat riser is not blocked.
Water in the fuel	Engine sputters and stalls; may not start.	Pump a small amount of fuel into a glass jar. Allow to stand, and inspect for droplets or a layer of water.	High humidity, extreme temperature changes.	For droplets, use one or two cans of commercial gas dryer (Dry Gas) For a layer of water, the tank must be drained, and the fuel lines blown out with compressed air.

Test and Procedure	*Results and Indications*	*Proceed to*
6.1—Test engine compression: Remove all spark plugs. Insert a compression gauge into a spark plug port, crank the engine to obtain the maximum reading, and record.	If compression is within limits on all cylinders:	7.1
	If gauge reading is extremely low on all cylinders:	6.2
	If gauge reading is low on one or two cylinders:	6.2
	(If gauge readings are identical and low on two or more adjacent cylinders, the head gasket must be replaced.)	

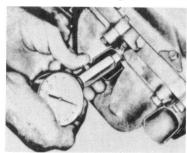

Testing compression
(© Chevrolet Div. G.M. Corp.)

Compression pressure limits
(© Buick Div. G.M. Corp.)

Maxi. Press. Lbs. Sq. In.	Min. Press. Lbs. Sq. In.	Maxi. Press. Lbs. Sq. In.	Min. Press. Lbs. Sq. In.	Max. Press. Lbs. Sq. In.	Min. Press. Lbs. Sq. In.	Max. Press. Lbs. Sq. In.	Min. Press. Lbs. Sq. In.
134	101	162	121	188	141	214	160
136	102	164	123	190	142	216	162
138	104	166	124	192	144	218	163
140	105	168	126	194	145	220	165
142	107	170	127	196	147	222	166
146	110	172	129	198	148	224	168
148	111	174	131	200	150	226	169
150	113	176	132	202	151	228	171
152	114	178	133	204	153	230	172
154	115	180	135	206	154	232	174
156	117	182	136	208	156	234	175
158	118	184	138	210	157	236	177
160	120	186	140	212	158	238	178

Test and Procedure	Results and Indications	Proceed to
6.2—Test engine compression (wet): Squirt approximately 30 cc. of engine oil into each cylinder, and retest per 6.1.	If the readings improve, worn or cracked rings or broken pistons are indicated:	Next Chapter
	If the readings do not improve, burned or excessively carboned valves or a jumped timing chain are indicated:	7.1
	NOTE: *A jumped timing chain is often indicated by difficult cranking.*	
7.1—Perform a vacuum check of the engine: Attach a vacuum gauge to the intake manifold beyond the throttle plate. Start the engine, and observe the action of the needle over the range of engine speeds.	See below.	See below

	Reading	Indications	Proceed to
	Steady, from 17-22 in. Hg.	Normal.	8.1
	Low and steady.	Late ignition or valve timing, or low compression:	6.1
	Very low	Vacuum leak:	7.2
	Needle fluctuates as engine speed increases.	Ignition miss, blown cylinder head gasket, leaking valve or weak valve spring:	6.1, 8.3
	Gradual drop in reading at idle.	Excessive back pressure in the exhaust system:	10.1
	Intermittent fluctuation at idle.	Ignition miss, sticking valve:	8.3, 9.1
	Drifting needle.	Improper idle mixture adjustment, carburetors not synchronized (where applicable), or minor intake leak. Synchronize the carburetors, adjust the idle, and retest. If the condition persists:	7.2
	High and steady.	Early ignition timing:	8.2

Test and Procedure	*Results and Indications*	*Proceed to*
7.2—Attach a vacuum gauge per 7.1, and test for an intake manifold leak. Squirt a small amount of oil around the intake manifold gaskets, carburetor gaskets, plugs and fittings. Observe the action of the vacuum gauge.	If the reading improves, replace the indicated gasket, or seal the indicated fitting or plug:	8.1
	If the reading remains low:	7.3
7.3—Test all vacuum hoses and accessories for leaks as described in 7.2. Also check the carburetor body (dashpots, automatic choke mechanism, throttle shafts) for leaks in the same manner.	If the reading improves, service or replace the offending part(s):	8.1
	If the reading remains low:	6.1
8.1—Check the point dwell angle: Connect a dwell meter between the distributor primary wire and ground. Start the engine, and observe the dwell angle from idle to 3000 rpm.	If necessary, adjust the dwell angle. NOTE: *Increasing the point gap reduces the dwell angle and vice-versa.* If the dwell angle moves outside specifications as engine speed increases, the distributor should be removed and checked for cam accuracy, shaft end-play and concentricity, bushing wear, and adequate point arm tension (NOTE: *Most of these items may be checked with the distributor installed in the engine, using an oscilloscope*):	8.2
8.2—Connect a timing light (per manufacturer's recommendation) and check the dynamic ignition timing. Disconnect and plug the vacuum hose(s) to the distributor if specified, start the engine, and observe the timing marks at the specified engine speed.	If the timing is not correct, adjust to specifications by rotating the distributor in the engine: (Advance timing by rotating distributor opposite normal direction of rotor rotation, retard timing by rotating distributor in same direction as rotor rotation.)	8.3
8.3—Check the operation of the distributor advance mechanism(s): To test the mechanical advance, disconnect all but the mechanical advance, and observe the timing marks with a timing light as the engine speed is increased from idle. If the mark moves smoothly, without hesitation, it may be assumed that the mechanical advance is functioning properly. To test vacuum advance and/or retard systems, alternately crimp and release the vacuum line, and observe the timing mark for movement. If movement is noted, the system is operating.	If the systems are functioning:	8.4
	If the systems are not functioning, remove the distributor, and test on a distributor tester:	8.4
8.4—Locate an ignition miss: With the engine running, remove each spark plug wire, one by one, until one is found that doesn't cause the engine to roughen and slow down.	When the missing cylinder is identified:	4.1

Test and Procedure	Results and Indications	Proceed to
9.1—Evaluate the valve train: Remove the valve cover, and ensure that the valves are adjusted to specifications. A mechanic's stethoscope may be used to aid in the diagnosis of the valve train. By pushing the probe on or near push rods or rockers, valve noise often can be isolated. A timing light also may be used to diagnose valve problems. Connect the light according to manufacturer's recommendations, and start the engine. Vary the firing moment of the light by increasing the engine speed (and therefore the ignition advance), and moving the trigger from cylinder to cylinder. Observe the movement of each valve.	See below	See below

Observation	Probable Cause	Remedy	Proceed to
Metallic tap heard through the stethoscope.	Sticking hydraulic lifter or excessive valve clearance.	Adjust valve. If tap persists, remove and replace the lifter:	10.1
Metallic tap through the stethoscope, able to push the rocker arm (lifter side) down by hand.	Collapsed valve lifter.	Remove and replace the lifter:	10.1
Erratic, irregular motion of the valve stem.*	Sticking valve, burned valve.	Recondition the valve and/or valve guide:	Next Chapter
Eccentric motion of the pushrod at the rocker arm.*	Bent pushrod.	Replace the pushrod:	10.1
Valve retainer bounces as the valve closes.*	Weak valve spring or damper.	Remove and test the spring and damper. Replace if necessary:	10.1

*—When observed with a timing light.

Test and Procedure	Results and Indications	Proceed to
9.2—Check the valve timing: Locate top dead center of the No. 1 piston, and install a degree wheel or tape on the crankshaft pulley or damper with zero corresponding to an index mark on the engine. Rotate the crankshaft in its direction of rotation, and observe the opening of the No. 1 cylinder intake valve. The opening should correspond with the correct mark on the degree wheel according to specifications.	If the timing is not correct, the timing cover must be removed for further investigation:	

Test and Procedure	Results and Indications	Proceed to
10.1—Determine whether the exhaust manifold heat control valve is operating: Operate the valve by hand to determine whether it is free to move. If the valve is free, run the engine to operating temperature and observe the action of the valve, to ensure that it is opening.	If the valve sticks, spray it with a suitable solvent, open and close the valve to free it, and retest. If the valve functions properly: If the valve does not free, or does not operate, replace the valve:	 10.2 10.2
10.2—Ensure that there are no exhaust restrictions: Visually inspect the exhaust system for kinks, dents, or crushing. Also note that gasses are flowing freely from the tailpipe at all engine speeds, indicating no restriction in the muffler or resonator.	Replace any damaged portion of the system:	11.1
11.1—Visually inspect the fan belt for glazing, cracks, and fraying, and replace if necessary. Tighten the belt so that the longest span has approximately ½" play at its midpoint under thumb pressure. Checking the fan belt tension (© Nissan Motor Co. Ltd.)	Replace or tighten the fan belt as necessary:	11.2
11.2—Check the fluid level of the cooling system.	If full or slightly low, fill as necessary: If extremely low:	11.5 11.3
11.3—Visually inspect the external portions of the cooling system (radiator, radiator hoses, thermostat elbow, water pump seals, heater hoses, etc.) for leaks. If none are found, pressurize the cooling system to 14-15 psi.	If cooling system holds the pressure: If cooling system loses pressure rapidly, reinspect external parts of the system for leaks under pressure. If none are found, check dipstick for coolant in crankcase. If no coolant is present, but pressure loss continues: If coolant is evident in crankcase, remove cylinder head(s), and check gasket(s). If gaskets are intact, block and cylinder head(s) should be checked for cracks or holes. If the gasket(s) is blown, replace, and purge the crankcase of coolant: NOTE: *Occasionally, due to atmospheric and driving conditions, condensation of water can occur in the crankcase. This causes the oil to appear milky white. To remedy, run the engine until hot, and change the oil and oil filter.*	11.5 11.4 12.6

Test and Procedure	Results and Indication	Proceed to
11.4—Check for combustion leaks into the cooling system: Pressurize the cooling system as above. Start the engine, and observe the pressure gauge. If the needle fluctuates, remove each spark plug wire, one by one, noting which cylinder(s) reduce or eliminate the fluctuation. **Radiator pressure tester** (© American Motors Corp.)	Cylinders which reduce or eliminate the fluctuation, when the spark plug wire is removed, are leaking into the cooling system. Replace the head gasket on the affected cylinder bank(s).	
11.5—Check the radiator pressure cap: Attach a radiator pressure tester to the radiator cap (wet the seal prior to installation). Quickly pump up the pressure, noting the point at which the cap releases. **Testing the radiator pressure cap** (© American Motors Corp.)	If the cap releases within ± 1 psi of the specified rating, it is operating properly: If the cap releases at more than ± 1 psi of the specified rating, it should be replaced:	11.6 11.6
11.6—Test the thermostat: Start the engine cold, remove the radiator cap, and insert a thermometer into the radiator. Allow the engine to idle. After a short while, there will be a sudden, rapid increase in coolant temperature. The temperature at which this sharp rise stops is the thermostat opening temperature.	If the thermostat opens at or about the specified temperature: If the temperature doesn't increase: (If the temperature increases slowly and gradually, replace the thermostat.)	11.7 11.7
11.7—Check the water pump: Remove the thermostat elbow and the thermostat, disconnect the coil high tension lead (to prevent starting), and crank the engine momentarily.	If coolant flows, replace the thermostat and retest per 11.6: If coolant doesn't flow, reverse flush the cooling system to alleviate any blockage that might exist. If system is not blocked, and coolant will not flow, recondition the water pump.	11.6 —
12.1—Check the oil pressure gauge or warning light: If the gauge shows low pressure, or the light is on, for no obvious reason, remove the oil pressure sender. Install an accurate oil pressure gauge and run the engine momentarily.	If oil pressure builds normally, run engine for a few moments to determine that it is functioning normally, and replace the sender. If the pressure remains low: If the pressure surges: If the oil pressure is zero:	— 12.2 12.3 12.3

Test and Procedure	Results and Indications	Proceed to
12.2—Visually inspect the oil: If the oil is watery or very thin, milky, or foamy, replace the oil and oil filter.	If the oil is normal:	12.3
	If after replacing oil the pressure remains low:	12.3
	If after replacing oil the pressure becomes normal:	—
12.3—Inspect the oil pressure relief valve and spring, to ensure that it is not sticking or stuck. Remove and thoroughly clean the valve, spring, and the valve body.	If the oil pressure improves:	—
	If no improvement is noted:	12.4

Oil pressure relief valve
(© British Leyland Motors)

Test and Procedure	Results and Indications	Proceed to
12.4—Check to ensure that the oil pump is not cavitating (sucking air instead of oil): See that the crankcase is neither over nor underfull, and that the pickup in the sump is in the proper position and free from sludge.	Fill or drain the crankcase to the proper capacity, and clean the pickup screen in solvent if necessary. If no improvement is noted:	12.5
12.5—Inspect the oil pump drive and the oil pump:	If the pump drive or the oil pump appear to be defective, service as necessary and retest per 12.1:	12.1
	If the pump drive and pump appear to be operating normally, the engine should be disassembled to determine where blockage exists:	Next Chapter
12.6—Purge the engine of ethylene glycol coolant: Completely drain the crankcase and the oil filter. Obtain a commercial butyl cellosolve base solvent, designated for this purpose, and follow the instructions precisely. Following this, install a new oil filter and refill the crankcase with the proper weight oil. The next oil and filter change should follow shortly thereafter (1000 miles).		

Chapter 3

Engine and Engine Rebuilding

Engine Electrical

DISTRIBUTOR

Removal

1. Remove the coil wire from the distributor cap terminal on point-type systems; disconnect the primary wiring harness connector on the solid-state system.

2. Remove the distributor cap.

3. Disconnect the vacuum advance line at the distributor.

4. Note the position of the rotor and scribe a mark on the distributor body, indicating its position. Scribe two more marks, one on the body of the distributor and another on the engine block, indicating the position of the distributor body in relation to the engine block. All of the scribe marks should be made in line with each other, starting with the metal tip of the rotor and ending with the mark on the engine block. These marks will be used as guides when installing the distributor in the correctly timed engine (not disturbed).

5. Remove the retaining bolt and lockwasher which hold the distributor in the engine.

6. Lift the distributor out of the engine block. Note that the rotor will turn slightly as it is removed. This is due to the curvature of the distributor drive gear. Take this into consideration in aligning the scribe marks, when installing the distributor.

Installation (Engine Not Disturbed)

1. Insert the distributor shaft into the engine. Align the marks on the distributor body with the metal tip of the rotor and the mark made on the engine block. Make sure that the vacuum advance diaphragm is pointed in the same direction as it was pointed originally. This will be done automatically if the marks on the engine and the distributor are aligned properly.

2. Install the distributor lockbolt and clamp. Leave the screw loose enough that you can turn the distributor with your hand.

3. Connect the distributor primary wire and install the distributor cap. Secure the distributor cap with the spring clips.

4. Install the spark plug wires. Make certain that the wires are pressed all the way into the top of the distributor cap and firmly onto the spark plugs.

5. Adjust the point dwell and set the ignition timing. Refer to the "Tune-Up" Section (Chapter 2).

Installation (Engine Disturbed)

If the engine has been disturbed, (i.e., crankshaft turned) while the distributor has been removed or the alignment marks were not drawn, it will be necessary to initially time the engine. Follow the procedure given below:

1. Place the No. 1 piston at TDC of the compression stroke. To determine this, remove the spark plug from the No. 1 cylinder and the high-tension coil wire from the distributor cap. Place your thumb over the spark plug hole while the engine is cranked. You will feel air being forced out of the cylinder as the piston comes up on its compression stroke. As soon as you feel this, stop cranking the engine. The final positioning adjustment for the No. 1 piston is to align the TDC timing mark with the pointer or notch in the crankshaft pulley.

2. Lightly oil the distributor housing, where the distributor mounts on the cylinder block.

3. Install the distributor so that the rotor, which is mounted on the shaft, points toward the No. 1 spark plug terminal of the distributor cap. To facilitate this operation, place the distributor cap on the distributor body in its normal position and make a mark on the body of the distributor just below the No. 1 spark plug terminal tower. Make sure that the metal tip of the rotor is pointing toward the mark when the distributor is installed.

4. When the distributor shaft has reached the bottom of the hole, move the rotor back and forth slightly until the drive gears of the distributor shaft and the camshaft mesh and the distributor assembly slides down into place.

5. When the distributor is correctly installed, the breaker point contacts should be in such a position that they are just ready to break contact with each other. On the solid-state system, align one armature tooth with the fixed stator. This is accomplished by rotating the distributor body after it has been installed in the engine.

6. Install the distributor retaining plate and lockbolt.

7. Install the spark plug into the No. 1 cylinder spark plug hole and continue from Step 3 of the distributor installation

procedure for engines that have not been disturbed.

ALTERNATOR

Alternator Precautions

To prevent damage to the alternator and regulator, the following precautionary measures must be taken when working with the electrical system.

1. Never reverse battery connections. Always check the battery polarity visually. This should be done before any connections are made to be sure that all of the connections correspond to the battery ground polarity of the van.

2. Booster batteries for starting must be connected properly. Make sure that the positive cable of the booster battery is connected to the positive terminal of the battery that is getting the boost. The same applies to the negative cables.

3. Disconnect the battery cables before using a fast charger; the charger has a tendency to force current through the diodes in the opposite direction for which they were designed. This burns out the diodes.

4. Never use a fast charger as a booster for starting the vehicle.

5. Never disconnect the voltage regulator while the engine is running.

6. Do not ground the alternator output terminal.

7. Do not operate the alternator on an open circuit with the field energized.

8. Do not attempt to polarize an alternator.

Removal and Installation

1. Open the hood and disconnect the battery ground cable.

2. From under the vehicle, remove the adjusting arm bolt.

3. Remove the alternator through-bolt. Remove the drive belt from the alternator pulley and lower the alternator.

4. Label all of the leads to the alternator so that you can install them correctly and disconnect the leads from the alternator.

5. Remove the alternator from the vehicle.

6. To install, reverse the above procedure.

Belt Tension Adjustment

The fan belt drives the alternator and water pump. If the belt is too loose, it will slip and the alternator will not be able to produce its rated current. Also, the water pump will not operate efficiently and the engine could overheat.

Check the tension of the fan belt by pushing your thumb down on the longest span of the belt, midway between the pulleys. Belt deflection should be approximately ½ in.

To adjust belt tension, proceed as follows:

1. Loosen the alternator mounting bolt and the adjusting arm bolts.

2. Apply pressure on the alternator front housing only, moving the alternator away from the engine to tighten the belt. Do not apply pressure to the rear of the cast aluminum housing of an alternator; damage to the housing could result.

3. Tighten the alternator mounting bolt and the adjusting arm bolts when the correct tension is reached.

REGULATOR

The alternator regulator has been designed to control the charging system's rate of charge and to compensate for seasonal temperature changes. The electromechanical regulator on 1968 and later vehicles, is calibrated at the factory and is not adjustable. The regulator on 1966–67 models is adjustable. The transistorized regulator used with the 1975–77 90 amp alternator has a voltage limit adjustment. The transistorized unit has a cover held on by screws rather than rivets. To adjust, remove the cover, and using a fiber or plastic rod, turn the adjusting screw clockwise to increase the voltage setting or counterclockwise to decrease.

Removal and Installation

1. Disconnect the positive terminal of the battery.

2. Disconnect all of the electrical leads at the regulator. Label them as removed, so that you can replace them in the correct order on the replacement unit. On late models, use a screwdriver to detach the plug.

3. Remove all of the hold-down screws, then remove the unit from the vehicle.

4. Install the new voltage regulator using the hold-down screws from the old one, or new ones if they are provided with the replacement regulator. Tighten the hold-down screws.

5. Connect all the leads to the new regulator.

Adjustment
(1966 and 1967 models only)

To make any adjustment to the voltage regulator, the unit has to be removed from the vehicle. See the "Removal and Installation" procedure above for instructions.

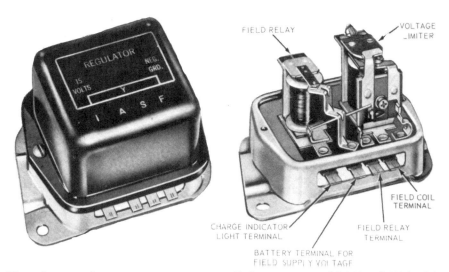

The voltage regulator components; cover installed, cover removed (1966 and 1967 only)

Alternator and Regulator Specifications

Year	Identi- fication Color Code	Field Current Draw (amps) @ 12 Volts	Output (amps)	Field Relay Air Gap (in.)	Field Relay Point Gap (in.)	Field Relay Volts to Close	Regulator Air Gap (in.)	Regulator Point Gap (in.)	Regulated Voltage @ 75° F
1966	Purple	2.5	38	0.010–0.018	——	2.5–4.0	0.049–0.056	0.017–0.022	14.1–14.9
	Black	2.9	45	0.010–0.018	——	2.5–4.0	0.049–0.056	0.017–0.022	14.1–14.9
	Red	2.9	55	0.010–0.018	——	2.5–4.0	0.049–0.056	0.017–0.022	14.1–14.9
1967	Purple	2.5	38	0.010–0.018	——	2.5–4.0	——	——	13.9–14.9
	Black	2.9	45	0.010–0.018	——	2.5–4.0	——	——	13.9–14.9
	Red	2.9	55	0.010–0.018	——	2.5–4.0	——	——	13.9–14.9
1968– 74	Purple	2.4	38	——	——	2.0–4.2	——	——	13.9–14.9
	Orange	2.9	42	——	——	2.0–4.2	——	——	13.9–14.9
	Red	2.9	55	——	——	2.0–4.2	——	——	13.9–14.9
1975– 77	Orange	2.9	40	——	——	——	——	——	13.9–14.9
	Green	2.9	60	——	——	——	——	——	13.9–14.9
	Red	2.9	90	——	——	——	——	——	13.9–14.9

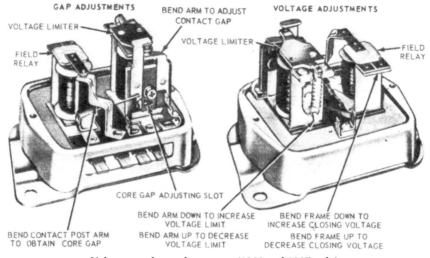

Voltage regulator adjustments (1966 and 1967 only)

Field Relay Adjustment

AIR GAP

Place a 0.010–0.018 in. feeler gauge on top of the coil core closest to the contact points. Hold the armature down on the gauge. Do not push down on the contact spring arm. Bend the contact post arm until the bottom contact just touches the upper contact. Remove the feeler gauge.

Voltage Limiter Adjustment

The voltage limiter is adjusted by bending the voltage limiter spring arm. To increase the voltage setting, bend the adjusting arm downward. To decrease the voltage setting, bend the adjusting arm upward. Final adjustment of the regulator must be made with the regulator at normal operating temperatures. The voltage limiter should be set to between 13.6 and 15.1 volts read with a voltmeter installed between the battery/alternator terminal of the starter relay and the positive terminal of the battery.

STARTER MOTOR

Removal

1. Disconnect the positive battery terminal.
2. Raise the vehicle and disconnect the starter cable at the starter terminal. With the 460 V8, turn the front wheels all the way to the right and unbolt the steering idler arm bracket from the frame.

3. Remove all of the starter attaching bolts that attach the starter to the bell-housing.
4. Remove the starter from the engine.
5. Install the starter in the reverse order of removal.

Starter Drive Replacement, Except 460 V8

1. Remove the cover of the starter drive's plunger lever arm, and the brush cover band. Remove the through-bolts, starter drive gear housing, and the return spring of the driver gear's actuating lever.
2. Remove the pivot pin which retains the starter gear plunger lever and remove the lever.
3. Remove the stop-ring retainer. Remove and discard the stop-ring which holds the drive gear to the armature shaft and then remove the drive gear assembly.

To install the drive gear assembly:

4. Lightly Lubriplate® the armature shaft splines and install the starter drive gear assembly on the shaft. Install a new stop-ring and stop-ring retainer.
5. Position the starter drive gear plunger lever to the frame and starter drive assembly.
6. Install the pivot pin.
7. Position the drive plunger lever return spring and the drive gear housing to the frame, then install and tighten the through-bolts. Be sure that the stop-

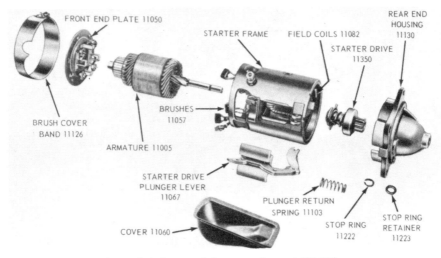

An exploded view of the starter (except 460 V8)

ring retainer is properly seated in the drive housing.

8. Position the starter drive plunger lever cover and the brush cover band on the starter. Tighten the brush cover band retaining screw.

Starter Relay Replacement

The starter relay is mounted on the inside of the left wheel well. To replace it, disconnect the positive battery cable from the battery, disconnect all of the electrical leads from the relay and remove the relay from the fender well. Replace in the reverse order of removal.

BATTERY

Removal and Installation

1. Loosen the nuts which secure the cable ends to the battery terminals. Lift the battery cables from the terminals with a twisting motion.

2. If there is a battery cable puller available, make use of it.

3. Remove the hold-down nuts from the battery hold-down bracket and remove the bracket and the battery. Lift the battery straight up and out of the vehicle, being sure to keep the battery level to avoid spilling the battery acid.

4. Before installing the battery in the vehicle, make sure that the battery terminals are clean and free from corrosion. Use a battery terminal cleaner on the terminals and on the inside of the battery cable ends. If a cleaner is not available, use coarse grade sandpaper to remove the corrosion. A mixture of baking soda and water poured over the terminals and cable ends will help remove and neutralize any acid buildup. Before installing the cables onto the terminals, cut a piece of felt cloth, or something similar into a circle about 3 in. across. Cut a hole in the middle about the size of the battery terminals at their base. Push the cloth pieces over the terminals so that they lay flat on the top of the battery. Soak the pieces of cloth with oil. This will keep the formation of oxidized acid to a minimum. Place the battery in the vehicle. Install the cables onto the terminals. Tighten the nuts on the cable ends. Smear a light coating of grease on the cable ends and tops of the terminals. This will further prevent the buildup of oxidized acid on the terminals and the cable ends. Install and tighten the nuts of the battery hold-down bracket.

Engine Mechanical

DESIGN

6 Cylinder Engines

The 170 cu in. 240 cu in. and 300 cu in. 6 cylinder engines installed in Ford vans are of an inline, overhead valve design.

The cylinder head carries the intake and exhaust valve assemblies and mechanism. Water passages in the cylinder head help keep the valves cool.

The distributor, located on the left-side of the engine, is gear-driven from the camshaft and also drives the oil pump through an intermediate shaft.

The 170 engine crankshaft has four main bearings with end thrust taken by the no. 3 bearing. The 240 and 300 have seven main bearings with thrust taken on no. 5.

The camshaft is mounted on 4 bearings and is driven by a sprocket and chain connection with the crankshaft in the

Starter Specifications

Starter Diameter (in.)	Engine	Lock Test		Torque (ft lbs)	No Load Test		Brush Spring Tension (oz)	Normal Current Draw (amps)
		Amps	Volts		Amps	Volts		
4	except 460	460	5	9	70	12	40	150–200
4½	except 460	670	5	15.5	70	12	40	150–180
4½	460	——	——	——	70	12	40	180–210

170; the 240 and 300 sixes use gears to drive the camshaft. An integral eccentric on the camshaft operates the fuel pump. The valve tappets are of the hydraulic type with solid type tappets installed in early 170 cu in. engines.

The engines are pressure lubricated by a rotor-type oil pump equipped with a pressure relief valve. Oil reaches the rocker arm shaft on the 170 through the No. 6 valve rocker arm shaft support at the rear of the engine.

General Engine Specifications

Year	Engine Displacement (cu in.)	Carb Type	Horsepower (@ rpm)	Torque @ rpm (ft lbs)	Bore x Stroke (in.)	Compression Ratio	Oil Pressure (psi) @ 2000 rpm
1966–67	6-170	1 bbl	105 @ 4400	158 @ 2400	3.500 x 2.940	9.1 : 1	35–55
	6-240	1 bbl	150 @ 4000	234 @ 2200	4.000 x 3.180	9.2 : 1	35–60
1968	6-170	1 bbl	100 @ 4000	158 @ 2200	3.500 x 2.940	9.3 : 1	35–55
	6-240	1 bbl	150 @ 4000	234 @ 2200	4.000 x 3.180	9.2 : 1	35–60
	8-302	2 bbl	205 @ 4600	300 @ 2600	4.000 x 3.000	8.6 : 1	35–60
1969	6-170	1 bbl	100 @ 4000	156 @ 2200	3.500 x 2.940	8.7 : 1	35–60
	6-240	1 bbl	150 @ 4000	234 @ 2200	4.000 x 3.180	9.2 : 1	35–60
	8-302	2 bbl	205 @ 4600	300 @ 2600	4.000 x 3.000	8.6 : 1	35–60
1970	6-170	1 bbl	100 @ 4000	156 @ 2200	3.500 x 2.940	8.7 : 1	35–60
	6-240	1 bbl	150 @ 4000	234 @ 2200	4.000 x 3.180	9.2 : 1	35–60
	8-302	2 bbl	205 @ 4600	300 @ 2600	4.000 x 3.000	8.6 : 1	35–60
1971	6-240	1 bbl	140 @ 4000	230 @ 2200	4.000 x 3.180	8.9 : 1	35–60
	8-302	2 bbl	205 @ 4600	300 @ 2600	4.000 x 3.000	8.6 : 1	35–60
1972	6-240	1 bbl	103 @ 3800	170 @ 2200	4.000 x 3.180	8.5 : 1	35–60
	8-302	2 bbl	140 @ 4000	242 @ 2000	4.000 x 3.000	8.5 : 1	35–60
1973–74	6-240	1 bbl	105 @ 3800	175 @ 2400	4.000 x 3.180	8.5 : 1	40–60
	6-300	1 bbl	114 @ 3400	222 @ 1600	4.000 x 3.980	8.4 : 1	40–60
	8-302	2 bbl	139 @ 3800	236 @ 2000	4.000 x 3.000	8.2 : 1	40–60
1975–77	6-300	1 bbl	114 @ 3400	222 @ 1600	4.000 x 3.980	8.3 : 1	40–60
	8-351	2 bbl	178 @ 4000	270 @ 2600	4.000 x 3.500	8.1 : 1	40–60
	8-400	4 bbl	243 @ 4200	371 @ 2000	4.000 x 3.050	8.0 : 1	35–65

Valve Specifications

Year	Engine Displacement (cu in.)	Seat Angle (deg)	Face Angle (deg)	Spring Test Pressure (lbs @ in.)	Spring Installed Height (in.)	Stem-to-Guide Clearance (in.)		Stem Diameter (in.)	
						Intake	Exhaust	Intake	Exhaust
1966–70	6-170	45	44	52 @ 1.6	$1\frac{9}{16}$–$1\frac{39}{64}$	0.0008–0.0025	0.0010–0.0027	0.3103	0.3128
1966	6-240	45	44	80 @ 1.7	$1\frac{43}{64}$–$1\frac{47}{64}$	0.0010–0.0027	0.0010–0.0027	0.3416–0.3423	0.3416–0.3423
1967	6-240	45	44	80 @ 1.7	$1\frac{35}{64}$–$1\frac{39}{64}$	0.0010–0.0027	0.0010–0.0027	0.3416–0.3423	0.3416–0.3423
1968–69	6-240	45	44	80 @ 1.7	$1\frac{43}{64}$–$1\frac{47}{64}$	0.0010–0.0027	0.0010–0.0027	0.3416–0.3423	0.3416–0.3423
	8-302	45	44	75 @ 1.66	$1\frac{5}{8}$–$1\frac{11}{16}$	0.0010–0.0027	0.0010–0.0027	0.3416–0.3423	0.3416–0.3423
1970–71	6-240	45	44	80 @ 1.7	$1\frac{21}{32}$–$1\frac{23}{32}$	0.0010–0.0027	0.0010–0.0027	0.3416–0.3423	0.3416–0.3423
	8-302	45	44	75 @ 1.66	$1\frac{5}{8}$–$1\frac{21}{32}$	0.0010–0.0027	0.0010–0.0027	0.3416–0.3423	0.3416–0.3423
1972	6-240	45	44	80 @ 1.7	$1\frac{21}{32}$–$1\frac{23}{32}$	0.0010–0.0027	0.0010–0.0027	0.3416–0.3423	0.3416–0.3423
	8-302	45	44	75 @ 1.66	$1\frac{5}{8}$–$1\frac{21}{32}$	0.0015–0.0032	0.0010–0.0027	0.3416–0.3423	0.3416–0.3423
1973	6-240 6-300	45	44	80 @ 1.7	$1\frac{11}{16}$–$1\frac{23}{32}$ ①	0.0010–0.0027	0.0010–0.0027	0.3416–0.3423	0.3416–0.3423
	8-302	45	44	80 @ 1.69	$1\frac{43}{64}$–$1\frac{45}{64}$	0.0010–0.0027	0.0015–0.0032	0.3416–0.3423	0.3416–0.3423
1974	6-240 6-300	45	44	80 @ 1.7	$1\frac{11}{16}$–$1\frac{23}{32}$ ①	0.0010–0.0027	0.0010–0.0027	0.3416–0.3423	0.3416–0.3423
	8-302	45	44	80 @ 1.7	$1\frac{43}{64}$–$1\frac{45}{64}$ ②	0.0010–0.0027	0.0015–0.0032	0.3416–0.3423	0.3411–0.3418
1975–77	6-300	45	44	80 @ 1.7	$1\frac{11}{16}$–$1\frac{23}{32}$ ①	0.0010–0.0027	0.0010–0.0027	0.3416–0.3423	0.3416–0.3423
	8-351	45	44	75 @ 1.8	$1\frac{49}{64}$–$1\frac{13}{16}$ ③	0.0010–0.0027	0.0015–0.0032	0.3416–0.3423	0.3411–0.3418
	8-460	45	44	80 @ 1.8	$1\frac{51}{64}$–$1\frac{53}{64}$	0.0010–0.0027	0.0010–0.0027	0.3416–0.3423	0.3416–0.3423

① Intake given; Exhaust—$1\frac{9}{16}$–$1\frac{19}{32}$ in.
② Intake given; Exhaust—$1\frac{19}{32}$–$1\frac{39}{64}$ in.
③ Intake given; Exhaust—$1\frac{13}{16}$–$1\frac{27}{32}$ in.

Crankshaft and Connecting Rod Specifications

(All measurements given in in.)

Year	Engine Displacement (cu in.)	Crankshaft				Connecting Rod		
		Main Brg Journal Dia	Main Brg Oil Clearance	Shaft End-Play	Thrust on No.	Journal Dia	Oil Clearance	Side Clearance
1966–70	6-170	2.2482–2.2490	0.0005–0.0022	0.004–0.008	3	2.1232–2.1240	0.0008–0.0024	0.0035–0.0105
1966–77	6-240, 300	2.3986–2.3990①	0.0008–0.0024②	0.004–0.008	5	2.1228–2.1236③	0.0010–0.0015④	0.006–0.013
1969–74	8-302	2.2482–2.2490	0.0005–0.0015⑤	0.004–0.008	3	2.1228–2.1236	0.0008–0.0015	0.010–0.020
1975–77	8-351	2.9994–3.0002	0.0008–0.0015⑥	0.004–0.008	3	2.3103–2.3111	0.0008–0.0015	0.010–0.020
1975–77	8-460	2.9994–3.0002	0.0008–0.0026⑦	0.004–0.008	3	2.4992–2.5000	0.0008–0.0015	0.010–0.020

① 1966 to 1968 given; 1969 to 1977—2.3982–2.3990 in.
② 1966 to 1968 given; 1969 to 1974—0.0005–0.0015 in.; 1975 to 1977—0.0008–0.0015 in.
③ 1968 only—2.1232–2.1246 in.
④ 1970 to 1972 given; 1966 to 1969 and 1973–77—0.0008–0.0015 in.
⑤ 1971 to 1974 No. 1 only—0.0001–0.0015 in.
⑥ No. 1—0.0005–0.0015
⑦ No. 1—0.0080–0.0026

Piston Clearance

Year	Engine Displacement (cu in.)	Minimum (in.)	Maximum (in.)
1966–70	6-170	0.0014	0.0020
1966–77	6-240, 300	0.0014	0.0022
1968–77	8-302	0.0018	0.0026
	8-351	0.0022	0.0030
1975–77	8-460	0.0022	0.0030

Ring Gap

Year	Engine Displacement (cu in.)	Top Compression (in.)		Bottom Compression (in.)		Year	Engine	Oil Control (in.)	
		Min.	Max.	Min.	Max.			Min.	Max.
1966–77	All	0.010	0.020	0.010	0.020	1966–70	6-170	0.015	0.055
						1966–77	6-240, 300	0.015	0.055
						1968–71	8-302	0.015	0.069
						1972–77	8-302, 351, 460	0.015	0.055

Ring Side Clearance

Year	Engine Displacement (cu in.)	Top Compression (in.)			Bottom Compression (in.)			Oil Control (in.)	
		Min.	Max.	Replace	Min.	Max.	Replace	Min.	Max.
1966	6-170	0.0009	0.0026	0.0060	0.0020	0.0040	0.0060	All engines—snug	
	6-240	0.0019	0.0036	0.0060	0.0020	0.0040	0.0060	All engines—snug	
1967	6-170, 240	0.0019	0.0036	0.0060	0.0020	0.0040	0.0060	All engines—snug	
1968–77	All	0.0020	0.0040	0.0060	0.0020	0.0040	0.0060	All engines—snug	

Torque Specifications
All readings in ft lbs

Year	Engine Displacement (cu in.)	Cylinder Head Bolts	Rod Bearing Bolts	Main Bearing Bolts	Crankshaft Pulley Bolt	Flywheel-to-Crankshaft Bolts	Manifold	
							Intake	Exhaust
1966–70	6-170	70–75	19–24	60–70	85–100	75–85	——	13–18
1966–77	6-240, 300	70–75②	40–45	60–70①	130–150	75–85	25	25
1968–74	8-302	65–72	19–24	60–70	70–90	75–85	24	14
1975–77	8-351	65–70	40–45	95–105	70–90	75–85	23–25	18–24
1975–77	8-460	130–140	40–45	95–105	70–90	75–85	28–33	28–33

① 1974—65–72
② 1975–77—70–85

V8

The V8 engines are of the standard, two-bank, V-design with the banks of cylinders opposed to each other at a 90° angle.

The crankshaft is supported by 5 main bearings, with crankshaft end thrust controlled by the flanged No. 3 bearing.

The camshaft, which is located in the center of the V-design of the engine, is mounted on 5 bearings and is driven by a sprocket and chain which are connected to a sprocket on the crankshaft. An eccentric bolted to the front of the camshaft operates the fuel pump. A gear on the front of the camshaft drives the distributor, which in turn drives the oil pump through an intermediate shaft. The oil pump is located in the left front of the oil pan.

All of the V8s are equipped with hydraulic valve lifters.

Engine Removal and Installation

170 SIX-CYLINDER

1. Drain the cooling system.
2. Remove the engine cover.
3. Remove the right-hand seat.
4. Raise the vehicle on a hoist.
5. Disconnect the driveshaft at the transmission flange. Remove the midship bearing support-to-chassis and position the driveshaft out of the way.
6. Disconnect the speedometer cable and housing at the transmission.
7. Disconnect the transmission shift rods at the transmission shift levers.
8. Disconnect the clutch retracting

spring. Remove the equalizer bracket at the chassis side rail and remove the clutch equalizer arm and clutch linkage from the cylinder block. Position the assembly out of the way.

9. Position an engine support bar to the chassis and the engine to support the rear of the engine.

10. Remove the bolt and nut attaching the rear engine support to the crossmember to the chassis and remove the crossmember.

11. Position a transmission jack under the transmission and secure it.

12. Remove the bolts attaching the transmission to the clutch housing and remove the transmission.

13. Disconnect the muffler inlet pipe at the exhaust manifold.

14. Disconnect the ground wire at the cylinder block.

15. Disconnect the ground wire at the starter retaining bolt.

16. Drain the crankcase.

17. Remove the oil filter.

18. Remove the nuts attaching the engine supports to the chassis.

19. Lower the vehicle.

20. Disconnect the battery.

21. Disconnect the radiator upper hose at the radiator.

22. Disconnect the radiator lower hose at the radiator and drain the radiator.

23. Remove the radiator.

24. Remove the fan assembly and the spacer.

25. Disconnect the heater hose at the water pump.

26. Remove the air cleaner assembly.

27. Disconnect the tank-to-pump fuel line at the fuel pump and plug the line.

28. Disconnect the accelerator cable at the carburetor.

29. Disconnect the choke cable, remove it from the mounting bracket and position it out of the way.

30. Remove the accelerator cable mounting bracket from the carburetor and the cylinder head.

31. Disconnect the heater hose at the cylinder head.

32. Disconnect the oil filler pipe at the rocker arm cover and remove the oil filler pipe.

33. Remove the oil dipstick and tube from the cylinder block.

34. Disconnect the engine wire loom and position it out of the way (temp., oil, coil).

35. Disconnect the starter cable at the starter.

36. Remove the alternator from the mounting and adjusting brackets and position the alternator out of the way.

37. Position an engine lifting device to the engine and attach it to a crane boom and lift the engine out of the vehicle through the right front door.

To install the 170 six:

1. Install the engine into the engine compartment through the right front door and allow it to rest on the front engine supports and the engine support bar at the rear of the engine.

2. Raise the vehicle on a hoist.

3. Install the engine support insulator attaching nuts to the chassis mounts.

4. Position the transmission to the clutch housing and install the attaching bolts.

5. Raise the transmission and position the crossmember to the chassis and the rear engine support. Install the bolts and nut attaching the crossmember to the transmission and chassis.

6. Remove the transmission jack and the engine support bar.

7. Position the equalizer arm to the cylinder block mount, position the linkage to the bearing fork, install the equalizer arm mounting bracket retracting spring.

8. Connect the shift rods at the transmission.

9. Connect the speedometer cable at the transmission.

10. Position the driveshaft to the transmission flange and install the "U" bolts and nuts. Position the midship bearing support to the chassis and install the attaching bolts.

11. Connect the muffler inlet pipe at the exhaust manifold and tighten the retaining clamp at the cylinder block.

12. Connect the ground wire to the starter.

13. Lower the vehicle.

14. Unplug and connect the fuel line from the tank to the fuel pump at the pump. Connect the fuel line from the fuel pump to the carburetor at the filter.

15. Position the engine wire loom in the retainers and connect at the respective locations (i.e., coil, oil, temp).

16. Position the alternator to the mounting brackets and install the attaching bolts.

17. Connect the alternator and battery ground wires.

18. Connect the starter cable at the starter.

19. Install the dipstick and tube to the cylinder block and support bracket.

20. Connect the heater hose at the cylinder head.

21. Install the accelerator cable mounting bracket to the cylinder head.

22. Connect the accelerator cable to the carburetor and mounting bracket and the retracting spring.

23. Connect the choke cable to the carburetor, if applicable.

24. Connect the oil filler pipe to the rocker arm cover.

25. Connect the heater hose at the water pump.

26. Position the alternator drive belt to the pulley and the water pump pulley to the water pump shaft.

27. Install the fan and spacer to the water pump shaft.

28. Adjust the alternator drive belt tension and tighten the attaching bolts.

29. Position the radiator to the radiator support and install the retaining bolts.

30. Connect the radiator upper and lower hoses.

31. Clean the oil filter mating surface and install the oil filter.

32. Fill the crankcase with oil.

33. Fill the cooling system.

34. Connect the battery.

35. Start the engine and check for leaks.

36. Adjust the carburetor idle speed and mixture as necessary.

37. Install the air cleaner assembly.

38. Install the right-hand seat and the engine cover.

240 AND 300 SIX-CYLINDER THROUGH 1972

1. Drain the cooling system and the crankcase. Remove the engine cover and remove the air cleaner assembly.

2. Disconnect the battery positive cable. Disconnect the heater hose from the water pump and the coolant outlet housing. Disconnect the flexible fuel line from the fuel pump.

3. Remove the radiator.

4. Remove the cooling fan, water pump pulley and the fan drive belt.

5. Disconnect the accelerator cable and the choke cable at the carburetor. Remove the cable retracting spring.

6. On a vehicle with power brakes, disconnect the vacuum line at the intake manifold.

7. On a vehicle with an automatic transmission, disconnect the transmission kick-down rod at the bellcrank assembly.

8. Disconnect the exhaust manifold from the muffler inlet pipe. Disconnect the body ground strap and the battery ground cable at the engine.

9. Disconnect the engine wiring harness at the ignition coil, coolant temperature sending unit and the oil pressure sending unit. Position the harness out of the way.

10. Remove the alternator mounting bolts and position the alternator out of the way, leaving the wires attached.

11. On a vehicle with power steering, remove the power steering pump from the mounting brackets and position it right-side up and to one side, leaving the lines attached.

12. Raise the vehicle. Remove the starter and the automatic transmission filler tube bracket, if applicable. Remove the engine rear plate upper right bolt.

On a vehicle with a manual transmission, remove all the flywheel housing lower attaching bolts. Disconnect the clutch retracting spring. On a vehicle with an automatic transmission, remove the converter housing access cover assembly. Remove the flywheel-to-converter nuts; then secure the converter assembly in the housing. Remove the transmission oil cooler lines from the retaining clip at the engine. Remove the converter housing-to-engine lower attaching bolts.

13. Remove the engine from the support insulator bolt.

14. Lower the vehicle and position a transmission jack under the transmission to support it. Remove the remaining flywheel or converter housing-to-engine bolts.

15. Attach the engine lifting device and raise the engine slightly. Carefully pull the engine from the transmission. Lift the engine out of the vehicle.

NOTE: *The 240–300 six is removed from the vehicle in the same manner as the 170 six, through the right-side door; consequently, the seat will have to be removed from the right-side if it hasn't already been done. The driver's seat should also be removed to afford the maximum amount of room for working.*

To install the engine:

1. Place a new gasket on the muffler inlet pipe.

2. Lower the engine carefully into the vehicle. Make sure that the studs on the exhaust manifold are aligned with the holes in the muffler inlet pipe and the dowels in the block engage the holes in the flywheel or converter housing.

On a vehicle with an automatic transmission, start the converter pilot into the crankshaft. Remove the retainer securing the converter in the housing.

On a vehicle with a manual transmission, start the transmission main drive gear into the clutch disc. It may be necessary to adjust the position of the transmission with relation to the engine if the transmission input shaft will not enter the clutch disc. If the engine hangs up after the shaft enters, turn the crankshaft slowly with the transmission in gear until the shaft splines mesh with the clutch disc.

3. Install the converter or flywheel housing upper attaching bolts. Remove the jack supporting the transmission.

4. Lower the engine until it rests on the engine support and remove the lifting device.

5. Install the front support bolt and nut. Install the bracket for the automatic transmission oil cooler lines.

6. Install the remaining converter or flywheel housing attaching bolts. Connect the clutch return spring.

7. Install the starter and connect the starter cable. Attach the automatic transmission oil cooler lines in the bracket at the engine block.

8. Install the exhaust manifold to the muffler inlet pipe lockwashers and nuts.

9. Connect the engine ground strap and the battery ground cable.

10. On a vehicle with an automatic transmission, connect the kick-down rod to the bellcrank assembly on the intake manifold.

11. Connect the accelerator linkage to the carburetor and install the retracting spring. Connect the choke cable to the carburetor and hand throttle, if so equipped.

12. On a vehicle with power brakes, connect the brake vacuum line to the intake manifold.

13. Connect the coil primary wire, oil pressure and coolant temperature sending unit wires, flexible fuel line, heater hoses, and the battery positive cable.

14. Install the alternator on the mounting bracket. On a vehicle with power steering, install the power steering pump on the mounting bracket.

15. Install the water pump pulley, spacer, cooling fan and drive belt. Adjust all the belt tensions and tighten the accesories' mounting bolts.

16. Install the radiator. Connect the radiator lower hose to the water pump and the radiator upper hose to the coolant outlet housing. On a vehicle with an automatic transmission, connect the oil cooler lines to the radiator.

17. Install and adjust the hood, if it was removed.

18. Fill the cooling system. Fill the crankcase. Operate the engine at a fast idle and check for leaks.

19. Adjust the carburetor idle speed and mixture. On a vehicle with a manual transmission, adjust the clutch pedal free-play. On a vehicle with an automatic transmission, adjust the transmission control linkage. Check the fluid level in the automatic tranmission and add as necessary.

20. Install the carburetor air cleaner.

1974–75 240 AND 300
SIX-CYLINDER

1. Disconnect the battery and drain the cooling system. Remove the engine cover and the right hand seat. Remove the grille and bumper.

2. Remove the hood lock support bracket, right and left headlight doors, and grille.

3. Disconnect all hoses and lines to the radiator, and remove the battery deflector. Remove the radiator.

4. Disconnect:

A. The heater hoses, at the engine.

B. Temperature, oil, and ignition wires.

C. Starter solenoid, neutral safety switch, and back-up light wiring.

5. Remove the engine oil dipstick and oil filler tube. Remove hoses connecting the rocker cover and air filter. Remove the air cleaner and brackets.

6. Disconnect the choke and accelerator cables at the carburetor. Disconnect the auxiliary heater hose at the front heater. Disconnect the hoses at the right front of the engine, and position them out of the way.

7. Disconnect the fuel pump discharge line at the pump. Disconnect the alternator, and remove it from the brackets.

8. Disconnect the ground wires at the block, and the muffler inlet pipe at the manifold. Disconnect the modulator line at the intake manifold.

9. Put the vehicle on a hoist. Drain the crankcase and remove the oil filter.

10. Disconnect the starter wiring, and remove the starter.

11. Position an engine support bar to the chassis and engine, and adjust it.

12. On manual transmission vehicles:

A. Disconnect the driveshaft, and remove it. Install a plug in the transmission extension housing.

B. Disconnect the speedometer cable and housing, and secure the assembly out of the way.

C. Remove the nut and bolt holding the rear support to the crossmember. Raise the transmission, remove the mounting bolts, and remove the crossmember.

D. Remove the clutch equalizer arm bolts from the engine. Disconnect the retracting spring, and move the assembly away.

E. Remove the bolts connecting transmission and clutch, and remove the transmission.

13. On automatic transmission vehicles:

A. Remove the bolts connecting the adapter plate and inspection cover to the torque converter.

B. Unbolt and remove the transmission dipstick tube. Drain the transmission.

C. Remove the nuts attaching the converter to the flex plate. Disconnect the fluid cooler and modulator lines at the transmission.

D. Disconnect the driveshaft at the companion flange.

E. Disconnect the speedometer cable and housing from the transmission. Disconnect the shift rod at the lever on the transmission. Jack the transmission up slightly.

F. Remove the nuts and bolts attaching the rear engine mount bracket to the crossmember. Remove the side support bolts, and remove the crossmember.

G. Secure the transmission to the jack with a safety chain, remove the remaining bolts attaching the transmission to the cylinder block, and remove the transmission from the vehicle.

14. Remove the nuts which attach the engine front support insulator, remove the bellcrank bolt from the block, and position it out of the way.

15. Lower the vehicle, and remove the fan spacer, and water pump pulley. Lift the engine from the vehicle with a lifting hook. Remove the clutch housing on vehicles with manual transmission.

16. Install the clutch housing on manual transmission vehicles. Hoist the engine into the vehicle, and allow it to rest on the front supports and support tool.

17. Raise the vehicle on a hoist.

18. On manual transmission:

A. Raise the transmission and position it behind the clutch housing. Install the mounting bolts.

B. Raise the transmission slightly further, position the crossmember to the chassis and rear support, and install the attaching bolts. Torque crossmember to body bolts to 20–30 ft-lbs.

C. Remove the jack and engine support tool. Connect the shift linkage and the speedometer cable housing.

D. Install and connect the drive shaft.

19. Install the engine front support insulator bolts, and torque to 45–55 ft-lbs.

20. Install the transmission bellcrank.

21. On automatic transmission equipped vehicles:

A. Position the transmission against the block and install the mounting bolts. Torque to 23–33 ft-lbs.

B. Position the crossmember to the rear mount bracket and frame side members. Install the attaching nuts and bolts, and torque to 20–30 ft-lbs.

C. Remove the transmission safety chain, and remove the jack. Remove the engine support bar.

D. Install the converter to the flex plate. Connect the vacuum and oil cooler lines to the transmission.

E. Install the dipstick and tube into the transmission oil pan. Install the tube and vacuum line bracket attaching bolt to the block.

F. Connect the driveshaft to the transmission companion flange. Connect the speedometer cable and housing to the transmission. Connect the shift rods to the transmission levers.

G. Install the adapter plate and inspection cover.

22. Install the starter. Connect the muffler inlet pipe at the manifold.

23. Install the clutch equalizer arm bracket (on manual transmission models). Install the attaching bolts, and connect the retractor spring.

24. Lower the vehicle to the floor, install the remaining automatic transmission mounting bolts.

25. Install the starter ground wire and remaining starter attaching bolt. Connect the starter cable at the starter.

26. Install the water pump pulley, spacer, and fan assembly.

27. Install the alternator onto its mounting brackets, and install and tension the V-belt.

28. Connect the alternator wiring, and back-up light and neutral safety switch leads.

29. Connect the alternator and battery ground wires to the block.

30. Connect the transmission modulator line to the manifold.

31. Connect the fuel line from the tank to the fuel pump.

32. Connect the choke and accelerator cables to the carburetor. Install the dipstick tube, and bolt it to the cylinder head.

33. Connect remaining neutral safety switch and back-up light wires. Position the wiring harness, and connect the coil, oil, and temperature leads.

34. Connect the auxiliary heater hoses. Connect the oil filler tube to the rocker arm cover and install the retaining clamp. Install the filler tube bracket to the dash panel.

35. Install the radiator and battery deflector. Connect the radiator hoses and oil cooler lines.

36. Install the grille, head light and hood lock bracket.

37. Fill the crankcase and cooling system. Fill the automatic transmission.

38. Connect the positive battery cable, and operate the engine to check for leaks. Adjust idle speed and mixture, and automatic transmission linkage.

39. Install the air cleaner and brackets, engine front cover, and right front seat, grille and bumper.

1975–77 300 SIX-CYLINDER

1. Take off the engine cover, drain the coolant, remove the air cleaner, and disconnect the battery.

2. Remove the bumper, grille, and gravel deflector.

3. Detach the upper radiator hose at the engine. Remove the alternator splash shield and detach the lower hose at the radiator. Remove the radiator and shroud, if any.

4. Disconnect the engine heater hoses and the alternator wires. Remove the power steering pump and support.

5. Disconnect and plug the fuel line at the pump.

6. Detach from the engine: distributor and gauge sending unit wires, brake booster hose, accelerator cable and bracket.

7. Disconnect the automatic transmission kickdown linkage at the bellcrank.

8. Remove the exhaust manifold heat deflector and unbolt the pipe from the manifold.

9. Disconnect the automatic transmission vacuum line from the intake manifold and from the junction. Remove the transmission dipstick tube support bolt at the intake manifold.

10. Remove the upper engine to transmission bolts.

11. Remove the starter. Remove the flywheel inspection cover. Remove the four automatic transmission torque converter nuts, then remove the front engine support nuts. Take off the oil filter.

12. Remove the rest of the transmission to engine fasteners, then lift the engine out from the engine compartment with a floor crane.

13. To replace the engine, lower it into place and start the mounting bolts. Install the upper transmission bolts, the converter nuts, and the lower transmission bolts. Tighten the mounting bolts. Replace all the items removed in the previous steps.

302 V8

1. Remove the engine cover.

2. Remove the right front seat. Also remove the driver's seat if more room to work is desired.

3. Drain the cooling system.

4. Remove the air cleaner and intake duct assembly, including the crankcase ventilation hose.

5. Disconnect the battery and alternator ground cables at the cylinder block.

6. Remove the oil filler tube at the dash panel and disconnect it at the rocker arm cover.

7. Disconnect the radiator upper and lower hoses at the radiator and the automatic transmission oil cooler lines, if so equipped.

8. Disconnect the radiator attaching bolts and remove the radiator.

9. Disconnect the heater hoses at the engine and position them out of the way.

10. Remove the fan, spacer, pulley, and the drive belt.

11. Disconnect the accelerator linkage at the accelerator shaft on the left cylinder head. Disconnect the automatic transmission kick-down rod at the carburetor and the vacuum line at the intake manifold, if so equipped.

12. Disconnect the engine wire harness from the left rocker arm cover and position it out of the way.

13. Remove the upper nut attaching the right exhaust manifolds to the muffler inlet pipe.

14. Raise the vehicle on a hoist.

15. Drain the crankcase and remove the oil filter.

16. Disconnect the fuel line (tank-to-pump) at the fuel pump.

17. Disconnect the oil dipstick tube bracket from the exhaust manifold and oil pan.

18. On manual transmissions, remove the bolts attaching the equalizer arm bracket to the cylinder block and the clutch housing. This includes the clutch linkage connection and the retracting springs. Remove the bracket.

19. Disconnect the starter cable at the starter and remove the starter.

20. On a vehicle with a manual transmission, disconnect the driveshaft at the rear axle and remove the driveshaft. Install a plug in the end of the transmission. On vehicles with automatic transmissions, disconnect the driveshaft at the companion flange.

21. Disconnect the speedometer cable and the transmission linkage at the transmission.

22. Position a transmission jack under the transmission. Raise the transmission and remove the bolts attaching the crossmember to the chassis. Lower the transmission slightly and remove the bolt and nut attaching the engine rear support to the crossmember. Remove the crossmember.

23. Remove the bolts attaching the manual transmission to the clutch housing and remove the transmission.

24. On a vehicle with an automatic transmission, remove the lower front cover from the converter housing. Remove the transmission dipstick tube and drain the transmission. Install a plug in the transmission oil pan. Remove the nuts attaching the transmission converter to the flywheel. Disconnect the oil cooler lines and the vacuum lines at the transmission. Remove the remaining bolts fastening the transmission to the engine and remove the transmission.

25. Position an engine support bar under the engine to steady it.

26. Disconnect the muffler inlet pipes at the exhaust manifolds.

27. Remove the engine front support attaching nuts and washers.

28. Remove the bellcrank bolt from the side of the cylinder block and position the bellcrank assembly out of the way.

29. Lower the vehicle.

30. Remove the bolts attaching the alternator to the cylinder block and the water pump and position it out of the way.

31. Remove the carburetor air horn stud and disconnect the fuel line (pump-to-carburetor) at the fuel pump.

32. Install an engine lifting device and remove the engine through the right-side door.

To install the 302 V8 engine:

1. Lift the engine into place through the right-side door.

2. Connect the fuel line (pump-to-carburetor) at the fuel pump.

3. Position the alternator and adjusting arm to the cylinder block and water pump housing. Install and tighten the attaching bolts.

4. Lift the engine and position it to the chassis and supporting bar.

5. Raise the vehicle on a hoist.

6. Install the engine front support attaching nuts and washers.

7. On a vehicle with an automatic transmission, position the bellcrank assembly to the cylinder block and install the attaching bolt. Position the transmission to the engine and install the attaching bolts.

8. On a vehicle with a manual transmission, position the transmission to the clutch housing and install the attaching bolts.

9. Remove the engine support bar.

10. Position the engine rear support crossmember to the chassis and install the attaching bolts. Position the transmission with the engine rear support attached to the crossmember. Install and tighten the bolt and nut. Remove the jack.

11. On a vehicle with an automatic transmission, install and tighten the converter-to-flywheel attaching nuts. Connect the oil cooler and vacuum lines at the transmission. Install the transmission dipstick tube in the pan. Install the dipstick tube and vacuum line retaining bracket bolt to the cylinder block.

12. Connect the transmission shift linkages and the speedometer cable.

13. On a vehicle with an automatic transmission, connect the driveshaft to the transmission companion flange. On a vehicle with a manual transmission, remove the plug from the transmission and install the driveshaft into the transmission. Connect the rear end of the driveshaft at the rear axle.

14. Install the starter and connect the cable to the starter.

15. Install the muffler inlet pipe attaching bolts and nuts (except the upper nut on the right-side exhaust manifold).

16. On a manual transmission, install the bolts connecting the equalizer arm bracket to the cylinder block and clutch housing. This includes connecting the clutch linkage and retracting spring.

17. Install the oil filter.

18. Install the oil dipstick tube bracket to the oil pan and the exhaust manifold.

19. Connect the fuel line (tank-to-pump) at the fuel pump.

20. Lower the vehicle.

21. Install the upper nut attaching the right exhaust manifold to the muffler inlet pipe.

22. Connect the engine wire harness at the left rocker arm cover. Connect the battery and the alternator ground cables at the cylinder block.

23. Connect the automatic transmission vacuum line at the intake manifold and the transmission kick-down rod at the carburetor, if so equipped. Connect the accelerator linkage to accelerator shaft on the left-side cylinder head.

24. Install the drive belt, pulley, spacer and fan, then tighten the belt tension.

25. Connect the heater hoses at the engine.

26. Position the radiator and install the attaching bolts. Connect the radiator upper and lower hoses and the automatic transmission cooler lines, if so equipped.

27. Install the oil filler tube.

28. Install the air cleaner and intake duct assembly, including the crankcase ventilation hose.

29. Fill and bleed the cooling system.

30. Fill the crankcase and the automatic transmission, if so equipped.

31. Install the engine cover and the right front seat.

32. Operate the engine at a fast idle and check for leaks.

351 AND 460 V8

1. Take off the engine cover, drain the coolant, remove the air cleaner, and disconnect the battery. Remove the bumper, grille, and gravel deflector. Remove the upper grille support bracket, hood lock support, and air conditioning condenser upper mounting brackets.

2. With air conditioning, the system must be discharged to remove the condenser. Do not attempt to do this yourself, unless you are trained in air conditioning. Disconnect the lines at the compressor.

3. Remove the accelerator cable bracket and the heater hoses. Detach the

radiator hoses and the automatic transmission cooler lines, if any. Remove the fan shroud, fan, and radiator.

4. Pivot the alternator in and detach the wires.

5. Remove the air cleaner, duct and valve, exhaust manifold shroud, and flex tube.

6. Disconnect the automatic transmission shift rod.

7. Disconnect the fuel and choke lines, detach the vacuum lines, and remove the carburetor and spacer.

8. Remove the oil filter. Detach the exhaust pipe from the manifold. Unbolt the automatic transmission tube bracket from the cylinder head. Remove the starter.

9. Remove the engine mount bolts. With automatic, remove the converter inspection cover and unbolt the converter from the flex plate.

10. Unbolt the engine ground cable and support the transmission.

11. Remove the power steering front bracket. Detach only one vacuum line at the rear of the intake manifold. Disconnect the engine wiring loom. Remove the speed control servo from the manifold. Detach the compressor clutch wire.

12. Install a lifting bracket to the intake manifold and attach a floor crane. Remove the transmission to engine bolts, making sure the transmission is supported. Remove the engine.

13. To install the engine, align the converter to the flex plate and the engine dowels to the transmission. With manual transmission, start the transmission shaft into the clutch disc. You may have to turn the crankshaft slowly with the transmission in gear. Install the transmission bolts, then the mounting bolts. Replace all the items removed in the previous steps.

CYLINDER HEAD

Removal and Installation

170, 240 AND 300 SIX-CYLINDER

1. Drain the cooling system. Remove the air cleaner. Remove the oil filler tube. Disconnect the battery cable at the cylinder head.

2. Disconnect the muffler inlet pipe at the exhaust manifold. Pull the muffler inlet pipe down. Remove the gasket.

3. Disconnect the accelerator rod retracting spring. Disconnect the choke control cable if applicable and the accelerator rod at the carburetor.

4. Disconnect the transmission kickdown rod. Disconnect the accelerator linkage at the bellcrank assembly.

5. Disconnect the fuel inlet line at the fuel filter hose, and the distributor vacuum line at the carburetor. Disconnect other vacuum lines as necessary for accessibility and identify them for proper connection.

6. Remove the radiator upper hose at the coolant outlet housing.

7. Disconnect the distributor vacuum line at the distributor. Disconnect the carburetor fuel inlet line at the fuel pump. Remove the lines as an assembly.

8. Disconnect the spark plug wires at the spark plugs and the temperature sending unit wire at the sending unit.

9. Grasp the crankcase vent hose near the regulator valve and pull the regulator valve out of the grommet in the valve rocker arm cover. Disconnect the crankcase vent hose at the hose fitting in the intake manifold spacer and remove the vent hose and regulator valve.

10. Disconnect the carburetor air vent tube and remove the valve rocker arm cover.

11. Remove the valve rocker arm shaft assembly on the 170; on the 240 and 300 loosen the rocker arm stud nuts and move the rocker arms aside. Remove the pushrods in sequence so that they can be identified and reinstalled in their original positions.

12. Remove the cylinder head bolts and remove the cylinder head. Do not pry between the cylinder head and the block as the gasket surfaces may be damaged. Two $5/16$ in. lifting eyes may be installed on the right side of the 240 and 300 head.

To install the cylinder head:

1. Clean the head and block gasket surfaces. If the cylinder head was removed for a gasket change, check the flatness of the cylinder head and block.

2. Apply sealer to both sides of the new 170 cylinder head gasket. Position the gasket on the cylinder block.

3. Install a new gasket on the flange of the muffler inlet pipe.

4. Lift the cylinder head above the

Cylinder head bolt tightening sequence for the 170 six-cylinder

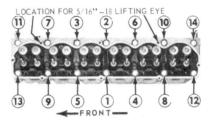

Cylinder head bolt tightening sequence for the 240, 300 six-cylinder

cylinder block and lower it into position using two head bolts installed through the head as guides.

5. Coat the threads of the No. 1 and 6 bolts for the right-side of the 170 cylinder head with a small amount of water-resistant sealer. Oil the threads of the remaining bolts. Install, but do not tighten, two bolts at the opposite ends of the head to hold the head and gasket in position.

6. The cylinder head bolts are tightened in 3 progressive steps. Torque them (in the proper sequence) to the specified torque.

7. Apply Lubriplate® to both ends of the pushrods and install them in their original positions.

8. Install the valve rocker shaft assembly.

9. Adjust the valves on the 170. See Chapter 2.

10. Install the muffler inlet pipe lockwashers and attaching nuts.

11. Connect the radiator upper hose at the coolant outlet housing.

12. Position the distributor vacuum line and the carburetor fuel inlet line on the engine. Connect the fuel line at the fuel filter hose and install a new clamp. Install the distributor vacuum line at the carburetor. Connect the accelerator linkage at the bellcrank assembly. Connect the transmission kick-down rod.

13. Connect the accelerator rod retracting spring. Connect the choke control cable (if applicable) and the accelerator rod at the carburetor.

14. Connect the distributor vacuum line at the distributor. Connect the carburetor fuel inlet line at the fuel pump. Connect all the vacuum lines using their previous identification for proper connection.

15. Connect the temperature sending unit wire at the sending unit. Connect the spark plug wires. Connect the battery cable at the cylinder head.

16. Fill the cooling system.

17. Install the valve rocker cover. Connect the carburetor air vent tube.

18. Connect the crankcase vent hose at the carburetor spacer fitting. Insert the regulator valve with the vent hose attached, into the valve rocker arm cover grommet. Install the air cleaner, start the engine and check for leaks.

302 AND 351 V8

1. Remove the intake manifold and the carburetor as an assembly.

2. Remove the rocker arm cover(s).

3. If the right cylinder head is to be removed, loosen the alternator adjusting arm bolt and remove the alternator mounting bracket bolt and spacer. Swing the alternator down and out of the way. Remove the ignition coil and the air cleaner inlet duct from the right cylinder head assembly.

If the left cylinder head is being removed, remove the bolts fastening the accelerator shaft assembly at the front of the cylinder head.

4. Disconnect the exhaust manifold(s) from the muffler inlet pipe(s).

5. Loosen the rocker arm stud nuts so that the rocker arms can be rotated to the side. Remove the pushrods and identify them so that they can be reinstalled in their original positions.

6. Remove the cylinder head bolts and lift the cylinder head from the block.

To install the cylinder head(s):

1. Clean the cylinder head, intake manifold, and the valve cover and head gasket surfaces.

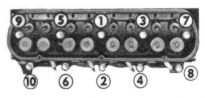

Cylinder head bolt tightening sequence for the V8

2. A specially treated composition head gasket is used. Do not apply sealer to a composition gasket. Position the new gasket over the locating dowels on the cylinder block. Then, position the cylinder head on the block and install the attaching bolts.

3. The cylinder head bolts are tightened in 3 progressive steps. Tighten all the bolts in the proper sequence to 50 ft lbs, 60 ft lbs, and finally to 70 ft lbs of torque.

4. Clean the pushrods. Blow out the oil passage in the rods with compressed air. Check the pushrods for straightness. Never try to straighten a pushrod; always replace it.

5. Apply Lubriplate to the ends of the pushrods and install them in their original positions.

6. Apply Lubriplate to the rocker arms and their fulcrum seats and install the rocker arms. Adjust the 302 valves as detailed in Chapter 2.

7. Position a new gasket(s) on the muffler inlet (pipe(s) as necessary. Connect the exhaust manifold(s) at the muffler inlet pipe(s).

8. If the right cylinder head was removed, install the alternator, ignition coil and air cleaner duct on the right cylinder head. Adjust the drive belt.

If the left cylinder head was removed, install the accelerator shaft assembly at the front of the cylinder head.

9. Clean the valve rocker arm cover and the cylinder head gasket surfaces. Place the new gaskets in the covers, making sure that the tabs of the gasket engage the notches provided in the cover.

10. Install the intake manifold and related parts.

460 V8

1. Remove the intake manifold and carburetor as an assembly.

2. Disconnect the exhaust pipe from the exhaust manifold.

3. Loosen the air conditioning compressor drive belt, if so equipped.

4. Loosen the alternator attaching bolts and remove the bolt attaching the alternator bracket to the right cylinder head.

5. Disconnect the air conditioning compressor from the engine and move it

aside, out of the way. Do not discharge the air conditioning system.

6. Remove the bolts securing the power steering reservoir bracket to the left cylinder head. Position the reservoir and bracket out of the way.

7. Remove the valve rocker arm covers. Remove the rocker arm bolts, rocker arms, oil deflectors, fulcrums and pushrods in sequence so that they can be reinstalled in their original positions.

8. Remove the cylinder head bolts and lift the head and exhaust manifold off the engine. If necessary, pry at the forward corners of the cylinder head against the casting bosses provided on the cylinder block. Do not damage the gasket mating surfaces of the cylinder head and block by prying against them.

9. Remove all gasket material from the cylinder head and block. Clean all gasket material from the mating surfaces of the intake manifold. If the exhaust manifold was removed, clean the mating surfaces of the cylinder head exhaust port areas and install the exhaust manifold.

10. Position the two long cylinder head bolts in the two rear lower bolt holes of the left cylinder head. Place a long cylinder head bolt in the rear lower bolt hole of the right cylinder head. Use rubber bands to keep the bolts in position until the cylinder heads are installed on the cylinder block.

11. Position new cylinder head gaskets on the cylinder block dowels. Do not apply sealer to the gaskets, heads, or block.

12. Place the cylinder heads on the block, guiding the exhaust pipe connections. Install the remaining cylinder head bolts. The longer bolts go in the lower row of holes.

13. Tighten all the cylinder head attaching bolts in the proper sequence in three stages: 75 ft lbs, 105 ft lbs, and finally, to 135 ft lbs. When this procedure is used, it is not necessary to retorque the heads after extended use.

14. Connect the exhaust pipes to the exhaust manifolds.

15. Install the intake manifold and carburetor assembly. Tighten the intake manifold attaching bolts in the proper sequence to 25–30 ft lbs.

16. Install the air conditioning compressor to the engine.

17. Install the power steering reservoir to the engine.

18. Apply oil-resistant sealer to one side of the new valve cover gaskets and lay the cemented side in place in the valve covers. Install the covers.

19. Install the alternator to the right cylinder head and adjust the alternator drive belt tension.

20. Adjust the air conditioning compressor drive belt tension.

21. Fill the radiator with coolant.

22. Start the engine and check for leaks.

INTAKE MANIFOLD

Removal and Installation

SIX-CYLINDER

See the exhaust manifold removal and installation procedure.

302 AND 351 V8

1. Drain cooling system.

2. Remove air cleaner and intake duct assembly, including crankcase ventilation hose.

3. Disconnect accelerator rod, choke cable and automatic transmission kickdown rod (if applicable) at the carburetor. Remove the accelerator retracting spring, where so equipped.

4. Disconnect high tension lead and wires from the coil.

5. Remove spark plug wire from plugs and harness brackets, then remove distributor cap and spark plug wire assembly.

6. Disconnect fuel inlet line at carburetor.

7. Disconnect distributor vacuum hoses and remove distributor.

8. Remove heater hose, radiator hose and water temperature sending unit wire from manifold.

9. Remove water pump bypass hose from coolant outlet housing.

10. Disconnect crankcase ventilation hose from valve rocker cover.

11. Remove intake manifold and carburetor as an assembly, prying manifold from cylinder head if necessary. Throw away gaskets and bolt sealing washers.

12. When disassembling, identify all vacuum hoses before disconnecting them. Remove coolant outlet housing and gasket. Remove ignition coil and engine

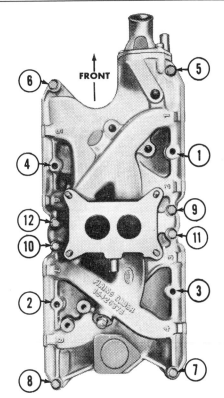

302 and 351 V8 intake manifold bolt torque sequence

identification tag, temperature sending unit, carburetor, spacer, gasket, vacuum fitting, accelerator retracting spring bracket and choke cable bracket.

13. To install, first assemble manifold/carburetor unit by installing all components removed in Step 12, making sure vacuum lines are positioned correctly.

14. Clean all mating surfaces, using a suitable solvent to remove all oil. Apply block surfaces with adhesive sealer.

15. Position new gaskets and front and rear seals, using a nonhardening sealer at four gasket-seal junctions. Interlock gaskets with seal tabs and be sure all holes are aligned.

16. Carefully position manifold, making sure that gaskets and seals do not shift. Install bolts and new bolt seal washers, tightening in the sequence illustrated to the specified torque. *Retighten after engine has been operated until warmed up.*

17. Install water bypass hose to coolant outlet housing, radiator upper hose and heater hose.

18. Install distributor as described in "Distributor Removal and Installation."

Install distributor cap and spark plug wires, positioning wires in harness brackets on valve rocker covers.

19. Connect crankcase ventilation hose, high tension lead and coil wires, accelerator rod and retracting spring, choke cable and automatic transmission kickdown rod (if applicable).

20. Fill and bleed cooling system.

21. Adjust ignition timing.

22. Connect vacuum hoses at distributor.

23. Operate engine until warmed up, checking for leaks.

24. Retorque manifold bolts.

25. Adjust transmission throttle linkage, if so equipped.

26. Install air cleaner and intake duct assembly including closed crankcase ventilation hose.

460 V8

1. Drain the cooling system and remove the air cleaner assembly.

2. Disconnect the upper radiator hose at the engine.

3. Disconnect the heater hoses at the intake manifold and the water pump. Position them out of the way. Loosen the water pump by-pass hose clamp at the intake manifold.

4. Disconnect the PCV valve and hose at the right valve cover. Disconnect all of the vacuum lines at the rear of the intake manifold and tag them for proper reinstallation.

5. Disconnect the wires at the spark plugs, and remove the wires from the brackets on the valve covers. Disconnect the high-tension wire from the coil and remove the distributor cap and wires as an assembly.

6. Disconnect all of the distributor vacuum lines at the carburetor and vacuum control valve and tag them for proper installation. Remove the distributor and vacuum lines as an assembly.

7. Disconnect the accelerator linkage at the carburetor. Remove the speed control linkage bracket, if so equipped, from the manifold and carburetor.

8. Remove the bolts holding the accelerator linkage bellcrank and position the linkage and return springs out of the way.

9. Disconnect the fuel line at the carburetor.

10. Disconnect the wiring harness at the coil battery terminal, engine temperature sending unit, oil pressure sending unit, and other connections as necessary. Disconnect the wiring harness from the clips at the left valve cover the position the harness out of the way.

11. Remove the coil and bracket assembly.

12. Remove the intake manifold attaching bolts and lift the manifold and carburetor from the engine as an assembly. It may be necessary to pry the manifold away from the cylinder heads. Do not damage the gasket sealing surfaces.

13. Install the intake manifold in the reverse order of removal. Clean all gasket material from the mating surfaces of the manifold and cylinder heads and block. Glue the intake manifold end seals in place before installing the manifold. Use sealer at each end of the intake manifold-to-cylinder head gaskets for the full width of the gasket. When the manifold is placed on top of the engine run your fingers around the end seal areas to make sure that the end seals have not shifted. If they have, remove the manifold and reposition the seals. Tighten the intake manifold bolts in two stages in the proper sequence. After the engine has been started and has reached normal operating temperature, retorque the intake manifold bolts.

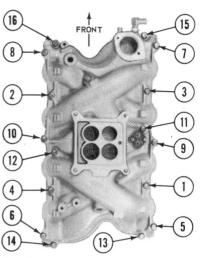

460 V8 intake manifold bolt torque sequence

EXHAUST MANIFOLD

Removal and Installation

170 SIX-CYLINDER

1. Raise the vehicle on a hoist and remove the air cleaner hot air duct.

2. Disconnect the muffler inlet pipe from the exhaust manifold.

3. Remove the attaching bolts and the exhaust manifold.

4. Clean the mating surfaces of the exhaust manifold and the cylinder head.

5. Apply graphite grease to the mating surface of the exhaust manifold.

6. Position the exhaust manifold on the cylinder head and install the attaching bolts and tab washers. Working from the center to the ends, torque the bolts to 18 ft lbs. Lock the bolts by bending one tab of the washer over a flat on the bolt.

7. Place a new gasket on the muffler inlet pipe and install the pipe to the exhaust manifold. Install the air cleaner hot air duct and lower the vehicle.

240 AND 300 SIX-CYLINDER

1. Remove the air cleaner. Disconnect the choke cable at the carburetor. Disconnect the accelerator cable or rod at the carburetor. Remove the accelerator retracting spring.

2. On a vehicle with automatic transmission, remove the kick-down rod retracting spring. Remove the accelerator rod bellcrank assembly.

3. Disconnect the fuel inlet line and the distributor vacuum line from the carburetor.

4. Disconnect the muffler inlet pipe from the exhaust manifold.

5. Disconnect the power brake vacuum line, if so equipped.

6. Remove the bolts and nuts attaching the manifolds to the cylinder head. Lift the manifold assemblies from the engine. Remove and discard the gaskets.

7. To separate the manifolds, remove the nuts joining the intake and exhaust manifolds.

8. Clean the mating surfaces of the cylinder head and the manifolds.

9. If the intake and exhaust manifolds have been separated, coat the mating surfaces lightly with graphite grease and place the exhaust manifold over the studs on the intake manifold. Install the lockwashers and nuts. Tighten them finger-tight.

10. Install a new intake manifold gasket.

11. Coat the mating surfaces lightly with graphite grease. Place the manifold assemblies in position against the cylinder head. Make sure that the gaskets have not become dislodged. Install the attaching washers, bolts and nuts. Tighten the attaching nuts and bolts in the proper sequence to 26 ft lbs. If the intake and exhaust manifolds were separated, tighten the nuts joining them.

12. Position a new gasket on the muffler inlet pipe and connect the inlet pipe to the exhaust manifold.

13. Connect the crankcase vent hose to the intake manifold inlet tube and position the hose clamp.

14. Connect the fuel inlet line and the distributor vacuum line to the carburetor.

15. Connect the accelerator cable to the carburetor and install the retracting

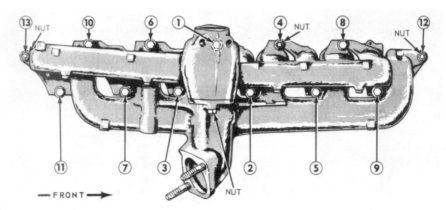

The 240, 300 six-cylinder intake and exhaust manifold torque sequence for the attaching bolts

spring. Connect the choke cable to the carburetor.

16. On a vehicle with an automatic transmission, install the bellcrank assembly and the kick-down rod retracting spring. Adjust the transmission control linkage.

17. Install the air cleaner.

V8

1. Remove the air cleaner and intake duct assembly, including the crankcase ventilation hose.

2. Disconnect the exhaust manifold(s) from the inlet pipe(s).

3. Remove the attaching bolts and flat washers, then remove the exhaust manifold.

4. Clean the mating surfaces of the exhaust manifold(s) and cylinder head(s). Clean the mounting flange of the exhaust manifold and muffler inlet pipe.

5. Apply graphite grease to the mating surface of the exhaust manifold(s).

6. Position the exhaust manifold on the cylinder head and install the attaching bolts and flat washers. Working from the center to the ends, tighten the bolts to the specified torque.

7. Position the air cleaner and intake duct assembly, including the crankcase ventilation hose.

TIMING GEAR COVER

Oil Seal Replacement

170 Six-Cylinder

1. Drain the cooling system and disconnect the radiator upper hose at the coolant outlet elbow and remove the two upper radiator retaining bolts.

2. Raise the vehicle and drain the crankcase.

3. Remove the splash shield and the automatic transmission oil cooling lines, if so equipped, then remove the radiator.

4. Loosen and remove the fan belt, fan and pulley.

5. Use a gear puller to remove the crankshaft pulley damper.

6. Remove the cylinder front cover retaining bolts and gently pry the cover away from the block. Remove the gasket.

7. Drive out the old seal with a pin punch from the rear of the cover. Clean out the recess in the cover.

8. Coat the new seal with grease and drive it into the cover until it is fully seated. Check the seal to make sure that the spring around the seal is in the proper position.

9. Clean the cylinder front cover and the gasket surface of the cylinder block. Apply an oil-resistant sealer to the new front cover gasket and install the gasket onto the cover.

10. Install the cylinder front cover onto the engine.

NOTE: *Trim away the exposed portion of the old oil pan gasket flush with the front of the engine block. Cut and position the required portion of a new gasket to the oil pan and apply sealer to both sides.*

11. Lubricate the hub of the crankshaft damper pulley with Lubriplate to prevent damage to the seal during installation or on initial starting of the engine.

12. Install and assemble the remaining components in the reverse order of removal, starting from Step 4. Start the engine and check for leaks.

240 and 300 Six-Cylinder

1. Drain the coolant and remove the radiator. Remove the fan, belts, and pulley.

2. Remove the bolt and washer and pull off the damper with a gear puller.

3. Remove the oil pan.

4. Remove the front cover and clean off the old gasket.

5. Drive out the crankshaft seal with a pin punch and clean out the cover recess. Coat the new seal with grease and drive it in until it is fully seated in the recess.

6. Use sealer on the gasket surfaces of the block and cover. Install the cover with a new gasket.

7. Lubricate the crankshaft and the damper seal rubbing surface. Align the damper keyway with the crankshaft key and install the damper.

8. Apply sealant to the cavities between the rear main bearing cap and cylinder block. Install a new oil pan rear seal in the rear main bearing cap and apply a bead of sealant to the tapered seal ends. Install new pan side gaskets with sealer. Place a new front cover seal on the pan.

9. Replace the oil pan and all the other parts removed.

V8

1. Drain the cooling system and the crankcase.

2. Disconnect the upper and lower radiator hoses from the water pump and remove the radiator.

3. Disconnect the heater hose from the water pump. Slide the water pump by-pass hose clamp toward the water pump.

4. Loosen the alternator pivot bolt and the bolt which secures the alternator adjusting arm to the water pump.

5. Remove the bolts holding the fan shroud to the radiator, if so equipped. Remove the fan, spacer, pulley and drive belts.

6. Remove the crankshaft pulley from the crankshaft damper. Remove the damper attaching bolt and washer and remove the damper with a puller.

7. Disconnect the fuel pump outlet line at the fuel pump. Disconnect the vacuum inlet and outlet lines from the fuel pump. Remove the fuel pump attaching bolts and lay the pump to one side with the fuel inlet line still attached.

8. Remove the oil level dipstick and the bolt holding the disptick tube to the exhaust manifold.

9. Remove the oil pan-to-cylinder front cover attaching bolts. Use a sharp, thin cutting blade to cut the oil pan gasket flush with the cylinder block. Remove the front cover and water pump as an assembly.

10. Discard the front cover gasket.

11. See Steps 7 and 8 of the front cover oil seal replacement procedure for 170 6 cylinder engines.

12. Assemble the engine in the reverse order of disassembly, referring to Steps 9, 10 and 12 of the procedure for

170 6 cylinder engines. It may be necessary to force the cover downward slightly to compress the pan gasket and align the attaching bolt holes in the cover and the cylinder block. This operation can be accomplished by inserting a dowel or drift pin in the holes and aligning the cover with the block.

TIMING CHAIN

Removal and Installation

170 Six-Cylinder and V8

1. Remove the front cover and the crankshaft front oil slinger.

2. With a socket wrench of the proper size on the crankshaft pulley bolt, gently rotate the crankshaft in a clockwise direction until all slack is removed from the left-side of the timing chain. Scribe a mark on the engine block parallel to the present position of the left-side of the chain. Next, turn the crankshaft in a counterclockwise direction to remove all slack from the right-side of the chain. Force the left-side of the chain outward with the fingers and measure the distance between the reference point and the present position of the chain. If the distance is more than ½ in., replace the chain and/or the sprockets.

3. Crank the engine until the timing marks are aligned.

TIMING MARKS

Alignment of the timing marks on the crankshaft and camshaft timing chain sprockets on the V8

TIMING MARKS

Alignment of the timing marks on the crankshaft and camshaft timing chain sprockets on the 170 six-cylinder

4. Remove the camshaft sprocket cap-screw, washers and fuel pump eccentric on the V8 engine. Slide both sprockets and the timing chain forward and remove them as an assembly.

5. Install the sprockets and chain in the reverse order of removal, making sure that when they are positioned onto the camshaft and crankshaft, the timing marks are aligned.

TIMING GEARS

Removal and Installation

240 AND 300 SIX-CYLINDER ONLY

1. Drain the cooling system and remove the front cover.

2. Crank the engine until the timing marks on the camshaft and crankshaft gears are aligned.

3. Use a gear puller to remove both of the timing gears. Some 300 engines have a bolted-on camshaft gear.

4. Before installing the timing gears, be sure that the key and spacer are properly installed. Align the gear key way with the key and install the gear on the camshaft. Be sure that the timing marks line up on the camshaft and the crankshaft gears and install the crankshaft gear.

Alignment of the timing marks on the crankshaft and camshaft timing gears on the 240, 300 six-cylinder

5. Install the front cover, and assemble the rest of the engine in the reverse order of disassembly. Fill the cooling system.

CAMSHAFT

Removal and Installation

NOTE: *This procedure will probably require removal of the engine for 1966–67 models.*

170 SIX-CYLINDER

1. Remove the front cover, align the timing marks, and remove the timing chain and related parts as stated before.

2. Remove the cylinder head as previously outlined.

3. Disconnect the distributor primary wire at the ignition coil. Loosen the distributor lockbolt and remove the distributor.

4. Disconnect and plug the fuel inlet line at the fuel pump. Remove the fuel pump and gasket.

5. Remove the valve tappets with a magnet. Note that the tappets must be replaced in the same positions from which they are removed.

6. Remove the oil level dipstick.

7. Remove the headlight doors and disconnect the light ground wires and the screws. Disconnect the headlights and parking lights.

8. Remove the grille and hood lock as an assembly.

9. Remove the camshaft thrust plate.

10. Carefully withdraw the camshaft from the engine.

11. In preparation for installing the camshaft, clean the passage that feeds the rocker arm shaft by blowing compressed air into the opening in the block. Oil the camshaft journals and apply Lubriplate to all of the camshaft lobes. If a new camshaft is being installed, the spacer and dowel from the old camshaft must be used. Carefully slide the camshaft through the bearings.

12. Assemble the engine in the reverse order of disassembly.

240 AND 300 SIX-CYLINDER

1. Remove the grille, radiator, and timing cover.

2. Remove the distributor, fuel pump, oil pan and oil pump.

3. Align the timing marks. Unbolt the camshaft thrust plate, working through the holes in the camshaft gear.

4. Loosen the rocker arms, remove the pushrods, take off the side cover and remove the valve lifters with a magnet.

5. Remove the camshaft very carefully to prevent nicking the bearings.

6. Oil the camshaft bearing journals and use Lubriplate® or something similar on the lobes. Install the camshaft, gear, and thrust plate, aligning the gear marks.

Tighten down the thrust plate. Make sure that the camshaft end-play is not excessive.

7. The last item to be replaced is the distributor. The rotor should be at the firing position for no. 1 cylinder, with the timing gear marks aligned.

V8

1. Remove the grille, front cover, timing chain, and sprockets.

2. Disconnect the spark plug wires from the ignition harness bracket on the valve covers. Disconnect the ignition coil high-tension lead at the coil. Remove the distributor cap and the spark plug wire assembly.

3. Disconnect the wires from the ignition coil side terminals.

4. Disconnect the distributor vacuum line from the carburetor. Remove the distributor lockbolt and clamp and remove the distributor from the engine.

5. Disconnect the heater hose from the intake manifold, the upper and lower radiator hoses at the engine and remove the radiator.

6. Disconnect the accelerator rod from the carburetor and the accelerator retracting spring.

7. Disconnect the water temperature sending unit wire from the sending unit and the engine ground strap at the engine.

8. Remove the PCV valve from the valve cover. Remove the valve covers. Loosen the rocker arm retaining nuts and rotate the rockers to the side, off the valve stems and pushrods.

9. Remove the intake manifold and carburetor as an assembly. Remove the intake manifold gaskets and seals.

10. Remove the valve pushrods in sequence so that they can be reinstalled in the same positions from which they were removed.

11. Remove the lifters and place them in order so that they too can be reinstalled in their original positions. Use either a magnet, or if the lifters are coated with varnish, a pair of pliers to remove them.

12. Remove the camshaft thrust plate and *carefully* remove the camshaft by sliding it out of the front of the engine.

13. In preparation for installation, oil the camshaft journals and apply Lubri-

plate to the lobes. Carefully slide the camshaft through the bearings and install the camshaft thrust plate.

NOTE: *Do not hammer the camshaft sprocket onto the camshaft because you might drive the plug out of the rear of the engine and cause an oil leak.*

14. Assemble the rest of the engine in the reverse order of disassembly.

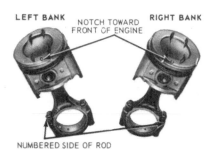

The proper positioning of the pistons and connecting rods in the 302 V8

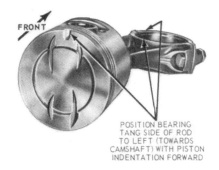

The proper positioning of the pistons and connecting rods in the 240, 300 six-cylinder

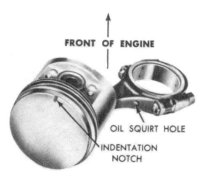

The proper positionining of the pistons and connecting rods in the 170 six-cylinder

Engine Lubrication

OIL PAN

Removal and Installation

170, 240 AND 300 SIX-CYLINDER

1. Drain the crankcase and cooling system. Remove the oil level dipstick.

2. Remove the fan and water pump pulley.

3. Disconnect the radiator upper hose at the coolant outlet elbow.

4. Disconnect the flexible fuel line at the fuel pump.

5. Raise the vehicle and remove the air deflector shield (if so equipped) from below the radiator. Disconnect the radiator lower hose at the radiator.

6. Disconnect the starter cable at the starter. Remove the retaining bolts and remove the starter. Remove the air cleaner and carburetor on 1975–77 models.

7. Remove the attaching nuts and washers from the motor mounts, raise the front of the engine with a transmission jack and a block of wood. Place 2 in. thick wood blocks between the motor mounts on the engine and the mounting brackets. Lower the engine and remove the transmission jack.

8. Remove the oil pan retaining bolts. Remove the oil pump inlet tube retaining bolts, and remove the inlet tube and screen assembly from the oil pump. Leave it in the bottom of the oil pan. Remove the oil pan and gaskets. Remove the inlet tube and screen from the oil pan.

9. In preparation for installation,

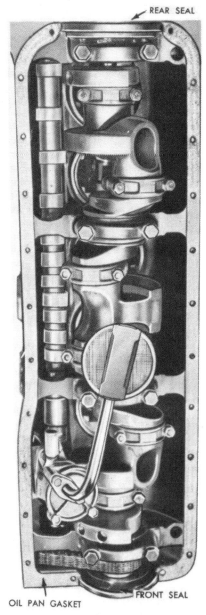

Positioning of the oil pan gaskets and seals on the 170 six-cylinder

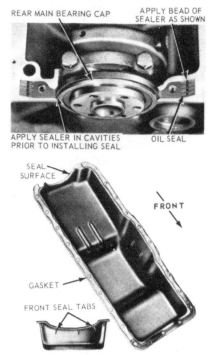

Positioning of the oil pan gaskets and seals on the 240, 300 six-cylinder

clean the gasket surfaces of the oil pump, oil pan and cylinder block. Remove the rear main bearing cap-to-oil pan seal and engine front cover-to-oil pan seal. Clean the seal grooves.

10. Position the oil pan front and rear seal on the engine front cover and the rear main bearing cap, respectively. Be sure that the tabs on the seals are over the oil pan gasket.

11. Clean the inlet tube and screen assembly and place it in the oil pan.

12. Position the oil pan under the engine and install the inlet tube and screen assembly on the oil pump with a new gasket. Position the oil pan against the cylinder block and install the retaining bolts.

13. Assemble the rest of the engine in the reverse order of disassembly, starting with Step 7.

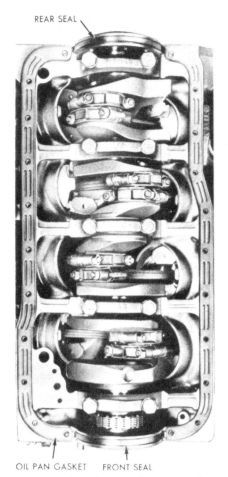

REAR SEAL

OIL PAN GASKET   FRONT SEAL

Positioning of the oil pan gaskets and seals on the 302 V8

302 V8

1. Raise the vehicle on a hoist.

2. Remove the bolts fastening the oil dipstick tube to the exhaust manifold and the oil pan. Position it to one side.

3. Drain the crankcase and remove the oil filter.

4. Disconnect the steering rod end at the idler arm.

5. Remove the nuts and washers attaching the engine front supports to the engine support crossmember.

6. Position a support jack under the damper and raise the engine as required.

7. Remove the nuts attaching the engine support crossmember to the side rails and frame. Remove the engine support crossmember.

8. Lower the support jack and remove the oil pan attaching bolts and the oil pan with the inlet tube.

9. Clean the oil pan, inlet tube and gasket surfaces.

10. Position a new oil pan gasket and end seals to the cylinder block, then install the oil pump inlet tube.

11. Position the oil pan to the cylinder block and install the attaching bolts and tighten them.

12. Position a support jack under the damper and raise the engine as required.

13. Position the engine support crossmember to the side rails and frame. Install the attaching bolts and nuts and tighten them.

14. Lower the engine and remove the jack.

15. Install the washers and nuts attaching the engine supports and tighten.

16. Connect the steering rod end at the idler arm.

17. Connect the oil dipstick tube to the oil pan and exhaust manifold.

18. Install the oil filter.

19. Lower the vehicle and fill the crankcase. Start the engine and check for leaks.

351 AND 460 V8

1. Remove the engine cover. Remove the air cleaner. Disconnect the battery. Remove or set aside the power steering pump, air conditioning compressor, fan shroud, dipstick tube, fuel line, fan and pulleys, transmission cooler lines, exhaust pipe, shift linkage, and driveshaft. The engine is going to be raised about

4 in. so virtually everything will have to be disconnected from the engine and transmission to prevent damage.

2. Unbolt the engine mounts and carefully raise the engine with a padded transmission jack about 4 in. off the mounts. Block it up for safety.

3. The oil pan may now be unbolted and removed.

REAR MAIN OIL SEAL

Replacement

NOTE: *There are seal removal and installation tools available to make this job a lot easier.*

240 AND 300 SIX-CYLINDER

1. Remove the starter.
2. Remove the transmission (see Transmission Removal and Installation). On standard transmission, remove pressure plate and cover assembly and the clutch disc.
3. Remove flywheel and engine rear cover plate.
4. Punch two holes with an awl on each side of the crankshaft just above the bearing cap to cylinder block splint line.
5. Install two sheet metal screws, then pry on both at once to remove seal. Be careful not to damage or scratch oil seal surface. Clean out seal recess in cap and block.
6. Lightly oil crankshaft and seal, then carefully drive the seal straight in.
7. Install engine rear cover plate and flywheel. Coat the flywheel attaching bolt threads with oil-resistant sealer and tighten to the specified torque.
8. On standard transmission, install the clutch disc and pressure plate assembly (see Clutch Removal and Installation).
9. Install transmission.

170 SIX-CYLINDER, ALL V8

1. Drain the crankcase and remove the oil pan, and as necessary, the oil pump.
2. Remove the lower half of the rear main bearing cap and, after removing the oil seal from the cap, drive out the pin in the bottom of the seal groove with a punch.
3. Loosen all the main bearing caps

and allow the crankshaft to lower slightly.

NOTE: *Do not allow the crankshaft to drop more than $1/32$ in.*

4. With a 6 in. length of $3/16$ in. brazing rod, drive up on either exposed end of the top half of the oil seal. When the opposite end of the seal starts to protrude, grasp it with a pair of pliers and gently pull, while the driven end is being tapped.

5. After removing both halves of the old original rope seal and the retaining pin from the lower half of the bearing cap, carefully clean the seal grooves in the cap and block with solvent.

6. Soak the new rubber replacement seals in clean engine oil.

7. Install the upper half of the seal in the block with the undercut side of the seal toward the front of the engine. Slide the seal around the crankshaft journal until $3/8$ in. protrudes beyond the base of the block.

8. Repeat the above procedure for the lower seal, allowing an equal amount of the seal to protrude beyond the opposite end of the bearing cap.

9. Install the rear bearing cap and torque all the main bearings to the proper specification. Apply sealer only to the rear of the seals.

10. Dip the bearing cap side seals in oil, then immediately install them. Do not use any sealer on the side seals. Tap the seals into place and do not clip the protruding ends.

11. Install the oil pump and oil pan. Fill the crankcase with oil, start the engine and check for leaks.

OIL PUMP

Removal and Installation

1. Remove the oil pan.
2. Remove the oil pump inlet tube and screen assembly.
3. Remove the oil pump attaching bolts and remove the oil pump gasket and intermediate driveshaft, if used.
4. Before installing the oil pump, prime it by filling the inlet and outlet port with engine oil and rotating the shaft of the pump to distribute it.
5. Position the intermediate driveshaft into the distributor socket.
6. Position the new gasket on the

pump body and insert the intermediate driveshaft into the pump body.

7. Install the pump and intermediate driveshaft as an assembly. Do not force the pump if it does not seat readily. The driveshaft may be misaligned with the distributor shaft. To align it, rotate the intermediate driveshaft into a new position.

8. Install the oil pump attaching bolts and torque them to 12–15 ft lbs on the 6 cylinder engines and to 20–25 ft lbs on the V8 engines.

9. Install the oil pan.

Engine Cooling

The satisfactory performance of any engine is controlled to a great extent by the proper operation of the cooling system. The engine block is fully water-jacketed to prevent distortion of the cylinder walls. Directed cooling and water holes in the cylinder head causes water to flow past the valve seats, which are one of the hottest parts of any engine, to carry heat away from the valves and seats.

The minimum temperature of the coolant is controlled by the thermostat, mounted in the coolant outlet passage of the engine. When the coolant temperature is below the temperature rating of the thermostat, the thermostat remains closed and the coolant is directed through the radiator by-pass hose to the water pump and back into the engine. When the coolant temperature reaches the temperature rating of the thermostat, the thermostat opens and allows coolant to flow past it and into the top of the radiator. The radiator dissipates the excess engine heat before the coolant is recirculated through the engine.

The cooling system is pressurized and operating pressure is regulated by the rating of the radiator cap which contains a relief valve. The reason for a pressurized cooling system is to allow for higher engine operating temperatures with a higher coolant boiling point.

RADIATOR

Removal and Installation

1. Drain the cooling system.
2. Disconnect the transmission cooling lines from the bottom of the radiator, if so equipped.

3. Remove the retaining bolts at each of the 4 corners of the shroud, if so equipped, and position the shroud over the fan, clear of the radiator.

4. Disconnect the upper and lower hoses from the radiator.

5. Remove the radiator retaining bolts or the upper supports and lift the radiator from the vehicle. On some 240 sixes only, remove the right hood lock bracket and bolts from the radiator grille before removing the radiator.

6. Install the radiator in the reverse order of removal. Fill the cooling system and check for leaks.

WATER PUMP

Removal and Installation

170, 240 AND 300 SIX-CYLINDER

1. Drain the cooling system.
2. Disconnect the lower radiator hose from the water pump.
3. Remove the drive belt, fan and water pump pulley.
4. Disconnect the heater hose at the water pump.
5. Remove the water pump.
6. Before installing the old water pump, clean the gasket mounting surfaces on the pump and on the cylinder block. If a new water pump is being installed, remove the heater hose fitting from the old pump and install it on the new one. Coat the new gaskets with sealer on both sides and install the water pump in the reverse order of removal.

V8

1. Remove the air cleaner and intake duct assembly, including the crankcase ventilation hose.

2. Drain the cooling system.

3. Disconnect the radiator upper hose at the engine and the lower hose at the radiator. Remove the radiator attaching bolts and nuts. Remove the radiator.

4. Loosen the alternator pivot bolt and the bolt attaching the alternator adjusting arm to the water pump.

5. Remove the drive belts, fan, spacer and the water pump pulley.

6. Disconnect the heater hose and the by-pass hose at the water pump.

7. Remove the bolts attaching the water pump to the cylinder front cover. Remove the water pump.

8. Remove all gasket material from the mounting surfaces of the cylinder front cover and the water pump.

9. Position a new gasket, coated on both sides with sealer, on the cylinder front cover; then install the water pump.

10. Connect the heater hose and the by-pass hose at the water pump.

11. Tighten the alternator pivot bolt and the bolt attaching the alternator adjusting arm to the water pump.

12. Install the water pump pulley, spacer and the fan drive belts.

12. Install the radiator, connecting the lower hose at the radiator and the upper hose at the engine.

13. Fill and bleed the cooling system. Operate the engine until normal operating temperatures have been reached and check for leaks.

14. Install the air cleaner and the intake duct assembly, including the crankcase ventilation hose.

THERMOSTAT

Removal and Installation

1. Drain the cooling system to a level below the coolant outlet housing. Use the petcock valve at the bottom of the radia-tor to drain the system; it is not necessary to remove any of the hoses.

2. Remove the coolant outlet housing retaining bolts and slide the housing with the hose attached to one side.

3. Turn the thermostat counterclockwise to unlock it from the outlet.

4. Remove the gasket from the engine block and clean both mating surfaces.

5. To install the thermostat, coat a new gasket with water-resistant sealer and position it on the outlet of the engine. The gasket must be in place before the thermostat is installed.

6. Install the thermostat with the bridge (opposite end from the spring) inside the elbow connection and turn it clockwise to lock it in position with the bridge against the flats cast into the elbow connection.

7. Position the elbow connection onto the mounting surface of the outlet so that the thermostat flange is resting on the gasket and install the retaining bolts.

8. Fill the radiator and operate the engine until it reaches operating temperature. Check the coolant level and adjust as necessary.

NOTE: *It is a good practice to check the operation of a new thermostat before it is installed in an engine. Place the thermostat in a pan of boiling water. If it does not open more than ¼ in., do not install it in the engine.*

Engine Rebuilding

This section describes, in detail, the procedures involved in rebuilding a typical engine. The procedures specifically refer to an inline engine, however, they are basically identical to those used in rebuilding engines of nearly all design and configurations. Procedures for servicing atypical engines (i.e., horizontally opposed) are described in the appropriate section, although in most cases, cylinder head reconditioning procedures described in this chapter will apply.

The section is divided into two sections. The first, Cylinder Head Reconditioning, assumes that the cylinder head is removed from the engine, all manifolds are removed, and the cylinder head is on a workbench. The camshaft should be removed from overhead cam cylinder heads. The second section, Cylinder Block Reconditioning, covers the block, pistons, connecting rods and crankshaft. It is assumed that the engine is mounted on a work stand, and the cylinder head and all accessories are removed.

Procedures are identified as follows:

Unmarked—Basic procedures that must be performed in order to successfully complete the rebuilding process.

Starred (*)—Procedures that should be performed to ensure maximum performance and engine life.

Double starred (**)—Procedures that may be performed to increase engine performance and reliability. These procedures are usually reserved for extremely heavy-duty or competition usage.

In many cases, a choice of methods is also provided. Methods are identified in the same manner as procedures. The choice of method for a procedure is at the discretion of the user.

The tools required for the basic rebuilding procedure should, with minor exceptions, be those

TORQUE (ft. lbs.) *

U.S.

Bolt Diameter (inches)	Bolt Grade (SAE)				Wrench Size (inches)	
	⬡ 1 and 2	⬡ 5	⬡ 6	⬡ 8	Bolt	Nut
1/4	5	7	10	10.5	3/8	7/16
5/16	9	14	19	22	1/2	9/16
3/8	15	25	34	37	9/16	5/8
7/16	24	40	55	60	5/8	3/4
1/2	37	60	85	92	3/4	13/16
9/16	53	88	120	132	7/8	7/8
5/8	74	120	167	180	15/16	1
3/4	120	200	280	296	1-1/8	1-1/8
7/8	190	302	440	473	1-5/16	1-5/16
1	282	466	660	714	1-1/2	1-1/2

Metric

Bolt Diameter (mm)	Bolt Grade				Wrench Size (mm)
	5D 5D	8G 8G	10K 10K	12K 12K	Bolt and Nut
6	5	6	8	10	10
8	10	16	22	27	14
10	19	31	40	49	17
12	34	54	70	86	19
14	55	89	117	137	22
16	83	132	175	208	24
18	111	182	236	283	27
22	182	284	394	464	32
24	261	419	570	689	36

*—Torque values are for lightly oiled bolts. CAUTION: Bolts threaded into aluminum require much less torque.

General Torque Specifications

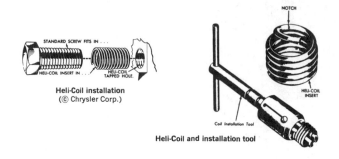

Heli-Coil installation
(© Chrysler Corp.)

Heli-Coil and installation tool

Heli-Coil Insert			Drill	Tap	Insert. Tool	Extract- ing Tool
Thread Size	Part No.	Insert Length (In.)	Size	Part No.	Part No.	Part No.
1/2 -20	1185-4	3/8	17/64(.266)	4 CPB	528-4N	1227-6
5/16-18	1185-5	15/32	Q (.332)	5 CPB	528-5N	1227-6
3/8 -16	1185-6	9/16	X (.397)	6 CPB	528-6N	1227-6
7/16-14	1185-7	21/32	29/64(.453)	7 CPB	528-7N	1227-16
1/2 -13	1185-8	3/4	33/64(.516)	8 CPB	528-8N	1227-16

Heli-Coil Specifications

included in a mechanic's tool kit. An accurate torque wrench, and a dial indicator (reading in thousandths) mounted on a universal base should be available. Bolts and nuts with no torque specification should be tightened according to size (see chart). Special tools, where required, all are readily available from the major tool suppliers (i.e., Craftsman, Snap-On, K-D). The services of a competent automotive machine shop must also be readily available.

When assembling the engine, any parts that will be in frictional contact must be pre-lubricated, to provide protection on initial start-up. Vortex Pre-Lube, STP, or any product specifically formulated for this purpose may be used. NOTE: *Do not use engine oil.* Where semi-permanent (locked but removable) installation of bolts or nuts is desired, threads should be cleaned and coated with Loctite. Studs may be permanently installed using Loctite Stud and Bearing Mount.

Aluminum has become increasingly popular for use in engines, due to its low weight and excellent heat transfer characteristics. The following precautions

must be observed when handling aluminum engine parts:
—Never hot-tank aluminum parts.
—Remove all aluminum parts (identification tags, etc.) from engine parts before hot-tanking (otherwise they will be removed during the process).
—Always coat threads lightly with engine oil or anti-seize compounds before installation, to prevent seizure.
—Never over-torque bolts or spark plugs in aluminum threads. Should stripping occur, threads can be restored according to the following procedure, using Heli-Coil thread inserts:

Tap drill the hole with the stripped threads to the specified size (see chart). Using the specified tap (NOTE: *Heli-Coil tap sizes refer to the size thread being replaced, rather than the actual tap size*), tap the hole for the Heli-Coil. Place the insert on the proper installation tool (see chart). Apply pressure on the insert while winding it clockwise into the hole, until the top of the insert is one turn below the surface. Remove the installation tool, and break the installation tang from the bottom of the in-

sert by moving it up and down. If the Heli-Coil must be removed, tap the removal tool firmly into the hole, so that it engages the top thread, and turn the tool counter-clockwise to extract the insert.

Snapped bolts or studs may be removed, using a stud extractor (unthreaded) or Vise-Grip pliers (threaded). Penetrating oil (e.g., Liquid Wrench) will often aid in breaking frozen threads. In cases where the stud or bolt is flush with, or below the surface, proceed as follows:

Drill a hole in the broken stud or bolt, approximately 1/2 its diameter. Select a screw extractor (e.g., Easy-Out) of the proper size, and tap it into the stud or bolt. Turn the extractor counter-clockwise to remove the stud or bolt.

Magnaflux and Zyglo are inspection techniques used to locate material flaws, such as stress cracks. Magnafluxing coats the part with fine magnetic particles, and subjects the part to a magnetic field. Cracks cause breaks

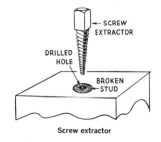

Screw extractor

in the magnetic field, which are outlined by the particles. Since Magnaflux is a magnetic process, it is applicable only to ferrous materials. The Zyglo process coats the material with a fluorescent dye penetrant, and then subjects it to blacklight inspection, under which cracks glow bright-

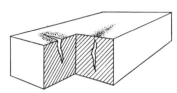

Magnaflux indication of cracks

ly. Parts made of any material may be tested using Zyglo. While Magnaflux and Zyglo are excellent for general inspection, and locating hidden defects, specific checks of suspected cracks may be made at lower cost and more readily using spot check dye. The dye is sprayed onto the suspected area, wiped off, and the area is then sprayed with a developer. Cracks then will show up brightly. Spot check dyes will only indicate surface cracks; therefore, structural cracks below the surface may escape detection. When questionable, the part should be tested using Magnaflux or Zyglo.

CYLINDER HEAD RECONDITIONING

Procedure	Method
Identify the valves:  **Valve identification** (© SAAB)	Invert the cylinder head, and number the valve faces front to rear, using a permanent felt-tip marker.
Remove the rocker arms:	Remove the rocker arms with shaft(s) or balls and nuts. Wire the sets of rockers, balls and nuts together, and identify according to the corresponding valve.
Remove the valves and springs:	Using an appropriate valve spring compressor (depending on the configuration of the cylinder head), compress the valve springs. Lift out the keepers with needlenose pliers, release the compressor, and remove the valve, spring, and spring retainer.
Check the valve stem-to-guide clearance:  **Checking the valve stem-to-guide clearance** (© American Motors Corp.)	Clean the valve stem with lacquer thinner or a similar solvent to remove all gum and varnish. Clean the valve guides using solvent and an expanding wire-type valve guide cleaner. Mount a dial indicator so that the stem is at 90° to the valve stem, as close to the valve guide as possible. Move the valve off its seat, and measure the valve guide-to-stem clearance by moving the stem back and forth to actuate the dial indicator. Measure the valve stems using a micrometer, and compare to specifications, to determine whether stem or guide wear is responsible for excessive clearance.
De-carbon the cylinder head and valves: 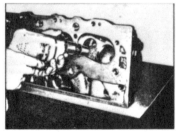 **Removing carbon from the cylinder head** (© Chevrolet Div. G.M. Corp.)	Chip carbon away from the valve heads, combustion chambers, and ports, using a chisel made of hardwood. Remove the remaining deposits with a stiff wire brush. NOTE: *Ensure that the deposits are actually removed, rather than burnished.*

Procedure	Method
Hot-tank the cylinder head:	Have the cylinder head hot-tanked to remove grease, corrosion, and scale from the water passages. NOTE: *In the case of overhead cam cylinder heads, consult the operator to determine whether the camshaft bearings will be damaged by the caustic solution.*
Degrease the remaining cylinder head parts:	Using solvent (i.e., Gunk), clean the rockers, rocker shaft(s) (where applicable), rocker balls and nuts, springs, spring retainers, and keepers. Do not remove the protective coating from the springs.
Check the cylinder head for warpage:  **Checking the cylinder head for warpage** (© Ford Motor Co.)	Place a straight-edge across the gasket surface of the cylinder head. Using feeler gauges, determine the clearance at the center of the straight-edge. Measure across both diagonals, along the longitudinal centerline, and across the cylinder head at several points. If warpage exceeds .003″ in a 6″ span, or .006″ over the total length, the cylinder head must be resurfaced. NOTE: *If warpage exceeds the manufacturers maximum tolerance for material removal, the cylinder head must be replaced.* When milling the cylinder heads of V-type engines, the intake manifold mounting position is altered, and must be corrected by milling the manifold flange a proportionate amount.
** Porting and gasket matching:  **Marking the cylinder head for gasket matching** (© Petersen Publishing Co.)  **Port configuration before and after gasket matching** (© Petersen Publishing Co.)	** Coat the manifold flanges of the cylinder head with Prussian blue dye. Glue intake and exhaust gaskets to the cylinder head in their installed position using rubber cement and scribe the outline of the ports on the manifold flanges. Remove the gaskets. Using a small cutter in a hand-held power tool (i.e., Dremel Moto-Tool), gradually taper the walls of the port out to the scribed outline of the gasket. Further enlargement of the ports should include the removal of sharp edges and radiusing of sharp corners. Do not alter the valve guides. NOTE: *The most efficient port configuration is determined only by extensive testing. Therefore, it is best to consult someone experienced with the head in question to determine the optimum alterations.*

Procedure	Method
** Polish the ports:	** Using a grinding stone with the above mentioned tool, polish the walls of the intake and exhaust ports, and combustion chamber. Use progressively finer stones until all surface imperfections are removed. NOTE: *Through testing, it has been determined that a smooth surface is more effective than a mirror polished surface in intake ports, and vice-versa in exhaust ports.*

Relieved and polished ports
(© Petersen Publishing Co.)

Polished combustion chamber
(© Petersen Publishing Co.)

Procedure	Method
* Knurling the valve guides:	* Valve guides which are not excessively worn or distorted may, in some cases, be knurled rather than replaced. Knurling is a process in which metal is displaced and raised, thereby reducing clearance. Knurling also provides excellent oil control. The possibility of knurling rather than replacing valve guides should be discussed with a machinist.

Cut-away view of a knurled valve guide
(© Petersen Publishing Co.)

Replacing the valve guides: NOTE: *Valve guides should only be replaced if damaged or if an oversize valve stem is not available.*

Depending on the type of cylinder head, valve guides may be pressed, hammered, or shrunk in. In cases where the guides are shrunk into the head, replacement should be left to an equipped machine shop. In other cases, the guides are replaced as follows: Press or tap the valve guides out of the head using a stepped drift (see illustration). Determine the height above the boss that the guide must extend, and obtain a stack of washers, their I.D. similar to the guide's O.D., of that height. Place the stack of washers on the guide, and insert the guide into the boss. NOTE: *Valve guides are often tapered or beveled for installation.* Using the stepped installation tool (see illustration), press or tap the guides into position. Ream the guides according to the size of the valve stem.

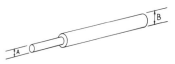

A-VALVE GUIDE I.D.
B-SLIGHTLY SMALLER THAN VALVE GUIDE O.D.

Valve guide removal tool

WASHERS

A-VALVE GUIDE I.D.
B-LARGER THAN THE VALVE GUIDE O.D.

Valve guide installation tool (with
washers used during installation)

Procedure	Method
Replacing valve seat inserts:	Replacement of valve seat inserts which are worn beyond resurfacing or broken, if feasible, must be done by a machine shop.
Resurfacing (grinding) the valve face:  Grinding a valve (© Subaru) 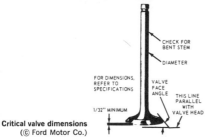 Critical valve dimensions (© Ford Motor Co.)	Using a valve grinder, resurface the valves according to specifications. CAUTION: *Valve face angle is not always identical to valve seat angle.* A minimum margin of 1/32″ should remain after grinding the valve. The valve stem tip should also be squared and resurfaced, by placing the stem in the V-block of the grinder, and turning it while pressing lightly against the grinding wheel.
Resurfacing the valve seats using reamers:  Reaming the valve seat (© S.p.A. Fiat) Valve seat width and centering (© Ford Motor Co.)	Select a reamer of the correct seat angle, slightly larger than the diameter of the valve seat, and assemble it with a pilot of the correct size. Install the pilot into the valve guide, and using steady pressure, turn the reamer clockwise. CAUTION: *Do not turn the reamer counter-clockwise.* Remove only as much material as necessary to clean the seat. Check the concentricity of the seat (see below). If the dye method is not used, coat the valve face with Prussian blue dye, install and rotate it on the valve seat. Using the dye marked area as a centering guide, center and narrow the valve seat to specifications with correction cutters. NOTE: *When no specifications are available, minimum seat width for exhaust valves should be 5/64″, intake valves 1/16″.* After making correction cuts, check the position of the valve seat on the valve face using Prussian blue dye.
* Resurfacing the valve seats using a grinder:  Grinding a valve seat (© Subaru)	Select a pilot of the correct size, and a coarse stone of the correct seat angle. Lubricate the pilot if necessary, and install the tool in the valve guide. Move the stone on and off the seat at approximately two cycles per second, until all flaws are removed from the seat. Install a fine stone, and finish the seat. Center and narrow the seat using correction stones, as described above.

Procedure	Method
Checking the valve seat concentricity: 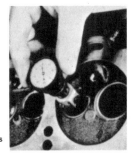 **Checking the valve seat concentricity using a dial gauge** (© American Motors Corp.)	Coat the valve face with Prussian blue dye, install the valve, and rotate it on the valve seat. If the entire seat becomes coated, and the valve is known to be concentric, the seat is concentric.
	* Install the dial gauge pilot into the guide, and rest the arm on the valve seat. Zero the gauge, and rotate the arm around the seat. Run-out should not exceed .002″.
* Lapping the valves: NOTE: *Valve lapping is done to ensure efficient sealing of resurfaced valves and seats. Valve lapping alone is not recommended for use as a resurfacing procedure.*  **Hand lapping the valves** 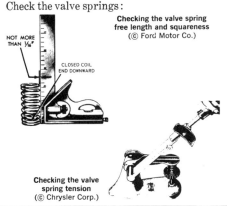 HAND DRILL ROD SUCTION CUP Home made mechanical valve lapping tool	* Invert the cylinder head, lightly lubricate the valve stems, and install the valves in the head as numbered. Coat valve seats with fine grinding compound, and attach the lapping tool suction cup to a valve head (NOTE: *Moisten the suction cup*). Rotate the tool between the palms, changing position and lifting the tool often to prevent grooving. Lap the valve until a smooth, polished seat is evident. Remove the valve and tool, and rinse away all traces of grinding compound.
	** Fasten a suction cup to a piece of drill rod, and mount the rod in a hand drill. Proceed as above, using the hand drill as a lapping tool. CAUTION: *Due to the higher speeds involved when using the hand drill, care must be exercised to avoid grooving the seat.* Lift the tool and change direction of rotation often.
Check the valve springs:  NOT MORE THAN ⅟₁₆″ CLOSED COIL END DOWNWARD **Checking the valve spring free length and squareness** (© Ford Motor Co.) **Checking the valve spring tension** (© Chrysler Corp.)	Place the spring on a flat surface next to a square. Measure the height of the spring, and rotate it against the edge of the square to measure distortion. If spring height varies (by comparison) by more than 1/16″ or if distortion exceeds 1/16″, replace the spring.
	** In addition to evaluating the spring as above, test the spring pressure at the installed and compressed (installed height minus valve lift) height using a valve spring tester. Springs used on small displacement engines (up to 3 liters) should be ± 1 lb. of all other springs in either position. A tolerance of ± 5 lbs. is permissible on larger engines.

Procedure	*Method*
* Install valve stem seals:  **Valve stem seal installation** (© Ford Motor Co.) SEAL	* Due to the pressure differential that exists at the ends of the intake valve guides (atmospheric pressure above, manifold vacuum below), oil is drawn through the valve guides into the intake port. This has been alleviated somewhat since the addition of positive crankcase ventilation, which lowers the pressure above the guides. Several types of valve stem seals are available to reduce blow-by. Certain seals simply slip over the stem and guide boss, while others require that the boss be machined. Recently, Teflon guide seals have become popular. Consult a parts supplier or machinist concerning availability and suggested usages. NOTE: *When installing seals, ensure that a small amount of oil is able to pass the seal to lubricate the valve guides; otherwise, excessive wear may result.*
Install the valves:	Lubricate the valve stems, and install the valves in the cylinder head as numbered. Lubricate and position the seals (if used, see above) and the valve springs. Install the spring retainers, compress the springs, and insert the keys using needlenose pliers or a tool designed for this purpose. NOTE: *Retain the keys with wheel bearing grease during installation.*
Checking valve spring installed height: 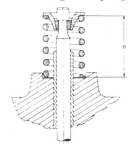 **Valve spring installed height dimension** (© Porsche)  **Measuring valve spring installed height** (© Petersen Publishing Co.)	Measure the distance between the spring pad and the lower edge of the spring retainer, and compare to specifications. If the installed height is incorrect, add shim washers between the spring pad and the spring. CAUTION: *Use only washers designed for this purpose.*
** CC'ing the combustion chambers:	** Invert the cylinder head and place a bead of sealer around a combustion chamber. Install an apparatus designed for this purpose (burette mounted on a clear plate; see illustration) over the combustion chamber, and fill with the specified fluid to an even mark on the burette. Record the burette reading, and fill the combustion chamber with fluid. (NOTE: *A hole drilled in the plate will permit air to escape*). Subtract the burette reading, with the combustion chamber filled, from the previous reading, to determine combustion chamber volume in cc's. Duplicate this procedure in all combustion

Procedure	*Method*

CC'ing the combustion chamber
(ⓒ Petersen Publishing Co.)

chambers on the cylinder head, and compare the readings. The volume of all combustion chambers should be made equal to that of the largest. Combustion chamber volume may be increased in two ways. When only a small change is required (usually), a small cutter or coarse stone may be used to remove material from the combustion chamber. NOTE: *Check volume frequently.* Remove material over a wide area, so as not to change the configuration of the combustion chamber. When a larger change is required, the valve seat may be sunk (lowered into the head). NOTE: *When altering valve seat, remember to compensate for the change in spring installed height.*

Inspect the rocker arms, balls, studs, and nuts (where applicable):

Stress cracks in rocker nuts
(ⓒ Ford Motor Co.)

Visually inspect the rocker arms, balls, studs, and nuts for cracks, galling, burning, scoring, or wear. If all parts are intact, liberally lubricate the rocker arms and balls, and install them on the cylinder head. If wear is noted on a rocker arm at the point of valve contact, grind it smooth and square, removing as little material as possible. Replace the rocker arm if excessively worn. If a rocker stud shows signs of wear, it must be replaced (see below). If a rocker nut shows stress cracks, replace it. If an exhaust ball is galled or burned, substitute the intake ball from the same cylinder (if it is intact), and install a new intake ball. NOTE: *Avoid using new rocker balls on exhaust valves.*

Replacing rocker studs:

Reaming the stud bore for oversize rocker studs
(ⓒ Buick Div. G.M. Corp.)

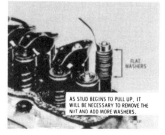

Extracting a pressed in rocker stud
(ⓒ Buick Div. G.M. Corp.)

AS STUD BEGINS TO PULL UP, IT WILL BE NECESSARY TO REMOVE THE NUT AND ADD MORE WASHERS.

In order to remove a threaded stud, lock two nuts on the stud, and unscrew the stud using the lower nut. Coat the lower threads of the new stud with Loctite, and install.

Two alternative methods are available for replacing pressed in studs. Remove the damaged stud using a stack of washers and a nut (see illustration). In the first, the boss is reamed .005-.006″ oversize, and an oversize stud pressed in. Control the stud extension over the boss using washers, in the same manner as valve guides. Before installing the stud, coat it with white lead and grease. To retain the stud more positively, drill a hole through the stud and boss, and install a roll pin. In the second method, the boss is tapped, and a threaded stud installed. Retain the stud using Loctite Stud and Bearing Mount.

Procedure	Method
Inspect the rocker shaft(s) and rocker arms (where applicable):  Disassembled rocker shaft parts arranged for inspection (© American Motors Corp.) 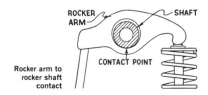 Rocker arm to rocker shaft contact	Remove rocker arms, springs and washers from rocker shaft. NOTE: *Lay out parts in the order they are removed.* Inspect rocker arms for pitting or wear on the valve contact point, or excessive bushing wear. Bushings need only be replaced if wear is excessive, because the rocker arm normally contacts the shaft at one point only. Grind the valve contact point of rocker arm smooth if necessary, removing as little material as possible. If excessive material must be removed to smooth and square the arm, it should be replaced. Clean out all oil holes and passages in rocker shaft. If shaft is grooved or worn, replace it. Lubricate and assemble the rocker shaft.
Inspect the camshaft bushings and the camshaft (overhead cam engines):	See next section.
Inspect the pushrods:	Remove the pushrods, and, if hollow, clean out the oil passages using fine wire. Roll each pushrod over a piece of clean glass. If a distinct clicking sound is heard as the pushrod rolls, the rod is bent, and must be replaced.
	* The length of all pushrods must be equal. Measure the length of the pushrods, compare to specifications, and replace as necessary.
Inspect the valve lifters:  Check for Concave Wear on Face of Tappet Using Tappet for Straight Edge Checking the lifter face (© American Motors Corp.)	Remove lifters from their bores, and remove gum and varnish, using solvent. Clean walls of lifter bores. Check lifters for concave wear as illustrated. If face is worn concave, replace lifter, and carefully inspect the camshaft. Lightly lubricate lifter and insert it into its bore. If play is excessive, an oversize lifter must be installed (where possible). Consult a machinist concerning feasibility. If play is satisfactory, remove, lubricate, and reinstall the lifter.
* Testing hydraulic lifter leak down: 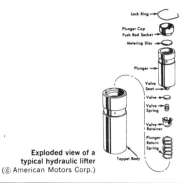 Lock Ring Plunger Cap Push Rod Socket Metering Disc Plunger Valve Seat Valve Valve Spring Valve Retainer Plunger Return Spring Tappet Body Exploded view of a typical hydraulic lifter (© American Motors Corp.)	Submerge lifter in a container of kerosene. Chuck a used pushrod or its equivalent into a drill press. Position container of kerosene so pushrod acts on the lifter plunger. Pump lifter with the drill press, until resistance increases. Pump several more times to bleed any air out of lifter. Apply very firm, constant pressure to the lifter, and observe rate at which fluid bleeds out of lifter. If the fluid bleeds very quickly (less than 15 seconds), lifter is defective. If the time exceeds 60 seconds, lifter is sticking. In either case, recondition or replace lifter. If lifter is operating properly (leak down time 15-60 seconds), lubricate and install it.

CYLINDER BLOCK RECONDITIONING

Procedure	*Method*

Checking the main bearing clearance:

Plastigage installed on main bearing journal
(© Chevrolet Div. G.M. Corp.)

**Measuring Plastigage to determine
main bearing clearance**
(© Chevrolet Div. G.M. Corp.)

Causes of bearing failure
(© Ford Motor Co.)

Invert engine, and remove cap from the bearing to be checked. Using a clean, dry rag, thoroughly clean all oil from crankshaft journal and bearing insert. NOTE: *Plastigage is soluble in oil; therefore, oil on the journal or bearing could result in erroneous readings.* Place a piece of Plastigage along the full length of journal, reinstall cap, and torque to specifications. Remove bearing cap, and determine bearing clearance by comparing width of Plastigage to the scale on Plastigage envelope. Journal taper is determined by comparing width of the Plastigage strip near its ends. Rotate crankshaft 90° and retest, to determine journal eccentricity. NOTE: *Do not rotate crankshaft with Plastigage installed.* If bearing insert and journal appear intact, and are within tolerances, no further main bearing service is required. If bearing or journal appear defective, cause of failure should be determined before replacement.

* Remove crankshaft from block (see below). Measure the main bearing journals at each end twice (90° apart) using a micrometer, to determine diameter, journal taper and eccentricity. If journals are within tolerances, reinstall bearing caps at their specified torque. Using a telescope gauge and micrometer, measure bearing I.D. parallel to piston axis and at 30° on each side of piston axis. Subtract journal O.D. from bearing I.D. to determine oil clearance. If crankshaft journals appear defective, or do not meet tolerances, there is no need to measure bearings; for the crankshaft will require grinding and/or undersize bearings will be required. If bearing appears defective, cause for failure should be determined prior to replacement.

Checking the connecting rod bearing clearance:

**Plastigage installed on connecting rod
bearing journal**
(© Chevrolet Div. G.M. Corp.)

Connecting rod bearing clearance is checked in the same manner as main bearing clearance, using Plastigage. Before removing the crankshaft, connecting rod side clearance also should be measured and recorded.

* Checking connecting rod bearing clearance, using a micrometer, is identical to checking main bearing clearance. If no other service

Procedure	*Method*

Measuring Plastigage to determine connecting rod bearing clearance
(© Chevrolet Div. G.M. Corp.)

is required, the piston and rod assemblies need not be removed.

Removing the crankshaft:

Connecting rod matching marks
(© Ford Motor Co.)

Using a punch, mark the corresponding main bearing caps and saddles according to position (i.e., one punch on the front main cap and saddle, two on the second, three on the third, etc.). Using number stamps, identify the corresponding connecting rods and caps, according to cylinder (if no numbers are present). Remove the main and connecting rod caps, and place sleeves of plastic tubing over the connecting rod bolts, to protect the journals as the crankshaft is removed. Lift the crankshaft out of the block.

Remove the ridge from the top of the cylinder:

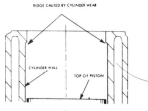

Cylinder bore ridge
(© Pontiac Div. G.M. Corp.)

In order to facilitate removal of the piston and connecting rod, the ridge at the top of the cylinder (unworn area; see illustration) must be removed. Place the piston at the bottom of the bore, and cover it with a rag. Cut the ridge away using a ridge reamer, exercising extreme care to avoid cutting too deeply. Remove the rag, and remove cuttings that remain on the piston. CAUTION: *If the ridge is not removed, and new rings are installed, damage to rings will result.*

Removing the piston and connecting rod:

Removing the piston
(© SAAB)

Invert the engine, and push the pistons and connecting rods out of the cylinders. If necessary, tap the connecting rod boss with a wooden hammer handle, to force the piston out. CAUTION: *Do not attempt to force the piston past the cylinder ridge* (see above).

Procedure	Method
Service the crankshaft:	Ensure that all oil holes and passages in the crankshaft are open and free of sludge. If necessary, have the crankshaft ground to the largest possible undersize.
	** Have the crankshaft Magnafluxed, to locate stress cracks. Consult a machinist concerning additional service procedures, such as surface hardening (e.g., nitriding, Tuftriding) to improve wear characteristics, cross drilling and chamfering the oil holes to improve lubrication, and balancing.
Removing freeze plugs:	Drill a small hole in the center of the freeze plugs. Thread a large sheet metal screw into the hole and remove the plug with a slide hammer.
Remove the oil gallery plugs:	Threaded plugs should be removed using an appropriate (usually square) wrench. To remove soft, pressed in plugs, drill a hole in the plug, and thread in a sheet metal screw. Pull the plug out by the screw using a slide hammer.
Hot-tank the block:	Have the block hot-tanked to remove grease, corrosion, and scale from the water jackets. NOTE: *Consult the operator to determine whether the camshaft bearings will be damaged during the hot-tank process.*
Check the block for cracks:	Visually inspect the block for cracks or chips. The most common locations are as follows: Adjacent to freeze plugs. Between the cylinders and water jackets. Adjacent to the main bearing saddles. At the extreme bottom of the cylinders. Check only suspected cracks using spot check dye (see introduction). If a crack is located, consult a machinist concerning possible repairs.
	** Magnaflux the block to locate hidden cracks. If cracks are located, consult a machinist about feasibility of repair.
Install the oil gallery plugs and freeze plugs:	Coat freeze plugs with sealer and tap into position using a piece of pipe, slightly smaller than the plug, as a driver. To ensure retention, stake the edges of the plugs. Coat threaded oil gallery plugs with sealer and install. Drive replacement soft plugs into block using a large drift as a driver.
	* Rather than reinstalling lead plugs, drill and tap the holes, and install threaded plugs.

Procedure	*Method*

Check the bore diameter and surface:

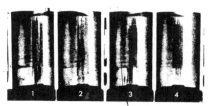

1, 2, 3 Piston skirt seizure resulted in this pattern. Engine must be rebored

4. Piston skirt and oil ring seizure caused this damage. Engine must be rebored

5, 6 Score marks caused by a split piston skirt. Damage is not serious enough to warrant reboring

7. Ring seized longitudinally, causing a score mark 1 3/16" wide, on the land side of the piston groove. The honing pattern is destroyed and the cylinder must be rebored

8. Result of oil ring seizure. Engine must be rebored

9. Oil ring seizure here was not serious enough to warrant reboring. The honing marks are still visible

Cylinder wall damage
(© Daimler-Benz A.G.)

Visually inspect the cylinder bores for roughness, scoring, or scuffing. If evident, the cylinder bore must be bored or honed oversize to eliminate imperfections, and the smallest possible oversize piston used. The new pistons should be given to the machinist with the block, so that the cylinders can be bored or honed exactly to the piston size (plus clearance). If no flaws are evident, measure the bore diameter using a telescope gauge and micrometer, or dial gauge, parallel and perpendicular to the engine centerline, at the top (below the ridge) and bottom of the bore. Subtract the bottom measurements from the top to determine taper, and the parallel to the centerline measurements from the perpendicular measurements to determine eccentricity. If the measurements are not within specifications, the cylinder must be bored or honed, and an oversize piston installed. If the measurements are within specifications the cylinder may be used as is, with only finish honing (see below). NOTE: *Prior to submitting the block for boring, perform the following operation(s).*

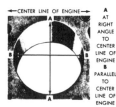 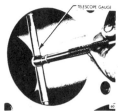  

Cylinder bore measuring positions
(© Ford Motor Co.)

Measuring the cylinder bore with a telescope gauge
(© Buick Div. G.M. Corp.)

Determining the cylinder bore by measuring the telescope gauge with a micrometer
(© Buick Div. G.M. Corp.)

Measuring the cylinder bore with a dial gauge
(© Chevrolet Div. G.M. Corp.)

Procedure	Method
Check the block deck for warpage:	Using a straightedge and feeler gauges, check the block deck for warpage in the same manner that the cylinder head is checked (see Cylinder Head Reconditioning). If warpage exceeds specifications, have the deck resurfaced. NOTE: *In certain cases a specification for total material removal (Cylinder head and block deck) is provided. This specification must not be exceeded.*
* Check the deck height:	The deck height is the distance from the crankshaft centerline to the block deck. To measure, invert the engine, and install the crankshaft, retaining it with the center main cap. Measure the distance from the crankshaft journal to the block deck, parallel to the cylinder centerline. Measure the diameter of the end (front and rear) main journals, parallel to the centerline of the cylinders, divide the diameter in half, and subtract it from the previous measurement. The results of the front and rear measurements should be identical. If the difference exceeds .005″, the deck height should be corrected. NOTE: *Block deck height and warpage should be corrected concurrently.*
Check the cylinder block bearing alignment:  **Checking main bearing saddle alignment** (© Petersen Publishing Co.)	Remove the upper bearing inserts. Place a straightedge in the bearing saddles along the centerline of the crankshaft. If clearance exists between the straightedge and the center saddle, the block must be align-bored.
Clean and inspect the pistons and connecting rods: 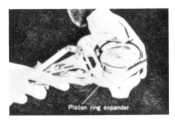 Piston ring expander **Removing the piston rings** (© Subaru)	Using a ring expander, remove the rings from the piston. Remove the retaining rings (if so equipped) and remove piston pin. NOTE: *If the piston pin must be pressed out, determine the proper method and use the proper tools; otherwise the piston will distort.* Clean the ring grooves using an appropriate tool, exercising care to avoid cutting too deeply. Thoroughly clean all carbon and varnish from the piston with solvent. CAUTION: *Do not use a wire brush or caustic solvent on pistons.* Inspect the pistons for scuffing, scoring, cracks, pitting, or excessive ring groove wear. If wear is evident, the piston must be replaced. Check the connecting rod length by measuring the rod from the inside of the large end to the inside of the small end using calipers (see

Procedure	*Method*

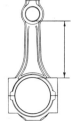

Cleaning the piston ring grooves
(© Ford Motor Co.)

Connecting rod
length checking
dimension

illustration). All connecting rods should be equal length. Replace any rod that differs from the others in the engine.

* Have the connecting rod alignment checked in an alignment fixture by a machinist. Replace any twisted or bent rods.

* Magnaflux the connecting rods to locate stress cracks. If cracks are found, replace the connecting rod.

Fit the pistons to the cylinders:

Measuring the cylinder
with a telescope gauge
for piston fitting
(© Buick Div.
G.M. Corp.)

Measuring the piston
for fitting
(© Buick Div.
G.M. Corp.)

Using a telescope gauge and micrometer, or a dial gauge, measure the cylinder bore diameter perpendicular to the piston pin, 2½″ below the deck. Measure the piston perpendicular to its pin on the skirt. The difference between the two measurements is the piston clearance. If the clearance is within specifications or slightly below (after boring or honing), finish honing is all that is required. If the clearance is excessive, try to obtain a slightly larger piston to bring clearance within specifications. Where this is not possible, obtain the first oversize piston, and hone (or if necessary, bore) the cylinder to size.

Assemble the pistons and connecting rods:

Installing piston pin lock rings
(© Nissan Motor Co., Ltd.)

Inspect piston pin, connecting rod small end bushing, and piston bore for galling, scoring, or excessive wear. If evident, replace defective part(s). Measure the I.D. of the piston boss and connecting rod small end, and the O.D. of the piston pin. If within specifications, assemble piston pin and rod. CAUTION: *If piston pin must be pressed in, determine the proper method and use the proper tools; otherwise the piston will distort.* Install the lock rings; ensure that they seat properly. If the parts are not within specifications, determine the service method for the type of engine. In some cases, piston and pin are serviced as an assembly when either is defective. Others specify reaming the piston and connecting rods for an oversize pin. If the connecting rod bushing is worn, it may in many cases be replaced. Reaming the piston and replacing the rod bushing are machine shop operations.

Procedure	*Method*

Clean and inspect the camshaft:

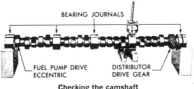

BEARING JOURNALS

FUEL PUMP DRIVE ECCENTRIC   DISTRIBUTOR DRIVE GEAR

Checking the camshaft for straightness
(© Chevrolet Motor Div. G.M. Corp.)

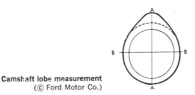

Camshaft lobe measurement
(© Ford Motor Co.)

Degrease the camshaft, using solvent, and clean out all oil holes. Visually inspect cam lobes and bearing journals for excessive wear. If a lobe is questionable, check all lobes as indicated below. If a journal or lobe is worn, the camshaft must be reground or replaced. NOTE: *If a journal is worn, there is a good chance that the bushings are worn.* If lobes and journals appear intact, place the front and rear journals in V-blocks, and rest a dial indicator on the center journal. Rotate the camshaft to check straightness. If deviation exceeds .001″, replace the camshaft.

* Check the camshaft lobes with a micrometer, by measuring the lobes from the nose to base and again at 90° (see illustration). The lift is determined by subtracting the second measurement from the first. If all exhaust lobes and all intake lobes are not identical, the camshaft must be reground or replaced.

Replace the camshaft bearings:

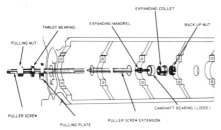

EXPANDING COLLET

THRUST BEARING   EXPANDING MANDREL   BACK-UP NUT

PULLING NUT

PULLER SCREW   CAMSHAFT BEARING (LOOSE)

PULLER SCREW EXTENSION

PULLING PLATE

Camshaft removal and installation tool (typical)
(© Ford Motor Co.)

If excessive wear is indicated, or if the engine is being completely rebuilt, camshaft bearings should be replaced as follows: Drive the camshaft rear plug from the block. Assemble the removal puller with its shoulder on the bearing to be removed. Gradually tighten the puller nut until bearing is removed. Remove remaining bearings, leaving the front and rear for last. To remove front and rear bearings, reverse position of the tool, so as to pull the bearings in toward the center of the block. Leave the tool in this position, pilot the new front and rear bearings on the installer, and pull them into position. Return the tool to its original position and pull remaining bearings into position. NOTE: *Ensure that oil holes align when installing bearings.* Replace camshaft rear plug, and stake it into position to aid retention.

Finish hone the cylinders:

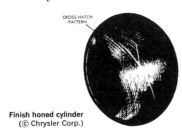

CROSS-HATCH PATTERN

Finish honed cylinder
(© Chrysler Corp.)

Chuck a flexible drive hone into a power drill, and insert it into the cylinder. Start the hone, and move it up and down in the cylinder at a rate which will produce approximately a 60° cross-hatch pattern (see illustration). NOTE: *Do not extend the hone below the cylinder bore.* After developing the pattern, remove the hone and recheck piston fit. Wash the cylinders with a detergent and water solution to remove abrasive dust, dry, and wipe several times with a rag soaked in engine oil.

Procedure	*Method*

Check piston ring end-gap:

Checking ring end-gap
(© Chevrolet Motor Div. G.M. Corp.)

Compress the piston rings to be used in a cylinder, one at a time, into that cylinder, and press them approximately 1″ below the deck with an inverted piston. Using feeler gauges, measure the ring end-gap, and compare to specifications. Pull the ring out of the cylinder and file the ends with a fine file to obtain proper clearance. CAUTION: *If inadequate ring end-gap is utilized, ring breakage will result.*

Install the piston rings:

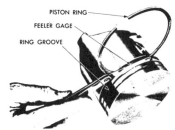

Checking ring side clearance
(© Chrysler Corp.)

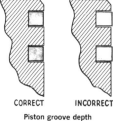

CORRECT INCORRECT
Piston groove depth

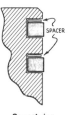

Correct ring spacer installation

Inspect the ring grooves in the piston for excessive wear or taper. If necessary, recut the groove(s) for use with an overwidth ring or a standard ring and spacer. If the groove is worn uniformly, overwidth rings, or standard rings and spacers may be installed without recutting. Roll the outside of the ring around the groove to check for burrs or deposits. If any are found, remove with a fine file. Hold the ring in the groove, and measure side clearance. If necessary, correct as indicated above. NOTE: *Always install any additional spacers above the piston ring.* The ring groove must be deep enough to allow the ring to seat below the lands (see illustration). In many cases, a "go-no-go" depth gauge will be provided with the piston rings. Shallow grooves may be corrected by recutting, while deep grooves require some type of filler or expander behind the piston. Consult the piston ring supplier concerning the suggested method. Install the rings on the piston, lowest ring first, using a ring expander. NOTE: *Position the ring markings as specified by the manufacturer (see car section).*

Install the camshaft:

Liberally lubricate the camshaft lobes and journals, and slide the camshaft into the block. CAUTION: *Exercise extreme care to avoid damaging the bearings when inserting the camshaft.* Install and tighten the camshaft thrust plate retaining bolts.

Check camshaft end-play:

Checking camshaft end-play with a feeler gauge
(© Ford Motor Co.)

Using feeler gauges, determine whether the clearance between the camshaft boss (or gear) and backing plate is within specifications. Install shims behind the thrust plate, or reposition the camshaft gear and retest end-play.

Procedure	*Method*

Checking camshaft end-play with a dial indicator

* Mount a dial indicator stand so that the stem of the dial indicator rests on the nose of the camshaft, parallel to the camshaft axis. Push the camshaft as far in as possible and zero the gauge. Move the camshaft outward to determine the amount of camshaft end-play. If the end-play is not within tolerance, install shims behind the thrust plate, or re-position the camshaft gear and retest.

Install the rear main seal (where applicable):

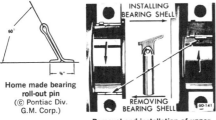

Seating the rear main seal
(© Buick Div. G.M. Corp.)

Position the block with the bearing saddles facing upward. Lay the rear main seal in its groove and press it lightly into its seat. Place a piece of pipe the same diameter as the crankshaft journal into the saddle, and firmly seat the seal. Hold the pipe in position, and trim the ends of the seal flush if required.

Install the crankshaft:

Home made bearing roll-out pin
(© Pontiac Div. G.M. Corp.)

Removal and installation of upper bearing insert using a roll-out pin
(© Buick Div. G.M. Corp.)

Thoroughly clean the main bearing saddles and caps. Place the upper halves of the bearing inserts on the saddles and press into position. NOTE: *Ensure that the oil holes align.* Press the corresponding bearing inserts into the main bearing caps. Lubricate the upper main bearings, and lay the crankshaft in position. Place a strip of Plastigage on each of the crankshaft journals, install the main caps, and torque to specifications. Remove the main caps, and compare the Plastigage to the scale on the Plastigage envelope. If clearances are within tolerances, remove the Plastigage, turn the crankshaft 90°, wipe off all oil and retest. If all clearances are correct, remove all Plastigage, thoroughly

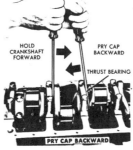

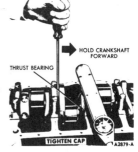

Aligning the thrust bearing
(© Ford Motor Co.)

Procedure	*Method*
	lubricate the main caps and bearing journals, and install the main caps. If clearances are not within tolerance, the upper bearing inserts may be removed, without removing the crankshaft, using a bearing roll out pin (see illustration). Roll in a bearing that will provide proper clearance, and retest. Torque all main caps, excluding the thrust bearing cap, to specifications. Tighten the thrust bearing cap finger tight. To properly align the thrust bearing, pry the crankshaft the extent of its axial travel several times, the last movement held toward the front of the engine, and torque the thrust bearing cap to specifications. Determine the crankshaft end-play (see below), and bring within tolerance with thrust washers.
Measure crankshaft end-play:  **Checking crankshaft end-play with a dial indicator** (© Ford Motor Co.)  **Checking crankshaft end-play with a feeler gauge** (© Chevrolet Div. (G.M. Corp.)	Mount a dial indicator stand on the front of the block, with the dial indicator stem resting on the nose of the crankshaft, parallel to the crankshaft axis. Pry the crankshaft the extent of its travel rearward, and zero the indicator. Pry the crankshaft forward and record crankshaft end-play. NOTE: *Crankshaft end-play also may be measured at the thrust bearing, using feeler gauges* (see illustration).
Install the pistons:	Press the upper connecting rod bearing halves into the connecting rods, and the lower halves into the connecting rod caps. Position the piston ring gaps according to specifications (see car section), and lubricate the pistons. Install a ring compresser on a piston, and press two long (8″) pieces of plastic tubing over the rod bolts. Using the plastic tubes as a guide, press the pistons into the bores and onto the crankshaft with a wooden hammer handle. After seating the rod on the crankshaft journal, remove the tubes and install the cap finger tight. Install the remaining pistons in the same man-

Procedure	*Method*

Tubing used as guide when installing
a piston
(© Oldsmobile Div. G.M. Corp.)

ner. Invert the engine and check the bearing clearance at two points (90° apart) on each journal with Plastigage. NOTE: *Do not turn the crankshaft with Plastigage installed.* If clearance is within tolerances, remove *all* Plastigage, thoroughly lubricate the journals, and torque the rod caps to specifications. If clearance is not within specifications, install different thickness bearing inserts and recheck. CAUTION: *Never shim or file the connecting rods or caps.* Always install plastic tube sleeves over the rod bolts when the caps are not installed, to protect the crankshaft journals.

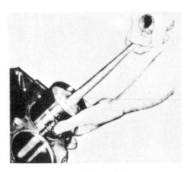

Installing a piston
(© Chevrolet Div. G.M. Corp.)

Check connecting rod side clearance:

Checking connecting rod side clearance
(© Chevrolet Div. G.M. Corp.)

Determine the clearance between the sides of the connecting rods and the crankshaft, using feeler gauges. If clearance is below the minimum tolerance, the rod may be machined to provide adequate clearance. If clearance is excessive, substitute an unworn rod, and recheck. If clearance is still outside specifications, the crankshaft must be welded and reground, or replaced.

Inspect the timing chain:

Visually inspect the timing chain for broken or loose links, and replace the chain if any are found. If the chain will flex sideways, it must be replaced. Install the timing chain as specified. NOTE: *If the original timing chain is to be reused, install it in its original position.*

Procedure	*Method*
Check timing gear backlash and runout:  **Checking camshaft gear backlash** (© Chevrolet Div. G.M. Corp.)  **Checking camshaft gear runout** (© Chevrolet Div. G.M. Corp.)	Mount a dial indicator with its stem resting on a tooth of the camshaft gear (as illustrated). Rotate the gear until all slack is removed, and zero the indicator. Rotate the gear in the opposite direction until slack is removed, and record gear backlash. Mount the indicator with its stem resting on the edge of the camshaft gear, parallel to the axis of the camshaft. Zero the indicator, and turn the camshaft gear one full turn, recording the runout. If either backlash or runout exceed specifications, replace the worn gear(s).

Completing the Rebuilding Process

Following the above procedures, complete the rebuilding process as follows:

Fill the oil pump with oil, to prevent cavitating (sucking air) on initial engine start up. Install the oil pump and the pickup tube on the engine. Coat the oil pan gasket as necessary, and install the gasket and the oil pan. Mount the flywheel and the crankshaft vibrational damper or pulley on the crankshaft. NOTE: *Always use new bolts when installing the flywheel.* Inspect the clutch shaft pilot bushing in the crankshaft. If the bushing is excessively worn, remove it with an expanding puller and a slide hammer, and tap a new bushing into place.

Position the engine, cylinder head side up. Lubricate the lifters, and install them into their bores. Install the cylinder head, and torque it as specified in the car section. Insert the pushrods (where applicable), and install the rocker shaft(s) (if so equipped) or position the rocker arms on the pushrods. If solid lifters are utilized, adjust the valves to the "cold" specifications.

Mount the intake and exhaust manifolds, the carburetor(s), the distributor and spark plugs. Adjust the point gap and the static ignition timing. Mount all accessories and install the engine in the car. Fill the radiator with coolant, and the crankcase with high quality engine oil.

Break-in Procedure

Start the engine, and allow it to run at low speed for a few minutes, while checking for leaks. Stop the engine, check the oil level, and fill as necessary. Restart the engine, and fill the cooling system to capacity. Check the point dwell angle and adjust the ignition timing and the valves. Run the engine at low to medium speed (800-2500 rpm) for approximately ½ hour, and retorque the cylinder head bolts. Road test the car, and check again for leaks.

Follow the manufacturer's recommended engine break-in procedure and maintenance schedule for new engines.

Chapter 4

Emission Controls and Fuel System

Emission Controls

There are three types of automobile pollutants that concern automotive engineers: crankcase fumes, exhaust gases and gasoline vapors from evaporation. The devices and systems used to limit these pollutants are commonly called emission control equipment.

CRANKCASE EMISSION CONTROLS

The crankcase emission control equipment consists of a positive crankcase ventilation (PCV) valve, a closed or open oil filler cap and the hoses that connect this equipment.

When the engine is running, a small portion of the gases which are formed in the combustion chamber leak by the piston rings and enter the crankcase. Since these gases are under pressure they tend to escape from the crankcase and enter into the atmosphere. If these gases were allowed to remain in the crankcase for any length of time, they would contaminate the engine oil and cause sludge to build up. If the gases are allowed to escape into the atmosphere, they would pollute the air, as they contain unburned

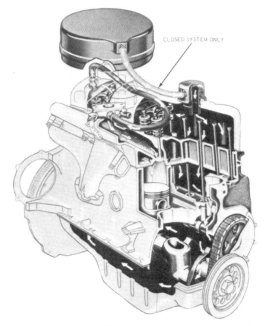

A cutaway view of the positive crankcase ventilation system of the 170 six. The 240, 300 six PCV system is very similar

hydrocarbons. The crankcase emission control equipment recycles these gases back into the engine combustion chamber, where they are burned.

Crankcase gases are recycled in the following manner. While the engine is running, clean filtered air is drawn into the crankcase either directly through the oil filler cap or through the carburetor air filter and then through a hose leading to the oil filler cap. As the air passes through the crankcase it picks up the combustion gases and carries them out of the crankcase, up through the PCV valve and into the intake manifold. After they enter the intake manifold they are drawn into the combustion chamber and are burned.

The most critical component of the system is the PCV valve. This vacuum-controlled valve regulates the amount of gases which are recycled into the combustion chamber. At low engine speeds the valve is partially closed, limiting the flow of gases into the intake manifold. As engine speed increases, the valve opens to admit greater quantities of the gases into the intake manifold. If the valve should become blocked or plugged, the gases will be prevented from escaping the crankcase by the normal route. Since these gases are under pressure, they will find their own way out of the crankcase. This alternate route is usually a weak oil seal or gasket in the engine. As the gas escapes by the gasket, it also creates an oil leak. Besides causing oil leaks, a clogged PCV valve also allows these gases to remain in the crankcase for an extended period of time, promoting the formation of sludge in the engine.

The above explanation and the troubleshooting procedure which follows applies to all of the engines installed in Ford vans, since all are equipped with PCV systems.

TROUBLESHOOTING

With the engine running, pull the PCV valve and hose from the valve rocker cover rubber grommet. Block off the end of the valve with your finger. A strong vacuum should be felt. Shake the valve; a clicking noise indicates it is free. Replace the valve if it is suspected of being blocked.

Removal

1. Pull the PCV valve and hose from the rubber grommet in the rocker cover.

2. Remove the PCV valve from the hose. Inspect the inside of the PCV valve. If it is dirty, disconnect it from the intake manifold and clean it in a suitable, safe solvent.

To install, proceed as follows:

1. If the PCV valve hose was removed, connect it to the intake manifold.

2. Connect the PCV valve to its hose.

3. Install the PCV valve into the rubber grommet in the valve rocker cover.

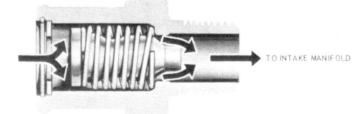

FROM CRANKCASE
AND/OR ROCKER
ARM COVER

TO INTAKE MANIFOLD

LOW SPEED OPERATION — HIGH MANIFOLD VACUUM

HIGH SPEED OPERATION — LOW MANIFOLD VACUUM

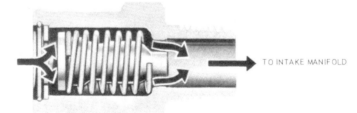

FROM CRANKCASE
AND/OR ROCKER
ARM COVER

TO INTAKE MANIFOLD

A cutaway view of a PCV valve showing its operation

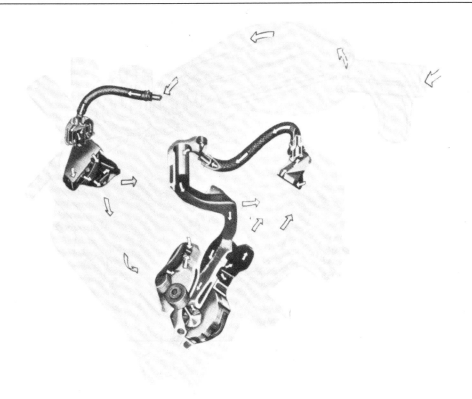

A cutaway view of the PCV system of the 302 V8

Exhaust Emission Controls

AIR PUMP

The Ford terminology for the air injection type emission control system is "Thermactor" exhaust emission control system. Since this type of system is common to all of the engines, it will be explained here.

The exhaust emission control air injection system consists of a belt-driven air pump, which directs compressed air through connecting hoses to an air manifold or to internal passages and through air nozzles in the exhaust ports adjacent to each exhaust valve. The air, with it normal oxygen content, reacts with the hot, but incompletely burned exhaust gases and permits further combustion in the exhaust port or manifold.

The air injection pump is a positive-displacement vane type which is permanently lubricated and requires little periodic maintenance. The only serviceable parts on the air pump are the exhaust tube and relief valve. The relief valve decreases the airflow when the pump pressure reaches a preset level. This occurs at high engine rpm. The relief valve also serves to prevent damage to the pump and to limit maximum exhaust manifold temperatures.

Inlet air for the Thermactor system is cleaned by a centrifugal filter fan mounted on the air pump driveshaft or an element-type air cleaner (filter).

The air supply from the air pump is controlled by the air by-pass valve. Normally, the air by-pass valve is closed and the air is directed to the check valve(s) and air manifold(s) for distribution to the cylinder head exhaust ports. During engine deceleration, the air by-pass valve opens and air delivery to the cylinder head exhaust ports is momentarily diverted to the atmosphere.

A check valve is used in the inlet air side of the air manifold(s) to prevent exhaust gases from flowing back into the air

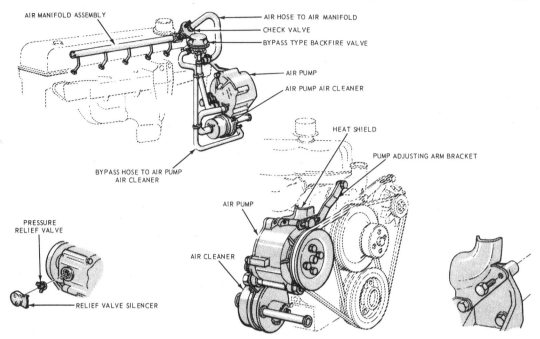

AIR MANIFOLD ASSEMBLY
AIR HOSE TO AIR MANIFOLD
CHECK VALVE
BYPASS TYPE BACKFIRE VALVE
AIR PUMP
AIR PUMP AIR CLEANER
HEAT SHIELD
PUMP ADJUSTING ARM BRACKET
BYPASS HOSE TO AIR PUMP AIR CLEANER
AIR PUMP
PRESSURE RELIEF VALVE
AIR CLEANER
RELIEF VALVE SILENCER

The Thermactor exhaust emission control system installed on a 240 six.

pump and air by-pass valve during the air by-pass cycle or during air pump and/or drive belt failure.

AIR DELIVERY MANIFOLD

The air delivery manifold distributes the air from the pump to each of the air delivery tubes in a uniform manner. This applies only to the 6 cylinder engines, as the air delivery manifold is integral with the cylinder head on the 302 V8 engines.

AIR BY-PASS VALVE

The air by-pass valve prevents engine backfire by briefly interrupting the air being injected into the exhaust manifold during periods of deceleration or rapid throttle closure. The valve opens when a sudden increase in manifold vacuum overcomes the diaphragm spring tension. With the valve in the open position, the airflow is vented to the atmosphere. In addition to preventing backfiring in the exhaust manifold as previously mentioned, the valve also prevents possible damage to the engine by not allowing the overly rich fuel mixture from being burned in the exhaust manifold. A rich mixture in the exhaust manifold is the result of deceleration or rapid throttle closure and to promote its further com-

bustion by injecting air would cause backfiring.

CARBURETOR

The carburetors used on engines equipped with emission controls have specific flow characteristics that differ from the carburetors used on vehicles not equipped with emission control devices. Also, since 1968, all carburetors have limiter caps installed on the idle fuel mixture adjustment screws. These limiter caps prevent an overly rich mixture adjustment from being made. The correct adjustment can usually be reached within the range of the limiter caps. These carburetors are identified by number. The same type carburetor should be used when replacement is necessary.

THERMOSTATICALLY CONTROLLED AIR CLEANER SYSTEM (TAC)

This system consists of a heat shroud which is integral with the right-side exhaust manifold, a hot air hose and a special air cleaner assembly equipped with a thermal sensor and vacuum motor and air valve assembly.

The temperature of the carburetor intake air is thermostatically controlled by

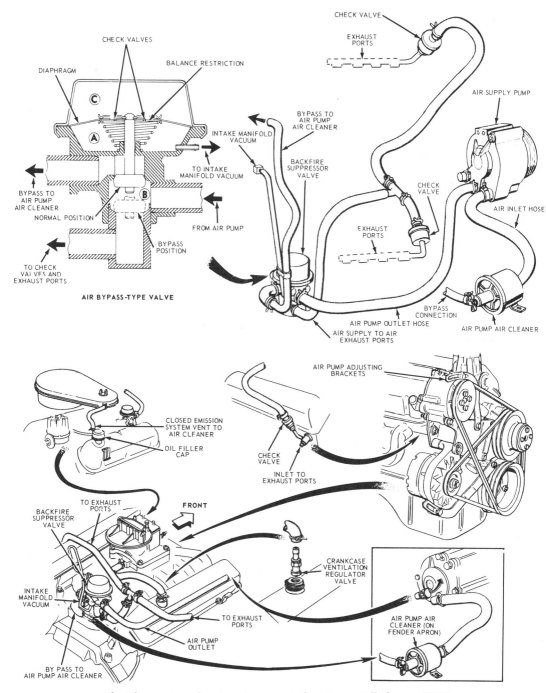

The Thermactor exhaust emission control system installed on a 302 V8

means of a valve plate and a vacuum override built into a duct assembly attached to the air cleaner. The exhaust manifold shroud tube is attached to the shroud over the exhaust manifold for the source of heated air.

The thermal sensor is attached to the air valve actuating lever, along with the vacuum motor lever, both of which control the position of the air valve to supply either heated air from the exhaust manifold or cooler air from the engine compartment.

During the warm-up period, when the under-the-hood temperatures are low, the thermal sensor doesn't exert enough

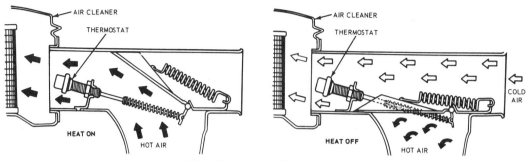

Operation of the thermostatically controlled air cleaner

tension on the air valve actuating lever to close (heat off) the air valve. Thus, the carburetor receives heated air from around the exhaust manifold.

As the temperature of the air entering the air cleaner approaches approximately 110°F, the thermal sensor begins to push on the air valve actuating lever and overcome the spring tension which holds the air valve in the open (heat on) position. The air valve begins to move to the closed (heat off) position, allowing only under-the-hood air to enter the air cleaner.

The air valve in the air cleaner will also open, regardless of the air temperature, during heavy acceleration to obtain maximum airflow through the air cleaner. The extreme decrease in intake manifold vacuum during heavy acceleration permits the vacuum motor to override the thermostatic control. This opens the system to both heated air and air from the engine compartment.

DUAL DIAPHRAGM DISTRIBUTOR

The dual diaphragm distributor has two diaphragms which operate independently. The outer (primary) diaphragm makes use of carburetor vacuum to advance the ignition timing. The inner secondary) diaphragm uses intake manifold vacuum to provide additional retardation of ignition timing during closed-throttle decleration and idle, resulting in the reduction of hydrocarbon emissions.

PORTED VACUUM SWITCH VALVE (PVS)

The PVS valve is a temperature sensing valve found on the distributor vacuum

advance line, and is installed in the coolant outlet elbow. During prolonged periods of idle, or any other situation which causes engine operating temperatures to be higher than normal, the valve, which under normal conditions simply connects the vacuum advance diaphragm to its vacuum source within the carburetor, closes the normal source vacuum port and engages an alternate source vacuum port. This alternate source is from the intake manifold which, under idle conditions, maintains a high vacuum. This increase in vacuum supply to the distributor diaphragm advances the timing, increasing the idle speed. The increase in idle speed causes a directly proportional increase in the operation of the cooling system. When the engine has cooled sufficiently, the vacuum supply is returned to its normal source, the carburetor.

DECELERATION VALVE

Beginning 1969, some engines were equipped with a distributor vacuum advance control valve (deceleration valve) which is used with dual diaphragm distributors to further aid in controlling ignition timing. The deceleration valve is in the vacuum line which runs from the outer (advance) diaphragm to the carburetor, the normal vacuum supply for the distributor. During deceleration, the intake manifold vacuum rises causing the deceleration valve to close off the carburetor vacuum source and connect the intake manifold vacuum source to the distributor advance diaphragm. The increase in vacuum provides maximum ignition timing advance, thus providing more complete fuel combustion and decreasing exhaust system backfiring.

EXHAUST GAS RECIRCULATION SYSTEM (EGR)

In this sytem, a vacuum-operated EGR flow valve is attached to the carburetor spacer. A passage in the carburetor spacer mates with a hole in the mounting face of the EGR valve or the intake manifold. The most common system allows exhaust gases to flow from the exhaust crossover, through the control valve and through the spacer into the intake manifold below the carburetor. For those engines where exhaust gases cannot be picked up from the exhaust crossover (6 cylinder) as described above, the gases are picked up from the choke stove located on the exhaust manifold or directly

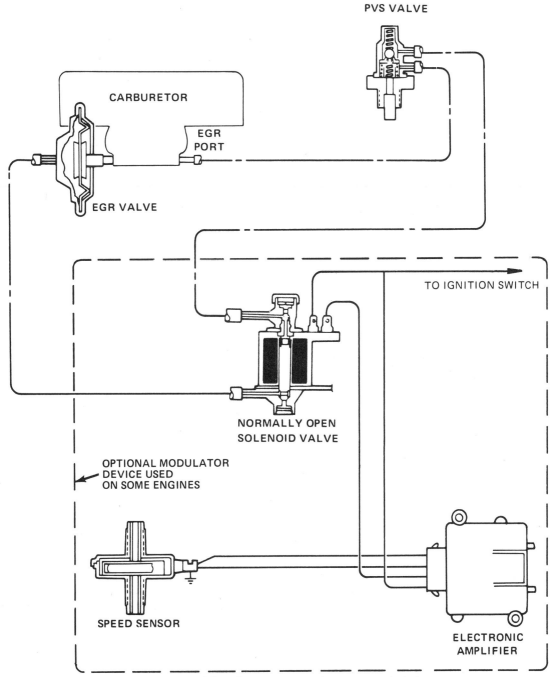

Schematic of the exhaust gas recirculation system (EGR)

from the exhaust manifold. The exhaust gases are routed to the carburetor spacer through steel tubing.

The vacuum signal which operates the EGR valve originates at the EGR vacuum port in the carburetor. This signal is controlled by at least one, and sometimes, two series of valves.

A water temperature sensing valve (the EGR PVS) which is closed until the water temperature reaches either 60° F or 125°F, depending on application, is always used.

The position of the EGR vacuum port in the carburetor and calibration of the EGR valve can be varied to give the required modulation of EGR during acceleration and low speed cruise conditions. However, a more complicated system using a second series valve is sometimes needed to provide control of EGR for engine operation at high speed cruise conditions. The second valve: the high speed modulator valve, is controlled as a function of vehicle speed.

The high speed EGR modulator subsystem consists of a speed sensor, an electronic module and a solenoid vacuum valve. The speed sensor, driven by the speedometer cable, provides an AC signal in relation to engine speed, to the electronic module. The electronic module processes the information from the speed sensor and sends a signal to the high speed modulator (vacuum solenoid) valve. When the vehicle speed exceeds the module trigger speed, the solenoid vacuum valve closes which, in turn, causes the EGR valve to close.

SPARK DELAY VALVE

The spark delay valve is a plastic spring-loaded, color-coded valve in the vacuum line to the distributor vacuum advance chamber on some 1972 models. Under heavy throttle application, the valve will close, blocking carburetor vacuum to the distributor vacuum advance mechanism. After the designated period of time, the valve opens, restoring normal carburetor vacuum to the distributor.

CATALYTIC CONVERTER

Starting 1975, most models under 6000 lbs. GVW have an exhaust system catalytic converter. The converter is in the exhaust system ahead of the muffler. It contains a catalytic agent made of platinum and palladium, used to oxodize hydrocarbons (HC) and carbon monoxide (CO). The catalyst is expected to function without service of any kind for at least 50,000 miles. Use of leaded fuel would quickly cause catalyst failure; for this reason, a tank filler restriction prevents the entry of service station leaded fuel nozzles.

VACUUM HEAT RISER

Some 1975–76 V8s have a vacuum-operated heat riser. This is quite similar to the old style heat riser that is operated by a thermostatic spring. It preheats the fuel-air mixture by directing some exhaust gases through passages in the intake manifold during warmup. The valve is operated by a vacuum diaphragm controlled by a coolant temperature sensing vacuum valve.

Evaporative Emission Controls

Beginning 1970, Ford vans produced for sale in California were equipped with evaporative emission controls on the fuel system. For 1971, the system was modified somewhat and used on all Ford vans as standard equipment.

Changes in atmospheric temperature cause fuel tanks to "breathe"; that is, the air within the tank expands and contracts with outside temperature changes. As the temperature rises, air escapes through the tank vent tube or the vent in the tank cap. The air which escapes contains gasoline vapors. In a similar manner, the gasoline which fills the carburetor float bowl expands when the engine is stopped. Engine heat causes this expansion. The vapors escape through the carburetor and air cleaner.

The Evaporative Emission Control System provides a sealed fuel system with the capability to store and condense fuel vapors. The system has three parts: a fill control vent system; a vapor vent and storage system; and a pressure and vacuum relief system (special fill cap).

The fill control vent system is a modification to the fuel tank. It uses an air space within the tank which is 10–12% of the tank's volume. The air space is sufficient to provide for the thermal expansion of the fuel. The space also serves as part of the in-tank vapor vent system.

The in-tank vent system consists of the air space previously described and a vapor separator assembly. The separator assembly is mounted to the top of the fuel tank and is secured by a cam-lockring, similar to the one which secures the fuel sending unit. Foam material fills the vapor separator assembly. The foam material separates raw fuel and vapors, thus retarding the entrance of fuel into the vapor line.

The sealed filler cap has a pressure-vacuum relief valve. Under normal operating conditions, the filler cap operates as a check valve, allowing air to enter the tank to replace the fuel consumed. At the same time, it prevents vapors from escaping through the cap. In case of excessive pressure within the tank, the filler cap valve opens to relieve the pressure.

Because the filler cap is sealed, fuel vapors have but one place through which they may escape—the vapor separator assembly at the top of the fuel tank. The vapors pass through the foam material and continue through a single vapor line which leads to a canister in the engine compartment. The canister is filled with activated charcoal.

Another vapor line runs from the top of the carburetor float chamber to the charcoal canister.

As the fuel vapors (hydrocarbons), enter the charcoal canister, they are absorbed by the charcoal. The air is dispelled through the open bottom of the charcoal canister, leaving the hydrocarbons trapped within the charcoal. When the engine is started, vacuum causes fresh air to be drawn into the canister from its open bottom. The fresh air passes through the charcoal picking up the hydrocarbons which are trapped there and feeding them into the carburetor for burning with the fuel mixture.

Emission Control Service

NOTE: *Complete and detailed procedures for the servicing of the crank-* *case ventilation system are found in the "Maintenance" Section of Chapter 1.*

THERMACTOR SYSTEM

Air By-Pass Valve Replacement

1. Disconnect the air and vacuum hoses at the air by-pass valve body.

2. Position the air by-pass valve and connect the respective hoses.

Check Valve Replacement

1. Disconnect the air supply hose at the valve. Use a 1¼ in. crowfoot wrench. The valve has a standard, right-hand pipe thread.

2. Clean the threads on the air manifold adapter (air supply tube on the V8 engines) with a wire brush. Do not blow compressed air through the check valve in either direction.

3. Install the check valve and tighten.

4. Connect the air supply hose.

Air Manifold Replacement

Six-Cylinder Engines

1. Disconnect the air supply hose at the check valve, position the hose out of the way and remove the valve.

2. Loosen all of the air manifold-to-cylinder head tube coupling nuts (compression fittings). Inspect the air manifold for damaged threads and fittings and for leaking connections. Repair or replace as required. Clean the manifold and associated parts with kerosene. Do not dry the parts with compressed air.

3. Position the air manifold on the cylinder head. Be sure that all of the tube coupling nuts are aligned with the cylinder head.

4. Screw each coupling nut into the cylinder head, one or two threads. Tighten the tube coupling nuts.

5. Install the check valve and tighten it.

6. Connect the air supply hose to the check valve.

Air Supply Tube Replacement

V8 Engine Only

1. Disconnect the air supply hose at the check valve and position the hose out of the way.

2. Remove the check valve.

3. Remove the air supply tube bolt and seal washer.

4. Carefully remove the air supply tube and seal washer from the cylinder head. Inspect the air supply tube for evidence of leaking threads or seal surfaces. Examine the attaching bolt head, seal washers, and supply tube surface for leaks. Inspect the attaching bolt and cylinder head threads for damage. Clean the air supply tube, seal washers, and bolt with kerosene. Do not dry the parts with compressed air.

5. Install the seal washer and air supply tube on the cylinder head. Be sure that it is positioned in the same manner as before removal.

6. Install the seal washer and mounting bolt. Tighten the bolt.

7. Install the check valve and tighten it.

8. Connect the air supply hose to the check valve.

Air Nozzle Replacement

Six-Cylinder Engines Only

Normally, air nozzles should be replaced during cylinder head reconditioning. A nozzle may be replaced, however, without removing the cylinder head, by removing the air manifold and using a hooked tool.

Clean the nozzle with kerosene and a stiff brush. Inspect the air nozzles for eroded tips.

Air Pump and Filter Fan Replacement

1. Loosen the air pump attaching bolts.

2. Remove the drive pulley attaching bolts and pull the pulley off the air pump shaft.

3. Pry the outer disc loose, then remove the centrifugal filter fan. Care must be used to prevent foreign matter from entering the air intake hole, especially if the fan breaks during removal. Do not attempt to remove the metal drive hub.

4. Install the new filter fan by drawing it into position with the pulley bolts.

NOTE: *Some 1966–67 air pumps have air filters with replaceable, noncleanable elements.*

Air Pump Replacement

1. Disconnect the air outlet hose at the air pump.

2. Loosen the pump belt tension adjuster.

3. Disengage the drive belt.

4. Remove the mounting bolt and air pump.

5. Position the air pump on the mounting bracket and install the mounting bolt.

6. Place the drive belt in the pulley and attach the adjusting arm to the air pump.

7. Adjust the drive belt tension and tighten the adjusting arm and mounting bolts.

8. Connect the air outlet hose to the air pump.

Relief Valve Replacement

Do not disassemble the air pump on the truck to replace the relief valve, but remove the pump from the engine.

1. Remove the relief valve with the aid of a slide hammer.

2. Position the relief valve on the pump housing and hold it in position with a block of wood.

3. Use a hammer to lightly tap the wood block until the relief valve is seated.

Relief Valve Pressure-Setting Plug Replacement

1. Compress the locking tabs inward (together) and remove the plastic pressure-setting plug.

2. Before installing the new plug, be sure that the plug is the correct one. The plugs are color-coded.

3. Insert the plug in the relief valve hole and push in until it snaps into place.

Distributor Temperature-Sensing Vacuum Control Valve Test

1. Check the routing and connection of all the vacuum hoses.

2. Attach a tachometer to the engine.

3. Bring the engine up to the normal operating temperature. The engine must not be overheated.

4. Note the engine rpm, with the transmission in Neutral, and the throttle at curb idle.

5. Disconnect the vacuum hose from

the intake manifold at the temperature-sensing valve. Plug or clamp the hose.

6. Note the idle rpm with the hose disconnected. If there is no change in rpm, the valve is good. If there is a drop of 100 or more rpm, the valve should be replaced. Replace the vacuum line.

7. Check to make sure that the all-season coolant mixture meets specifications and that the correct radiator cap is in place and functioning.

8. Block the radiator airflow to induce a higher-than-normal temperature condition.

9. Continue to operate the engine until the temperature or heat indicator shows above normal.

If the engine speed, by this time, has increased 100 or more rpm, the temperature-sensing valve is satisfactory. If not, it should be replaced.

Distributor Deceleration Vacuum Control Valve Test

1. Connect a tachometer to the engine and bring the engine to the normal operating temperature.

2. Check the idle speed and set it to specifications with the headlights on high beam, as necessary.

3. Turn off the headlights and note the idle rpm.

4. Remove the plastic cover from the valve. Slowly turn the adjusting screw counterclockwise without pressing in. After 5, and no more than 6 turns, the idle speed should suddenly increase to about 1000 rpm. If the speed does not increase after six turns, push inward on the valve spring retainer and release. Speed should now increase.

5. Slowly turn the adjusting screw clockwise until the idle speed drops to the speed noted in Step 3. Make one more turn clockwise.

6. Increase the engine speed to 2000 rpm, hold for 5 seconds, and release the throttle. The engine speed should return to idle speed within 4 seconds. If idle is not resumed in 4 seconds, back off the dashpot adjustment and repeat the check. If the idle is not resumed in 3 seconds with the dashpot back off, turn the deceleration valve adjustment screw an additional quarter turn clockwise and repeat the check. Repeat the quarter turn adjustment and idle return checks until the

engine returns to idle within the required time.

7. If it takes more than one complete turn from Step 5 to meet the idle return time specification, replace the valve.

Dual Diaphragm Vacuum Advance and Vacuum Retard Functional Check

1. To check vacuum advance, disconnect the vacuum lines from both the advance (outer) and retard (inner) diaphragms. Plug the line removed from the retard diaphragm

Connect a tachometer and timing light to the engine. Increase the idle speed by setting the screw on the first step of the fast idle cam. Note the ignition timing setting, using a timing light.

Connect the carburetor vacuum line to the advance diaphragm. If the timing advances immediately, the advance unit is functioning properly. Adjust the idle speed to 550–600 rpm.

2. Check the vacuum retardation as follows: using a timing light, note the ignition timing. Remove the plug from the manifold vacuum line and connect the line to the inner diaphragm. Timing should retard immediately.

3. If vacuum retardation is not to specifications, replace the dual diaphragm advance unit. If the advance (vacuum) does not function properly, calibrate the unit on a distributor test stand. If the advance part of the unit cannot be calibrated, or if either diaphragm is leaking, replace the dual diaphragm vacuum advance unit.

Evaporative Emission Control System Check

Other than a visual check to determine that none of the vapor lines are broken, there is no test for this equipment.

Electronic Spark Control System Operation Test

1. Raise the rear of the car until the rear wheels are clear of the ground by at least 4 in. Support the rear of the car with jackstands.

CAUTION: *The rear of the car must be firmly supported during this test. If one of the rear wheels should come in contact with the ground while it is turning, the car will move forward very rapidly and unexpectedly. As an extra precaution, chock the front*

(ESC) ELECTRONIC SPARK CONTROL

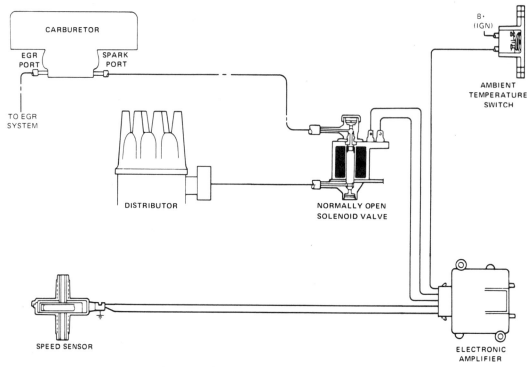

Schematic of the electronic spark control (ESC)

wheels and do not stand in front of the vehicle while the wheels are turning.

2. Disconnect the vacuum hose from the distributor vacuum advance chamber. This is the outer hose on cars with dual diaphragm vacuum advance units.

3. Connect the hose to a vacuum gauge.

4. Pour hot water on the temperature-sensing switch to make sure that it is above 65° F.

5. Start the engine and apply the foot brake. Depress the clutch and shift the transmission into High gear. Release the hand brake and slowly engage the clutch.

6. Have an assistant observe the vacuum gauge while you raise the speed of the engine until the speedometer reads 35 mph, at which time the vacuum gauge should show a reading.

9. If the vacuum gauge shows a reading below 35 mph, a component in the electronic spark control system is defective. If the vacuum gauge does not show a reading, even above 35 mph, there is either a defective component in the electronic spark control system, or there is a broken or clogged vacuum passage between the carburetor and the distributor.

Heated Air Intake Test

1. With the engine completely cold, look inside the cold air duct and make sure that the valve plate is fully in the up position (closing the cold air duct).

2. Start the engine and bring it to operating temperature.

3. Stop the engine and look inside the cold air duct again. The valve plate should be down, allowing an opening from the cold air duct into the air cleaner.

4. If the unit appears to be malfunctioning, remove it and examine it to make sure that the springs are not broken or disconnected, and replace the thermostat if all other parts appear intact and properly connected.

Transmission-Regulated Spark

TRANSMISSION VALVE TEST

1. Attach a test light to the wire which connects the transmission valve to the distributor modulator valve.

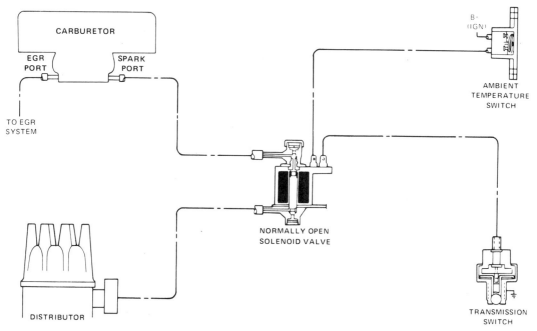

Schematic of the transmission regulated spark system

2. Jack up and support the vehicle, so that the rear wheels are free to turn.

3. Start the engine and engage the transmission in Low gear. Observe the test light, which should be lighted at this time.

4. On standard transmissions, engage High gear and check to see that the light goes out.

5. On automatic transmissions, place the vehicle in Drive and allow it to up-shift. Upon the shift into High gear, the test light should go out.

6. If the test lamp fails to function properly, replace the transmission valve.

Fuel System

FUEL PUMP

Ford van engines use a camshaft ec-centric-actuated combination fuel pump located on the lower left-side of the engine block on both 6 cylinder and V8 engines.

Removal

1. Disconnect the fuel inlet and outlet lines at the fuel pump. Discard the fuel inlet retaining clamp.

2. Remove the pump retaining bolts then remove the pump assembly and gas-ket from the engine. Discard the gasket.

Installation

1. If a new pump is to be installed, remove the fuel line connector fitting from the old pump and install it in the new pump.

2. Remove all gasket material from the mounting pad and pump flange. Apply oil-resistant sealer to both sides of a new gasket.

3. Position the new gasket on the pump flange and hold the pump in posi-tion against the mounting pad. Make sure that the rocker arm is riding on the cam-shaft eccentric.

4. Press the pump tight against the pad, install the retaining bolts and alter-nately torque them to 12–15 ft lbs on 6 cylinder engines and 20–24 ft lbs on the V8. Connect the fuel lines. Use a new clamp on the fuel inlet line.

5. Operate the engine and check for leaks.

Testing

Incorrect fuel pump pressure and low volume (flow rate) are the two most likely fuel pump troubles that will affect engine performance. Low pressure will cause a lean mixture and fuel starvation at high speeds and excessive pressure will cause high fuel consumption and carburetor flooding.

To determine that the fuel pump is in satisfactory operating condition, tests for both fuel pump pressure and volume should be performed.

The tests are performed with the fuel pump installed on the engine and the engine at normal operating temperature and at idle speed.

Before the test, make sure that the replaceable fuel filter has been changed at the proper mileage interval. If in doubt, install a new filter.

PRESSURE TEST

1. Remove the air cleaner assembly. Disconnect the fuel inlet line of the fuel filter at the carburetor. Use care to prevent fire, due to fuel spillage. Place an absorbent cloth under the connection before removing the line to catch any fuel that might flow out of the line.

2. Connect a pressure gauge, a restrictor and a flexible hose between the fuel filter and the carburetor.

3. Position the flexible hose and the restrictor so that the fuel can be discharged into a suitable, graduated container.

4. Before taking a pressure reading, operate the engine at the specified idle rpm and vent the system into the container by opening the hose restrictor momentarily.

5. Close the hose restrictor, allow the pressure to stabilize and note the reading. The pressure should be:

Six through 1976	4–6 psi
1977 six, V8 through 1976	5–7 psi
1977 V8, 1976 460 V8	6–8 psi

If the pump pressure is not within 4–6 psi and the fuel lines and filter are in satisfactory condition, the pump is defective and should be replaced.

If the pump pressure is within the proper range, perform the test for fuel volume.

VOLUME TEST

1. Operate the engine at the specified idle rpm.

2. Open the hose restrictor and catch the fuel in the container while observing the time it takes to pump 1 pint. It should take 30 seconds for 1 pint to be expelled on all vehicles made prior to the 1974 model year. On 1974–77 vehicles, 1 pint should be expelled in 20 seconds. If the pump does not pump to specifications, check for proper fuel tank venting or a restriction in the fuel line leading from the fuel tank to the carburetor before replacing the fuel pump.

CARBURETORS

In 1966 and 1967, the 170 and 240 sixes were equipped with the Ford 1100 and 1101 1-bbl carburetor. During 1968 through 1969, the 170 and 240 sixes were available with either the Ford 1100 1-bbl carburetor or the Carter Model YF 1-bbl carburetor. From 1970 to 1977, only the Carter Model YF has been used on all the sixes. The 302 V8 is equipped with an Autolite Model 2100 2-bbl carburetor. The 351 V8 uses the Motorcraft (formerly Autolite) 2150 2-bbl carburetor; the 460 V8 uses the Motorcraft 4350 4-bbl.

The carburetor identification tag is attached to the carburetor. The basic part number for all carburetors is 9510. To obtain replacement parts, it is necessary to know the part number prefix, suffix and, in some cases, the design change code. If the carburetor is ever replaced by a new unit, make sure that the identification tag stays with the new carburetor and the vehicle.

Removal and Installation

1. Remove the air cleaner.

2. Remove the throttle cable or rod from the throttle lever. Disconnect the distributor vacuum line, EGR vacuum line, if so equipped, the inline fuel filter and the choke heat tube at the carburetor.

3. Disconnect the choke clean air tube from the air horn. Disconnect the choke actuating cable, if so equipped.

4. Remove the carburetor retaining nuts then remove the carburetor. Remove the carburetor mounting gasket, spacer (if so equipped), and the lower gasket from the intake manifold.

5. Before installing the carburetor, clean the gasket mounting surfaces of the spacer and carburetor. Place the spacer between two new gaskets and position the spacer and gaskets on the intake manifold. Position the carburetor on the

spacer and gasket and secure it with the retaining nuts. To prevent leakage, distortion or damage to the carburetor body flange, snug the nuts, then alternately tighten each nut in a criss-cross pattern.

6. Connect the inline fuel filter, throttle cable, choke heat tube, distributor vacuum line, EGR vacuum line, and choke cable.

7. Connect the choke clean air line to the air horn.

8. Adjust the engine idle speed, the idle fuel mixture and anti-stall dashpot (if so equipped). Install the air cleaner.

Carburetor Troubleshooting

The best way to diagnose a bad carburetor is to eliminate all other possible sources of the problem. If the carburetor is suspected to be the problem, first perform all of the adjustments given in this Section. If this doesn't correct the difficulty, then check the following. Check the ignition system to make sure that the spark plugs, breaker points, and condenser are in good condition and adjusted to the proper specifications. Examine the emission control equipment to make sure that all the vacuum lines are connected and none are blocked or clogged. See the first half of this Chapter. Check the ignition timing adjustment. Check all of the vacuum lines on the engine for loose connections, splits or breaks. Torque the carburetor and intake manifold attaching bolts to the proper specifications. If, after performing all of these checks and adjustments, the problem is still not solved, then you can safely assume that the carburetor is the source of the problem.

OVERHAUL

Efficient carburetion depends greatly on careful cleaning and inspection during overhaul since dirt, gum, water or varnish in or on the carburetor parts are often responsible for poor performance.

Overhaul the carburetor in a clean, dust-free area. Carefully disassemble the carburetor, referring often to the exploded views. Keep all similar and look-alike parts segregated during disassembly and cleaning to avoid accidental interchange during assembly. Make a note of all jet sizes.

When the carburetor is disassembled, wash all parts (except diaphragms, electric choke units, pump plunger and any other plastic, leather, fiber, or rubber parts) in clean carburetor solvent. Do not leave the parts in the solvent any longer than is necessary to sufficiently loosen the dirt and deposits. Excessive cleaning may remove the special finish from the float bowl and choke valve bodies, leaving these parts unfit for service. Rinse all parts in clean solvent and blow them dry with compressed air or allow them to air dry, while resting on clean, lintless paper. Wipe clean all cork, plastic, leather and fiber parts with a clean, lint-free cloth.

Blow out all passages and jets with compressed air and be sure that there are no restrictions or blockages. Never use wire or similar tools to clean jets, fuel passages or air bleeds. Clean all jets and valves separately to avoid accidental interchange.

Examine all parts for wear or damage. If wear or damage is found, replace the defective parts. Especially, inspect the following:

1. Check the float needle and seat for wear. If wear is found, replace the complete assembly.

2. Check the float hinge pin for wear and the float(s) for dents or distortion. Replace the float if fuel has leaked into it.

3. Check the throttle and choke shaft bores for wear or an out-of-round condition. Damage or wear to the throttle arm, shaft or shaft bore will often require replacement of the throttle body. These parts require a close tolerance of fit; wear may allow air leakage, which could affect starting and idling.

NOTE: *Throttle shafts and bushings are not normally included in overhaul kits. They can be purchased separately.*

4. Inspect the idle mixture adjusting needles for burrs or grooves. Any such condition requires replacement of the needle, since you will not be able to obtain a satisfactory idle.

5. Test the accelerator pump check valves. They should pass air one way, but not the other. Test for proper seating by blowing and sucking on the valve. Replace the valve as necessary. If the valve is satisfactory, wash the valve again to remove moisture.

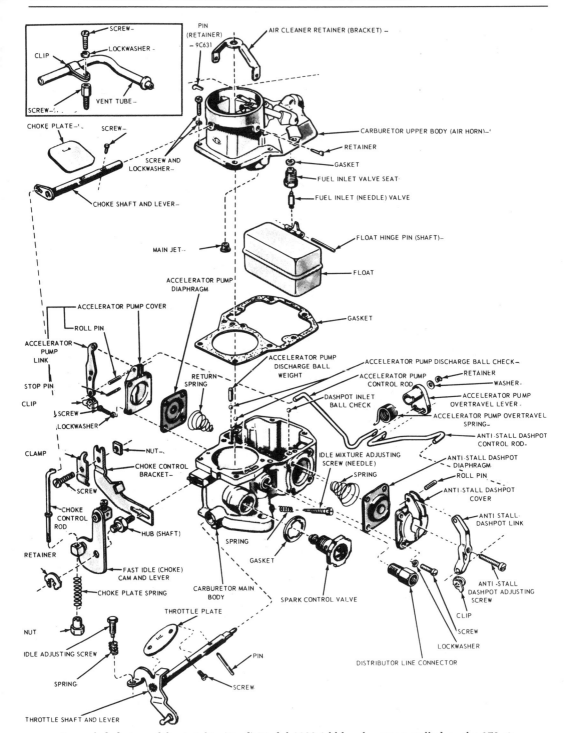

An exploded view of the Autolite (Ford) Model 1100 1-bbl carburetor installed on the 170 six

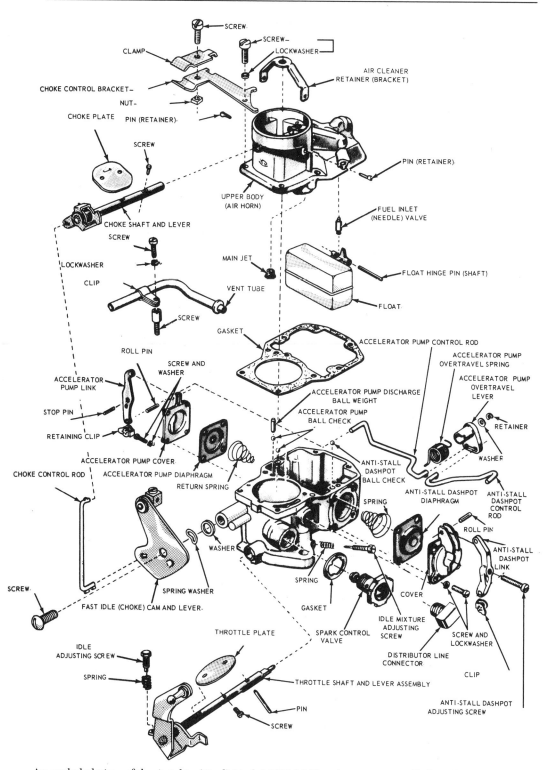

An exploded view of the Autolite (Ford) Model 1101 1-bbl carburetor as installed on the 240 six

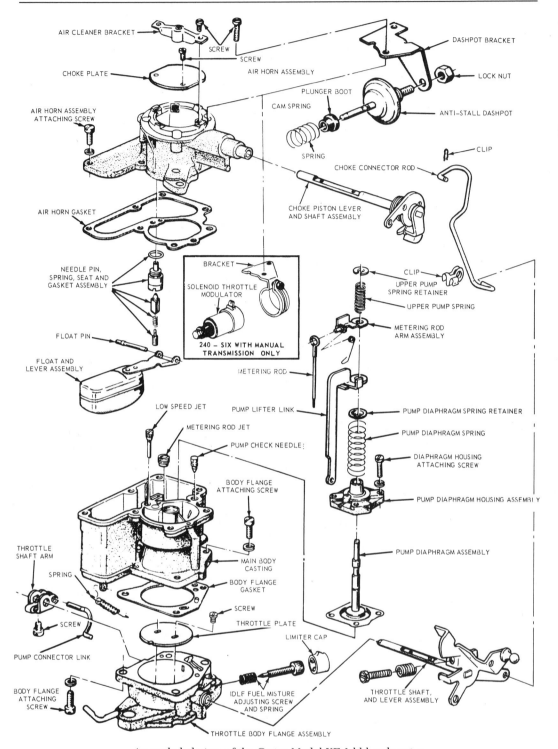

An exploded view of the Carter Model YF 1-bbl carburetor

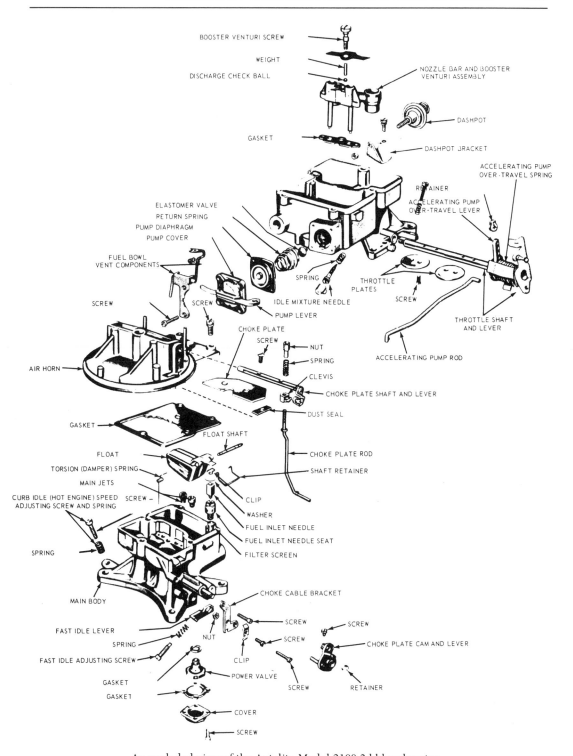

An exploded view of the Autolite Model 2100 2-bbl carburetor

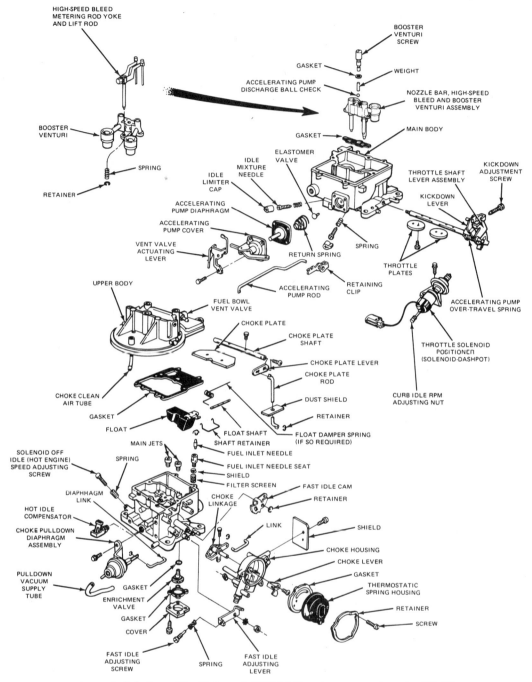

An exploded view of the Motorcraft 2150 2-bbl carburetor used on the 351 V8

6. Check the bowl cover for warped surfaces with a straightedge.

7. Closely inspect the valves and seats for wear and damage, replacing as necessary.

8. After the carburetor is assembled, check the choke valve for freedom of operation

Carburetor overhaul kits are recommended for each overhaul. These kits contain all gaskets and new parts to replace those which deteriorate most rapidly. Failure to replace all of the parts supplied with the kit (especially gaskets) can result in poor performance later.

Most carburetor manufacturers supply

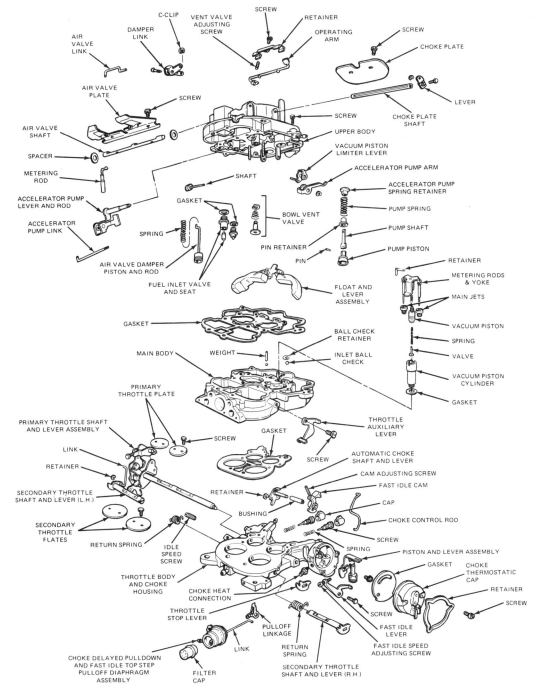

An exploded view of the Motorcraft 4350 4-bbl carburetor used on the 460 V8

overhaul kits of three basic types: minor repair; major repair; and gasket kits. Basically, they contain the following:

Minor Repair Kits:
   All gaskets
   Float needle valve
   Mixture adjusting screws
   All diaphragms

Spring for the pump diaphragm

Major Repair Kits:
   All jets and gaskets
   All diaphragms
   Float needle valve
   Mixture adjusting screws
   Pump ball valve
   Main jet carrier

Float
Some float bowl cover hold-down
screws and washers
Gasket Kits:
All gaskets

After cleaning and checking all components, reassemble the carburetor, using new parts and referring to the exploded view. When reassembling, make sure that all screws and jets are tight in their seats, but do not overtighten, as the tips will be distorted. Tighten all screws gradually, in rotation. Do not tighten needle valves into their seats; uneven jetting will result. Always use new gaskets. Be sure to adjust the float level.

Float and Fuel Level Adjustment

FORD MODEL 1100, 1101 1-BBL AND CARTER MODEL YF 1-BBL

1. Remove the carburetor air horn and gasket from the carburetor.

2. Invert the air horn assembly, and check the clearance from the top of the float to the bottom of the air horn. Hold the air horn at eye level when gauging the float level. The float arm (lever) should be resting on the needle pin. Do not load the needle when adjusting the float. Bend the float arm as necessary to adjust the float level (clearance). Do not bend the tab at the end of the float arm, because it prevents the float from striking the bottom of the fuel bowl when empty.

3. Turn the air horn over and hold it upright and let the float hang free. Measure the maximum clearance from the top of the float to the bottom of the air horn with the float gauge. Hold the air horn at eye level when gauging the dimension. To adjust the float drop, bend the tab at the end of the float arm.

4. Install the carburetor air horn with a new gasket.

AUTOLITE (MOTORCRAFT) MODEL 2100, 2150 2-BBL (WET ADJUSTMENT)

1. Operate the engine until it reaches normal operating temperature. Place the vehicle on a level surface and stop the engine.

2. Remove the carburetor air cleaner assembly.

3. Remove the air horn attaching screws and the carburetor identification

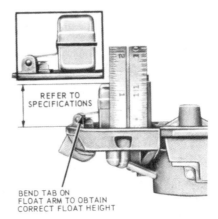

REFER TO SPECIFICATIONS

BEND TAB ON FLOAT ARM TO OBTAIN CORRECT FLOAT HEIGHT

Float level adjustment for the Autolite (Ford) Model 1100 1-bbl carburetor

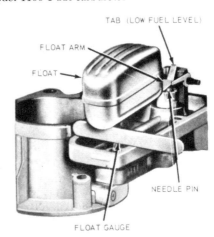

TAB (LOW FUEL LEVEL)

FLOAT ARM

FLOAT

NEEDLE PIN

FLOAT GAUGE

Float level adjustment for the Carter Model YF 1-bbl carburetor

tag. Temporarily, leave the air horn and gasket in position on the carburetor main body and start the engine. Let the engine idle for a few minutes, then rotate the air horn out of the way and remove the air horn gasket to provide access to the float assembly.

4. While the engine is idling, use a scale to measure the vertical distance from the top machined surface of the carburetor main body to the level of the fuel in the fuel bowl. The measurement must be made at least ¼ in. away from any vertical surface to assure an accurate reading, because the surface of the fuel is concave—being higher at the edges than in the center. Care must be exercised to measure the fuel level at the point of contact with the float.

5. If any adjustment is required, stop the engine to minimize the hazard of fire due to spilled gasoline. To adjust the fuel

level, bend the float tab contacting the fuel inlet valve upward in relation to the original position to raise the fuel level,

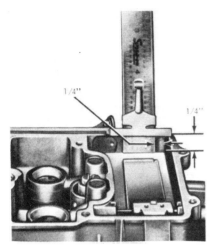

Float level adjustment for the Autolite Model 2100 and 2150 2-bbl carburetor

and downward to lower it. Each time the float is adjusted, the engine must be started and permitted to idle for a few minutes to stabilize the fuel level. Check the fuel level after each adjustment, until the specified level is obtained.

6. Assemble the carburetor in the reverse order of disassembly, using a new gasket between the air horn and the main carburetor body.

MOTORCRAFT MODEL 4350

1. Adjustments to the fuel level are best made with the carburetor removed from the engine.

2. Invert the air horn assembly and remove the gasket from the surface.

3. Use a T-scale to measure the distance from the floats to the air horn casting. Position the scale horizontally over the flat surface of both floats at the free ends and parallel to the air horn casting. Hold the lower end of the vertical scale in full contact with the smooth surface of the air horn.

CAUTION: *The end of the vertical scale must not come into contact with any gasket sealing ridges while measuring the float level.*

4. The free end of each float should just touch the horizontal scale. If one float is lower than the other, twist the float and lever assembly slightly to correct.

5. Adjust the float level by bending the tab which contacts the needle and seat assembly.

NOTE: *The illustrations show an alternate method of adjusting the floats on the model 4300 carburetor.*

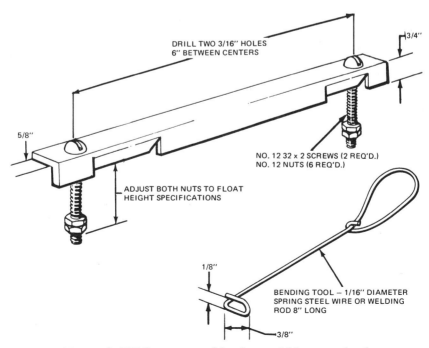

Motorcraft 4350 float gauge and bending tool fabrication details

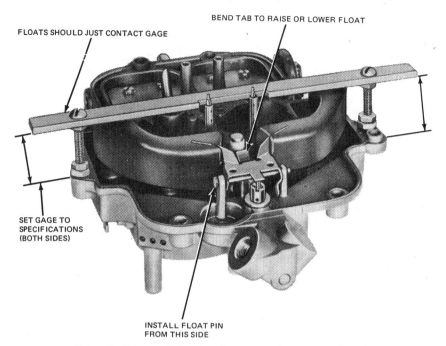

FLOATS SHOULD JUST CONTACT GAGE

BEND TAB TO RAISE OR LOWER FLOAT

SET GAGE TO
SPECIFICATIONS
(BOTH SIDES)

INSTALL FLOAT PIN
FROM THIS SIDE

Using the fabricated float level gauge on the Motorcraft 4350

The procedure includes the fabrication of a gauge and a bending device. After fabricating the gauge, it is possible to adjust it to the specified dimensions and insert it into the air horn outboard holes. Both pontoons should just touch the gauge.

A float tab bending tool is also shown and may be used in the following manner.

To raise the float: insert the open end of the bending tool to the RIGHT side of the float lever tab and between the needle and float hinge. Raise the float lever off of the needle and bend the tab downward.

To lower the float: insert the bending tool to the LEFT side of the float lever tab between the needle and float hinge, support the float lever, and bend the tab upward.

Fast Idle Speed Adjustment

FORD MODEL 1100, 1101 1-BBL

The fast idle is controlled by the idle adjusting screw bearing against the bottom of the choke cam and lever during idle or closed-throttle conditions. The choke cam and lever opens the throttle slightly, through contact of the idle adjusting screw with the cam, as the manual choke position is selected. Higher engine idle speeds are automatically provided through contact of the idle adjusting screw with the cam. The curb idle must be adjusted correctly for the fast idle to be proper during application of the choke.

CARTER MODEL YF 1-BBL

1. Position the fast idle screw on the kick-down step of the fast idle cam against the shoulder of the high step.

2. Adjust by bending the choke plate connecting rod to obtain the specified clearance between the lower edge of the choke plate and the carburetor air horn. Use a drill bit inserted between the lower edge of the choke plate and the carburetor air horn.

3. With the engine at operating temperature, air cleaner removed and a tachometer attached according to the manufacturer's instructions, manually rotate the fast idle cam to the top or second step as specified while holding the choke plate fully open. Turn the fast idle adjusting screw inward or outward as required to obtain the specified speed.

4. When setting the fast idle speed, all distributor vacuum and EGR controls must be disconnected and plugged to in-

sure proper speeds during cold operation.

AUTOLITE (MOTORCRAFT) MODEL 2100, 2150 2-BBL

The fast idle speed adjustment is made in the same manner as for the Model YF carburetor, starting at Step 3.

To adjust the model 2100 fast idle cam clearance, follow the procedure given below:

1. Rotate the choke thermostatic spring housing 90° in the rich direction.
2. Position the fast idle speed screw on the high step of the cam.
3. Depress the choke pulldown diaphragm against the diaphragm stop screw to place the choke in the pulldown position.
4. While holding the choke pulldown diaphragm depressed, open the throttle slightly and allow the fast idle cam to fall.
5. Close the throttle and check the position of the fast idle cam. The screw should contact the cam at the V mark on the cam.

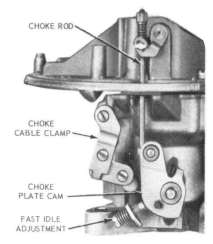

Fast idle speed adjustment on the Autolite Model 2100 2-bbl carburetor

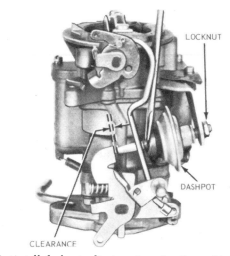

Anti-stall dashpot adjustment on the Carter Model YF 1-bbl carburetor

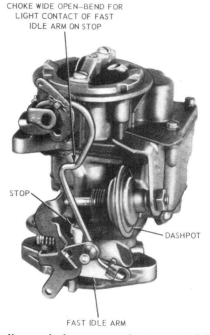

Fast idle speed adjustment on the Carter Model YF 1-bbl carburetor

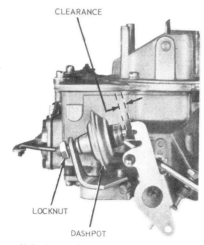

Anti-stall dashpot adjustment on the Autolite Model 2100 2-bbl carburetor

6. Adjust the fast idle cam adjusting screw to obtain the proper setting.

MOTORCRAFT 4350 4-BBL

The fast idle speed adjustment is made in the same manner as for the Model YF carburetor, starting with Step 3.

Dashpot Adjustment

1. Remove the air cleaner.
2. Loosen the anti-stall dashpot lock-nut.
3. With the choke plate open, hold the throttle plate closed (idle position), and check the clearance between the throttle lever and the dashpot plunger tip with a feeler gauge.
NOTE: *On the Ford Model 1100 1-bbl carburetor, turn the adjusting screw 3 turns in after the screw contacts the diaphragm assembly.*

Anti-stall dashpot adjustment on the Autolite (Ford) Model 1100 1-bbl carburetor

Carburetor Specifications

Model	Year	Fuel Float Level Adjustment (in. ± 1/32 in.)	Float Drop (in.)	Choke Plate Pulldown Clearance Adjustment (in. ± 0.010 in.)	Dechoke Clearance Adjustment— Minimum (in.)	Fast Idle Cam Index Setting (in.)	Fast Idle Speed (rpm)	Dashpot Adjustment (in. ± 1/64 in.)
Ford 1100, 1101	1966	1.090	——	0.350–0.400	——	——	——	3½ turns in
	1966 240 manual	1.020	——	——	——	——	——	3½ turns in
	1967	1³⁄₃₂	——	0.350–0.400	——	——	——	3½ turns in
	1967–69 240	1³⁄₃₂	——	0.359–0.391	——	——	——	——
Carter YF, YFA	1968–69	7/32	1¼	——	——	——	——	——
	1970	7/32	1¼	0.225	0.280	——	——	7/64
	1971	3/8	1¼	0.230	0.280	0.175	1750	7/64
	1972	3/8	1¼	0.230	0.280	0.175	——	0.100
	1973	3/8	1¼	0.230	0.280	0.175	1750	——
	1974	3/8	1¼	0.230	0.280	0.175	——	——
	1974 240 auto.	3/8	1¼	0.290	0.280	0.175	——	——

Carburetor Specifications (cont.)

Model	Year	Fuel Float Level Adjustment (in. ± 1/32 in.)	Float Drop (in.)	Choke Plate Pulldown Clearance Adjustment (in. ± 0.010 in.)	Dechoke Clearance Adjustment— Minimum (in.)	Fast Idle Cam Index Setting (in.)	Fast Idle Speed (rpm)	Dashpot Adjustment (in. ± 1/64 in.)
	1974 300	3/8	1¼	0.230	0.280	0.110	——	0.100
	1975	3/8	1¼	0.230	0.280	0.110	——	——
	1976–77, E-100, All Calif.	3/8	1¼	0.230	0.280	0.110	——	——
	1976–77	23/32	1¼	0.290	0.280	0.110	——	——
Auto-lite 2100	1968–69	3/4	——	0.250	——	——	——	——
	1970 manual	13/16	——	0.170	0.060	0.150	1400	5/64
	1970 auto.	13/16	——	0.170	0.060	0.140	1600	5/64
	1971	13/16	——	0.160	0.060	0.140	——	1/8
	1972	7/16	——	0.140	0.060	0.110	——	1/16
	1973 manual	13/16	——	——	——	0.110	1100	——
	1973 auto.	13/16	——	——	——	0.110	1400	0.065
	1974	13/16	——	——	——	——	——	——
Motor-craft 2150	1975–77	0.875	——	0.153	——	——	——	——
	1975–77 Calif.	0.875	——	0.160	——	——	——	——
Motor-craft 4350	1975	15/16	——	0.160	0.300	0.170	——	——
	1976–77	1.000	——	——	0.300	0.170	——	——

Chapter 5

Chassis Electrical

Understanding and Troubleshooting Electrical Systems

For any electrical system to operate, it must make a complete circuit. This simply means that the power flow from the battery must make a complete circle. When an electrical component is operating, power flows from the battery to the component, passes through the component causing it to perform its function (lighting a light bulb), and then returns to the battery through the ground of the circuit. This ground is usually (but not always) the metal part of the vehicle on which the electrical component is mounted.

Perhaps the easiest way to visualize this is to think of connecting a light bulb with two wires attached to it to your battery. The battery has two posts (negative and positive). If one of the two wires attached to the light bulb was attached to the negative post of the battery and the other wire was attached to the positive post of the battery, you would have a complete circuit. Current from the battery would flow out one post, through the wire attached to it and then to the light bulb, where it would pass through caus-

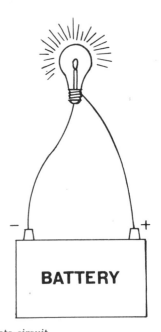

A complete circuit

ing it to light. It would then leave the light bulb, travel through the other wire, and return to the other post of the battery.

The normal automotive circuit differs from this simple example in two ways. First, instead of having a return wire from the bulb to the battery, the light bulb returns the current to the battery through the chassis of the vehicle. Since the negative battery cable is attached to the chassis and the chassis is made of elec-

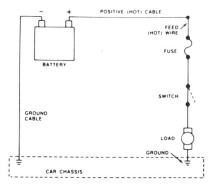

A simple automotive circuit

trically conductive metal, the chassis of the vehicle can serve as a ground wire to complete the circuit. Secondly, most automotive circuits contain switches to turn components on and off as required.

There are many types of switches, but the most common simply serves to prevent the passage of current when it is turned off. Since the switch is a part of the circle necessary for a complete circuit, it operates to leave an opening in the circuit, and thus an incomplete or open circuit, when it is turned off.

Some electrical components which require a large amount of current to operate also have a relay in their circuit. Since these circuits carry a large amount of current, the thickness of the wire in the circuit (gauge size) is also greater. If this large wire were connected from the component to the control switch on the instrument panel, and then back to the component, a voltage drop would occur in the circuit. To prevent this potential drop in voltage, an electromagnetic switch (relay) is used. The large wires in the circuit are connected from the car battery to one side of the relay, and from the opposite side of the relay to the component. The relay is normally open, preventing current from passing through the circuit. An additional, smaller, wire is connected from the relay to the control switch for the circuit. When the control switch is turned on, it grounds the smaller wire from the relay and completes the circuit. This closes the relay and allows current to flow from the battery to the component. The horn, headlight, and starter circuits are three which use relays.

Did you ever notice how your instrument panel lights get brighter the

faster your vehicle goes? This happens because your alternator (which supplies the battery) puts out more current at speeds above idle. This is normal. However, it is possible for larger surges of current to pass through the electrical system. If this surge of current were to reach an electrical component, it could burn it out. To prevent this from happening, fuses are connected into the current supply wires of most of the major electrical systems. The fuse serves to head off the surge at the pass. When an electrical current of excessive power passes through the component's fuse, the fuse melts and breaks the circuit, saving it from destruction.

The fuse also protects the component from damage if the power supply wire to the component is grounded before the current reaches the component.

Let us here interject another rule to the complete circle circuit. *Every complete circuit from a power source must include a component which is using the power from the power source.* If you were to disconnect the light bulb (from the previous example of a light bulb being connected to the battery by two wires) from the wires and touch the two wires together (please take my word for this; don't try it), the result would be shocking. You probably haven't seen so many sparks since the Fourth of July. A similar thing happens (on a smaller scale) when the power supply wire to a component or the electrical component itself becomes grounded before the normal ground connection for the circuit. To prevent damage to the system, the fuse for the circuit melts to interrupt the circuit—protecting the components from damage. Because grounding a wire from a power source makes a complete circuit—less the required component to use the power— this phenomenon is called a short circuit. The most common causes of short circuits are: the rubber insulation on a wire breaking or rubbing through to expose the current carrying core of the wire to a metal part of the car, or a shorted switch.

Some electrical systems are protected by a circuit breaker which is, basically, a self-repairing fuse. When either of the above-described events takes place in a system which is protected by a circuit breaker, the circuit breaker opens the circuit the same way a fuse does. However, when either the short is removed from the circuit or the surge subsides, the circuit breaker resets itself and does not have to be replaced as a fuse does.

The final protective device in the chassis electrical system is a fuse link. A fuse link is a wire that acts as a fuse. It is connected between the starter relay and the main wiring harness for the car. This connection is under the hood, very near a similar fuse link which protects the engine electrical system. Since the fuse link protects all the chassis electrical components, it is the probable cause of trouble when none of the electrical components function, unless the battery is disconnected or dead.

Electrical problems generally fall into one of three areas:

1. The component that is not functioning is not receiving current.

2. The component itself is not functioning.

3. The component is not properly grounded.

Problems that fall into the first category are by far the most complicated. It is the current supply system to the component which contains all the switches, relays, fuses, etc.

The electrical system can be checked with a test light and a jumper wire. A test light is a device that looks like a pointed screwdriver with a wire attached to it. It has a light bulb in its handle. A jumper wire is a piece of insulated wire with an alligator clip attached to each end. To check the system you must follow the wiring diagrams found in this chapter. A wiring diagram is a road map of the electrical system.

If a light bulb is not working, you must follow a systematic plan to determine which of the three causes is the villain.

1. Turn on the switch that controls the inoperable bulb.

2. Disconnect the power supply wire from the bulb.

3. Attach the ground wire on the test light to a good metal ground.

4. Touch the probe end of the test light to the end of the power supply wire that was disconnected from the bulb. If the bulb is receiving current, the test light will go on.

NOTE: *If the bulb is one which works only when the ignition key is turned on (turn signal), make sure that the key is turned on.*

If the test light does not go on, then the problem is in the circuit between the battery and the bulb. As mentioned before, this includes all the switches, fuses, and relays in the system. Turn to the wiring diagram and find the bulb on the diagram. Follow the wire that runs back to the battery. The problem is an open circuit between the battery and the bulb. If the fuse is blown and, when replaced, immediately blows again, there is a short circuit in the system which must be located and repaired. If there is a switch in the system, bypass it with a jumper wire. This is done by connecting one end of the jumper wire to the power supply wire into the switch and the other end of the jumper wire to the wire coming out of the switch. Again, consult the wiring diagram. If the test light lights with the jumper wire installed, the switch or whatever was bypassed is defective.

NOTE: *Never substitute the jumper wire for the bulb, as the bulb is the component required to use the power from the power source.*

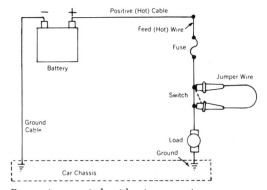

By-passing a switch with a jumper wire

5. If the bulb in the test light goes on, then the current is getting to the bulb that is not working. This eliminates the first of the three possible causes. Connect the power supply wire and connect a jumper wire from the bulb to a good metal ground. Do this with the switch which controls the bulb turned on, and also the ignition switch turned on if it is required for the light to work. If the bulb works with the jumper wire installed, then it

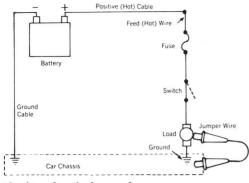

Checking for a bad ground

has a bad ground. This is usually caused by the metal area on which the bulb mounts being coated with some type of foreign matter.

6. If neither test located the source of the trouble, then the light bulb itself is defective.

The above test procedure can be applied to any of the components of the chassis electrical system by substituting the component that is not working for the light bulb. Remember that for any electrical system to work, all connections must be clean and tight.

Heater

BLOWER MOTOR AND/OR HEATER CORE

Removal and Installation

1966–74

1. Open the hood and remove the battery to gain access to the heater mounting bolts.

2. Drain the cooling system.

3. Disconnect the heater hoses at the heater.

4. Disconnect the heater resistor and motor leads.

5. From under the hood, remove the 3 heater-to-dash mounting bolts. Then, move the heater out of position to gain access to the control cable and disconnect the cable. Remove the heater assembly to a bench.

6. Separate the two halves of the heater case (16 screws and 1 clip).

For heater core replacement, use Steps 7, 8 and 14 through 18.

7. Remove the heater core.

8. Transfer the core pads to the new core, and position the core in the case.

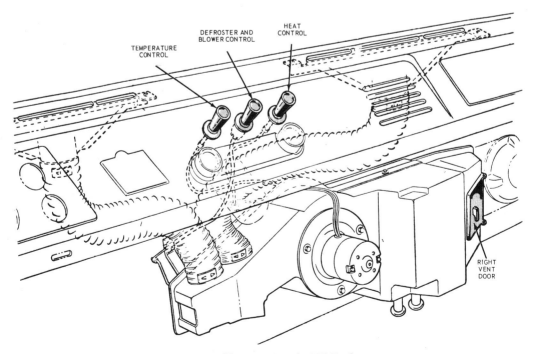

Heater assembly in 1966 and 1967 Ford vans

For blower motor replacement, use Steps 9 through 18.

9. Remove the two screws and lift the motor and wheel from the front half of the heater housing.

10. Remove the blower wheel and motor mounting bracket.

11. Position the new motor in the mounting bracket and install the mounting bolts and nuts.

12. Install the blower wheel.

13. Position the motor assembly in the housing and install the mounting screws.

14. Position both halves of the case together and install the screws and clip.

15. Place the heater controls in the Off position. Place the heater on the wheel housing as near the installed position as possible. Pull the air door closed (toward the rear of the vehicle) and connect the control cable.

16. Position the heater to the dash, and install the 3 mounting bolts. Use an assistant and make certain that the housing openings line up with the defroster and fresh air openings.

17. Connect the resistor and motor leads.

18. Connect the heater hoses.

19. Install the battery and fill the cooling system. Run the engine and check for leaks.

NOTE: *The heater assembly on 1966–67 vehicles is removed in a similar manner. Removal of the right-hand light door is required to gain access to 6 attaching screws. Removal of the heater blower motor is accomplished simply by removing the attaching bolts, disconnecting the electrical lead and lifting the motor from the plenum chamber.*

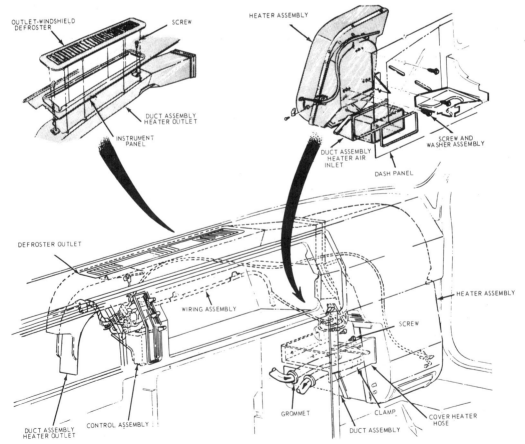

Heater assembly in 1970–74 Ford vans

1975–77 WITHOUT AIR CONDITIONING

Heater Core

1. Drain the coolant; remove the battery.
2. Disconnect the resistor wiring harness and the orange blower motor lead. Remove the ground wire screw from the firewall.
3. Detach the heater hoses and the plastic hose retaining strap.
4. Remove the five mounting screws inside the truck.
5. Remove the heater assembly.
6. Cut the seal at the top and bottom edge of the core retainer. Remove the two screws and the retainer. Slide the core and seal out of the case.
7. Reverse the procedure for installation.

Blower Motor

1. Disconnect the orange motor lead wire. Remove the ground wire screw from the firewall.
2. Disconnect the blower motor cooling tube.
3. Remove the four mounting plate screws and the motor assembly.
4. Reverse the procedure for installation.

1975–77 WITH AIR CONDITIONING

Heater Core

1. Disconnect the resistor electrical leads on the front of the blower cover inside the truck. Detach the vacuum line from the vacuum motor. Remove the blower cover.
2. Remove the nut and push washer from the air door shaft. Remove the control cable from the bracket and the air door shaft.
3. Remove the blower motor housing and the air door housing.
4. Drain the coolant and detach the heater hoses.
5. Remove the heater core retaining brackets. Remove the core and seal assembly.
6. Reverse the procedure for installation.

Blower Motor

1. Disconnect the resistor electrical leads on the front of the blower cover inside the truck.
2. Remove the blower cover.
3. Push the wiring grommet forward out of the housing hole.
4. Remove the blower motor mounting plate. Remove the blower motor.
5. Reverse the procedure for installation.

Radio

Removal and Installation

1966–67

1. Disconnect the lead wire at the fuse panel.
2. Detach the speaker leads at the radio.
3. Detach the antenna.
4. Pull off the control knobs. Remove the screws and take off the dial assembly.
5. Remove the shaft nuts and the retaining plate.
6. Remove the right and left support bracket nuts and remove the radio.
7. Reverse the procedure for installation.

1968–74

1. Disconnect the ground cable from the battery.
2. Remove the 8 screws attaching the instrument cluster to the instrument panel. Pull the cluster away from the instrument panel and disconnect the speedometer cable from the speedometer. Allow the instrument cluster to hang out of the opening.
3. Disconnect the radio power and light wires at the connectors.
4. From under the hood, remove the nut attaching the radio rear mounting bracket to the dash panel.
5. Remove the knobs from the radio control shafts.
6. Remove the 8 screws attaching the radio bezel to the instrument panel. Pull the bezel away from the radio and disconnect the speaker wires at the multiple connector.

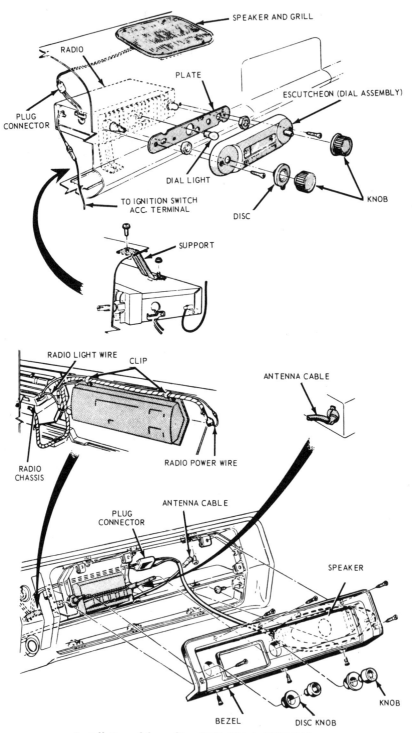

Installation of the radio—1966–67 top, 1968–74 bottom

7. Remove the radio power wire from the two clips over the instrument cluster opening.

8. Disconnect the antenna lead-in cable from the radio.

9. Remove the 3 screws attaching the radio and mounting bracket to the radio opening, and remove the radio and bracket from the vehicle.

To install the radio:

10. Position the radio and mounting bracket in the instrument panel opening. Route the power wire through the clips over the instrument cluster opening.

11. Install the 3 radio mounting bracket attaching screws.

12. Connect the antenna lead-in cable to the radio.

13. Connect the remaining components and install the instrument cluster in the reverse order of removal.

1975–77

1. Detach the battery ground cable.

2. Remove the heater and A/C control knobs. Remove the lighter.

3. Remove the radio knobs and discs.

4. If the truck has a lighter, snap out the name plate at the right side to remove the panel attaching screw.

5. Remove the five finish panel screws.

6. Very carefully pry out the cluster panel in two places.

7. Detach the antenna lead and speaker wires.

8. Remove the two nuts and washers and the mounting plate.

9. Remove the four front radio attaching screws. Remove the rear support nut and washer and remove the radio.

10. Reverse the procedure for installation.

Windshield Wipers

MOTOR

Removal and Installation

1967–74

1. Disconnect the battery ground cable.

2. Disconnect the wiper motor wires at the harness multiple connector or stud terminal.

3. Remove the clip which retains the motor drive arm to the linkage mounting arm and pivot shaft assembly.

4. Remove the wiper motor bracket attaching bolts and remove the motor and bracket from the vehicle. Then, remove the motor from the bracket.

5. Check the new motor to be sure that it is in the park position. Then, install the motor on the mounting bracket.

6. Remove the drive arm from the old motor and install it on the new motor in the park position (in the opposite direction from the ground strap).

7. Install the motor and bracket on the dash panel.

8. Connect the linkage mounting arm and pivot shaft assembly to the motor drive arm and install the retaining clip.

9. Connect the motor wires to the harness or stud terminal and the ground

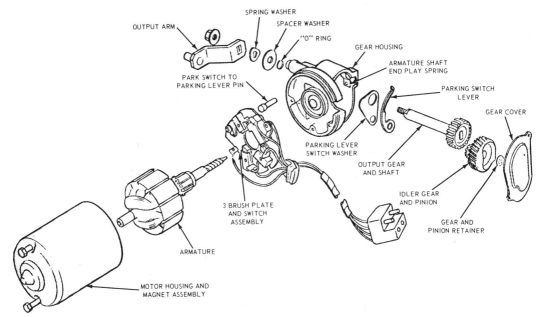

An exploded view of the windshield wiper motor

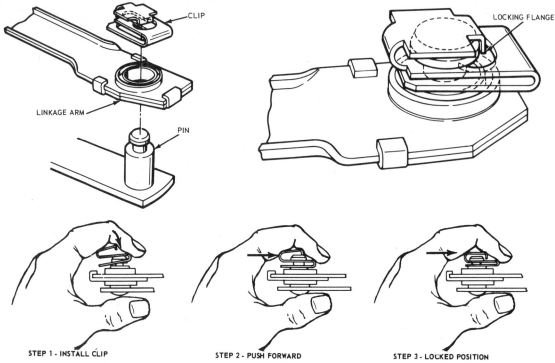

STEP 1 - INSTALL CLIP   STEP 2 - PUSH FORWARD   STEP 3 - LOCKED POSITION

Installation of the wiper arm connecting clip

cable to the battery. Then check the operation of the wipers.

1975–77

1. Disconnect the battery ground cable. Remove the fuse panel and bracket.

2. Disconnect the motor wires.

3. Remove the arms and blades.

4. Remove the outer air inlet cowl. Take off the motor linkage clip.

5. Unbolt and remove the motor.

6. Reverse the procedure for installation.

LINKAGE

Removal and Installation

1967–74

1. Remove the wiper blade and arm assembly from the pivot shaft.

2. Working under the instrument panel from inside the vehicle, remove the six screws retaining the pivot shafts. Remove the external retaining nut on 1966–67 models.

3. Remove the retaining clip that secures the linkage to the wiper motor arm and remove the linkage and pivot shafts from the vehicle.

4. Position the pivot shafts in the mounting holes on the front cowl panel. Secure the linkage to the motor arm with the retaining clip.

5. Install the six screws or two nuts retaining the pivot shafts to the cowl.

6. Install the wiper arm and blade assemblies to the pivot shafts and check the operation of the wipers.

1975–77

1. Disconnect the battery ground cable.

2. Remove the wiper blades and arms. Detach the washer hoses.

3. Remove the cowl grille.

4. Remove the linkage clips. Remove the pivot to cowl screws and remove the assembly.

Instrument Cluster

Removal and Installation

Disconnect the battery ground cable. From the front of the cluster, remove the screws which retain the cluster to the instrument panel, and position the cluster part way out of the panel for access to the back of the cluster. At the back of the cluster, disconnect the speedometer cable from the head and disconnect the multiple (feed) plug from the printed circuit. Disconnect the wire from the flasher unit at the upper left-hand corner of the cluster. Disconnect any other wires not included in the wiring harness. Remove the cluster assembly from the vehicle.

Install the instrument cluster in the reverse order of removal.

Headlights

Removal and Installation

1. Remove the attaching screws and remove the trim ring, or door. This isn't necessary on 1975–77 models.

2. Loosen or remove the headlight retaining ring screws and remove the retaining ring. Do not disturb the adjusting screw settings.

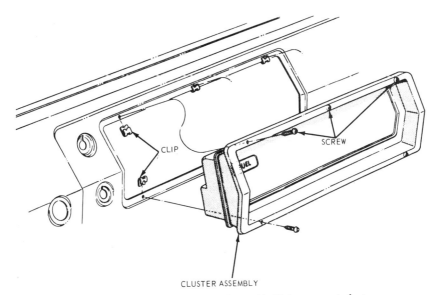

Removal and installation of the 1968–74 instrument cluster

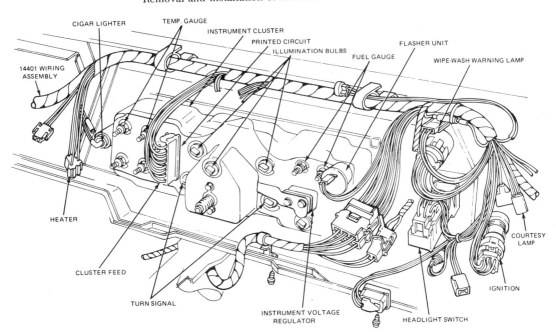

Rear view of a 1974 instrument cluster

3. Pull the headlight bulb forward and disconnect the wiring assembly plug from the bulb.

4. Connect the wiring assembly plug to the new bulb. Place the bulb in position, making sure that the locating tabs of the bulb are fitted in the positioning slots.

5. Install the headlight retaining ring.

6. Place the headlight trim ring or door into position, and install the retaining screws.

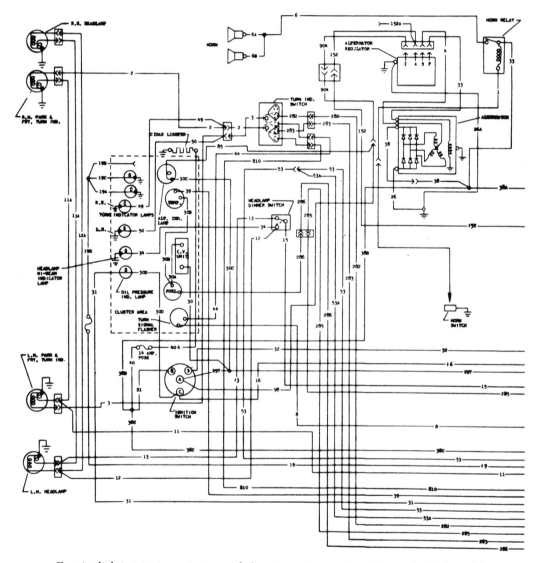

Exterior lighting, ignition, starting and charging systems wiring diagram for 1966 models

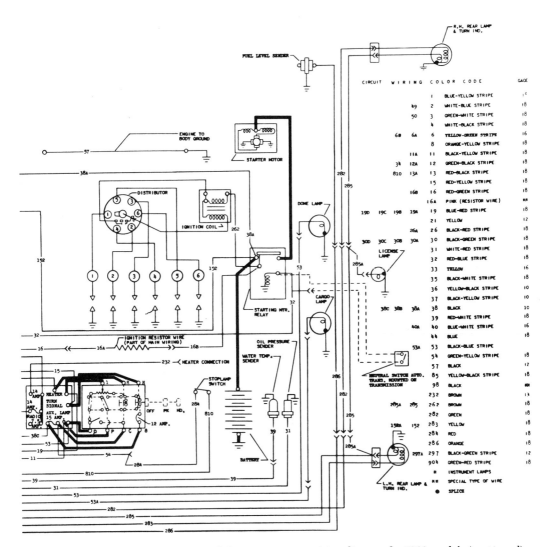

Exterior lighting, ignition, starting and charging systems wiring diagram for 1966 models (continued)

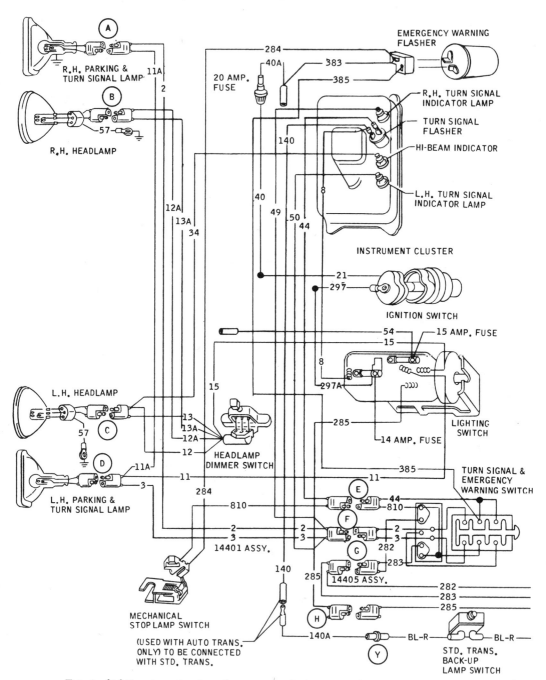

Exterior lighting, turn signals and emergency flasher wiring diagram for 1967 models

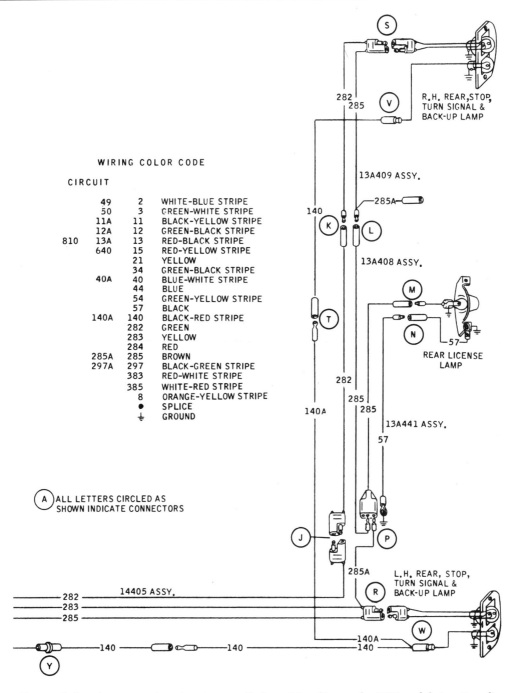

WIRING COLOR CODE

CIRCUIT

49	2	WHITE-BLUE STRIPE
50	3	GREEN-WHITE STRIPE
11A	11	BLACK-YELLOW STRIPE
12A	12	GREEN-BLACK STRIPE
810	13A	13	RED-BLACK STRIPE
640	15	RED-YELLOW STRIPE
	21	YELLOW
	34	GREEN-BLACK STRIPE
40A	40	BLUE-WHITE STRIPE
	44	BLUE
	54	GREEN-YELLOW STRIPE
	57	BLACK
140A	140	BLACK-RED STRIPE
	282	GREEN
	283	YELLOW
	284	RED
285A	285	BROWN
297A	297	BLACK-GREEN STRIPE
	383	RED-WHITE STRIPE
	385	WHITE-RED STRIPE
	8	ORANGE-YELLOW STRIPE
	●	SPLICE
	⏚	GROUND

R.H. REAR, STOP, TURN SIGNAL & BACK-UP LAMP

13A409 ASSY.

13A408 ASSY.

REAR LICENSE LAMP

13A441 ASSY.

A ALL LETTERS CIRCLED AS SHOWN INDICATE CONNECTORS

14405 ASSY.

L.H. REAR, STOP, TURN SIGNAL & BACK-UP LAMP

Exterior lighting, turn signals and emergency flasher wiring diagram for 1967 models (continued)

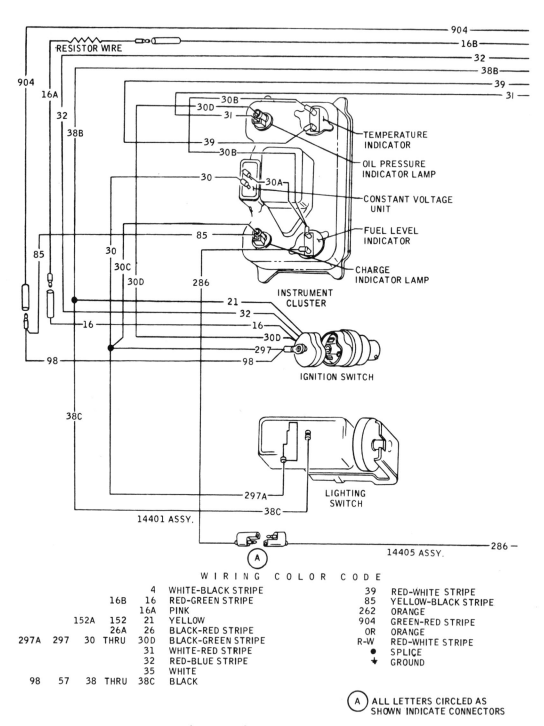

RESISTOR WIRE

904
16A
32
38B

30B
30D
31

39
30B

30

30A

85

85
30
30C
30D
286

904
16B
32
38B
39
31

TEMPERATURE
INDICATOR

OIL PRESSURE
INDICATOR LAMP

CONSTANT VOLTAGE
UNIT

FUEL LEVEL
INDICATOR

CHARGE
INDICATOR LAMP

INSTRUMENT
CLUSTER

21
32
16
30D
297
98

16

98

IGNITION SWITCH

38C

LIGHTING
SWITCH

297A
38C

14401 ASSY.

286

14405 ASSY.

A

WIRING COLOR CODE

			4	WHITE-BLACK STRIPE		39	RED-WHITE STRIPE
	16B	16	RED-GREEN STRIPE			85	YELLOW-BLACK STRIPE
		16A	PINK			262	ORANGE
	152A	152	21	YELLOW		904	GREEN-RED STRIPE
		26A	26	BLACK-RED STRIPE		OR	ORANGE
297A	297	30 THRU	30D	BLACK-GREEN STRIPE		R-W	RED-WHITE STRIPE
			31	WHITE-RED STRIPE		●	SPLICE
			32	RED-BLUE STRIPE		↓	GROUND
			35	WHITE			
98	57	38 THRU	38C	BLACK			

A ALL LETTERS CIRCLED AS
SHOWN INDICATE CONNECTORS

Ignition, starting, charging and gauge wiring diagram for 1967 models

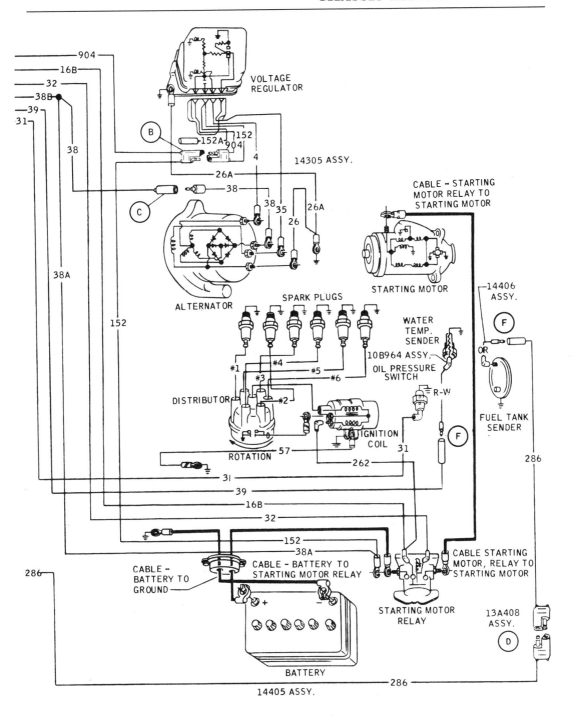

Ignition, starting, charging and gauge wiring diagram for 1967 models (continued)

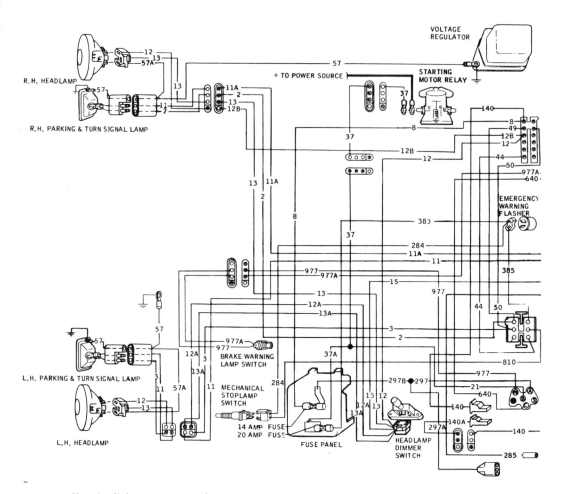

Exterior lighting, turn signals and emergency flasher wiring diagram for 1968 models

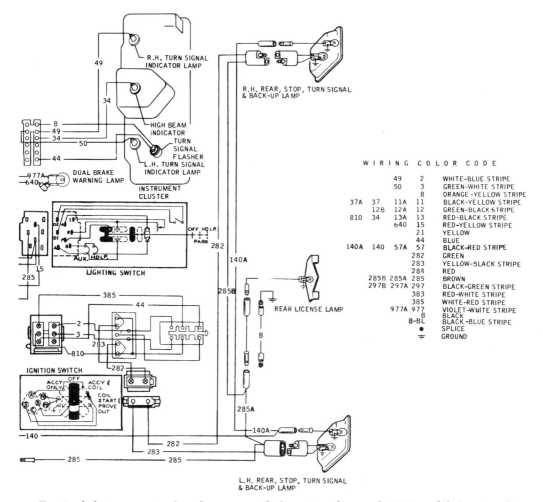

Exterior lighting, turn signals and emergency flasher wiring diagram for 1968 models (continued)

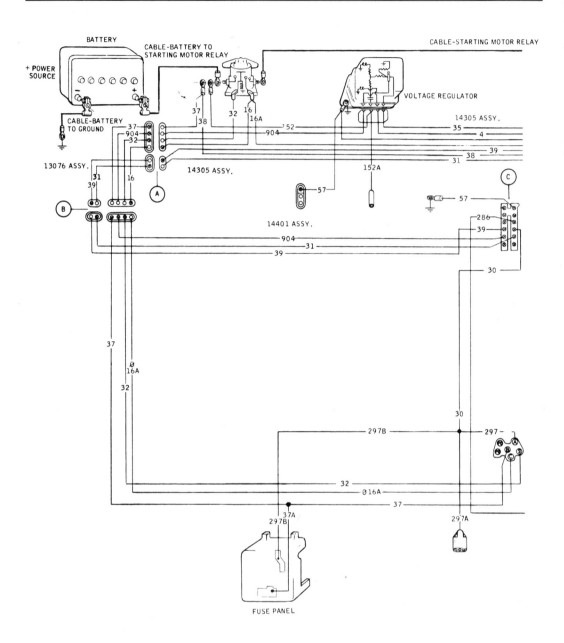

Ignition, starting, charging and gauge wiring diagram for 1968 models

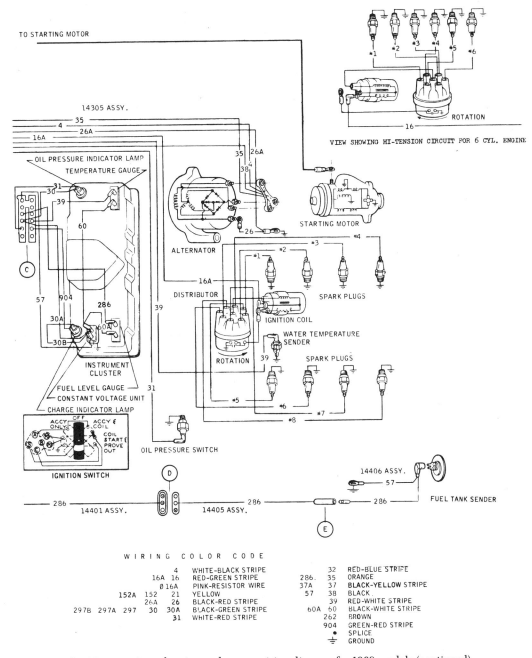

Ignition, starting, charging and gauge wiring diagram for 1968 models (continued)

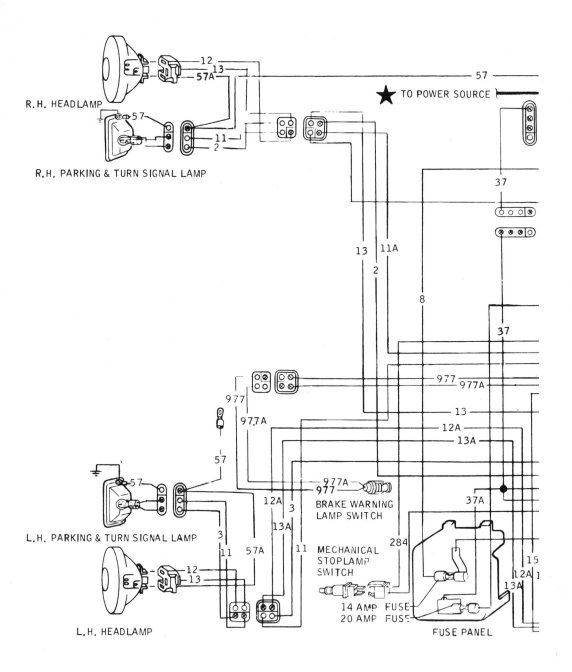

Exterior lighting and turn signals wiring diagram for 1969 models

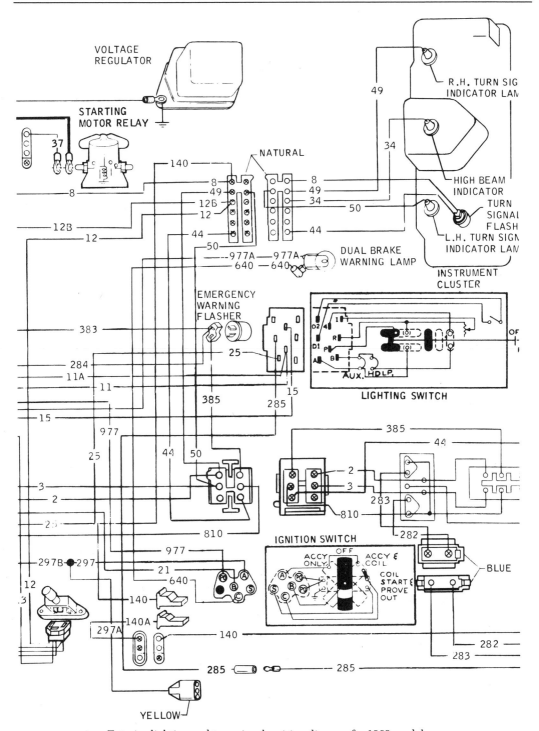

Exterior lighting and turn signals wiring diagram for 1969 models

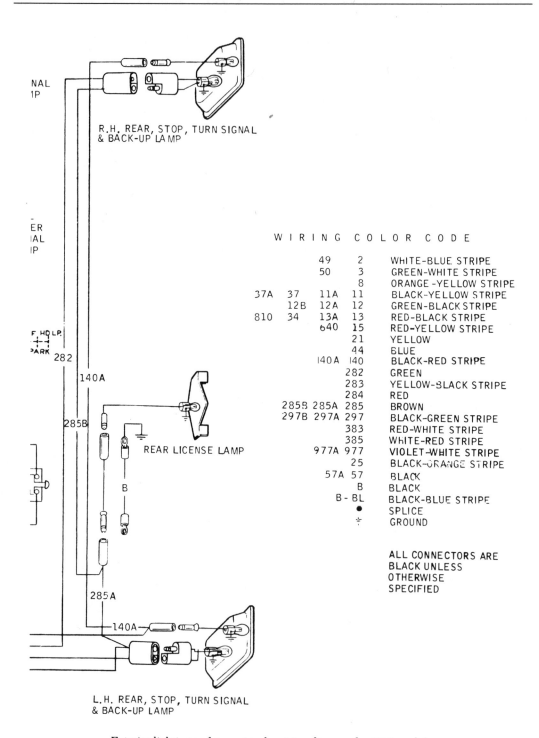

R.H. REAR, STOP, TURN SIGNAL
& BACK-UP LAMP

NAL
1P

-
ER
IAL
1P

F HD LP.
PARK   282

140A

285B

B

285A

140A

REAR LICENSE LAMP

WIRING COLOR CODE

		49	2	WHITE-BLUE STRIPE
		50	3	GREEN-WHITE STRIPE
			8	ORANGE-YELLOW STRIPE
37A	37	11A	11	BLACK-YELLOW STRIPE
	12B	12A	12	GREEN-BLACK STRIPE
810	34	13A	13	RED-BLACK STRIPE
		640	15	RED-YELLOW STRIPE
			21	YELLOW
			44	BLUE
		140A	140	BLACK-RED STRIPE
			282	GREEN
			283	YELLOW-BLACK STRIPE
			284	RED
	285B	285A	285	BROWN
	297B	297A	297	BLACK-GREEN STRIPE
			383	RED-WHITE STRIPE
			385	WHITE-RED STRIPE
		977A	977	VIOLET-WHITE STRIPE
			25	BLACK-ORANGE STRIPE
		57A	57	BLACK
			B	BLACK
		B-BL		BLACK-BLUE STRIPE
		●		SPLICE
		÷		GROUND

ALL CONNECTORS ARE
BLACK UNLESS
OTHERWISE
SPECIFIED

L.H. REAR, STOP, TURN SIGNAL
& BACK-UP LAMP

Exterior lighting and turn signals wiring diagram for 1969 models

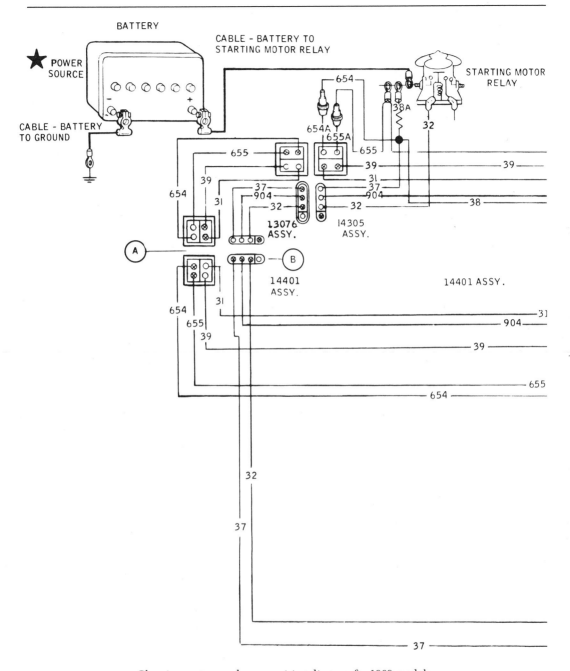

Charging system and gauge wiring diagram for 1969 models

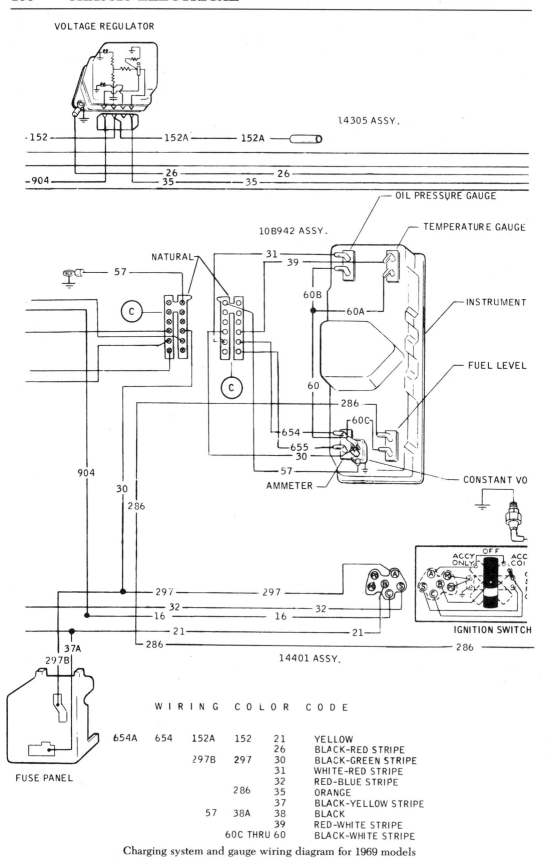

VOLTAGE REGULATOR

14305 ASSY.

-152- 152A- 152A

-904-

26 — 26
35 — 35

OIL PRESSURE GAUGE

TEMPERATURE GAUGE

10B942 ASSY.

NATURAL

57

31
39

60B

60A

INSTRUMENT

C

60

FUEL LEVEL

C

286

60C

654

655

30

57

CONSTANT VO

AMMETER

904

30

286

ACCY ONLY   OFF   ACC COI

A

B

S

C

297 — 297

32 — 32

16 — 16

21 — 21

IGNITION SWITCH

37A

286

286

14401 ASSY.

297B

FUSE PANEL

W I R I N G   C O L O R   C O D E

654A	654	152A	152	21	YELLOW
				26	BLACK-RED STRIPE
		297B	297	30	BLACK-GREEN STRIPE
				31	WHITE-RED STRIPE
				32	RED-BLUE STRIPE
			286	35	ORANGE
				37	BLACK-YELLOW STRIPE
	57	38A		38	BLACK
				39	RED-WHITE STRIPE
			60C THRU 60		BLACK-WHITE STRIPE

Charging system and gauge wiring diagram for 1969 models

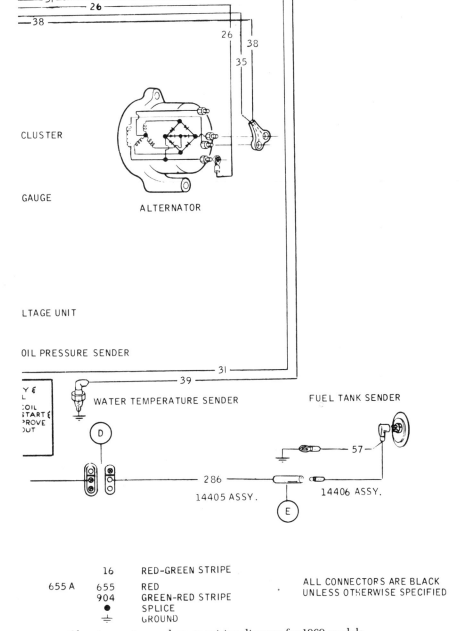

CLUSTER

GAUGE

ALTERNATOR

LTAGE UNIT

OIL PRESSURE SENDER

WATER TEMPERATURE SENDER

FUEL TANK SENDER

14405 ASSY.

14406 ASSY.

16	RED-GREEN STRIPE
655	RED
904	GREEN-RED STRIPE
●	SPLICE
⏚	GROUND

655 A

ALL CONNECTORS ARE BLACK
UNLESS OTHERWISE SPECIFIED

Charging system and gauge wiring diagram for 1969 models

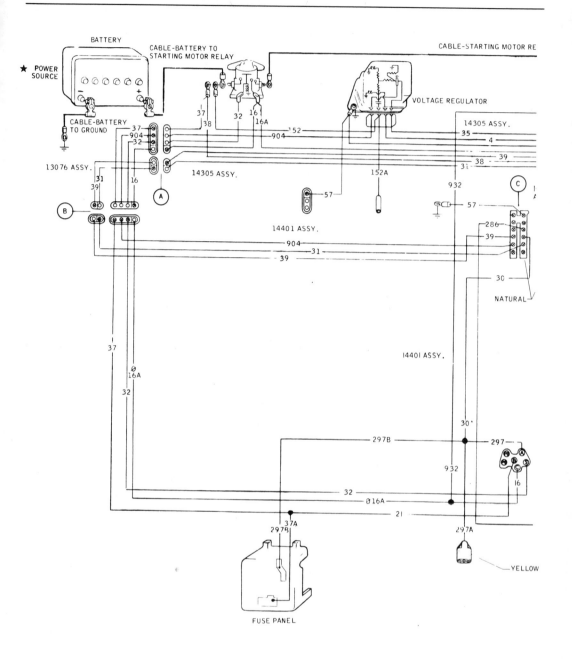

Ignition, starting, and charging systems and gauge wiring diagram for 1969 models

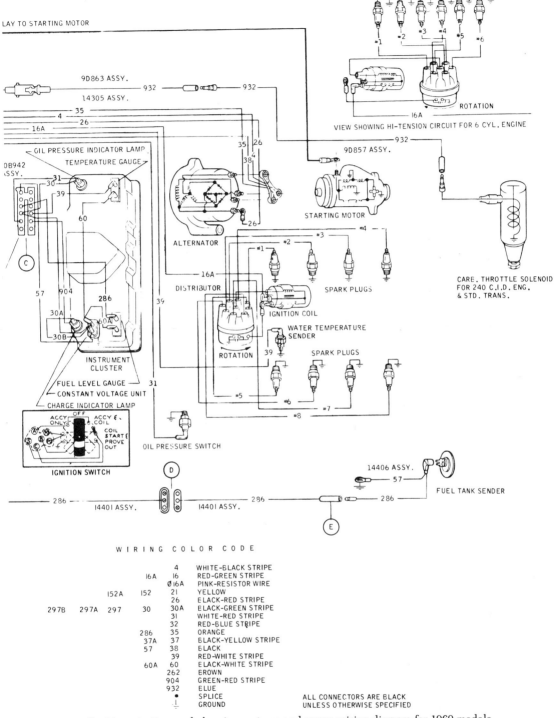

LAY TO STARTING MOTOR

9D863 ASSY.

14305 ASSY.

932   932

ROTATION

35
26
16A

VIEW SHOWING HI-TENSION CIRCUIT FOR 6 CYL. ENGINE

932

9D857 ASSY.

OIL PRESSURE INDICATOR LAMP
TEMPERATURE GAUGE

0B942
ASSY.

35 26
4
38

STARTING MOTOR

31
30
39

60

ALTERNATOR

CARE. THROTTLE SOLENOID
FOR 240 C.I.D. ENG.
& STD. TRANS.

#1 #2 #3 #4

SPARK PLUGS

57 904

286

16A

DISTRIBUTOR

30A

30B
60A

IGNITION COIL

WATER TEMPERATURE
SENDER

39
INSTRUMENT
CLUSTER

ROTATION

SPARK PLUGS

FUEL LEVEL GAUGE
CONSTANT VOLTAGE UNIT
CHARGE INDICATOR LAMP

31

#5   #6   #7

#8

OIL PRESSURE SWITCH

14406 ASSY.

57

ACCY.
ONLY
OFF
ACCY &
COIL

COIL
START &
PROVE
OUT

IGNITION SWITCH

D

FUEL TANK SENDER

286
14401 ASSY.

14401 ASSY.

286

286

E

Ignition, starting, and charging systems and gauge wiring diagram for 1969 models

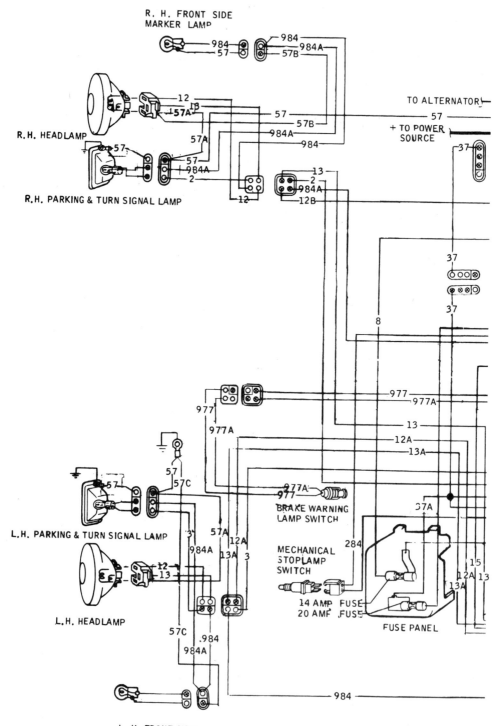

Exterior lighting and turn signals wiring diagram for 1970 models

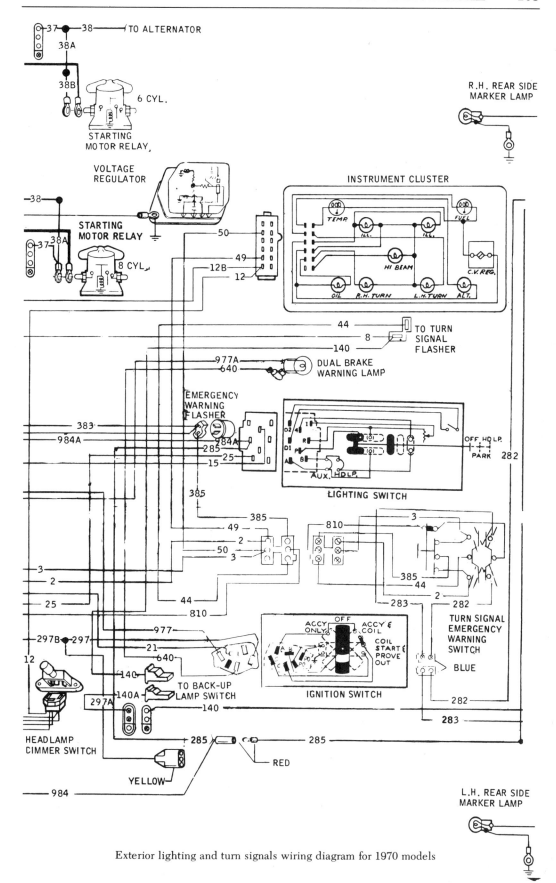

Exterior lighting and turn signals wiring diagram for 1970 models

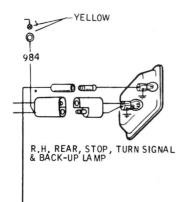

R.H. REAR, STOP, TURN SIGNAL
& BACK-UP LAMP

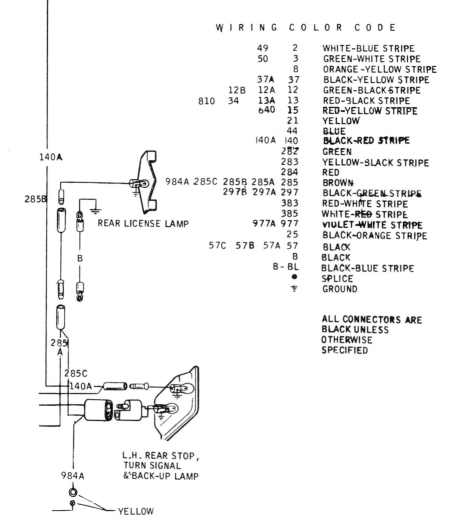

```
W I R I N G     C O L O R     C O D E
                     49    2      WHITE-BLUE STRIPE
                     50    3      GREEN-WHITE STRIPE
                           8      ORANGE-YELLOW STRIPE
                     37A   37     BLACK-YELLOW STRIPE
              12B    12A   12     GREEN-BLACK STRIPE
        810   34     13A   13     RED-BLACK STRIPE
                     640   15     RED-YELLOW STRIPE
                           21     YELLOW
                           44     BLUE
                     140A  140    BLACK-RED STRIPE
                           282    GREEN
                           283    YELLOW-BLACK STRIPE
                           284    RED
   984A 285C 285B 285A  285       BROWN
        297B 297A  297            BLACK-GREEN STRIPE
                     383          RED-WHITE STRIPE
                     385          WHITE-RED STRIPE
                977A  977         VIOLET-WHITE STRIPE
                      25          BLACK-ORANGE STRIPE
      57C 57B 57A  57             BLACK
                    B             BLACK
               B- BL              BLACK-BLUE STRIPE
                    ●             SPLICE
                    ⏚             GROUND
```

ALL CONNECTORS ARE
BLACK UNLESS
OTHERWISE
SPECIFIED

REAR LICENSE LAMP

L.H. REAR STOP,
TURN SIGNAL
& BACK-UP LAMP

Exterior lighting and turn signals wiring diagram for 1970 models

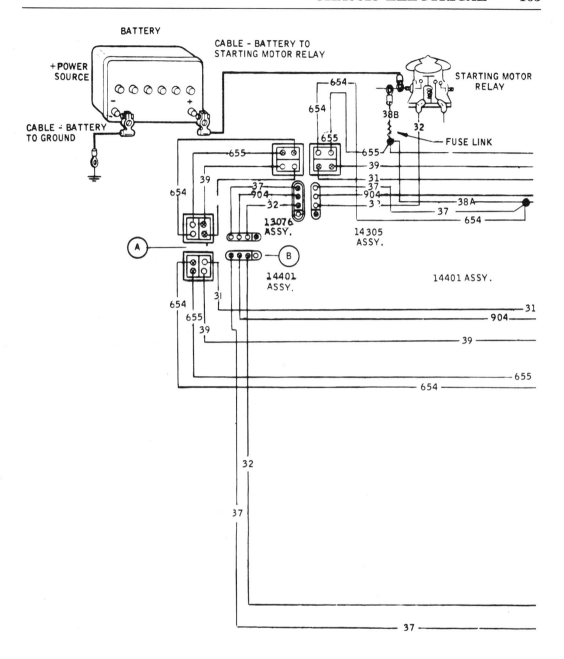

Charging system and gauge wiring diagram for 1970 models

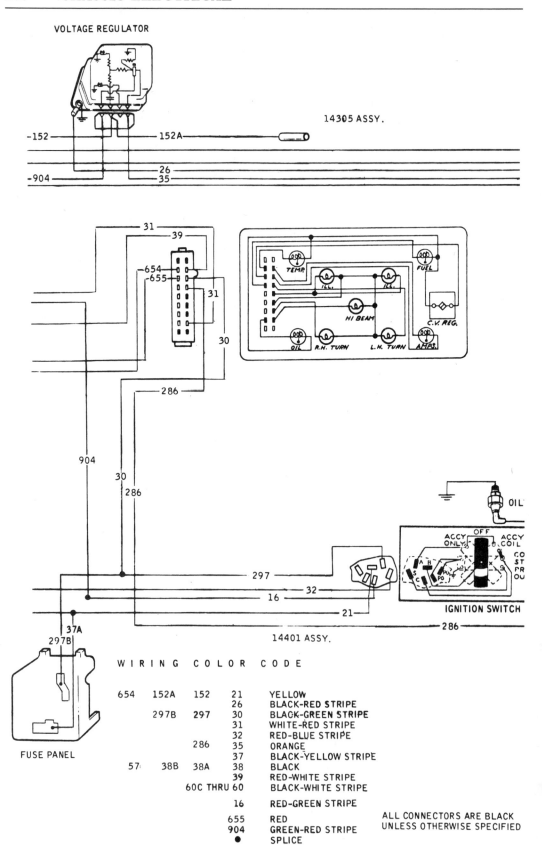

VOLTAGE REGULATOR

14305 ASSY.

WIRING COLOR CODE

654	152A	152	21	YELLOW
			26	BLACK-RED STRIPE
	297B	297	30	BLACK-GREEN STRIPE
			31	WHITE-RED STRIPE
			32	RED-BLUE STRIPE
		286	35	ORANGE
			37	BLACK-YELLOW STRIPE
57	38B	38A	38	BLACK
			39	RED-WHITE STRIPE
		60C THRU 60		BLACK-WHITE STRIPE
			16	RED-GREEN STRIPE
			655	RED
			904	GREEN-RED STRIPE
			●	SPLICE
			⏚	GROUND

ALL CONNECTORS ARE BLACK
UNLESS OTHERWISE SPECIFIED

Charging system and gauge wiring diagram for 1970 models

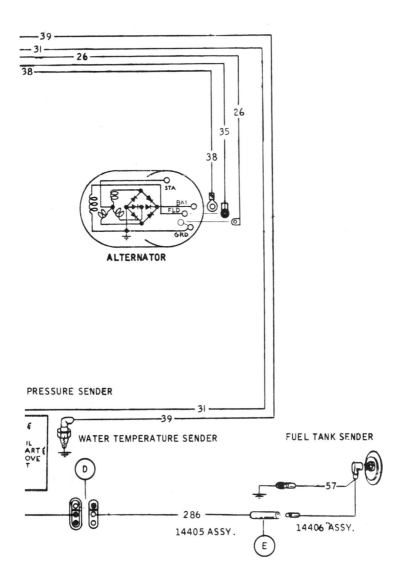

Charging system and gauge wiring diagram for 1970 models

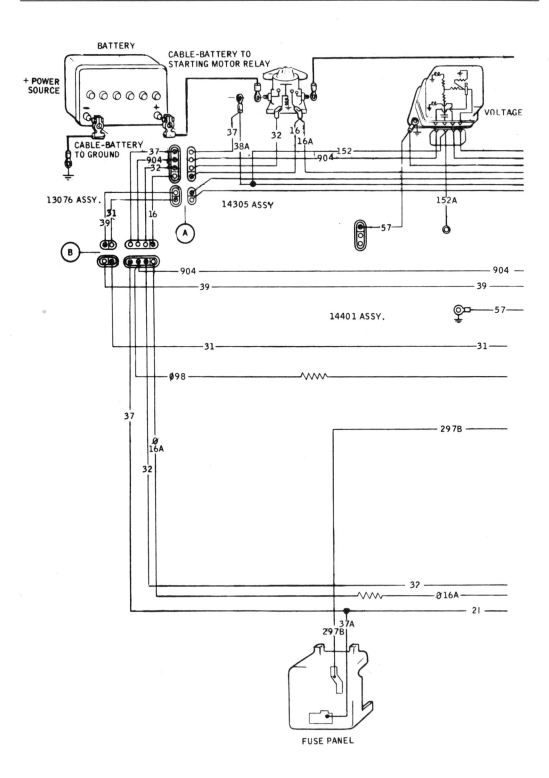

Ignition, starting, charging systems and gauge wiring diagram for 1970 models

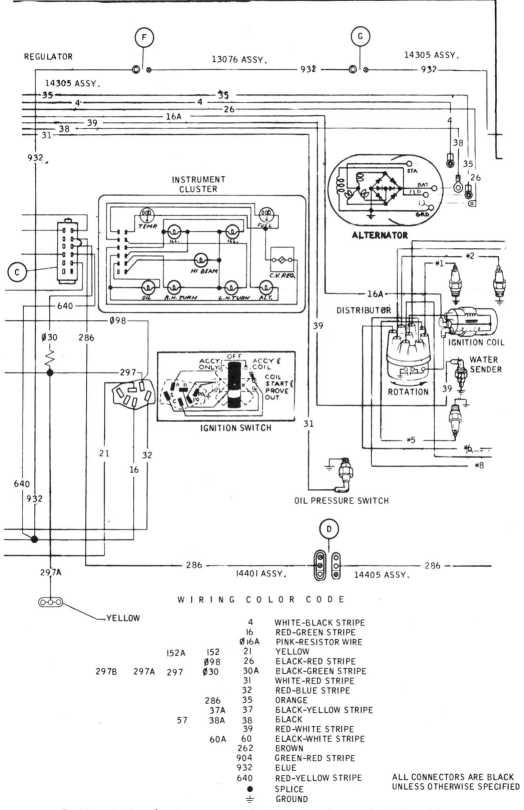

CABLE-STARTING MOTOR RELAY TO STARTING MOTOR

WIRING COLOR CODE

				4	WHITE-BLACK STRIPE
				16	RED-GREEN STRIPE
				Ø16A	PINK-RESISTOR WIRE
		152A	152	21	YELLOW
			Ø98	26	BLACK-RED STRIPE
297B	297A	297	Ø30	30A	BLACK-GREEN STRIPE
				31	WHITE-RED STRIPE
				32	RED-BLUE STRIPE
		286		35	ORANGE
		37A		37	BLACK-YELLOW STRIPE
		57	38A	38	BLACK
				39	RED-WHITE STRIPE
		60A		60	BLACK-WHITE STRIPE
				262	BROWN
				904	GREEN-RED STRIPE
				932	BLUE
				640	RED-YELLOW STRIPE
				●	SPLICE
				⏚	GROUND

ALL CONNECTORS ARE BLACK
UNLESS OTHERWISE SPECIFIED

Ignition, starting, charging systems and gauge wiring diagram for 1970 models

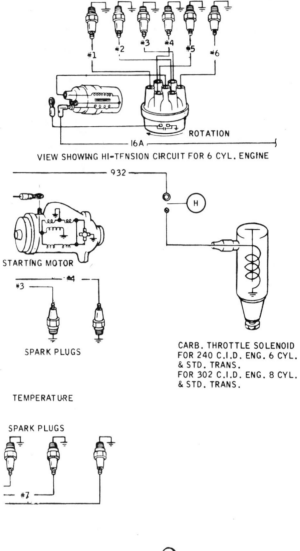

#1 #2 #3 #4 #5 #6

ROTATION

16A

VIEW SHOWING HI-TENSION CIRCUIT FOR 6 CYL. ENGINE

932

H

STARTING MOTOR

#3 #4

SPARK PLUGS

TEMPERATURE

SPARK PLUGS

#7

CARB. THROTTLE SOLENOID
FOR 240 C.I.D. ENG. 6 CYL.
& STD. TRANS.
FOR 302 C.I.D. ENG. 8 CYL.
& STD. TRANS.

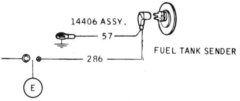

14406 ASSY.

57

286

FUEL TANK SENDER

E

Ignition, starting, charging systems and gauge wiring diagram for 1970 models

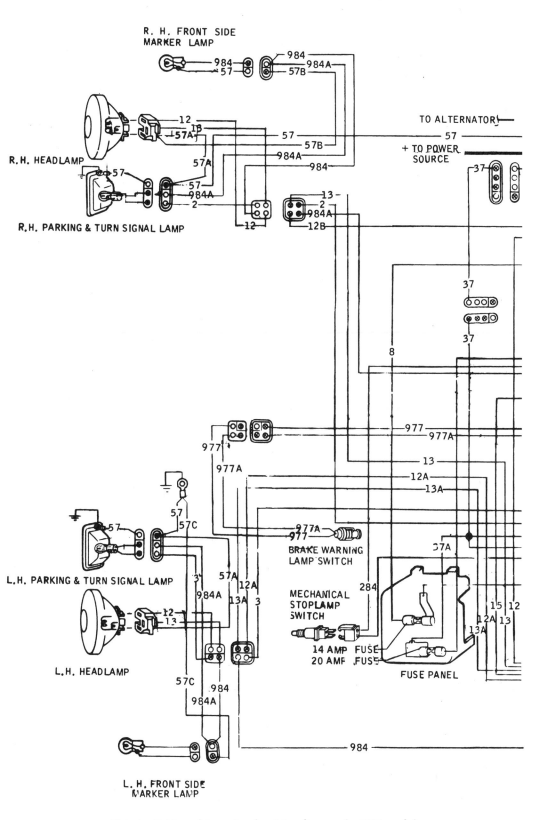

Exterior lights and turn signals wiring diagram for 1971 models

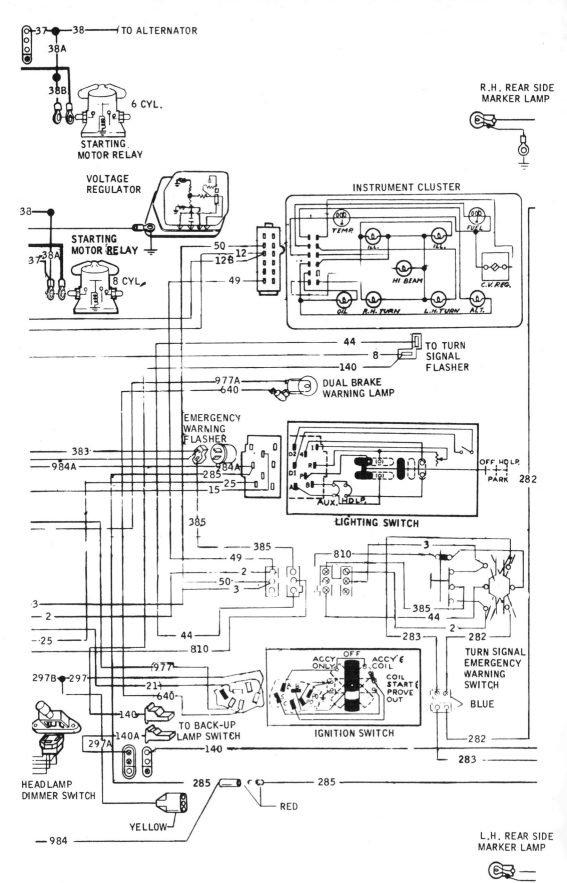

Exterior lights and turn signals wiring diagram for 1971 models

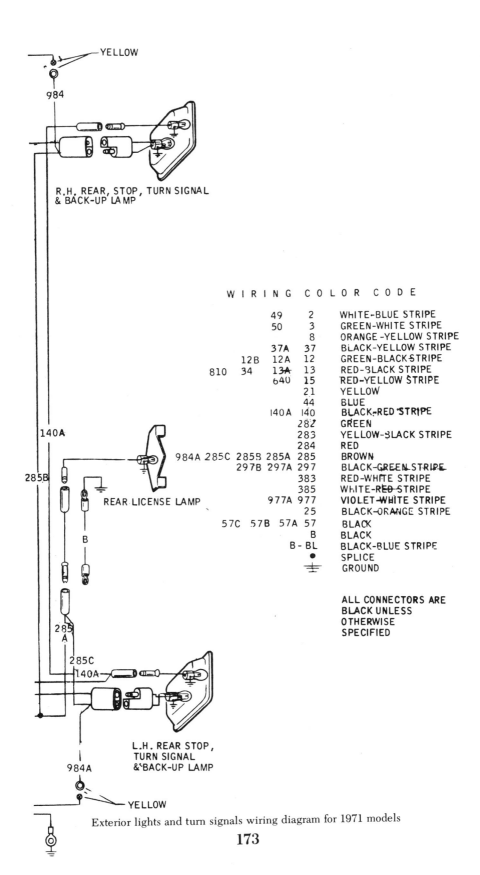

YELLOW

984

R.H. REAR, STOP, TURN SIGNAL & BACK-UP LAMP

W I R I N G   C O L O R   C O D E

			49	2	WHITE-BLUE STRIPE
			50	3	GREEN-WHITE STRIPE
				8	ORANGE-YELLOW STRIPE
			37A	37	BLACK-YELLOW STRIPE
		12B	12A	12	GREEN-BLACK STRIPE
810	34		13A	13	RED-BLACK STRIPE
			640	15	RED-YELLOW STRIPE
				21	YELLOW
				44	BLUE
			140A	140	BLACK-RED STRIPE
				282	GREEN
				283	YELLOW-BLACK STRIPE
				284	RED
984A	285C	285B	285A	285	BROWN
		297B	297A	297	BLACK-GREEN STRIPE
				383	RED-WHITE STRIPE
				385	WHITE-RED STRIPE
			977A	977	VIOLET-WHITE STRIPE
				25	BLACK-ORANGE STRIPE
57C	57B	57A	57		BLACK
				B	BLACK
			B - BL		BLACK-BLUE STRIPE
				●	SPLICE
				⏚	GROUND

ALL CONNECTORS ARE BLACK UNLESS OTHERWISE SPECIFIED

140A

285B

REAR LICENSE LAMP

B

285 A

285C

140A

L.H. REAR STOP, TURN SIGNAL & BACK-UP LAMP

984A

YELLOW

Exterior lights and turn signals wiring diagram for 1971 models

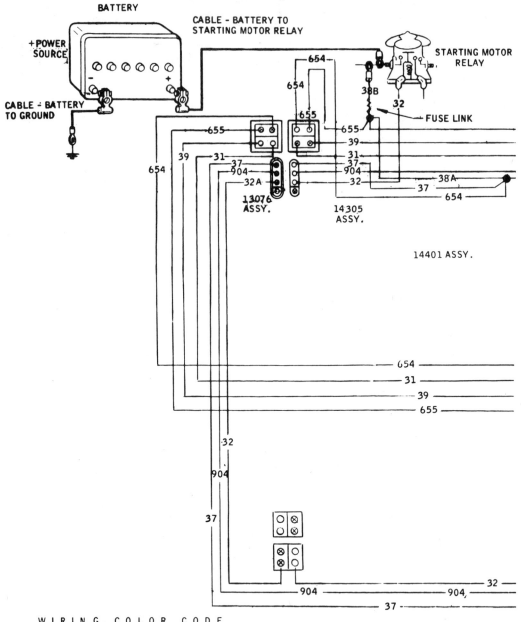

WIRING COLOR CODE

654	152A	152	21	YELLOW
			26	BLACK-RED STRIPE
	297B	297	30	BLACK-GREEN STRIPE
			31	WHITE-RED STRIPE
			32	RED-BLUE STRIPE
		286	35	ORANGE
			37	BLACK-YELLOW STRIPE
57	38B	38A	38	BLACK
			39	RED-WHITE STRIPE
		60C THRU 60		BLACK-WHITE STRIPE
			16	RED-GREEN STRIPE
			655	RED
			904	GREEN-RED STRIPE
			●	SPLICE
			⏚	GROUND

ALL CONNECTORS ARE BLACK
UNLESS OTHERWISE SPECIFIED

Ignition, starting, charging systems and gauge wiring diagrams for 1971 models

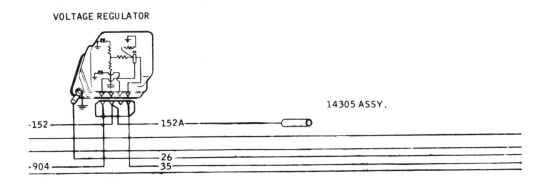

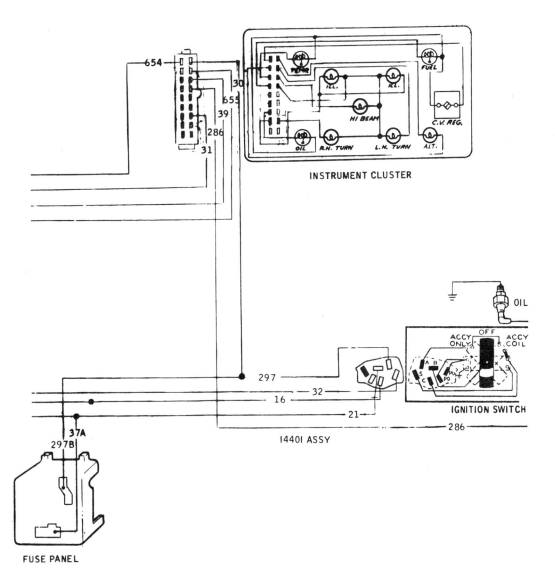

Ignition, starting, charging systems and gauge wiring diagrams for 1971 models

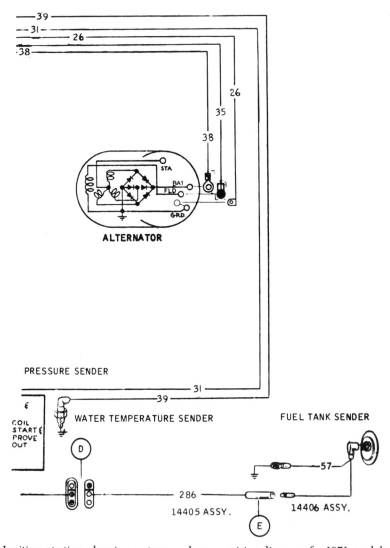

Ignition, starting, charging systems and gauge wiring diagrams for 1971 models

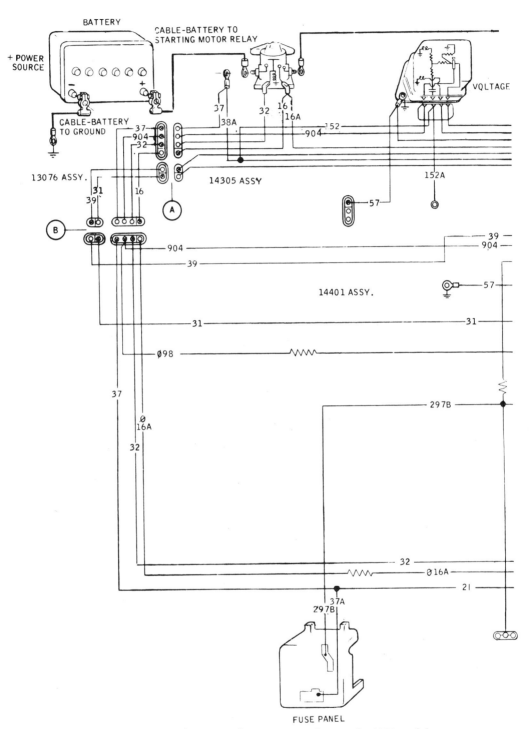

Ignition, starting, charging and gauge wiring diagram for 1971 models

CABLE-STARTING MOTOR RELAY TO STARTING MOTOR

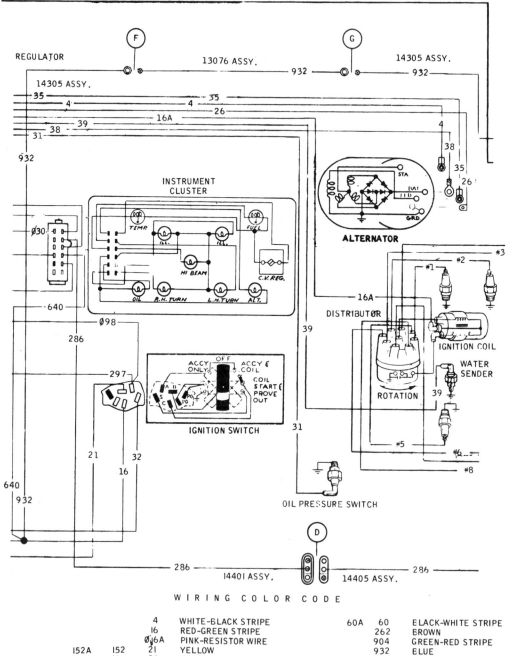

WIRING COLOR CODE

			4	WHITE-BLACK STRIPE	60A	60	BLACK-WHITE STRIPE
			16	RED-GREEN STRIPE		262	BROWN
			Ø16A	PINK-RESISTOR WIRE		904	GREEN-RED STRIPE
	152A	152	21	YELLOW		932	BLUE
		Ø98	26	BLACK-RED STRIPE		640	RED-YELLOW STRIPE
297B	297A	297	30A	BLACK-GREEN STRIPE		●	SPLICE
		Ø30	31	WHITE-RED STRIPE		⏚	GROUND
			32	RED-BLUE STRIPE			
		286	35	ORANGE			
		37A	37	BLACK-YELLOW STRIPE			
	57	38A	38	BLACK		ALL CONNECTORS ARE BLACK
			39	RED-WHITE STRIPE		UNLESS OTHERWISE SPECIFIED

Ignition, starting, charging and gauge wiring diagram for 1971 models

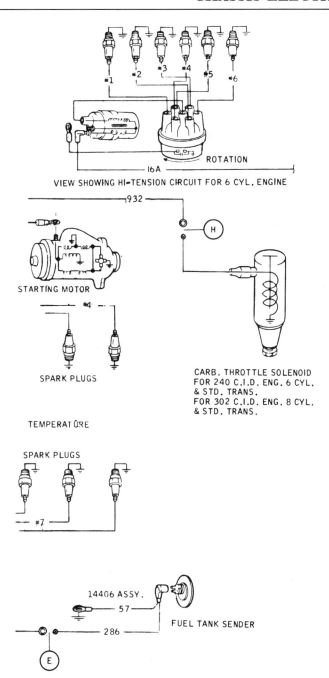

#1 #2 #3 #4 #5 #6

ROTATION

16A

VIEW SHOWING HI-TENSION CIRCUIT FOR 6 CYL. ENGINE

932

H

STARTING MOTOR

SPARK PLUGS

TEMPERATURE

CARB. THROTTLE SOLENOID
FOR 240 C.I.D. ENG. 6 CYL.
& STD. TRANS.
FOR 302 C.I.D. ENG. 8 CYL.
& STD. TRANS.

SPARK PLUGS

#7

14406 ASSY.

57

286

FUEL TANK SENDER

E

Ignition, starting, charging and gauge wiring diagram for 1971 models

INDEX

COMPONENT	LOCATION
AIR CONDITIONER:	
BLOWER MOTOR	H-34
BLOWER MOTOR & CLUTCH CONTROL SWITCH	E-34
CLUTCH SOLENOID	J-35
HIGH BLOWER RELAY	G-36
BLOWER MOTOR RESISTOR	G-34
THERMOSTAT SWITCH	E-35
ALTERNATOR	C-11
ALTERNATOR INDICATOR	B-10
ALTERNATOR REGULATOR	G-11
AMBIENT SENSOR SWITCH	D-14
AMMETER IN CLUSTER	D-13
BACK-UP LAMPS	K-27
BACK-UP LAMP SWITCH (STD. TRANS.)	F-27
BATTERY	C-2
CARBURETOR SOLENOID	J-17
CARGO LAMP	J-54
CIGAR LIGHTER ILLUMINATION LAMP	E-42
CIGAR LIGHTER	E-53
CLUSTER ILLUMINATION LAMPS	F-43
CONSTANT VOLTAGE REGULATOR	D-21
DISTRIBUTOR	J-2
DOME LAMP	H-54
DOOR SWITCHES:	
L.H. FRONT	G-53 & C-57
R.H. FRONT	G-53 & H-57
R.H. FRONT (CARGO)	F-57 & F-53
R.H. REAR	E-53 & E-57
DUAL BRAKE WARNING LAMP	H-18
DUAL BRAKE WARNING SWITCH	J-18
E.S.C. SOLENOID VACUUM VALVE	K-13
ELECTRONIC DIST. MODULATOR	G-13
EMERGENCY WARNING FLASHER	D-53
EMERGENCY WARNING SWITCH	C-51
ENGINE TEMPERATURE SWITCH	J-20
FUEL GAGE	E-21
FUEL SENDER	J-21
HEADLAMPS:	
DIMMER SWITCH	E-40
HI-BEAM INDICATOR LAMP	F-40
SWITCH	C-41
L.H.	J-41
R.H.	J-42
HEATER:	
AUXILIARY	J-31
AUXILIARY SWITCH	E-31
BLOWER MOTOR	D-30
BLOWER MOTOR RESISTOR	E-30
THERMOSTAT SWITCH	D-32
HEATER SWITCH	H-30
HORN:	
STANDARD	J-44
SWITCH	J-44
R.P.O.	J-45
RELAY	G-44
IGNITION COIL	F-3
IGNITION SWITCH	C-20
LICENSE LAMP	J-51
MARKER LAMPS:	
L.H. FRONT	J-47
R.H. FRONT	J-48
L.H. REAR	J-50
R.H. REAR	J-53
NEUTRAL START SWITCH	C-16
NEUTRAL START & BACK-UP LAMP SWITCH (AUTO. TRANS.)	F-28
OIL PRESSURE:	
GAGE	E-22
SENDER (GAGES)	J-22
SWITCH (LIGHTS)	J-23
WARNING LAMPS	E-23
PARK & TURN SIGNAL LAMPS:	
L.H.	J-46
R.H.	J-49
RADIO RECEIVER	F-32
RADIO SPEAKER	H-32
SCHOOL BUS WARNING LAMPS	
L.H. FRONT	K-56
R.H. FRONT	K-57
L.H. REAR	K-59
R.H. REAR	K-58
SPEEDO SENSOR	J-11
STARTER MOTOR RELAY	C-5
STARTER MOTOR	H-5
STOP LAMP SWITCH	D-48
STOP & TURN SIGNAL LAMPS:	
L.H.	J-51
R.H.	J-52
SUPPRESSION CAPACITOR	G-9 & G-12
T.R.S. SOLENOID VACUUM VALVE	K-15
TEMPERATURE GAGE	E-20
TRANSMISSION SENSOR SWITCH	K-14
TURN SIGNAL FLASHER	D-53 & C-27
TURN SIGNAL INDICATOR LAMPS:	
L.H.	F-50
R.H.	F-50
TURN SIGNAL SWITCH	C-50
WARNING LAMPS (SCHOOL BUS)	
FLASHER	C-59
RELAY	A-59
SWITCH	A-57
WINDSHIELD:	
WASHER MOTOR PUMP	H-25
WIPER MOTOR	J-24
WIPER SWITCH	D-24
WASHER SWITCH	E-25

WIRING COLOR KEY

PRIMARY COLORS

BLACK	BK
BROWN	BR
RED	R
PINK	PK
ORANGE	O
YELLOW	Y
GREEN	G
BLUE	B
GRAY	GY
WHITE	W
VIOLET	V

Wiring diagram for 1972 model Econolines

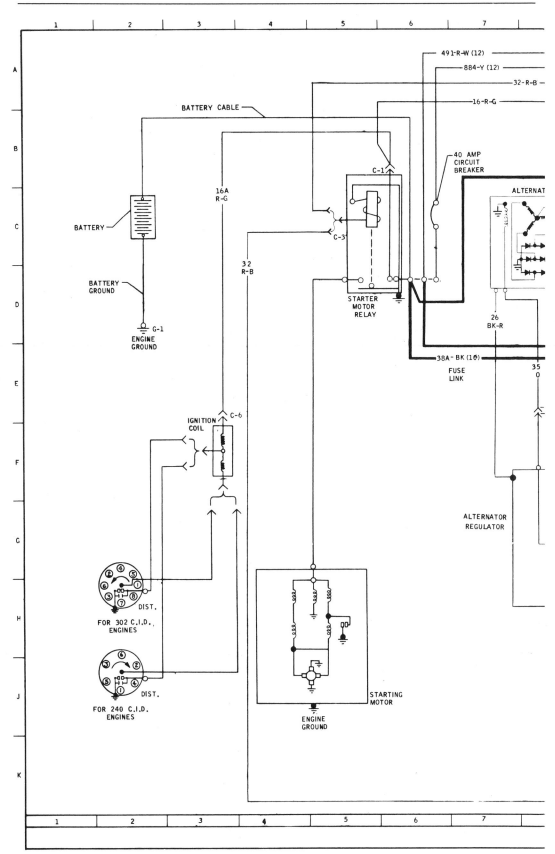

Wiring diagram for 1972 model Econolines

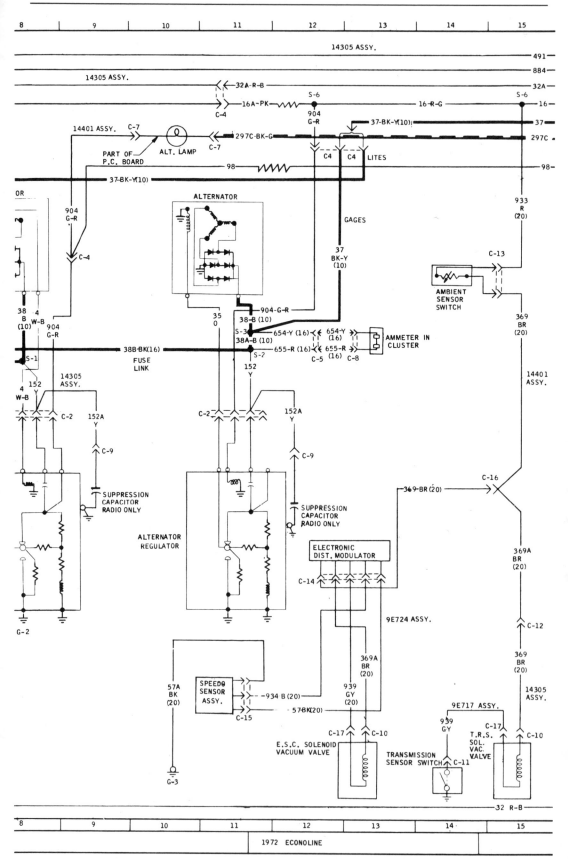

Wiring diagram for 1972 model Econolines

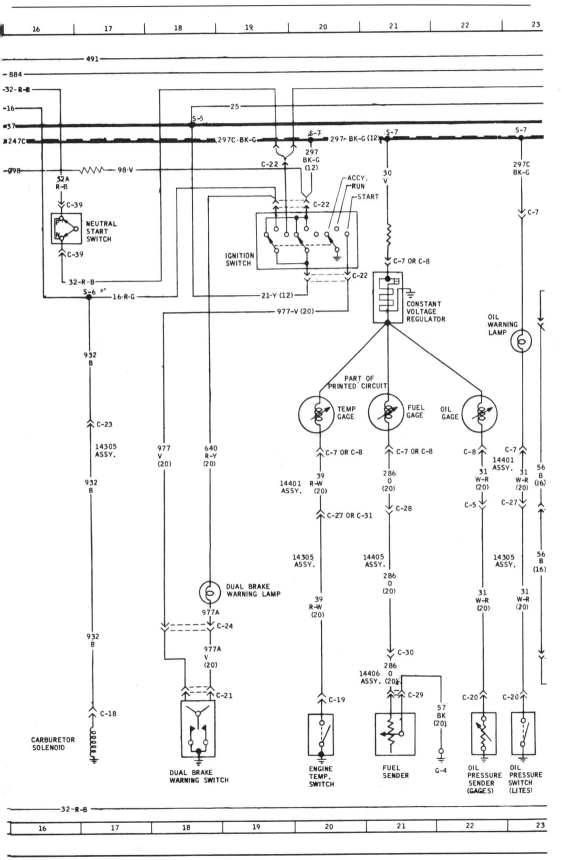

Wiring diagram for 1972 model Econolines

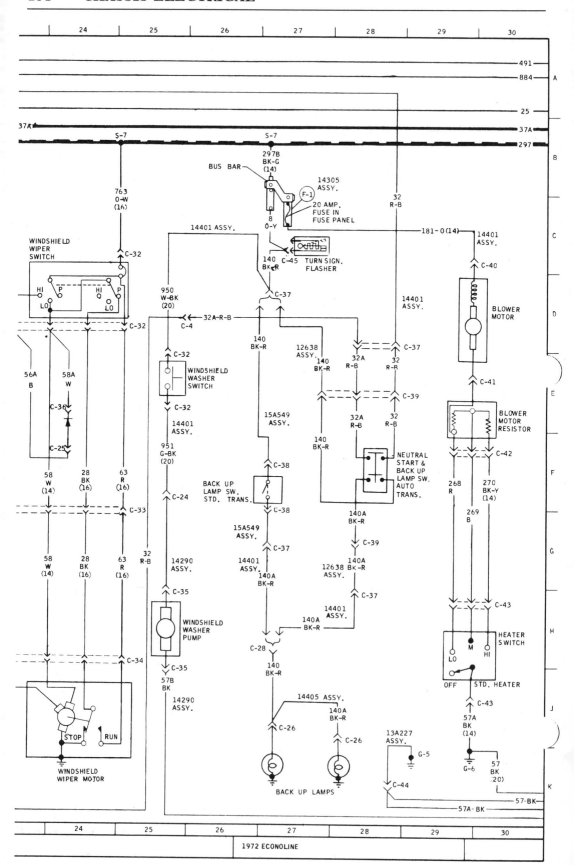

Wiring diagram for 1972 model Econolines

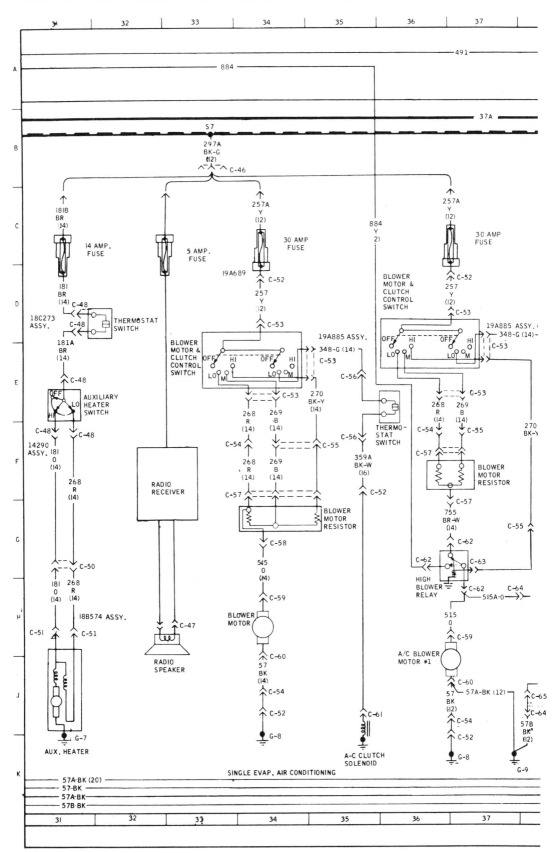

Wiring diagram for 1972 model Econolines

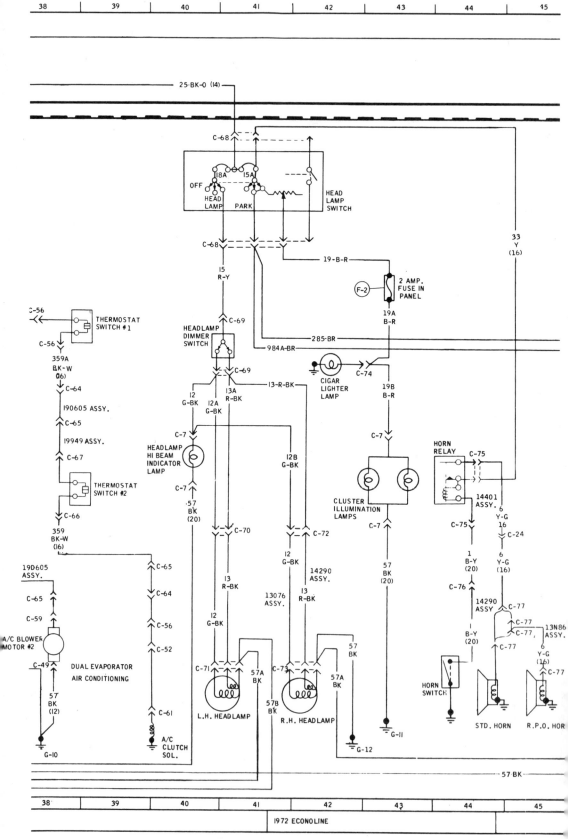

Wiring diagram for 1972 model Econolines

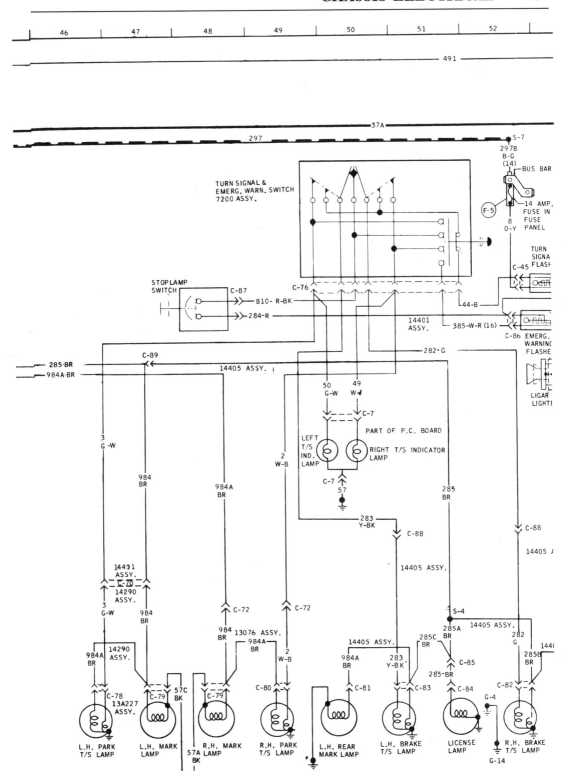

Wiring diagram for 1972 model Econolines

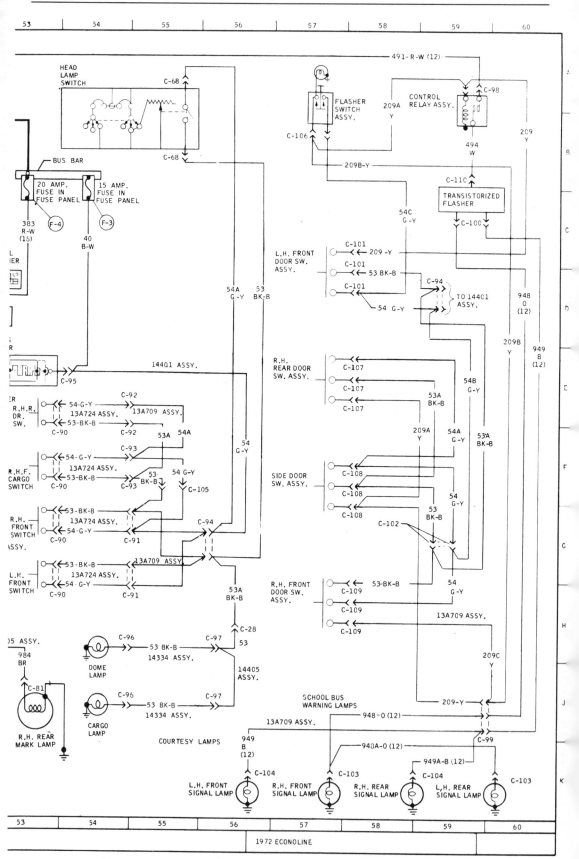

Wiring diagram for 1972 model Econolines

INDEX

WIRING COLOR KEY
PRIMARY COLORS

BLACK	BK	DARK BLUE	DB
BROWN	BR	LIGHT BLUE	LB
TAN	T	PURPLE	P
RED	R	GRAY	GY
PINK	PK	WHITE	W
ORANGE	O	HASH	(H)
YELLOW	Y	DOT	(D)
DARK GREEN	DG	STRIPE IS UNDERSTOOD	
LIGHT GREEN	LG	AND HAS NO COLOR KEY	

Wiring diagram for 1973–74 model

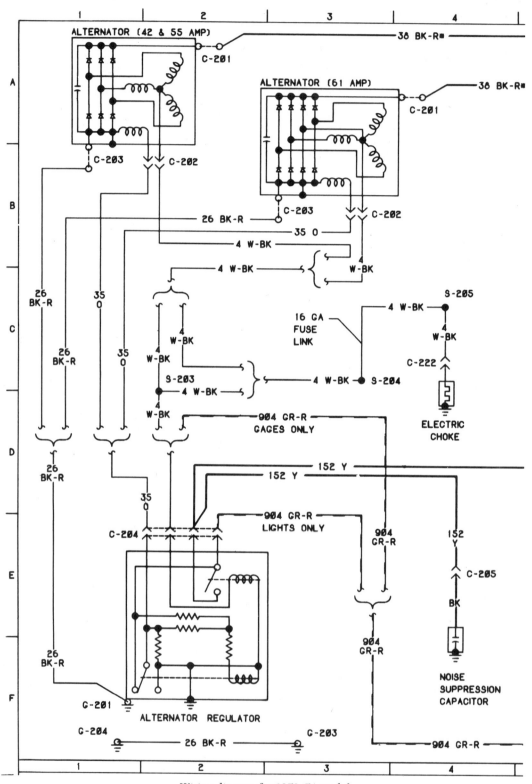

Wiring diagram for 1973–74 model

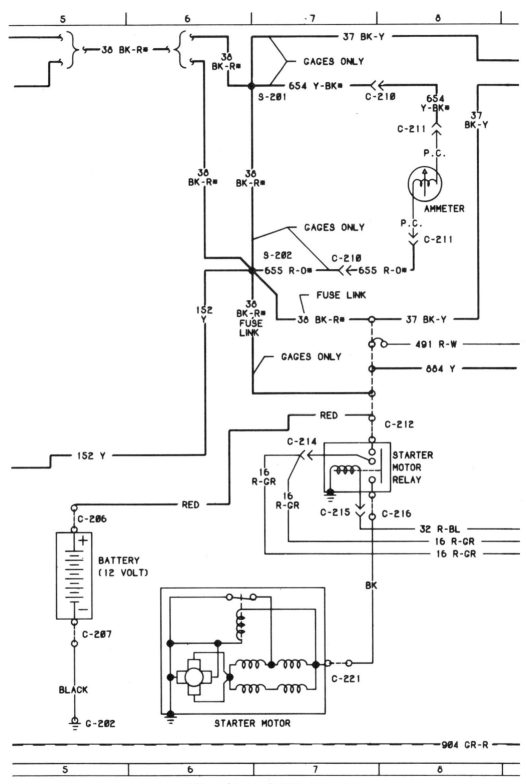

Wiring diagram for 1973–74 model

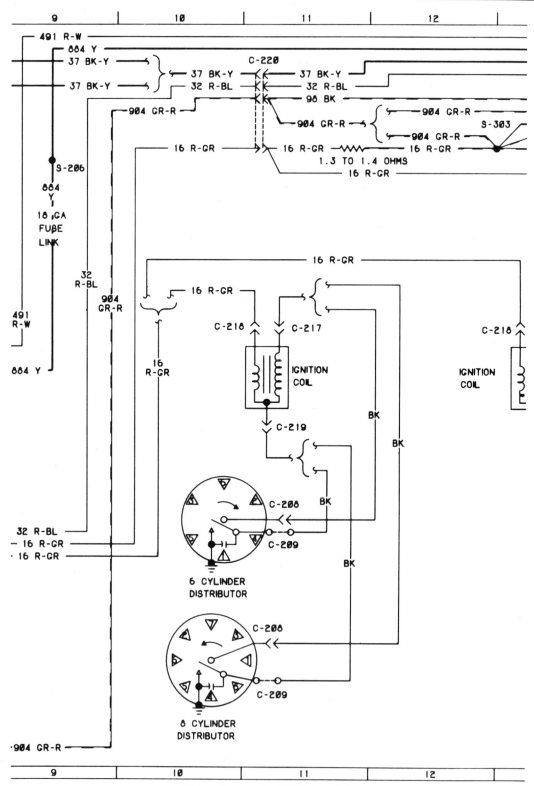

Wiring diagram for 1973–74 model

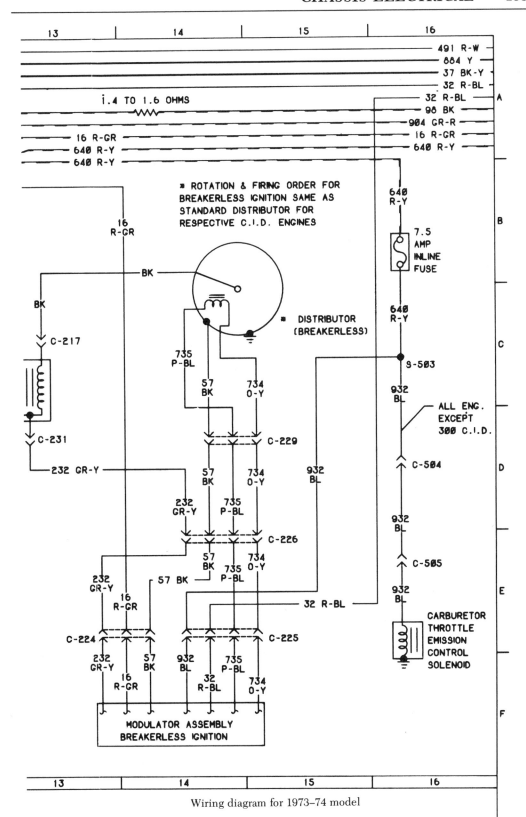

Wiring diagram for 1973–74 model

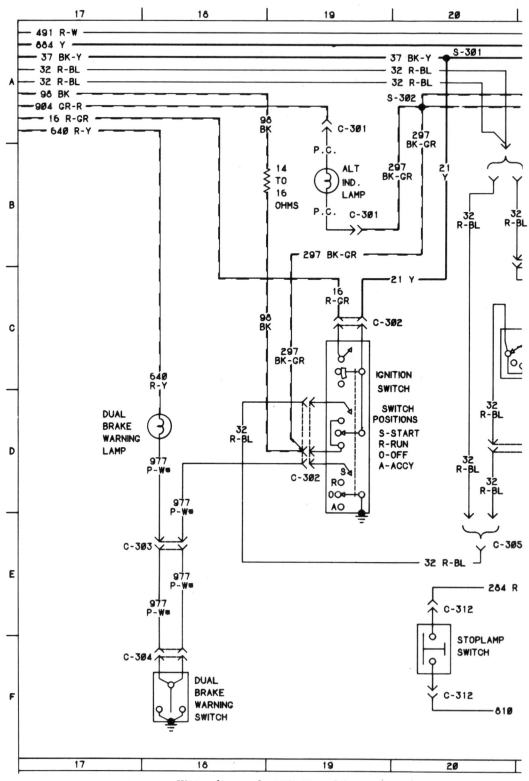

Wiring diagram for 1973–74 model

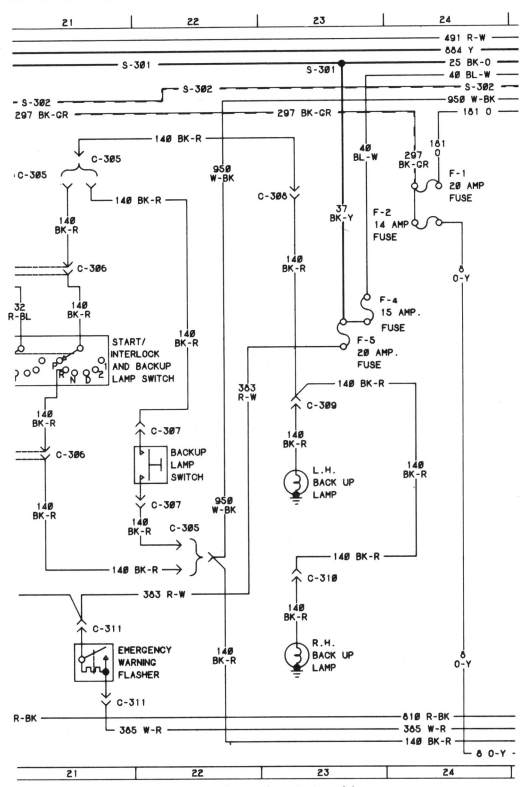

Wiring diagram for 1973–74 model

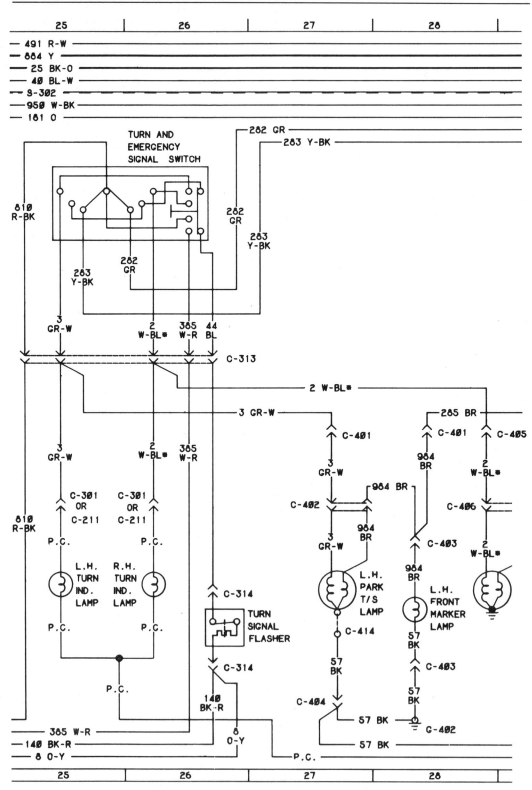

Wiring diagram for 1973–74 model

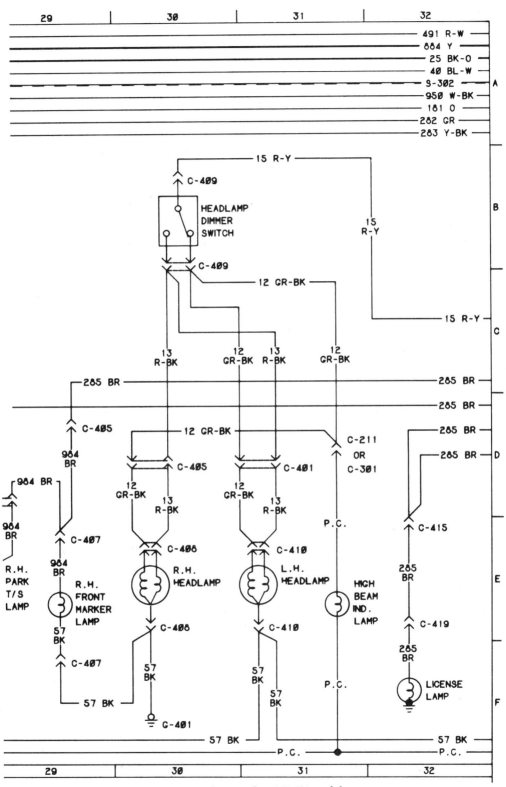

Wiring diagram for 1973–74 model

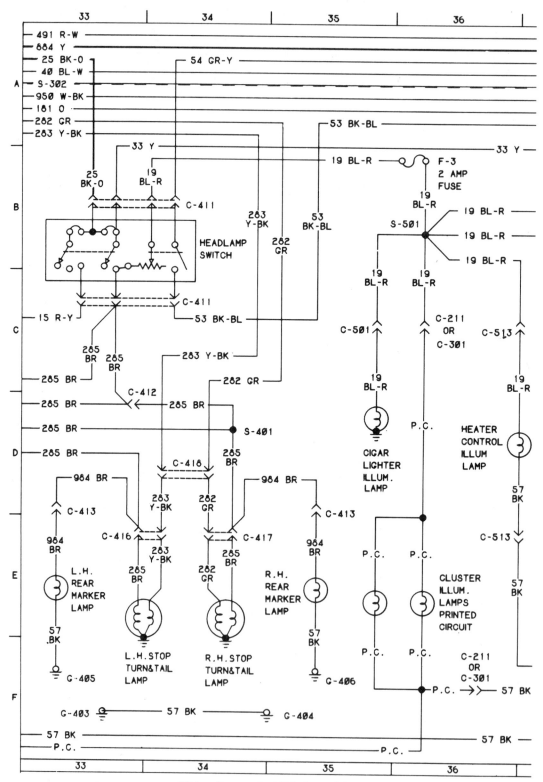

Wiring diagram for 1973–74 model

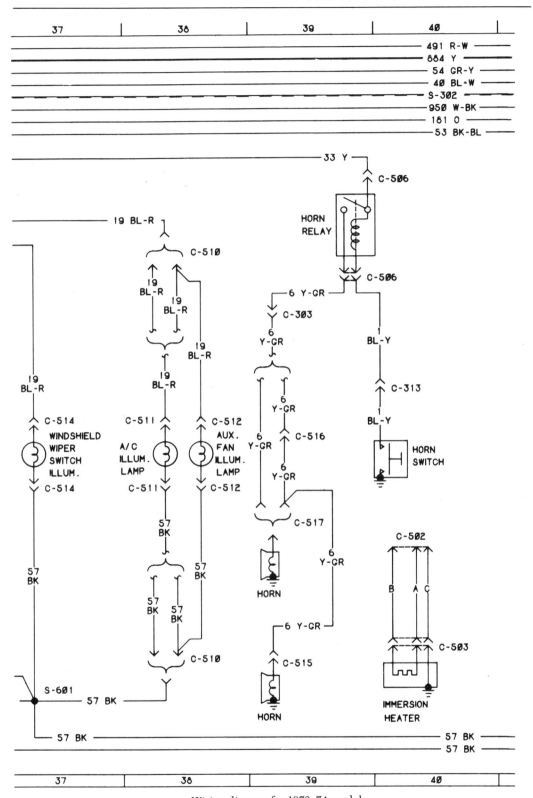

Wiring diagram for 1973–74 model

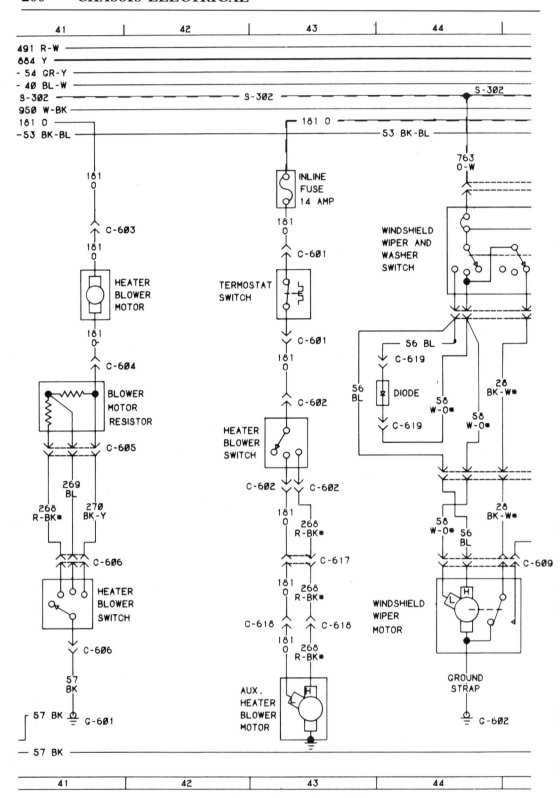

Wiring diagram for 1973–74 model

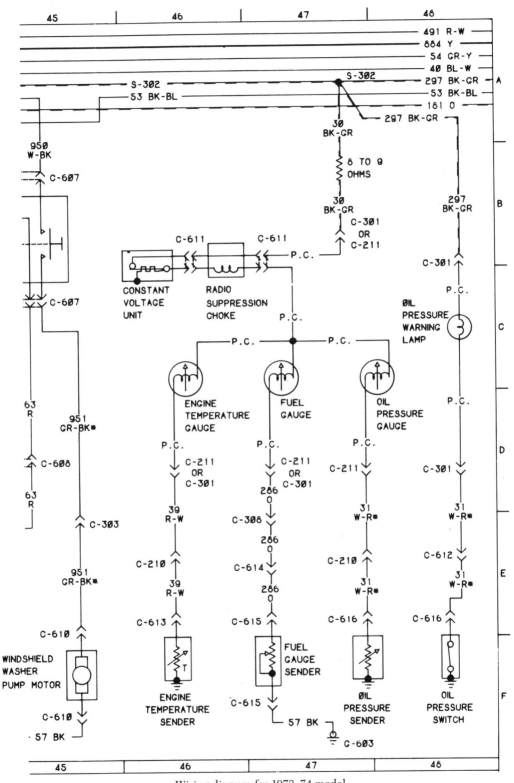

Wiring diagram for 1973–74 model

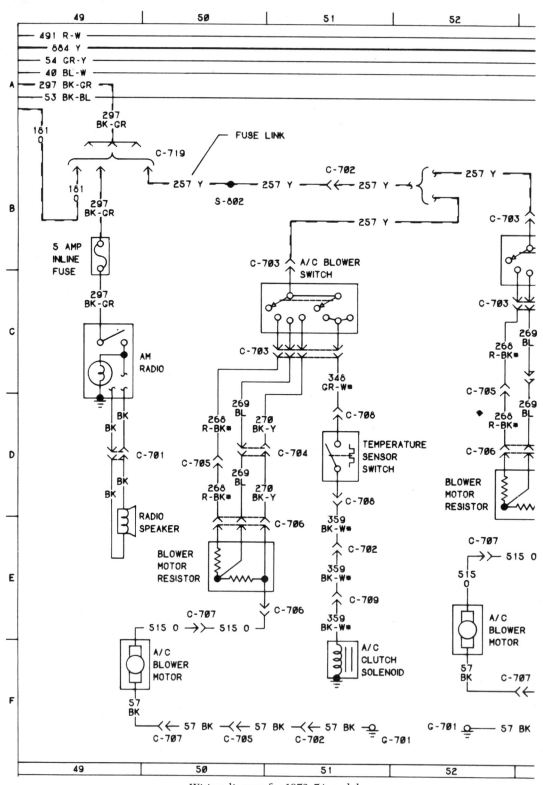

Wiring diagram for 1973–74 model

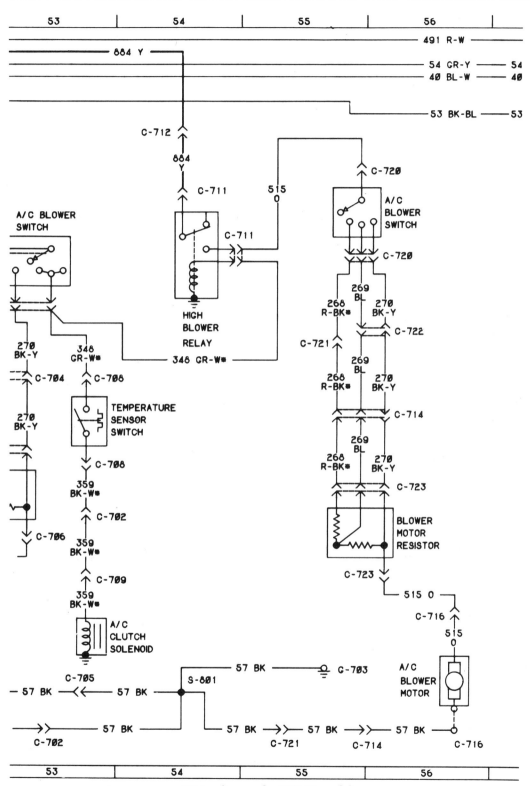

Wiring diagram for 1973–74 model

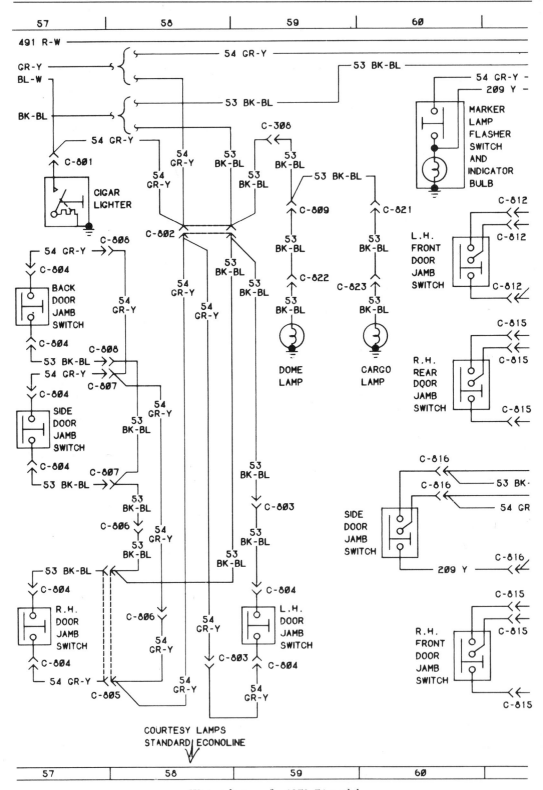

Wiring diagram for 1973–74 model

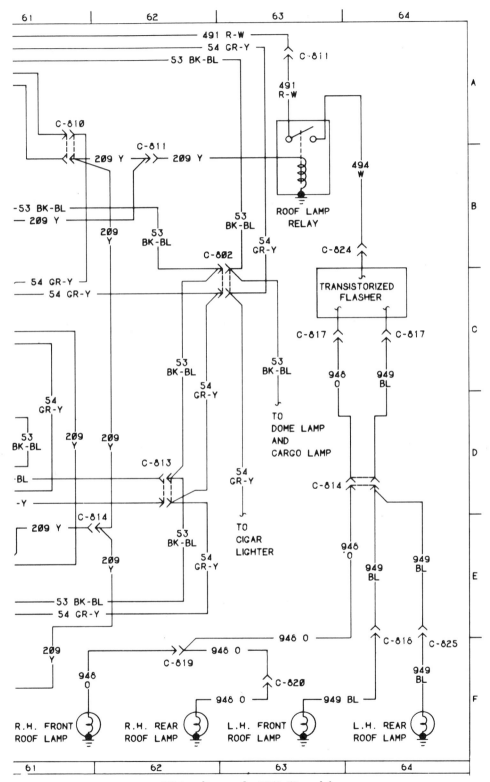

Wiring diagram for 1973–74 model

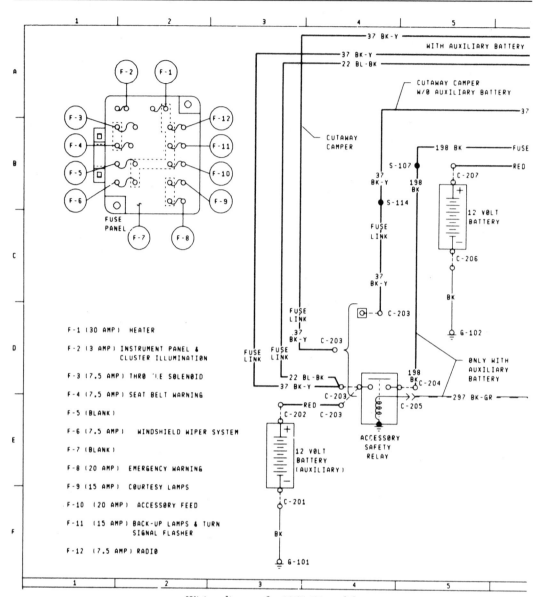

F-1 (30 AMP) HEATER

F-2 (3 AMP) INSTRUMENT PANEL &
CLUSTER ILLUMINATION

F-3 (7.5 AMP) THROTTLE SOLENOID

F-4 (7.5 AMP) SEAT BELT WARNING

F-5 (BLANK)

F-6 (7.5 AMP) WINDSHIELD WIPER SYSTEM

F-7 (BLANK)

F-8 (20 AMP) EMERGENCY WARNING

F-9 (15 AMP) COURTESY LAMPS

F-10 (20 AMP) ACCESSORY FEED

F-11 (15 AMP) BACK-UP LAMPS & TURN
SIGNAL FLASHER

F-12 (7.5 AMP) RADIO

Wiring diagram for 1975–77 models

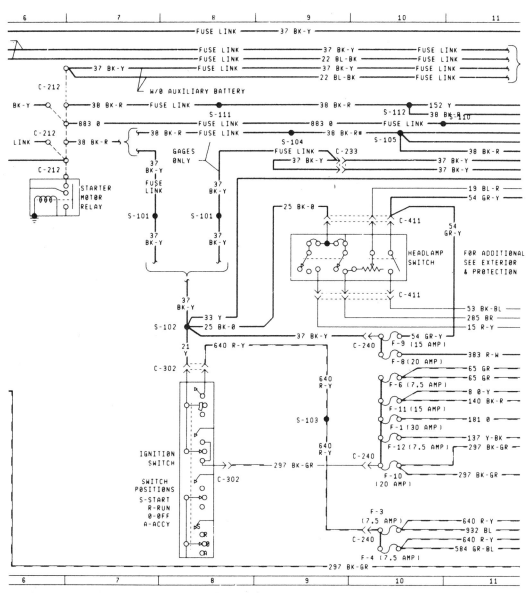

Wiring diagram for 1975–77 models

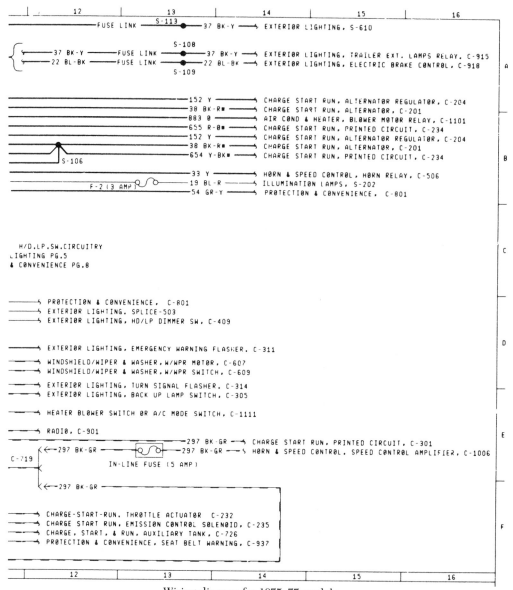

Wiring diagram for 1975–77 models

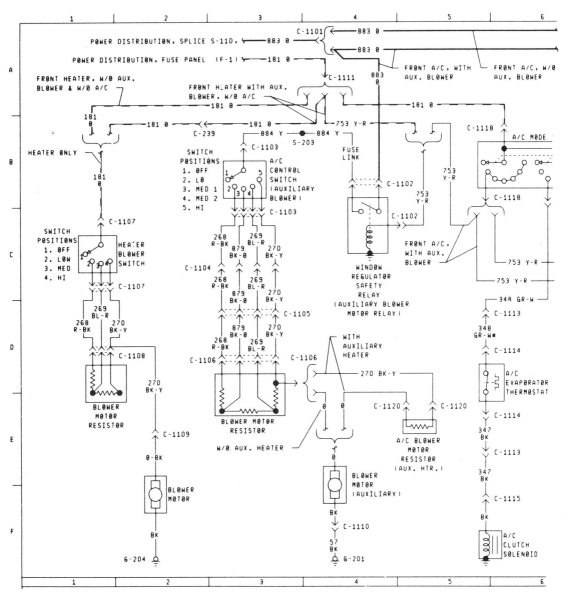

Wiring diagram for 1975–77 models

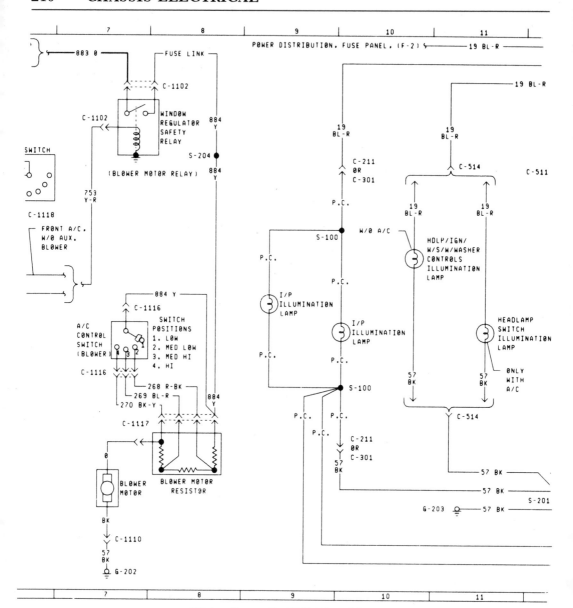

Wiring diagram for 1975–77 models

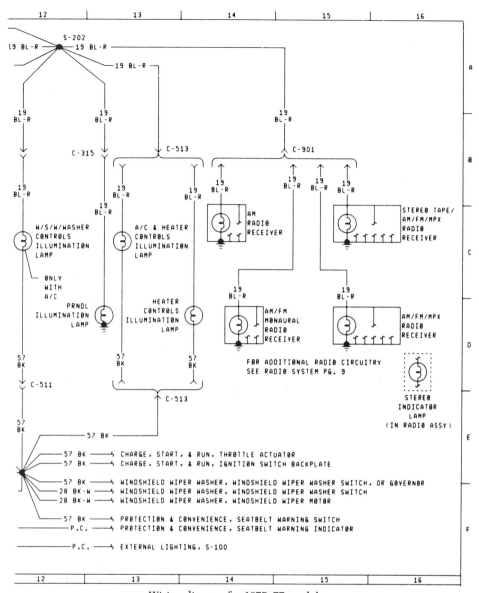

Wiring diagram for 1975–77 models

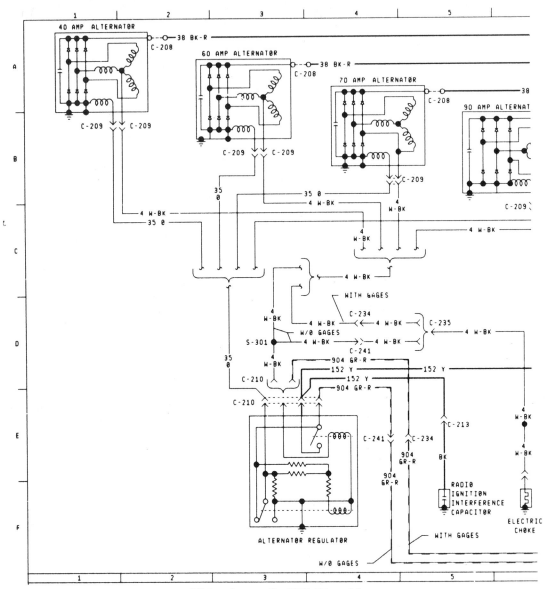

Wiring diagram for 1975–77 models

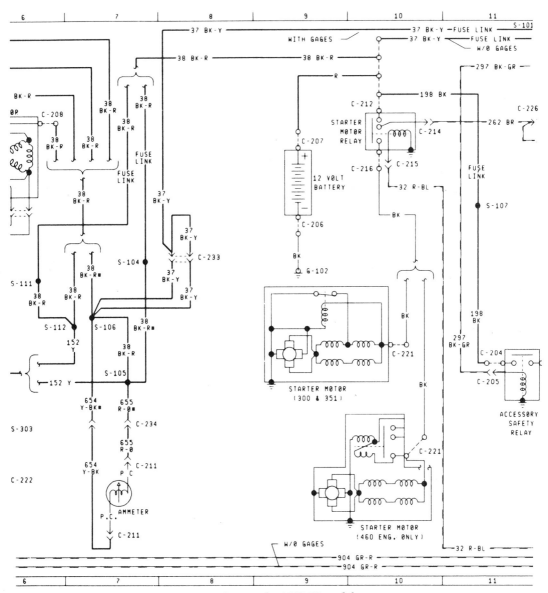

Wiring diagram for 1975–77 models

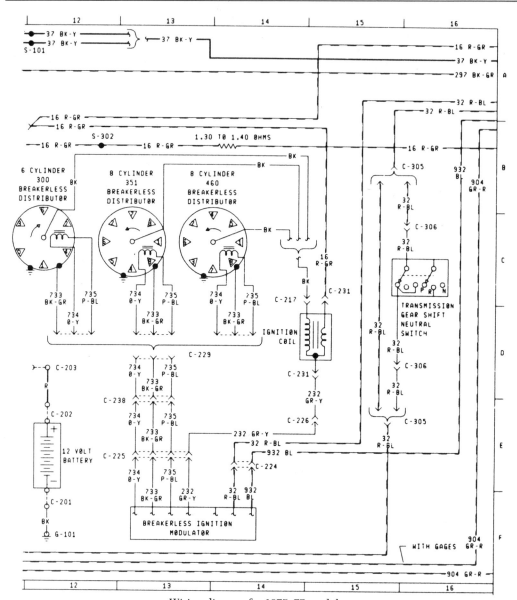

Wiring diagram for 1975–77 models

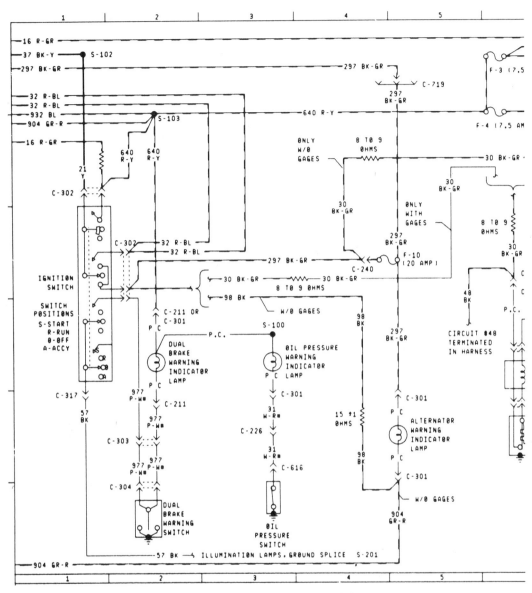

Wiring diagram for 1975–77 models

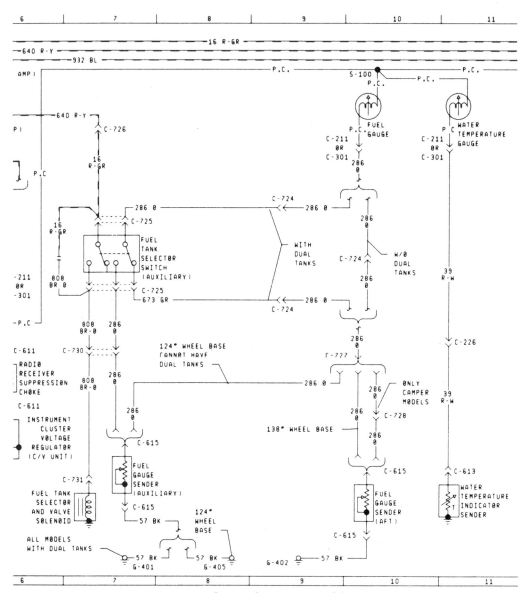

Wiring diagram for 1975–77 models

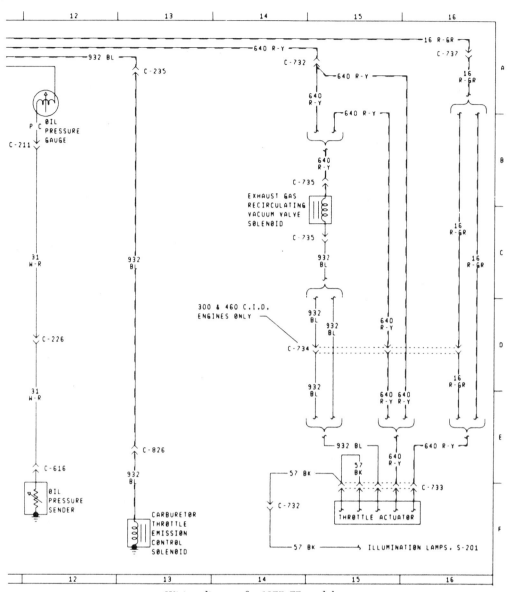

Wiring diagram for 1975–77 models

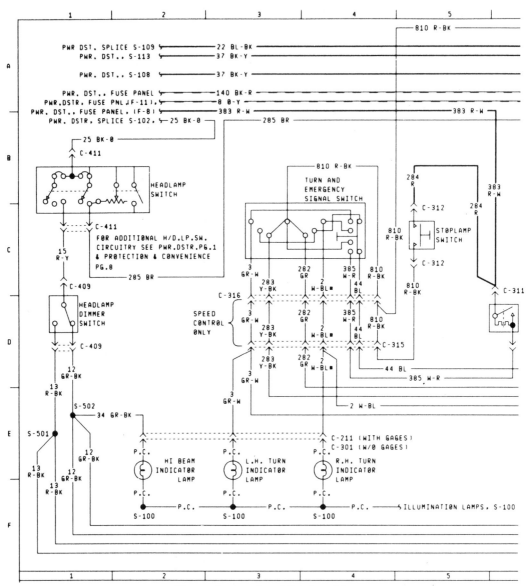

Wiring diagram for 1975–77 models

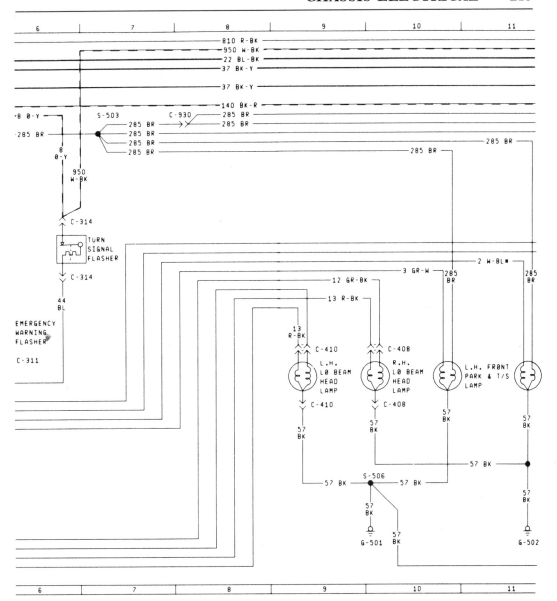

Wiring diagram for 1975–77 models

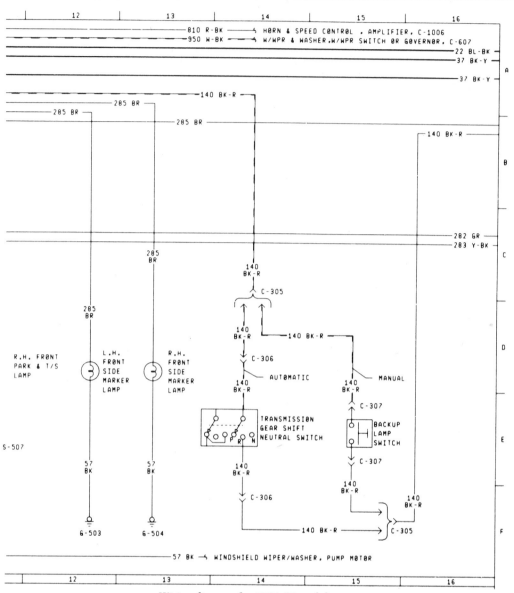

Wiring diagram for 1975–77 models

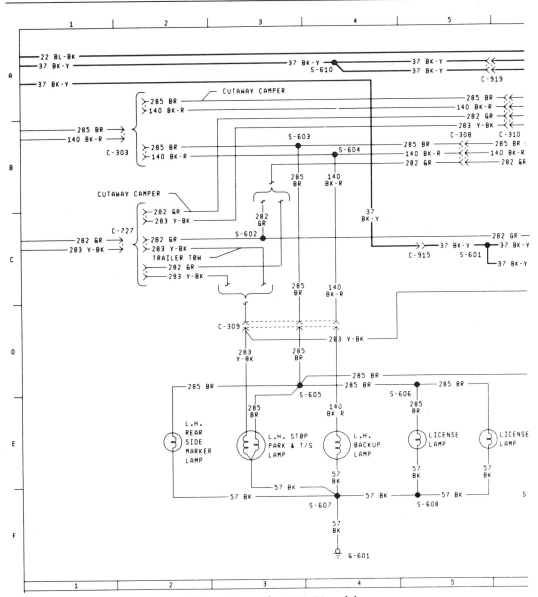

Wiring diagram for 1975–77 models

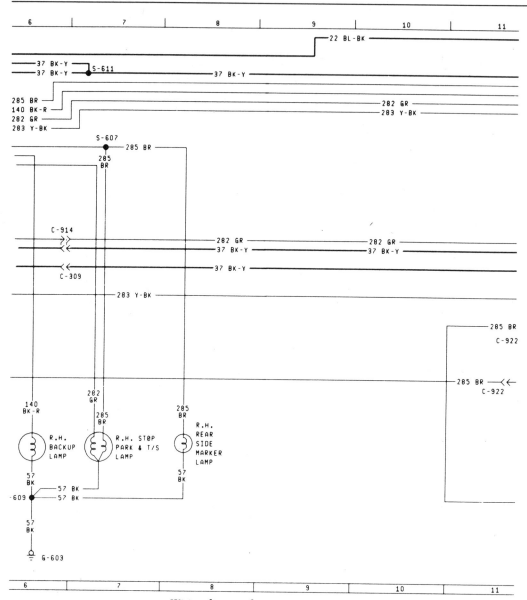

Wiring diagram for 1975–77 models

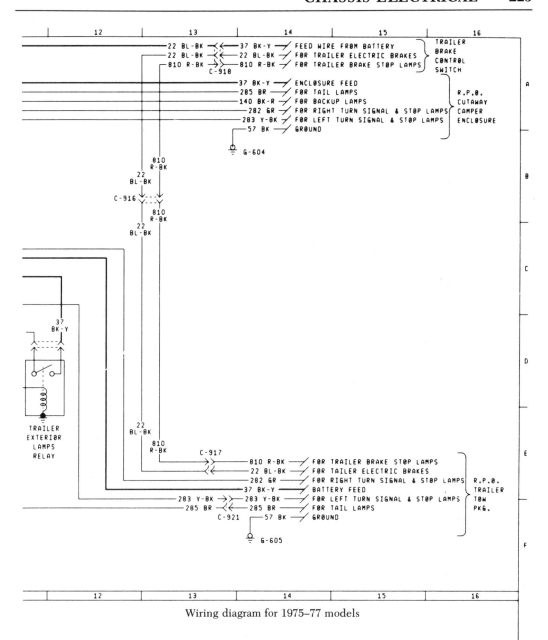

| | 12 | 13 | 14 | 15 | 16 |

22 BL-BK ←← 37 BK-Y FEED WIRE FROM BATTERY
22 BL-BK ←← 22 BL-BK FOR TRAILER ELECTRIC BRAKES
810 R-BK →→ 810 R-BK FOR TRAILER BRAKE STOP LAMPS
C-918

TRAILER
BRAKE
CONTROL
SWITCH

37 BK-Y ENCLOSURE FEED
285 BR FOR TAIL LAMPS
140 BK-R FOR BACKUP LAMPS
282 GR FOR RIGHT TURN SIGNAL & STOP LAMPS
283 Y-BK FOR LEFT TURN SIGNAL & STOP LAMPS
57 BK GROUND

R.P.O.
CUTAWAY
CAMPER
ENCLOSURE

G-604

810 R-BK
22 BL-BK
C-916
810 R-BK
22 BL-BK

22 BL-BK
810 R-BK
C-917

37 BK-Y

TRAILER
EXTERIOR
LAMPS
RELAY

810 R-BK FOR TRAILER BRAKE STOP LAMPS
22 BL-BK FOR TAILER ELECTRIC BRAKES
282 GR FOR RIGHT TURN SIGNAL & STOP LAMPS
37 BK-Y BATTERY FEED
283 Y-BK →→ 283 Y-BK FOR LEFT TURN SIGNAL & STOP LAMPS
285 BR ←← 285 BR FOR TAIL LAMPS
C-921   57 BK GROUND

R.P.O.
TRAILER
TOW
PKG.

G-605

Wiring diagram for 1975–77 models

| | 12 | 13 | 14 | 15 | 16 |

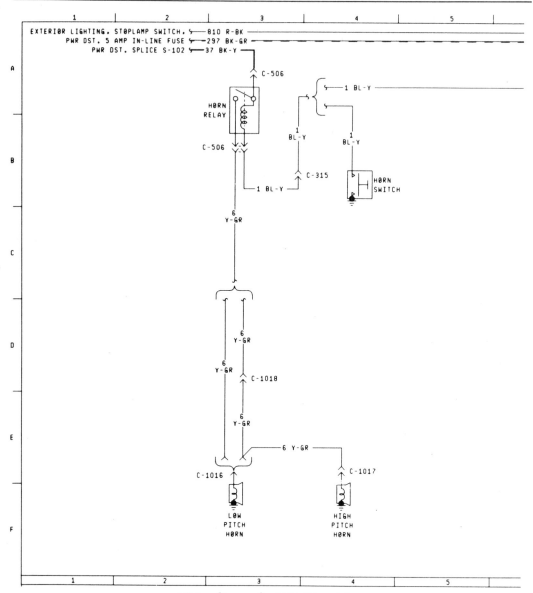

EXTERIOR LIGHTING, STOPLAMP SWITCH, ⎯ 810 R-BK
PWR DST. 5 AMP IN-LINE FUSE ⎯ 297 BK-GR
PWR DST. SPLICE S-102 ⎯ 37 BK-Y

C-506

HORN
RELAY

1 BL-Y

C-506

1
BL-Y

1
BL-Y

C-315

HORN
SWITCH

1 BL-Y

6
Y-GR

6
Y-GR

6
Y-GR

C-1018

6
Y-GR

6 Y-GR

C-1017

C-1016

LOW
PITCH
HORN

HIGH
PITCH
HORN

Wiring diagram for 1975–77 models

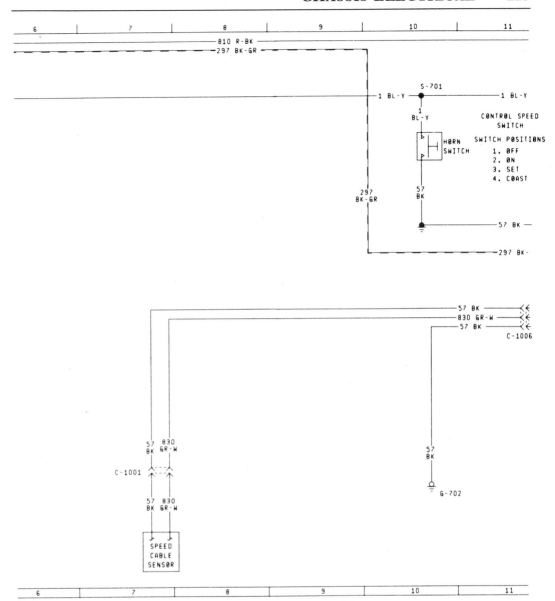

Wiring diagram for 1975–77 models

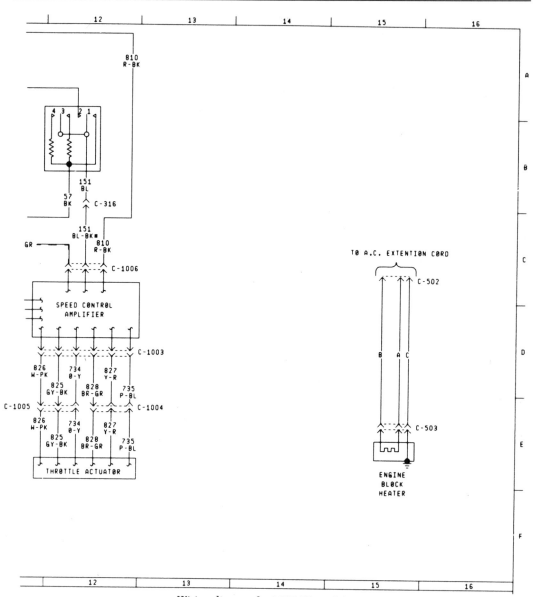

Wiring diagram for 1975–77 models

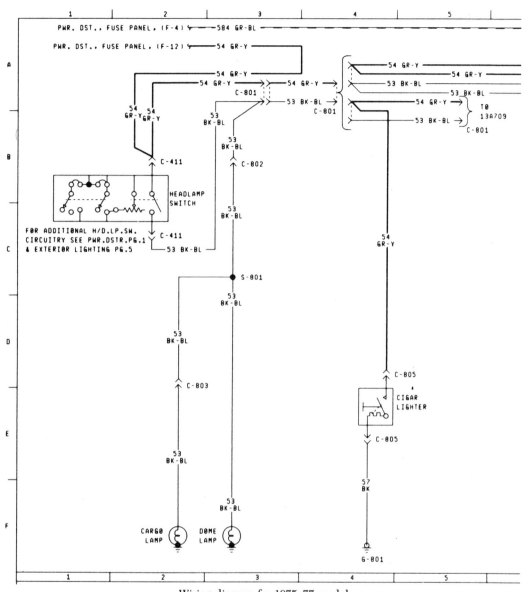

Wiring diagram for 1975–77 models

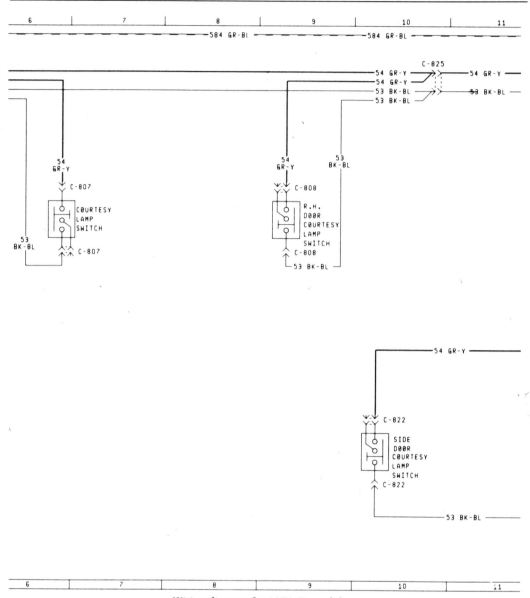

Wiring diagram for 1975–77 models

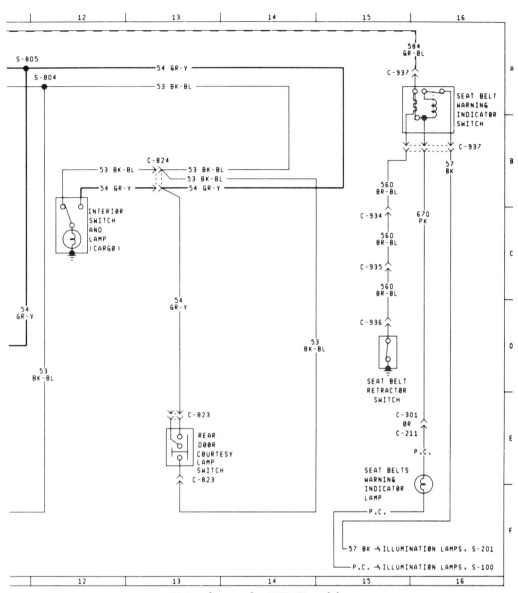

Wiring diagram for 1975–77 models

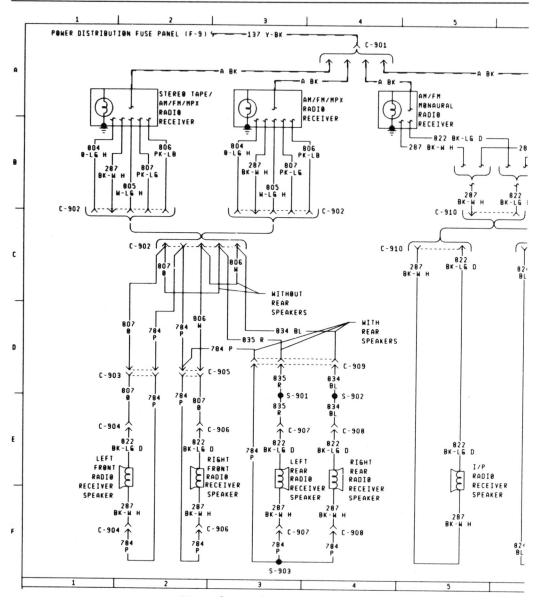

Wiring diagram for 1975–77 models

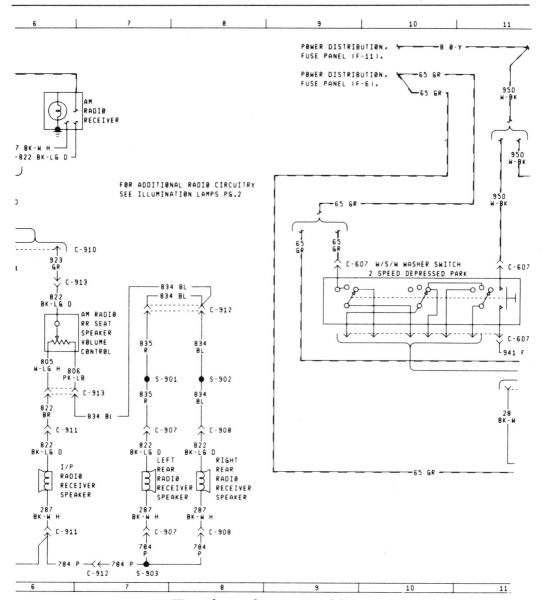

Wiring diagram for 1975–77 models

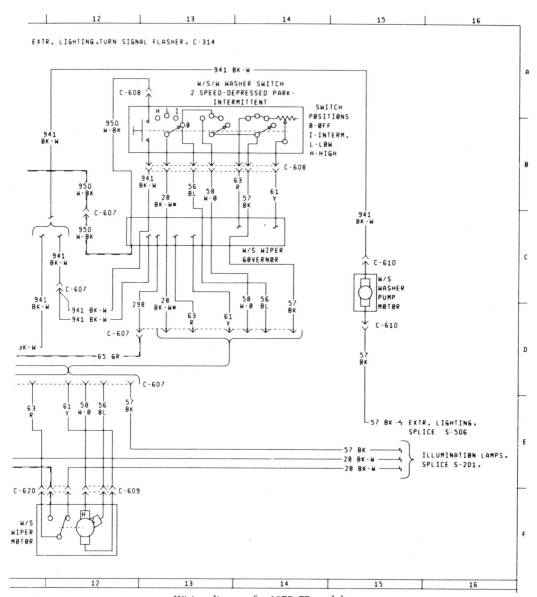

Wiring diagram for 1975–77 models

Clutch and Transmission

Manual Transmission

All Ford vans use a Ford Model 3.03 three-speed manual transmission; the shifter is mounted on the steering column. The number 3.03 is the distance in inches between the centerlines of the countershaft and the input shaft.

Removal and Installation

1. Raise the vehicle on a hoist and drain the lubricant from the transmission by removing the lower extension housing-to-transmission bolt.

2. Disconnect the driveshaft from the flange at the transmission. Secure the front end of the driveshaft out of the way by tying it up with a length of wire.

3. Disconnect the speedometer cable from the extension housing and disconnect the gearshift rods from the transmission. Disconnect the transmission regulated spark switch, if so equipped.

4. Position a transmission jack under the transmission. Chain the transmission to the jack.

5. On 1966 and 1967 vehicles, remove the transmission rear support bolts. Lower the engine enough to drop the transmission extension housing from the rear support.

On 1968 and later vehicles, raise the transmission slightly and remove the 4 bolts which retain the transmission support crossmember to the frame side rails. Remove the bolt which retains the transmission extension housing to the crossmember.

6. Remove the 4 transmission-to-flywheel housing bolts.

7. On the 1968 and later vehicles, position a bar under the rear of the engine to support it.

8. Remove the transmission from the vehicle by lowering the jack.

To install the transmission:

9. Make sure that the machined surfaces of the transmission case and the flywheel housing are free of dirt, paint, and burrs.

10. Install a guide pin in each lower mounting bolt hole.

11. Start the input shaft through the release bearing. Align the splines on the input shaft with the splines in the clutch disc. Move the transmission forward on the guide pins until the input shaft pilot enters the bearing or bushing in the crankshaft. If the transmission front bearing retainer binds up on the clutch release bearing hub, work the release bearing lever until the hub slides onto the transmission front bearing retainer. Install the two upper mounting bolts and lockwashers which attach the flywheel housing to the transmission. Remove the

two guide pins and install the lower mounting bolts and lockwashers.

12. On 1966 and 1967 vehicles, raise the jack enough to align the extension housing with the mounting holes in the hanger bracket. Install the attaching bolts. Remove the jack.

13. On 1968 and later vehicles, raise the jack slightly and remove the engine support bar. Position the support crossmember on the frame side rails and install the retaining bolts. Install the extension housing-to-crossmember retaining bolt.

14. Connect the gearshift rods and the speedometer cable. Connect the transmission regulated spark switch lead, if so equipped.

15. Install the driveshaft.

16. Fill the transmission to the bottom of the filler hole with the proper lubricant.

17. Adjust the clutch pedal free-play and the shift linkage as required.

Shift Linkage Adjustment

1. Place the gearshift lever in the Neutral position.

2. Loosen the adjustment nuts on the transmission shift levers sufficiently to allow the shift rods to slide freely on the transmission shift levers.

3. Insert a ¼ in. rod ($^3/_{16}$ in. for 1976–77) through the pilot hole in the shift tube mounting bracket (1967–75 only) until it enters the adjustment hole of both the upper and lower shift lever.

4. Place the transmission shift levers in the Neutral position and tighten the adjustment nuts on the transmission shift levers.

5. Remove the ¼ in. rod from the pilot hole, and check the operation of the gearshift lever in all gear positions.

Clutch

Removal and Installation

1. Disconnect the cable from the starter and remove the starter.

2. Remove the transmission.

3. Disconnect the release lever retracting spring and release the rod.

4. Remove the hub and release bearing assembly.

5. Remove the flywheel housing-to-

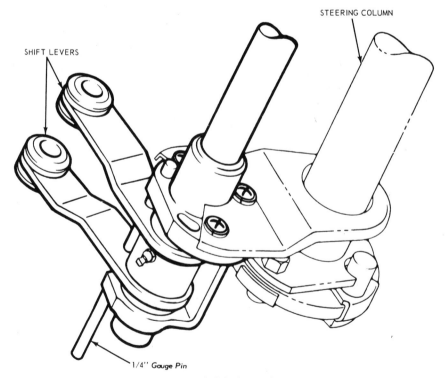

SHIFT LEVERS

STEERING COLUMN

1/4" Gauge Pin

1967–75 Gearshift linkage adjustment

engine bolts, and lower the flywheel housing.

6. Remove the pressure plate and the disc from the flywheel. Unscrew the attaching bolts a few turns at a time, in a staggered sequence to prevent distortion of the pressure plate.

7. Wash the flywheel surface with alcohol. Do not use an oil-base cleaner, carbon tetrachloride or gasoline.

To install the clutch:

8. Place the clutch disc and the pressure plate and cover assembly in position on the flywheel. Start the retaining bolts until finger-tight.

9. Align the clutch disc with a clutch arbor (an old mainshaft works well) and then evenly torque the bolts to 23–28 ft lbs.

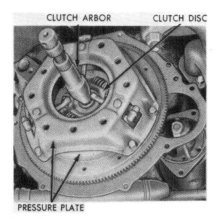

Installing the clutch, using an alignment arbor to align the clutch disc spline

10. Lightly lubricate the release lever fulcrum and ends with lithium-base grease and position the release lever in the flywheel housing. Do not grease the release lever pivot assembly on 1975–77 models. Crimp the dust seal tabs flush against the fly wheel housing. Attach the springs of the release bearing hub to the ends of the release fork. Be careful not to distort the springs.

11. Fill the groove in the clutch release bearing hub with lithium-base grease. Wipe the excess grease from the hub.

12. Position the flywheel housing and release lever assembly, and install the mounting bolts. Make sure that the muffler front hanger is in place on the flywheel housing. Install the dust cover, and tighten the attaching bolts.

13. Remove any dirt, paint, or burrs from the mounting surfaces of the flywheel housing and the transmission.

14. Install the transmission.

15. Install the starter and connect the starter cable.

16. Adjust the clutch pedal free-play and check the operation of the clutch.

Clutch Pedal Adjustment

To check and adjust the pedal free travel, measure and note the distance from the floor pan to the top of the pedal; then depress the pedal slowly until the clutch release fingers contact the clutch release bearing. Measure and record the distance. The difference between the reading with the pedal in the depressed position and the reading with the pedal in the fully released position is the pedal free travel. The free travel should be as specified. If the free travel is not within specifications, loosen the jam nut on the clutch release rod. Adjust the rod length until the free travel is correct, then tighten the nut.

The clutch pedal height should be within 7½–7¾ in. from the floor pan to the center of the clutch pedal on 1968–74 models. On other models, the pedal height is not adjustable. Pedal height is adjusted by loosening the nut securing the clutch pedal eccentric bumper and rotating the bumper until the proper clutch pedal height is within the proper range.

Clutch Pedal Free Travel (in.)

Year	Free Travel
1966–67	11⁄16–1⅛
1968–69	1⅛–1⅜
1970–72	1⅛–1½
1973–74	¾–1½
1975–77	¾–1½, 1¼–1½ preferred

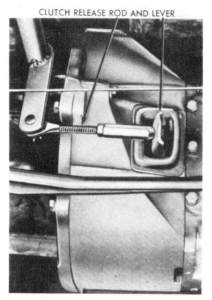

Clutch linkage (pedal travel) adjustment point at the bellhousing

Automatic Transmission

The C4 automatic transmission is used on all 1966–74 models and the 1975–77

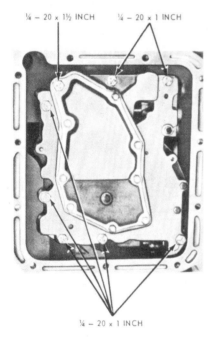

View of the underside of the C4 transmission with the pan removed showing the location of the transmission filter screen

E-100 and 150 sixes; the heavier-duty C6 is used on all other 1975–77 models. The C4 is identified by the letter G in the TRANS space on the Vehicle Certification Label; Z indicates the C6. Fluid changing and pan removal is covered in Chapter 1. The Maintenance Intervals Chart in Chapter 1 gives the recommended band adjustment intervals.

Front Band (Intermediate) Adjustment

C4 AND C6

1. Clean all dirt from the adjusting screw and remove and discard the locknut.
2. Install a new locknut on the adjusting screw. Using a torque wrench, tighten the adjusting screw to 10 ft lbs.
3. Back off the adjusting screw EXACTLY 1¾ TURNS FOR THE C4, 1½ TURNS FOR THE C6.
4. Hold the adjusting screw steady and tighten the locknut to 35–45 ft lbs.

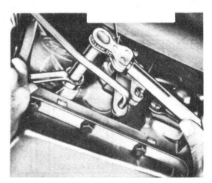

Adjusting the front (Intermediate) band

Rear Band (Low-Reverse) Adjustment

C4 ONLY

1. Clean all dirt from around the band adjusting screw and remove and discard the locknut.
2. Install a new locknut on the adjusting screw. Using a torque wrench, tighten the adjusting screw to 10 ft lbs.
3. Back off the adjusting screw EXACTLY 3 FULL TURNS.
4. Hold the adjusting screw steady and tighten the locknut to 35–45 ft lbs.

Shift Linkage Adjustment

1. On 1966 and 1967 Ford vans, place the shift lever in the Neutral position. On

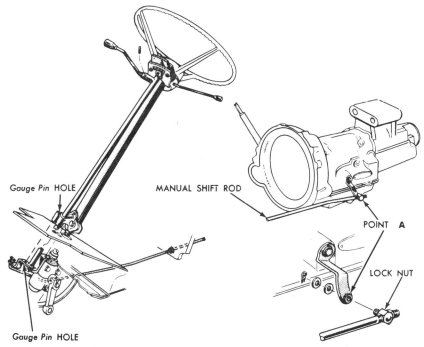

Gauge Pin HOLE   MANUAL SHIFT ROD

POINT **A**

LOCK NUT

Gauge Pin HOLE

Automatic transmission shift control linkage for 1966–67 models

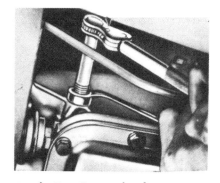

Adjusting the Low-Reverse band

all other model years, place the shift lever in the Drive position (parking brake applied, engine off).

2. Disconnect the manual shift rod from the shift lever on the transmission.

3. On 1966 and 1967 models, shift the transmission shift lever at the transmission into the Neutral position (fourth detent from the rear). On all other models, move the transmission shift lever at the transmission to the Drive position (second detent from the rear).

4. On the 1966 and 1967 models, insert a ¼ in. gauge pin through the steering column shift rod actuating lever and the steering column shift tube bracket to

hold the shift rod linkage in the Neutral position.

On all other models, just make sure that the steering column shift lever remains in the Drive position.

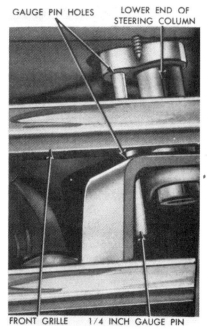

GAUGE PIN HOLES   LOWER END OF STEERING COLUMN

FRONT GRILLE   1/4 INCH GAUGE PIN

Installation of the gauge pin on 1966–67 models

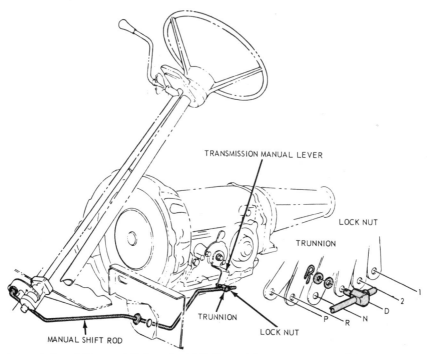

Automatic transmission shift control linkage for 1968–73 models. On 1972–73 models there are two locknuts on either side of the trunnion

5. With the linkage in the position mentioned above (Drive or Neutral) at the steering column shift lever and the shift lever on the transmission, adjust the trunnion on the transmission end of the shift rod so that it slips into the manual lever on the transmission easily.

NOTE: *On 1974–77 models, the end of*

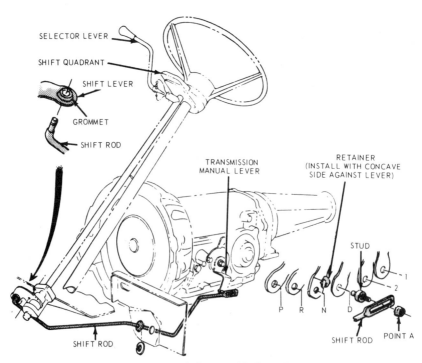

Automatic transmission shift control linkage for 1974–77 models

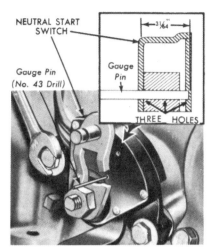

Neutral start switch adjustment

the shift rod is slotted and can be connected to the transmission at this point in the procedure. Tighten the attaching nut. This ends the linkage adjustment procedure for all 1974–77 models.

6. On 1966 and 1967 models, turn the trunnion 1 complete turn counter-clockwise to lengthen the rod. On 1968–71 models, turn the trunnion 4 complete turns counterclockwise to lengthen the rod. On 1972 and 1973 models, lock the trunnion in the original position described in Step 5.

7. Connect the trunnion to the shift lever at the transmission. Remove the gauge pin on 1966 and 1967 models.

8. Check the operation of the linkage and the transmission.

Neutral Start Switch Adjustment

1. With the manual shift linkage adjusted properly, loosen the two switch attaching bolts.

2. Place the transmission manual lever in Neutral. Rotate the switch and insert a No. 43 drill shank end into the gauge pin holes of the switch. The gauge pin (No. 43 drill) has to be inserted a full $^{31}/_{64}$ in. into the 3 holes of the switch.

3. Tighten the two neutral start switch attaching bolts 15 in. lbs. Remove the gauge pin from the switch.

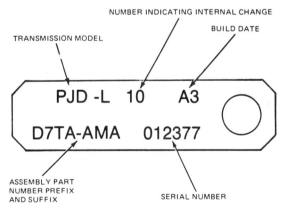

Typical automatic transmission identification tag

Chapter 7

Drive Train

Driveline

DRIVESHAFT

Short wheelbase vans use a single-piece driveshaft; long wheelbase models use a two-piece driveshaft with a support bearing and a sliding spline yoke at the center.

The driveshaft is joined to the transmission output shaft with sliding splines on all manual transmission short wheelbase models and 1973–77 automatic transmission models; it connects to a fixed yoke on the output shaft on all long

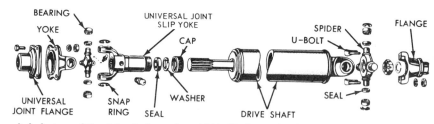

An exploded view of the driveshaft used on 1966–72 short wheelbase and automatic transmission

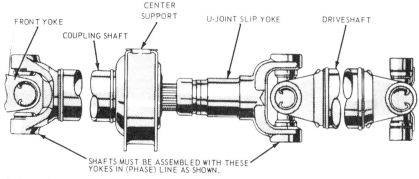

The driveshaft used on all long wheelbase manual transmission and 1966–72 long wheelbase automatic transmission

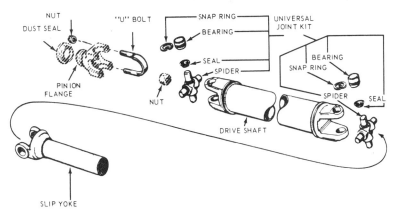

The driveshaft assembly used on all short wheelbase models with manual transmission and 1973–77 short wheelbase automatic transmission models

wheelbase manual transmission models and 1966–72 automatic transmission models.

Removal and Installation

One-Piece Driveshaft

1. If there are no alignment marks, matchmark the rear driveshaft yoke and the rear axle flange.

2. Unbolt the rear U-joint from the rear axle flange. Tape the bearing caps in place.

3. Unbolt the front U-joint from the transmission output shaft yoke on 1966–72 automatic transmission.

4. Pull the driveshaft back and remove it. You may have to plug the transmission extension housing to prevent leakage.

5. Reverse the procedure for installation. Grease the sliding splines used on all models except 1966–72 automatic transmission. Align the matchmarks.

NOTE: *If there is vibration in the driveline, try unbolting the driveshaft from the rear axle flange and turning it 180°.*

Two-Piece Driveshaft

1. If there are no alignment marks, matchmark the rear driveshaft yoke and the rear axle flange. Also matchmark the two driveshaft halves.

2. Unbolt the rear U-joint from the rear axle flange. Tape the bearing caps in place.

3. Slide the rear half of the driveshaft off the coupling shaft splines.

4. Unbolt and support the center bearing.

5. Unbolt the front U-joint from the transmission output shaft yoke except on 1973–77 automatic transmission.

6. Pull the front half of the driveshaft back and remove it. You may have to plug the transmission extension housing to prevent leakage.

7. Reverse the procedure for installation. Grease the sliding splines used on 1973–77 automatic transmission. Align all matchmarks, making sure that all U-joints are in the same horizontal plane.

U-JOINTS

Overhaul

1. Remove the driveshaft from the vehicle and place it in a vise, being careful not to damage it.

2. Remove the snap-rings which retain the bearings in the flange and in the driveshaft.

3. Remove the driveshaft tube from the vise and position the U-joint in the vise with a socket smaller than the bearing cap on one side and a socket larger than the bearing cap on the other side.

4. Slowly tighten the jaws of the vise so that the smaller socket forces the U-joint spider and the opposite bearing into the larger socket.

5. Remove the other side of the spider in the same manner (if applicable) and remove the spider assembly from the driveshaft. Discard the spider assemblies.

6. Clean all foreign matter from the yoke areas at the end of the driveshaft(s). Grease the new bearings.

7. Start the new spider and one of the bearing cap assemblies into a yoke by positioning the yoke in a vise with the spider positioned in place with one of the bearing cap assemblies positioned over one of the holes in the yoke. Slowly close the vise, pressing the bearing cap assembly in the yoke. Press the cap in far enough so that the retaining snap-ring can be installed. Use the smaller socket to recess the bearing cap.

8. Open the vise and position the opposite bearing cap assembly over the proper hole in the yoke with the socket that is smaller than the diameter of the bearing cap located on the cap. Slowly close the vise, pressing the bearing cap into the hole in the yoke with the socket. Make sure that the spider assembly is in line with the bearing cap as it is pressed in. Press the bearing cap in far enough so that the retaining snap-ring can be installed.

9. Install all remaining U-joints in the same manner.

10. Install the driveshaft.

CENTER BEARING

Removal and Installation

1. Remove the driveshafts.

2. Remove the two center support bearing attaching bolts and remove the assembly from the vehicle.

3. Do not immerse the sealed bearing in any type of cleaning fluid. Wipe the bearing and cushion clean with a cloth dampened with cleaning fluid.

4. Check the bearing for wear or rough action by rotating the inner race while holding the outer race. If wear or roughness is evident, replace the bearing.

Examine the rubber cushion for evidence of hardening, cracking, or deterioration. Replace it if it is damaged in any way.

5. Place the bearing in the rubber support and the rubber support in the U-shaped support and install the bearing in the reverse order of removal.

Rear Axle

The E-100, E-150, and E-200 models use the Ford removable carrier type rear axle with semi-floating axle shafts. The E-250, E-300, and E-350 models use the Dana integral carrier type rear axle with full-floating axle shafts. The Dana (Spicer) model 60 is used through 1974, the model 61 from 1975–77, and the model 70 in 1975–77 dual wheel and limited-slip differential applications.

The axle ratio is on a tag attached by one of the differential carrier or rear cover bolts. Ford axles with limited slip are indicated by an L replacing the axle ratio decimal point; Dana axles are marked L-S.

INTRODUCTION

The rear axle must transmit power through 90°. To accomplish this, straight

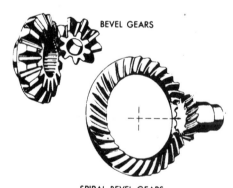

BEVEL GEARS

SPIRAL BEVEL GEARS
Bevel gear application
(© Chevrolet Div., G.M. Corp)

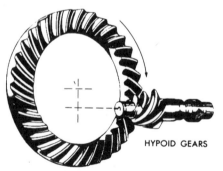

HYPOID GEARS

Hypoid gear application
(© Chevrolet Div., G.M. Corp)

The three different designs of ring and pinion gears

cut bevel gears or spiral bevel gears were used. This type of gear is satisfactory for differential side gears, but since the centerline of the gears must intersect, they rapidly became unsuited for ring and pinion gears. The lowering of the driveshaft brought about a variation of the bevel gear, which is called the hypoid gear. This type of gear does not require a meeting of the gear centerlines and can therefore be underslung, relative to the centerline of the ring gear.

Gear Ratios

The drive axle of a vehicle is said to have a certain axle ratio. This number (usually a whole number and a decimal fraction) is actually a comparison of the number of gear teeth on the ring gear and the pinion gear. For example, a 4.11 rear means that theoretically, there are 4.11 teeth on the ring gear and one tooth on the pinion. Actually on a 4.11 rear, there are 37 teeth on the ring gear and nine teeth on the pinion gear. By dividing the number of teeth on the pinion gear into the number of teeth on the ring gear, the numerical axle ratio (4.11) is obtained. This also provides a good method of ascertaining exactly which axle ratio one is dealing with.

Differential Operation

The differential is an arrangement of gears which permits the rear wheels to turn at different speeds when cornering and divides the torque between the axle shafts. The differential gears are mounted on a pinion shaft and the gears are free to rotate on this shaft. The pinion shaft is fitted in a bore in the differential case and is at right angles to the axle shafts.

Power flow through the differential is as follows. The drive pinion, which is turned by the driveshaft, turns the ring gear. The ring gear, which is bolted to the differential case, rotates the case. The differential pinion forces the pinion gears against the side gears. In cases where both wheels have equal traction, the pinion gears do not rotate on the pinion shaft, because the input force of the pinion gear is divided equally between the two side gears. Consequently the pinion gears revolve with the pinion shaft, although they do not revolve on the pinion

shaft itself. The side gears, which are splined to the axle shafts, and meshed with the pinion gears, rotate the axle shafts.

When it becomes necessary to turn a corner, the differential becomes effective and allows the axle shafts to rotate at different speeds. As the inner wheel slows down, the side gear splined to the inner wheel axle shaft also slows down. The pinion gears act as balancing levers by maintaining equal tooth loads to both gears while allowing unequal speeds of rotation at the axle shafts. If the vehicle speed remains constant, and the inner wheel slows down to 90 percent of vehicle speed, the outer wheel will speed up to 110 percent.

Limited-Slip Differential Operation

Limited-slip differentials provide driving force to the wheel with the best traction before the other wheel begins to spin. This is accomplished through clutch plates or cones. The clutch plates or cones are located between the side gears and inner wall of the differential case. When they are squeezed together through spring tension and outward force from the side gears, three reactions occur. Resistance on the side gears causes more torque to be exerted on the clutch packs or clutch cones. Rapid one-wheel spin cannot occur, because the side gear is forced to turn at the same speed as the case. Most important, with the side gear and the differential case turning at the same speed, the other wheel is forced to rotate in the same direction and at the same speed as the differential case. Thus driving force is applied to the wheel with the better traction.

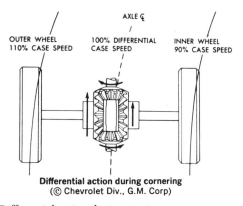

Differential action during cornering
(© Chevrolet Div., G.M. Corp)

Differential action during turning

Differential Diagnosis

The most essential part of rear axle service is proper diagnosis of the problem. Bent or broken axle shafts or broken gears pose little problem, but isolating an axle noise and correctly interpreting the problem can be extremely difficult, even for an experienced mechanic.

Any gear driven unit will produce a certain amount of noise, therefore, a specific diagnosis for each individual unit is the best practice. Acceptable or normal noise can be classified as a slight noise heard only at certain speeds or under unusual conditions. This noise tends to reach a peak at 40–60 mph, depending on the road condition, load, gear ratio and tire size. Frequently, other noises are mistakenly diagnosed as coming from the rear axle. Vehicle noises from tires, transmission, driveshaft, U-joints and front and rear wheel bearings will often be mistaken as emanating from the rear axle. Raising the tire pressure to eliminate tire noise (although this will not silence mud or snow treads), listening for noise at varying speeds and road conditions and listening for noise at drive and coast conditions will aid in diagnosing alleged rear axle noises.

External Noise Elimination

It is advisable to make a thorough road test to determine whether the noise originates in the rear axle or whether it originates from the tires, engine transmission, wheel bearings or road surface. Noise originating from other places cannot be corrected by overhauling the rear axle.

Road Noise

Brick roads or rough surfaced concrete, may cause a noise which can be mistaken as coming from the rear axle. Driving on a different type of road (smooth asphalt or dirt), will determine whether the road is the cause of the noise. Road noise is usually the same on drive or coast conditions.

Tire Noise

Tire noise can be mistaken as rear axle noises, even though the tires on the front are at fault. Snow tread and mud tread tires or tires worn unevenly will frequently cause vibrations which seem to originate elsewhere; *temporarily, and for test purposes only,* inflate the tires to 40–50 lbs. This will significantly alter the noise produced by the tires, but will not alter noise from the rear axle. Noises from the rear axle will normally cease at speeds below 30 mph on coast, while tire noise will continue at lower tone as speed is decreased. The rear axle noise will usually change from drive conditions to coast conditions, while tire noise will not. Do not forget to lower the tire pressure to normal after the test is complete.

Engine and Transmission Noise

Engine and transmission noises also seem to originate in the rear axle. Road test the vehicle and determine at which speeds the noise is most pronounced. Stop in a quiet place to avoid interfering noises. With the transmission in Neutral, run the engine slowly through the engine speeds corresponding to the speed at which the noise was most noticeable. If a similar noise was produced standing still, the noise is not in the rear axle, but somewhere in the engine or transmission.

Front Wheel Bearing Noise

Front wheel bearing noises, sometimes confused with rear axle noises, will not change when comparing drive and coast conditions. While holding the car speed steady, lightly apply the footbrake. This will often cause wheel bearing noise to lessen, as some of the weight is taken off the bearing. Front wheel bearings are easily checked by jacking up the wheels and spinning the wheels. Shaking the wheels will also determine if the wheel bearings are excessively loose.

Rear Axle Noises

If a logical test of the vehicle shows that the noise is not caused by external items, it can be assumed that the noise originates from the rear axle. The rear axle should be tested on a smooth level road to avoid road noise. It is not advisable to test the axle by jacking up the rear wheels and running the van.

True rear axle noises generally fall into two classes; gear noise and bearing noises, and can be caused by a faulty driveshaft, faulty wheel bearings, worn differential or pinion shaft bearings, U-joint misalignment, worn differential

General Drive Axle Diagnostic Guide

(Also see following text for further differential diagnosis.)

Condition	Possible Cause	Correction
Rear wheel noise	(a) Loose wheel.	(a) Tighten loose wheel nuts.
	(b) Spalled wheel bearing cup or cone.	(b) Check rear wheel bearings. If spalled or worn, replace.
	(c) Defective or brinelled wheel bearing.	(c) Defective or brinelled bearings must be replaced. Check rear axle shaft end-play.
	(d) Excessive axle shaft end-play.	(d) Readjust axle shaft end-play.
	(e) Bent or sprung axle shaft flange.	(e) Replace bent or sprung axle shaft.
Scoring of differential gears and pinions	(a) Insufficient lubrication.	(a) Replace scored gears. Scoring marks on the pressure face of gear teeth or in the bore are caused by instantaneous fusing of the mating surfaces. Scored gears should be replaced. Fill rear axle to required capacity with proper lubricant.
	(b) Improper grade of lubricant.	(b) Replace scored gears. Inspect all gears and bearings for possible damage. Clean and refill axle to required capacity with proper lubricant.
	(c) Excessive spinning of one wheel.	(c) Replace scored gears. Inspect all gears, pinion bores and shaft for scoring, or bearings for possible damage.
Tooth breakage (ring gear and pinion)	(a) Overloading.	(a) Replace gears. Examine other gears and bearings for possible damage. Avoid future overloading.
	(b) Erratic clutch operation.	(b) Replace gears, and examine remaining parts for possible damage. Avoid erratic clutch operation.
	(c) Ice-spotted pavements.	(c) Replace gears. Examine remaining parts for possible damage. Replace parts as required.
	(d) Improper adjustment.	(d) Replace gears. Examine other parts for possible damage. Be sure ring gear and pinion backlash is correct.
Rear axle noise	(a) Insufficient lubricant.	(a) Refill rear axle with correct amount of the proper lubricant. Also check for leaks and correct as necessary.
	(b) Improper ring gear and pinion adjustment.	(b) Check ring gear and pinion tooth contact.
	(c) Unmatched ring gear and pinion.	(c) Remove unmatched ring gear and pinion. Replace with a new matched gear and pinion set.
	(d) Worn teeth on ring gear or pinion.	(d) Check teeth on ring gear and pinion for contact. If necessary, replace with new matched set.
	(e) End-play in drive pinion bearings.	(e) Adjust drive pinion bearing preload.
	(f) Side play in differential bearings.	(f) Adjust differential bearing preload.
	(g) Incorrect drive gearlash.	(g) Correct drive gear lash.
	(h) Limited-slip differential—moan and chatter.	(h) Drain and flush lubricant. Refill with proper lubricant.

Loss of lubricant	(a) Lubricant level too high.	(a) Drain excess lubricant.
	(b) Worn axle shaft oil seals.	(b) Replace worn oil seals with new ones. Prepare new seals before replacement.
	(c) Cracked rear axle housing.	(c) Repair or replace housing as required.
	(d) Worn drive pinion oil seal.	(d) Replace worn drive pinion oil seal with a new one.
	(e) Scored and worn companion flange.	(e) Replace worn or scored companion flange and oil seal.
	(f) Clogged vent.	(f) Remove obstructions.
	(g) Loose carrier housing bolts or housing cover screws.	(g) Tighten bolts or cover screws to specifications and fill to correct level with proper lubricant.
Overheating of unit	(a) Lubricant level too low.	(a) Refill rear axle.
	(b) Incorrect grade of lubricant.	(b) Drain, flush and refill rear axle with correct amount of the proper lubricant.
	(c) Bearings adjusted too tightly.	(c) Readjust bearings.
	(d) Excessive wear in gears.	(d) Check gears for excessive wear or scoring. Replace as necessary.
	(e) Insufficient ring gear-to-pinion clearance.	(e) Readjust ring gear and pinion backlash and check gears for possible scoring.

A. Drive Noise:	Produced under vehicle acceleration.
B. Coast Noise:	Produced while the van coasts with a closed throttle.
C. Float Noise:	Occurs while maintaining constant speed on a level road.
D. Drive, Coast and Float Noise:	These noises will vary in tone with speed and be very rough or irregular if the differential or pinion shaft bearings are worn.

side gears and pinions, or mismatched, improperly adjusted, or scored ring and pinion gears.

REAR WHEEL BEARING NOISE

A rough rear wheel bearing causes a vibration or growl which will continue with the van coasting or in Neutral. A brinelled rear wheel bearing will also cause a knock or click approximately every two revolutions of the rear wheel, due to the fact that the bearing rollers do not travel at the same speed as the rear wheel and axle. Jack up the rear wheels and spin the wheel slowly, listening for signs of a rough or brinelled wheel bearing.

DIFFERENTIAL SIDE GEAR AND PINION NOISE

Differential side gears and pinions seldom cause noise, since their movement is relatively slight on straight-ahead driving. Noise produced by these gears will be more noticeable on turns.

PINION BEARING NOISE

Pinion bearing failures can be distinguished by their speed of rotation, which is higher than side bearings or axle bearings. Rough or brinelled pinion bearings cause a continuous low pitch whirring or scraping noise beginning at low speeds.

SIDE BEARING NOISE

Side bearings produce a constant rough noise, which is slower than the pinion bearing noise. Side bearing noise may also fluctuate in the above rear wheel bearing test.

GEAR NOISE

Two basic types of gear noise exist. First, is the type produced by bent or broken gear teeth which have been forcibly damaged. The noise from this type of damage is audible over the entire speed range. Scoring or damage to the hypoid gear teeth generally results from insufficient lubricant, improper lubricant, improper break-in, insufficient gear backlash, improper ring and pinion gear alignment or loss of torque on the drive pinion nut. If not corrected, the scoring will lead to eventual erosion or fracture of the gear teeth. Hypoid gear tooth fracture can also be caused by extended overloading of the gear set (fatigue fracture) or by shock overloading (sudden failure). Differential and side gears rarely give trouble, but common causes of differential failure are shock loading, extended overloading and differential pinion seizure at the cross-shaft, resulting from excessive wheel spin and consequent lubricant breakdown.

The second type of gear noise pertains to the mesh pattern between the ring and pinion gears. This type of abnormal gear noise can be recognized as a cycling pitch or whine audible in either drive, float or coast conditions. Gear noises can be recognized as they tend to peak out in a narrow speed range and remain constant in pitch, whereas bearing noises tend to vary in pitch with vehicle speeds. Noises produced by the ring and pinion gears will generally follow the pattern below.

AXLE SHAFT, BEARING, AND SEAL

Removal and Installation

E-100, E-150, AND E-200

1. Raise and support the vehicle and remove the wheel/tire assembly from the brake drum.
2. Remove the clips which secure the brake drum to the axle flange, then remove the drum from the flange.
3. Working through the hole provided in each axle shaft flange, remove the nuts which secure the wheel bearing retainer plate.
4. Pull the axle shaft assembly out of the axle housing. You may need a slide hammer.

NOTE: *The brake backing plate must not be dislodged. Install one nut to hold the plate in place after the axle shaft is removed.*

5. If the axle has ball bearings:
Loosen the bearing retainer ring by nicking it in several places with a cold chisel, then slide it off the axle shaft. On 1977 models, drill a ¼ to ½ in. hole part way through the ring, then break it with a cold chisel. A hydraulic press is needed to press the bearing off and to press the new one on. Press the new bearing and the new retainer ring on separately. Use a slide hammer to pull the old seal out of the axle housing. Use sealer on the outer edge of the new seal through 1975. Carefully drive the new seal evenly into the axle housing, preferably with a seal driver tool.

6. If the axle has tapered roller bearings (1974–77 only):
Use a slide hammer to remove the bearing cup from the axle housing. Drill a ¼ to ½ in. hole part way through the bearing retainer ring, then break it with a cold chisel. A hydraulic press is needed to press the bearing off and remove the seal. Press on the new seal and bearing, then the new retainer ring. Do not press the bearing and ring on together. Put the cup on the bearing, not in the housing, and lubricate the outer diameter of the cup and seal.

7. With ball bearings:
Place a new gasket between the housing flange and backing plate. Carefully slide the axle shaft into place. Turn the shaft to start the splines into the side gear and push it in.

8. With tapered roller bearings:
Move the seal out toward the axle shaft flange so there is at least ³/₃₂ between the edge of the outer seal and the bearing cup, to prevent snagging on installation. Carefully slide the axle shaft into place. Turn the shaft to start the splines into the side gear and push it in.

Noise Diagnosis Chart

Problem	*Cause*
1. Identical noise in drive or coast conditions	1. Road noise Tire noise Front wheel bearing noise
2. Noise changes on a different type of road	2. Road noise Tire noise
3. Noise tone lowers as speed is lowered	3. Tire noise
4. Similar noise is produced standing and driving	4. Engine noise Transmission noise
5. Vibration	5. Rough rear wheel bearing Unbalanced or damaged driveshaft Unbalanced tire Worn universal joint in driveshaft Misaligned driveshaft at companion flange Excessive companion flange runout
6. A knock or click approximately every two revolutions of rear wheel	6. Brinelled rear wheel bearing
7. Noise most pronounced on turns	7. Differential side gear and pinion wear or damage
8. A continuous low pitch whirring or scraping noise starting at relatively low speed	8. Damaged or worn pinion bearing
9. Drive noise, coast noise or float noise	9. Damaged or worn ring and pinion gear
10. Clunk on acceleration or deceleration	10. Worn differential cross-shaft in case
11. Clunk on stops	11. Insufficient grease in driveshaft slip yoke
12. Groan in Forward or Reverse	12. Improper differential lubricant
13. Chatter on turns	13. Improper differential lubricant Worn clutch plates
14. Clunk or knock during operation on rough roads	14. Excessive end-play of axle shafts to differential cross-shaft

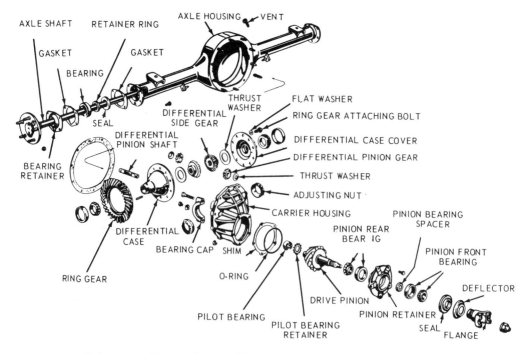

An exploded view of the Ford removable carrier rear axle with semi-floating axle shafts

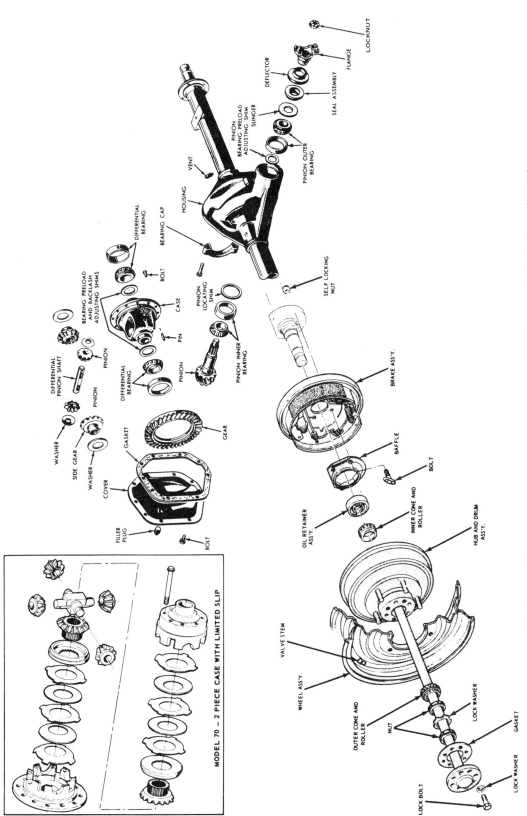

An exploded view of the Dana integral carrier rear axle with full-floating axle shafts (through 1974)

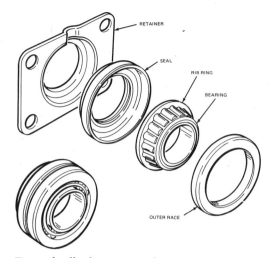

Tapered roller bearings used on some 1974–77 E-100, E-150, and E-200 axle shafts

9. Install the bearing retainer plate.

10. Replace the brake drum and the wheel and tire.

E-250, E-300, AND E-350

These procedures are thoroughly covered in Chapter 1 under Rear Wheel Bearing Packing and Adjustment.

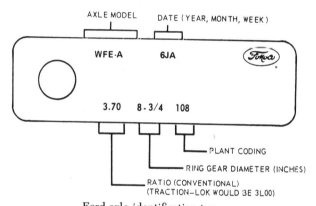

Ford axle identification tag

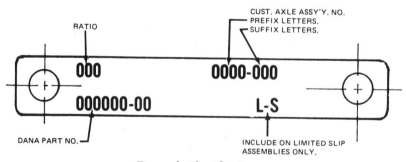

Dana axle identification tag

Chapter 8

Suspension and Steering

Front and Rear Suspension

The front axle in all 1966 and 1967 model Ford vans consists of a solid "I"-beam axle with the front wheel spindles attached to the ends of the axle spindle bolt (kingpin). Since 1968, all Ford vans have used two "I"-beam type front axles; one for each wheel. One end of each axle is attached to the spindle and a radius arm and the other end is attached to a frame pivot bracket on the opposite side of the vehicle. The spindles are held onto the axles by pivot bolts (kingpins).

Semi-elliptical leaf springs are used on the rear axles of all Ford vans. The front springs of 1966 and 1967 models are also semi-elliptical leaf springs. The front springs on 1968 and later models are coil type springs.

FRONT SPRINGS

Removal and Installation

COIL SPRINGS

1968–74

1. Remove the floor mat (if so equipped) retainer from the lower end of the door opening. Fold the mat to one side to gain access to the shock absorber cover plate.

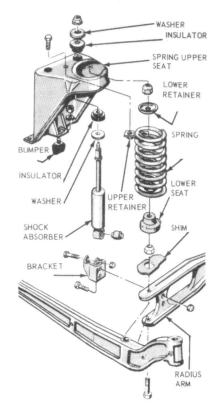

Typical 1968–77 front suspension

2. Remove the two cover plate attaching screws and remove the plate.

3. Remove the two spring upper retainer attaching screws and remove the retainer insulator and clamp.

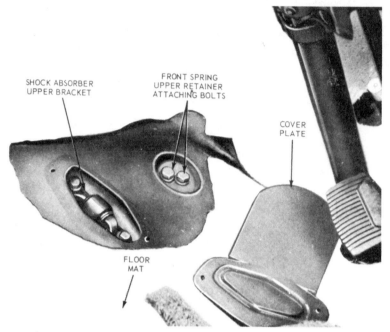

The 1968–74 upper shock absorber and spring mountings cover plate

4. Support the frame side rails with jackstands.

5. Place a jack under the axle, then remove the spring lower retainer attaching bolt. Remove the spring support and lower retainer.

6. Lower the jack slowly to relieve the spring tension, then remove the spring.

To install the front coil spring:

7. Position the spring on the axle with the pigtails toward the rear.

8. Position the spring lower support and retainer, and install the attaching bolt loosely.

9. Position the upper insulator on the spring.

10. Raise the jack high enough to apply light tension on the spring.

11. Install the spring upper retainer and the clamp in the following manner:

a. Check the retainer assembly to ensure that the bolts are approximately flush with the bottom of the clamp bar.

b. Insert the retainer assembly into the hole in the floor with the clamp bar pointing toward the right-side of the vehicle.

c. Rotate the retainer assembly about 90° clockwise until the oval retainer seats properly to the oval hole and secure the two bolts.

d. Visually inspect the spring to ensure that the clamp bar has trapped the tang on the upper end of the spring.

12. Tighten the upper and lower attaching bolts. Remove the jackstands.

13. Install the shock absorber cover plate and floor mat, if so equipped.

1975–77

1. Raise the van with jack stands under the frame and a jack under the axle.

2. Disconnect the lower end of the shock absorber.

3. Remove the two spring upper retainer bolts from the top of the upper spring seat. Take off the retainer strap.

4. Remove the nut holding the lower spring retainer disc to the seat and axle. Remove the retainer.

5. Carefully lower the axle and remove the extended spring.

6. On installation, put the spring in place and raise the axle. Install the lower retainer and nut. Install the upper retainer strap. Connect the shock absorber.

LEAF SPRINGS

1. Raise the front of the vehicle and support the chassis with jackstands. Support the front axle with a floor jack or hoist.

2. Remove the front splash shield.

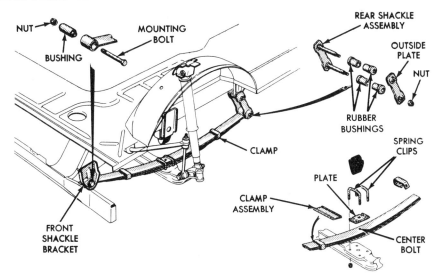

Front leaf spring assembly of 1966–67 Ford vans

3. Disconnect the lower end of the shock absorber from the anchor bolt in the front axle.

4. Remove the two spring clips (U-bolts) and the spring clip plate.

5. Lower the spring, and remove the rear shackle nuts and outside plate.

6. Pull the rear shackle assembly and rubber bushings from the bracket and spring.

7. Remove the nut and mounting bolt which secure the front end of the spring, and remove the spring from the front shackle bracket.

To install the front leaf spring:

8. Install new rubber bushings in the rear shackle bracket and in the rear eye of the replacement spring.

9. Position the spring assembly and connect the front eye of the spring to the front shackle bracket by installing the front mounting bolt and nut. Do not tighten the nut.

10. Mount the rear end of the spring by inserting the upper stud of the rear shackle assembly through the rear shackle bracket, and the lower stud through the rear eye of the spring.

11. Install the outside plate to the rear shackle studs, and install the shackle nuts. Do not tighten the nuts at this time.

12. Position the spring center bolt to the pilot hole in the axle, and install the spring clips and plate. Do not tighten the attaching nuts at this time.

13. Raise the axle with the floor jack

until the vehicle is free of the jackstands, and connect the lower end of the shock absorber to the anchor bolt in the front axle. Install the washer and nut.

14. Tighten the spring front mounting bolt and nut, the rear shackle nuts, and the spring clip nuts.

15. Install the front splash shield.

16. Remove the jackstands and lower the vehicle.

REAR SPRINGS

Removal and Installation

E-100, E-150, AND E-200

1. Raise the rear of the vehicle and support the chassis with jackstands. Support the rear axle with a floor jack or hoist.

2. Disconnect the lower end of the shock absorber from the bracket on the axle housing.

3. Remove the two U-bolts and plate.

4. Lower the axle and remove the upper and lower rear shackle bolts.

5. Pull the rear shackle assembly and rubber bushings from the bracket and spring.

6. Remove the nut and mounting bolt which secure the front end of the spring. Remove the spring assembly from the front shackle bracket.

7. Install new rubber bushings in the rear shackle bracket and in the rear eye of the replacement spring.

8. Assemble the front eye of the spring to the front shackle bracket with

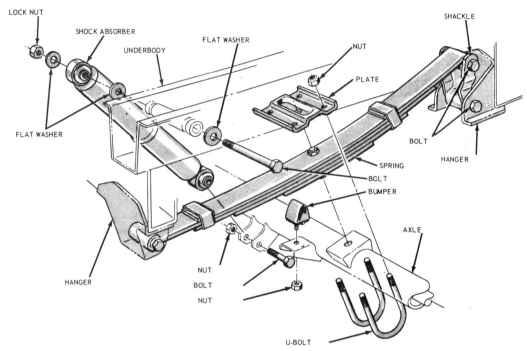

The rear spring assembly of E-100, E-150, and E-200 vans

the front mounting bolt and nut. Do not tighten the nut.

9. Mount the rear end of the spring with the upper bolt of the rear shackle assembly passing through the eye of the spring. Insert the lower bolt through the rear spring hanger.

10. Assemble the spring center bolt in the pilot hole in the axle and install the plate. Install the U-bolts through the plate. Do not tighten the attaching nuts at this time.

11. Raise the axle with a floor jack or hoist until the vehicle is free of the jackstands. Connect the lower end of the shock absorber to the bracket on the axle housing.

12. Tighten the spring front mounting bolt and nut, the rear shackle nuts and the U-bolt nuts.

13. Remove the jackstands and lower the vehicle.

E-250, E-300, AND E-350

1. Raise the rear of the vehicle and support the chassis with jackstands. Support the rear axle with a floor jack or hoist.

2. Disconnect the lower end of the shock absorber from the bracket on the axle housing.

3. Remove the two spring U-bolts and the spring cap.

4. Lower the axle and remove the spring front bolt from the hanger.

5. Remove the two attaching bolts from the rear of the spring. Remove the spring and shackle.

6. Assemble the upper end of the shackle to the spring with the attaching bolt.

7. Connect the front of the spring to the front bracket with the attaching bolt.

8. Assemble the spring and shackle to the rear bracket with the attaching bolt.

9. Place the spring plate over the head of the center bolt.

10. Raise the axle with a jack. Install the center bolt through the pilot hole in the pad on the axle housing.

11. Install the spring U-bolts, cap and attaching nuts. Tighten the nuts snugly.

12. Connect the lower end of the shock absorber to the lower bracket.

13. Tighten the spring front mounting bolt and nut, the rear shackle nuts and the spring U-bolt nuts.

14. Remove the jackstands and lower the vehicle.

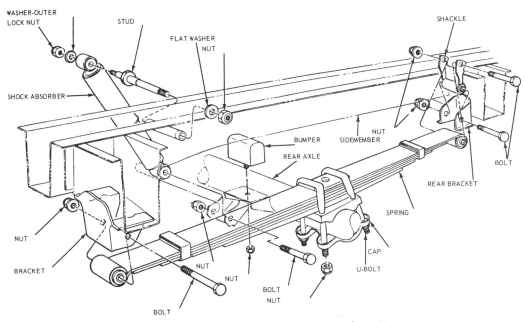

The rear spring assembly of E-250, E-300, and E-350 vans

The front shock absorber and stabilizer link lower connections on 1966–67 models

SHOCK ABSORBERS

Removal and Installation

1966–67

1. Raise the vehicle on a hoist.
2. Remove the shock absorber lower attaching nut and washer.
3. On the rear shock absorbers, swing the lower end free of the mounting bracket on the axle housing.

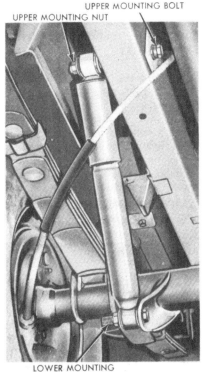

The rear shock absorber mounting for all models

4. Remove the upper attaching nut or bolt and remove the shock absorber from the vehicle.
5. Transfer the sleeves from the upper and lower bushings of the rear shocks

and only the lower bushing of the front shock absorber to the new shocks. If the sleeves are worn or damaged, replace them with new ones.

6. Install the shock absorbers in the reverse order of removal.

1968–74

NOTE: *Replace the rear shock absorbers in the same manner as outlined for 1966–67 vehicles.*

1. Remove the bolt which attaches the lower end of the shock absorber to the radius arm bracket.

2. Remove the floor mat retainer from the lower end of the door opening. Fold the mat to one side to gain access to the shock absorber cover plate.

3. Remove the two cover plate attaching screws and remove the plate.

4. Remove the two shock absorber bracket attaching bolts and lift the shock absorber and bracket up through the floor pan.

5. Position the shock absorber and install and tighten the two attaching bolts.

6. Install the shock absorber cover plate.

7. Position the floor mat and install the retainer.

8. Connect the lower end of the shock absorber to the bracket.

1975–77

NOTE: *Replace the rear shock absorbers in the same way as outlined previously for 1966–67 models.*

To replace front shocks:

1. Insert a wrench from the rear side of the upper spring seat to hold the upper shock retaining nut. Loosen the stud by using another wrench on the hex on the shaft.

2. Remove the bolt and nut at the lower end.

3. On installation, make sure to get the washers and insulators in the right place. Tighten the upper nut by turning the hext on the shaft. Replace the lower bolt. It is recommended that new rubber insulators be used.

FRONT WHEEL SPINDLES AND KING PINS

Removal and Installation

1. Raise the vehicle until the front wheel clears the floor and place a support under the axle.

2. Back off the brake adjustment as necessary, and remove the wheel, wheel bearing, hub and drum as an assembly.

3. On 1968–74 E-100 and E-200 models, remove the brake backing plate and spindle-to-spindle arm attaching bolt. Remove the spindle arm and the brake backing plate from the spindle. Support the brake backing plate hose. On disc brake models, remove the caliper assembly and wire it up. Remove the dust cap, cotter pin, nut, washer, outer bearing, and rotor (disc). Take off the inner bearing cone and seal. Remove the brake dust shield.

4. On 1968–74 E-300 and all 1975–77 models, disconnect the steering linkage from the integral spindle and the spindle arm.

5. Remove the nut and lockwasher from the locking pin, and remove the locking pin.

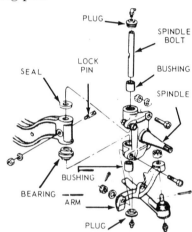

The front spindle assembly for 1968–74 E-100 and E-200 vans

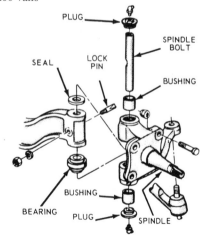

The front spindle assembly for 1968–74 E-300 and all 1975–77 models

6. Remove the upper and lower spindle bolt plugs; then, drive the spindle bolt out from the top of the axle and remove the spindle and bearing. Knock out the seal.

7. Make sure that the spindle bolt hole in the axle is free of nicks, burrs or foreign material. Install a new seal and coat the spindle bolt bushings and the spindle bolt hole in the axle with oil; then place the spindle in position on the axle.

8. Pack the spindle thrust bearing with chassis lubricant and insert the bearing into the spindle with the open end (lip side) of the bearing seal facing downward into the spindle.

9. Install the spindle pin in the spindle with the locking pin notch in the spindle bolt lined up with the locking pin hole in the axle. Drive the spindle bolt through the axle from the top side until the spindle bolt locking pin notch is lined up with the locking pin hole.

10. Make sure that the notch in the spindle pin is lined up with the locking pin hole in the axle and install a new locking pin. Install the locking pin lockwasher and nut. Tighten the nut and install the spindle bolt plugs at the top and bottom of the spindle.

11. On 1968–74 E-100 and E-200, install the brake backing plate and spindle arm. Torque the brake backing plate and spindle-to-spindle arm bolt and nut to 30–50 ft lbs. Advance the castellated nut as required to install the cotter in.

12. Connect the steering linkage to the spindle on 1968–74 E-300 and all 1975–77 models. Tighten the nut to 50–75 ft lbs and advance the nut as required to install the cotter pin.

13. Install the wheel, hub and drum or disc brake assembly, and adjust the wheel bearing.

14. Lubricate the spindle assembly.

15. Check and adjust the toe-in setting.

RADIUS ARM (1968–77)

Removal and Installation

1. Raise the front of the vehicle and place safety stands under the frame and a jack under the wheel or axle.

2. Disconnect the shock absorber from the radius arm bracket.

3. Remove the two spring upper retainer attaching bolts from the top of the spring upper seat and remove the retainer.

4. Remove the nut which attaches the spring lower retainer to the lower seat and axle and remove the retainer.

5. Lower the axle and remove the spring.

6. Disconnect the steering rod from the spindle arm.

7. Remove the spring lower seat and shim from the radius arm. Then, remove the bolt and nut which attach the radius arm to the axle.

8. Remove the cotter pin, nut and washer from the radius arm rear attachment.

9. Remove the bushing from the radius arm and remove the radius arm from the vehicle.

10. Remove the inner bushing from the radius arm.

11. Position the radius arm to the axle and install the bolt and nut finger-tight.

12. Install the inner bushing on the radius arm and position the arm to the frame bracket.

13. Install the bushing, washer, and attaching nut. Tighten the nut and install the cotter pin.

14. Connect the steering rod to the spindle arm and install the attaching nut. Tighten the nut and install the cotter pin.

15. Tighten the radius arm-to-axle attaching bolt and nut.

16. Position the shim over the radius arm-to-axle attaching nut and install the spring lower seat.

17. Place the spring in position and raise the front axle.

18. Position the spring lower retainer over the stud and lower the seat, and install the attaching nut.

19. Position the upper retainer over the spring coil and against the spring upper seat, and install the two attaching bolts.

20. Tighten the upper retainer attaching bolts and lower retainer attaching nut.

21. Connect the shock absorber to the lower bracket. Remove the jack and safety stands and lower the vehicle.

22. Check and adjust the toe-in setting.

FRONT END ALIGNMENT

Caster and Camber

The caster and camber angles of the front axle(s) of Ford vans are designed into the front axle(s) at the factory. Excessive negative camber on twin I-beams, causing wear on the inside edges of the tires, can be corrected by installation of front spring shims, available as Ford parts. Suspension misalignment caused by bent axles can be corrected by cold-bending in a shop with the suitable heavy equipment, probably a truck frame and alignment specialist. The caster angle of vehicles with solid front axles is adjusted by inserting tapered metal wedges between the springs and the spring pads on the axle. Toe-in is adjustable in the normal manner (by adjusting the tie-rods) and the procedure is given later on in this Section.

If you start to notice abnormal tire wear patterns and handling characteristics (steering wheel is hard to return to the straight-ahead position after negotiating a turn), then front end misalignment can be suspected.

NOTE: *It is very important that the tires be rotated at least at the intervals shown in the Maintenance Intervals Chart in Chapter 1 in order to get even tread wear on trucks with twin I-beam front suspension.*

However, toe-in alignment maladjustment, rather than caster or camber, is more likely to be the cause of excessive or uneven tire wear. Seldom is it necessary to correct caster or camber. The toe-in alignment should be checked before the caster and camber angles after making the following checks:

1. Check the air pressure in all the tires. Make sure that the pressures agree with those specified for the tires and vehicle model being checked.

2. Raise the front of the vehicle off the ground. Grasp each front tire at the top and bottom, and push the wheel inward and outward. If any free-play is noticed between the brake drum and the brake backing plate, adjust the wheel bearings.

NOTE: *There is supposed to be a very, very small amount of free-play present.*

A *common cause of excessive wear on the inside edge of the front tires is worn kingpins.*

3. Check all steering linkage for wear or maladjustment. Adjust and/or replace all worn parts.

4. Check the torque on the steering gear mounting bolts and tighten as necessary.

5. Rotate each front wheel slowly, and observe the amount of lateral or side run-out. If the wheel run-out exceeds ⅛ in., replace the wheel or install the wheel on the rear.

6. Inspect the twin I-beam radius arms to be sure that they are not bent or damaged. Inspect the bushings at the radius arm-to-axle attachment and radius arm-to-frame attachment points for wear or looseness. Repair or replace parts as required.

7. Raising the rear of the van, whether by suspension modifications or by using tall rear tires, will reduce the caster angle.

Toe-In Adjustment

Toe-in can be measured by either a front end alignment machine or by the following method:

With the front wheels in the straight-ahead position, measure the distance between the extreme front and the extreme rear of the front wheels. In other words, measure the distance across the under-carriage of the vehicle between the two front edges and the two rear edges of the two front wheels. Both of these measurements (front and rear of the two wheels) must be taken at an equal distance from the floor and at the approximate centerline of the spindle. The difference between these two distances is the amount that the wheels toe-in or toe-out. The wheels should always be adjusted to toe-in according to specifications.

1. Loosen the clamp bolts at each end of the tie-rod sleeve. Rotate the connecting rod tube until the correct toe-in is obtained, then tighten the clamp bolts.

2. Recheck the toe-in to make sure that no changes occurred when the bolts were tightened.

NOTE: *The clamps should be positioned with the clamp bolts in a vertical position in front of the tube, with the nut down.*

Wheel Alignment Specifications

Year	Model	Caster (deg)	Camber (deg)	Toe-In (in.)	Steering Knuckle Pin Inclination (deg)
1966	All	5¼	⅜	3/32	7½
1967	All	5	½	3/32	7½
1968–69	All	5	½	⅛	4
1970	All	3	2	3/32	——
1971	E-100, 200	3	2	3/32	——
1971	E-300	5	2	3/32	——
1972	E-100, 200	6	2	3/32	——
1972	E-300	5	2	3/32	——
1973	E-100, 200	6	2	1/32	——
1973	E-300	5	2	1/32	——
1974–76	E-100, 150, 200, 250	4½	2	1/32	——
1974–76	E-300, 350	5	2	1/32	——
1977	E-100, 150	3⅞	½	1/32	——
1977	E-250, 350	6⅛	1⅜	1/32	——

Steering

STEERING WHEEL

Removal and Installation

1. Disconnect the battery ground cable or the horn wire connector. Remove the horn button or ring by pressing down and turning counterclockwise. Remove the horn pad on later models by removing the screws on the back of the wheel spokes, unclip the wires, and remove the horn switch.

2. Remove the steering wheel nut.

3. Make sure that the wheels are in the straight-ahead position and mark the steering wheel and steering column so that the steering wheel can be reassembled in the same position from which it is removed.

4. Remove the steering wheel with a puller.

5. Install the steering wheel in the reverse order of removal. Tighten the nut to 35 ft lbs.

TURN SIGNAL/HAZARD WARNING SWITCH

Removal and Installation

1968–74

1. Disconnect the turn signal wires under the instrument panel.

2. Turn the turn signal lever counterclockwise to remove it. Remove the cover which retains the turn indicator wires to the steering column.

3. Remove the two retaining screws under the steering column cup, and lift the horn contact plate and turn the indicator assembly from the steering column cup.

4. Install the turn signal switch in the reverse order of removal.

1975–77

1. Disconnect the battery ground cable. Remove the steering wheel and horn switch.

2. Unscrew the turn signal switch lever.

3. Disconnect the switch wiring plug by lifting up on the tabs and separating. Remove the screws holding the switch to the column.

4. Remove the wires and terminals from the steering column connector plug, after noting the location and color of each.

5. Remove the protective wire cover from the harness and remove the switch and wires through the top of the column.

6. Tape the loose ends of the new switch wires to a wire and pull them through the steering column.

7. Install the switch retaining screws.

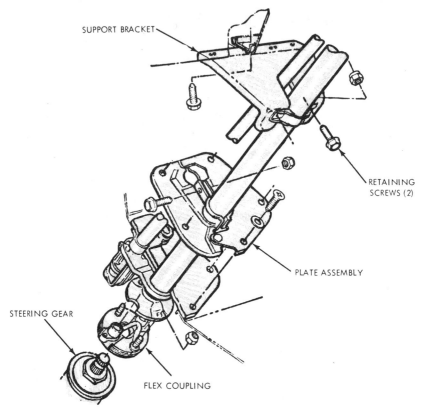

SUPPORT BRACKET

RETAINING SCREWS (2)

PLATE ASSEMBLY

STEERING GEAR

FLEX COUPLING

Installation of the 1968–74 steering column

8. Install the wires into the column wire connector and connect the terminals.

9. Replace the turn signal lever, the steering wheel, and the horn switch.

STEERING COLUMN

Removal and Installation

1966–77

1. Disconnect the horn and turn signal wires under the instrument panel.

2. Move the floormat, pull up the rubber seal, and remove the column floor pan cover.

3. Loosen the three column support attaching bolts. Remove the clamp bolts holding the support to the column.

4. Disconnect the shift rods at the lower end of the column.

5. Remove the three steering gear mounting bolts and the pitman arm clamp bolt. Spread the pitman arm with a chisel. Separate the pitman arm and the steering gear.

6. Lift the column and steering gear

assembly out through the inside of the van.

7. Reverse the procedure for installation.

1968–74

1. Disconnect the horn, turn signal and back-up lamp wires.

2. Remove the steering wheel.

3. Disconnect the shift rods at the column shift levers.

4. Disconnect the flex coupling from the steering gear.

5. Remove the clamp holding the column to the support bracket on the instrument panel.

6. Remove the screws holding the plate assembly to the floor pan.

7. Remove the bolt and nut from the plate assembly clamp.

8. Lift the column from the vehicle.

To install the steering column:

9. Position the column in the vehicle.

10. Install the screws which hold the column bracket to the support bracket on the instrument panel.

11. Align the flex coupling on the steering gear and install the retaining nuts.

12. Install the screws which hold the plate assembly to the floor pan.

13. Install the bolt and nut into the plate assembly clamp.

14. Connect the shift rods to the column shift levers.

15. Install the steering wheel.

16. Connect the back-up light, turn signal and horn wires.

1975–77

1. Remove the steering wheel as explained earlier.

2. Remove the two screws and the modesty cover from the instrument panel.

3. Disconnect the ignition switch wire connector and the backup and neutral start switch wires.

4. Disconnect the shift rods at the bottom of the column.

5. Remove the two nuts holding the steering shaft flange to the flexible coupling, after matchmarking it. Remove the three bolts holding the firewall opening cover plate.

6. Remove the column upper bracket to brake support bracket bolts.

7. Remove the column assembly through the inside of the truck.

8. Install the column, attach the flexible coupling, pull the column up slightly so that the coupling is either flat or curved up less than $^3/_{32}$ in., then tighten the column support brackets. Make sure that the flexible coupling pins are not binding. You can do this by putting a .010

in. shim around the right pin and turning the wheel. If it can be pulled out after turning the wheel, alignment is good.

MANUAL AND POWER ASSISTED STEERING GEAR (RECIRCULATING BALL TYPE)

Adjustments

These adjustments apply to the manual steering gear for all years and to the linkage-assisted power steering used through 1974. They do not apply to 1975–77 integral power steering.

Steering gear adjustments are normally required only after extensive mileage.

1. Be sure that the steering column is properly aligned and is not causing excessive turning effort.

2. On 1966–67 models, disconnect the steering linkage and remove the column floor pan cover for access. On 1968–77 models, the steering gear must be removed from the truck.

3. Be sure that the ball nut assembly and the sector gear are properly adjusted as follows to maintain minimum steering shaft endplay and backlash between the sector gear and ball nut (preload adjustment).

4. Loosen the sector shaft adjusting screw locknut and turn the adjusting screw counterclockwise approximately 3 times.

5. Measure the worm bearing preload by attaching an in. lbs torque wrench to the input shaft. Measure the torque required to rotate the input shaft about 1½ turns 2½ for 1975–77 in either direc-

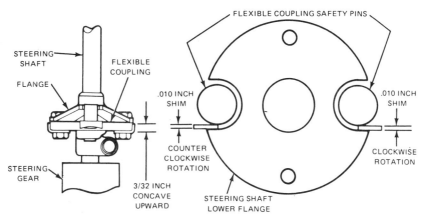

Checking 1975–77 steering column alignment

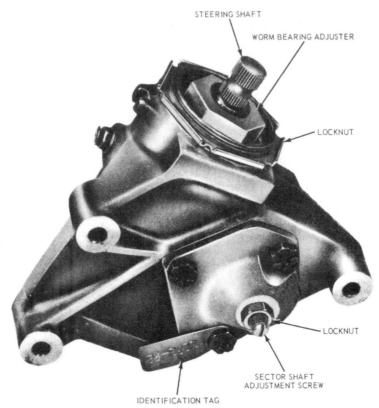

STEERING SHAFT

WORM BEARING ADJUSTER

LOCKNUT

LOCKNUT

SECTOR SHAFT
ADJUSTMENT SCREW

IDENTIFICATION TAG

The recirculating ball type steering gear used in all Ford vans

tion. The worm bearing preload should be as specified.

Model	Worm Bearing Preload (in. lbs)
1967–73 manual	4–5
1971–73 power	3–4
1974 manual	3–8
1974 power	2–6
1975–76 manual	5–8
1977 manual	3–8

6. To adjust the worm bearing preload, loosen the input shaft bearing adjuster locknut, and tighten or loosen the bearing adjuster to bring the preload within the specified limits. Tighten the locknut and recheck the preload.

7. Turn the input shaft slowly to either stop. Turn gently against the stop to avoid possible damage to the ball return guides. Then rotate the shaft approximately 3 turns to center the ball nut.

8. Turn the sector shaft adjusting screw clockwise until the specified pull is obtained to rotate the worm past its center.

With the steering gear in the center position, hold the sector shaft to prevent rotation and check the lash between the ball nuts, balls and worm shaft by applying a 15 in. lb torque on the steering gear input shaft, in both right and left turn direc-

Model	Total Center Meshload (in. lbs)
1967–73 manual	9–10
1971–73 power	8–9
1974 manual	10–16
1974 power	7–12
1975–76 manual	4–10
1977 manual	10–16

tions. Total travel of the wrench should not exceed 1¼ in. when applying a 15 in. lbs torque on the steering shaft.

9. Tighten the sector shaft adjusting screw locknut, and recheck the backlash adjustment.

POWER STEERING

Ford vans were first equipped with power steering in 1971. This is a hydraulically-controlled linkage assist type system which includes a power steering pump, a control valve, a power cylinder, 4 fluid lines, and the steering linkage. The only adjustments that can be made in addition to the steering gear (same as for manual steering) are the pitman arm stops.

1975–77 models have an integral power steering system in which the power assist is combined with the steering gear assembly.

Adjustments

PITMAN ARM STOPS—1971–74

1. Loosen the locknut on both pitman arm stops and turn the adjusting screws inward several turns.

2. Turn the steering wheel to the right, until the right spindle steering arm contacts the stop.

3. Adjust the forward pitman arm stop

outward until it contacts the pitman arm. Tighten the locknut.

4. Turn the steering wheel to the left until the left spindle steering arm contacts the stop.

5. Adjust the rearward pitman arm stop outward until it contacts the pitman arm. Tighten the locknut.

STEERING GEAR MESHLOAD—1975–77

This adjustment is only for the 1975–77 integral power steering. It is normally required only after extensive mileage.

1. Make sure that the steering column is correctly aligned as explained in Step 8 of Steering Column Removal and Installation.

2. Disconnect the steering linkage from the pitman arm on the steering gear. Remove the horn pad as explained under Steering Wheel Removal and Installation.

3. Disconnect the fluid reservoir return line and cap the reservoir return line tube. Place the end of the return line in a clean container and turn the steering wheel back and forth several times to empty the steering gear.

4. Turn the steering wheel nut with an inch pound torque wrench slowly. Find the torque required at: ½ turn off right and left stops, ½ turn off center both right

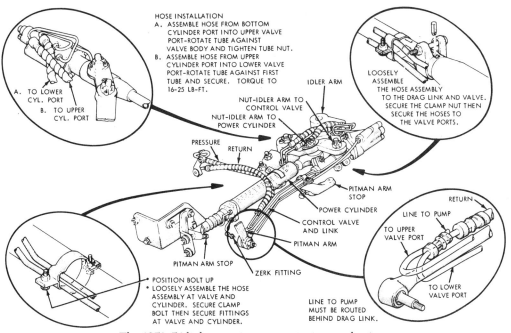

The 1971–74 linkage assist power steering mechanism

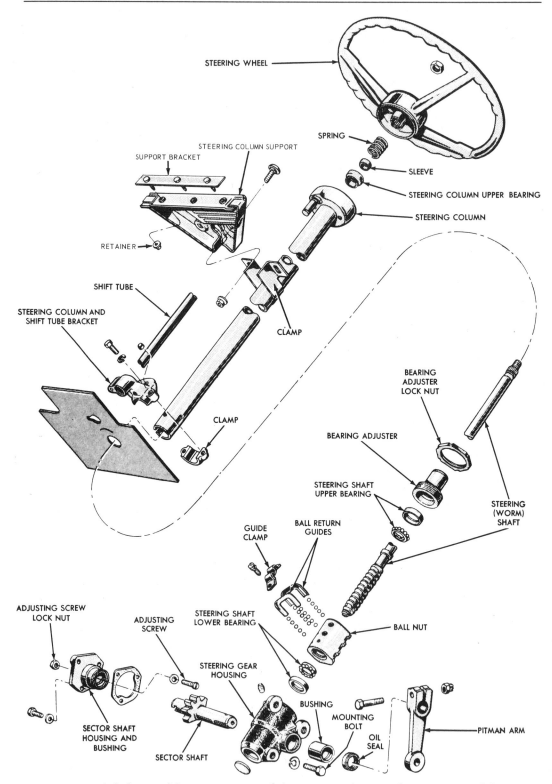

STEERING WHEEL

STEERING COLUMN SUPPORT

SUPPORT BRACKET

SPRING

SLEEVE

STEERING COLUMN UPPER BEARING

STEERING COLUMN

RETAINER

SHIFT TUBE

STEERING COLUMN AND
SHIFT TUBE BRACKET

CLAMP

BEARING
ADJUSTER
LOCK NUT

BEARING ADJUSTER

CLAMP

STEERING SHAFT
UPPER BEARING

STEERING
(WORM)
SHAFT

GUIDE
CLAMP

BALL RETURN
GUIDES

ADJUSTING SCREW
LOCK NUT

ADJUSTING
SCREW

STEERING SHAFT
LOWER BEARING

BALL NUT

STEERING GEAR
HOUSING

BUSHING

MOUNTING
BOLT

PITMAN ARM

SECTOR SHAFT
HOUSING AND
BUSHING

OIL
SEAL

SECTOR SHAFT

An exploded view of the steering gear and the steering column used in 1966–67 models and left, and over-center (full turn). The over-center torque should be 4–6 in. lb more than the end readings, but the total over-center torque must not exceed 14 in. lb.

5. To correct, back off the pitman shaft adjuster all the way, then back in ½ turn. Recheck the over-center torque. Loosen the locknut and tighten the sector shaft adjusting screw until the over-center torque reads 4–6 in. lb higher, but doesn't exceed 14 in. lb. Tighten the adjusting screw locknut and recheck.

6. Refill the system with the fluid specified in Chapter 1. Bleed the system of air by turning the steering wheel all the way to the right and left several times with the engine warmed up. Do not hold the steering against the stops or pump damage will result.

POWER STEERING PUMP

Removal and Installation

1971–74

1. Raise the vehicle on a hoist.
2. Place a drain pan beneath the power steering pump and disconnect the pressure and return lines at the pump and drain the pump. If a suction gun is available, use it to remove the fluid from the pump reservoir. Lower six-cylinder engine equipped vehicles.

3. Loosen the power steering pump retaining bolts and move the drive belt out of the way.

4. Disconnect the reservoir hose from the pump on those models equipped with a remote reservoir.

5. On six-cylinder engine equipped vehicles, remove the nuts which hold the pump bracket to the cylinder block. Remove the pump and bracket from under the vehicle.

6. On V8 engine equipped vehicles, remove the bolts which hold the pump to the mounting bracket and lay the pump on the crossmember. Loosen the bolts and nuts which hold the mounting bracket to the cylinder block, allowing the bracket to move forward, and remove the pump from the vehicle.

NOTE: *If the power steering pump is being removed from the engine in*

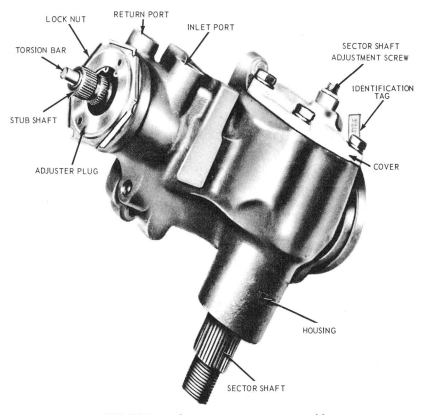

1975–77 Integral power steering gear assembly

order to facilitate the removal of some other component, and it is not necessary to completely remove the pump from the vehicle, it is not necessary and is not recommended that the pressure and return hoses be disconnected from the pump.

7. Install the power steering pump in the reverse order of removal. Follow the procedure given below for initial start-up after the power steering pump or power cylinder have been disconnected from the system. This procedure is necessary to remove any air that might be trapped in the system.

Initial Start-Up Procedure

Upon initial engine start-up after a power cylinder or pump replacement, there is, more often than not, much noise and aeration. This is due to air trapped in the replaced unit which mixes with the surging fluid and causes aeration. The problem can be minimized, if the following procedure is employed:

1. Disconnect the coil wire.
2. Fill the power steering reservoir with the proper power steering fluid.
3. Crank the engine with the starter and continue adding fluid until the level stabilizes.
4. Rotate the steering wheel about 30° to each side of center, while continuing to crank the engine.

5. Recheck the fluid level and fill as required.
6. Reconnect the coil wire
7. Start the engine and allow it to run for several minutes.
8. Rotate the steering wheel from stop to stop.
9. Shut off the engine and recheck the fluid level in the reservoir. Add fluid as necessary.

NOTE: *Check for fluid leaks before starting the engine and during the time the engine is running. If a leak is noticed, depending on its severity, shut the engine off and make the necessary adjustments to stop the leak. The pump could be damaged by being operated in the absence of fluid, since the fluid lubricates the pump.*

1975–77

1. Disconnect and plug the fluid lines.
2. Loosen the drive belt.
3. Unbolt the pump bracket from the air conditioning bracket, if any.
4. Remove the pump, mounting bracket, and pulley as an assembly.
5. Reverse the procedure for installation. Refill the system with the fluid specified in Chapter 1. Bleed the system of air by turning the steering wheel all the way to the right and left several times with the engine warmed up. Do not hold the steering against the stops or pump damage will result.

Chapter 9

Brakes

Single-anchor, internal-expanding, duo-servo, self-adjusting, hydraulic drum brakes with a safety, dual master cylinder are used on Ford vans. Disc front brakes are used on 1975–77 models; dual piston on E-250 and 350, single piston on E-100 and 150.

The dual, safety-type master cylinder contains a double hydraulic cylinder with two fluid reservoirs, two hydraulic pistons (a primary and a secondary), and two residual check valves on all-drum systems, located in the outlet ports. The master cylinder's primary and secondary pistons function simultaneously when both the primary and secondary systems are fully operative.

Failure in either the front or rear brake system does not result in failure of the entire hydraulic brake system. Should hydraulic failure occur in the rear system, the hydraulic pressure from the primary piston (which actuates the front brakes) causes the secondary piston to bottom out in its bore, due to the lack of hydraulic pressure. The primary piston then actuates the front brakes with the continued stroke of the brake pedal.

Clean, high-quality brake fluid is essential to the safe and proper operation of the brake system. You should always buy the highest quality brake fluid that is available. If the brake fluid becomes con-taminated, drain and flush the system and fill the master cylinder with new fluid.

NOTE: *Never reuse any brake fluid. Any brake fluid that is removed from the system should be discarded.*

The system has a pressure differential valve that activates a warning light if either hydraulic circuit is losing pressure. On 1975–77 models, the pressure differential valve is combined with a metering valve that restricts flow to the front brakes until the rear brakes overcome their retracting springs to prevent front brake lockup, and a proportioning valve that limits rear brake hydraulic pressure to prevent rear brake lockup.

Brake System

The drum brakes are self-adjusting; they require manual adjustment only after brake shoe replacement. The disc brakes are inherently self-adjusting and have no provision for manual adjustment.

To adjust the brakes, follow the procedure given below:

1. Raise the vehicle and support it with safety stands.

2. Remove the rubber plug from the adjusting slot on the backing plate.

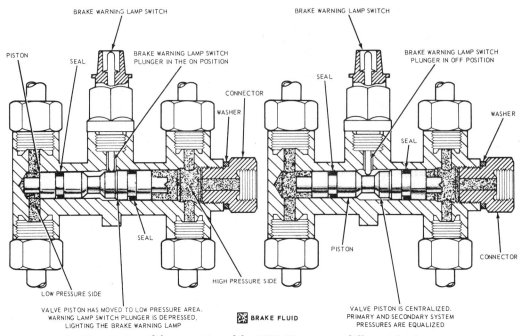

A cutaway view of the operation of the 1966–74 pressure differential valve system

3. Insert a brake adjusting spoon into the slot and engage the lowest possible tooth on the starwheel. Move the end of the brake spoon downward to expand the adjusting screw. Repeat this operation until the brakes lock the wheel.

4. Insert a small screwdriver or piece of firm wire (coathanger wire) into the adjusting slot and push the automatic adjusting lever out and free of the starwheel on the adjusting screw and hold it there.

5. Engage the topmost tooth possible on the starwheel with the brake adjusting spoon. Move the end of the adjusting spoon upward to contract the adjusting screw. Back off the adjusting screw starwheel until the wheel spins freely without any drag. Keep track of the number of turns that the starwheel is backed off, or the number of strokes taken with the brake adjusting spoon.

6. Repeat this operation for the other side. When backing off the brakes on the other side, the starwheel adjuster must

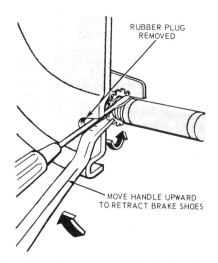

Positioning and operation of the brake adjusting tools during the adjustment procedure on E-100, E-150, and E-200 models—backing off the brakes

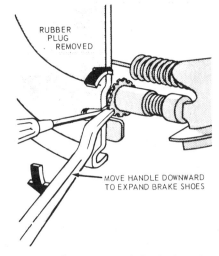

Positioning and operation of the brake adjusting tools during the adjustment procedure on E-250, E-300, and E-350 models—expanding the brakes

be backed off the same number of turns to prevent side-to-side brake pull.

7. Repeat this operation on the other drum brakes.

8. When all drum brakes are adjusted, make several stops while backing the vehicle, to equalize the brakes at all of the wheels.

9. Remove the safety stands and lower the vehicle. Road test the vehicle.

Hydraulic System

MASTER CYLINDER

Removal and Installation

1966–67

1. Unbolt the forward splash shield.
2. Disconnect the pedal return spring.
3. Remove the locknut and eccentric bolt connecting the return spring bracket and master cylinder pushrod to the brake panel bracket.
4. Remove the snap ring from the pedal pivot pin.
5. Disconnect the brake lines and the stoplight switch.
6. Remove the mounting bolts and swing the cylinder down. Remove it from the pedal pivot pin and remove the pivot pin bushings.

7. On installation, adjust the eccentric bolt so that there is $1/4$–$7/16$ in. pedal free-travel.

8. Bleed the system of air.

1968–74

1. Disconnect the wires from the stoplight switch.
2. Disconnect the hydraulic system brake lines at the master cylinder.
3. Remove the shoulder bolt and nut retaining the pushrod to the brake pedal. Remove the pushrod bushing.
4. Slide the master cylinder pushrod off the brake pedal pin. Remove the bushings and washers.
5. Remove the master cylinder retaining bolts and remove the master cylinder.

To install the master cylinder:

6. Position the master cylinder assembly on the firewall and install the retaining bolts.
7. Connect the hydraulic brake system lines to the master cylinder.
8. Lubricate the pushrod bushing. Insert the bushing in the pushrod and install the shoulder bolt which secures the pushrod to the brake pedal.

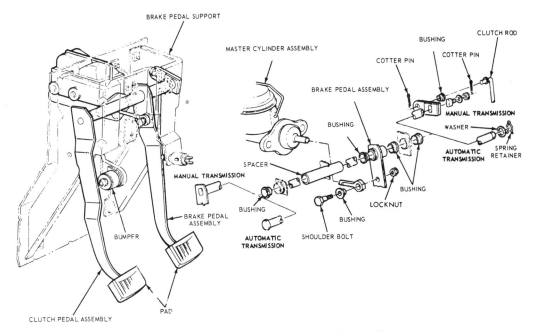

The 1968–74 master cylinder and brake pedal installation

9. Connect the stoplight switch wires to the switch.

10. Bleed the hydraulic brake system.

1975–77

Power Brakes

1. Push the pedal down to release the vacuum from the booster. Release the pedal.

2. Disconnect the hydraulic lines.

3. Unbolt the master cylinder from the booster.

4. Before installation, check that the booster pushrod protrudes .980–.995 in. for 1977 and .880–.895 in. for 1975–76 beyond the base of the master cylinder mounting studs. Adjust as necessary.

5. Bleed the system of air after installation.

Non-Power Brakes

1. Disconnect the stoplight switch. Disconnect the dust boot from the rear of the master cylinder at the firewall.

2. Remove the shoulder bolt holding the cylinder pushrod to the brake pedal. Remove the stoplight switch from the pedal.

3. Remove the boot from the pushrod.

4. Disconnect the hydraulic lines.

5. Unbolt the master cylinder from the firewall.

6. Reverse the procedure for installation. Grease the pushrod bushing. Bleed the system of air after installation.

Overhaul

The most important thing to remember when rebuilding the master cylinder is cleanliness. Work in clean surroundings with clean tools and clean cloths or paper for drying purposes. Have plenty of clean alcohol and brake fluid on hand to clean and lubricate the internal components. There are service repair kits available for overhauling the master cylinder. Rebuilt master cylinders are also available.

1. Clean the outside of the master cylinder and remove the filler cap and

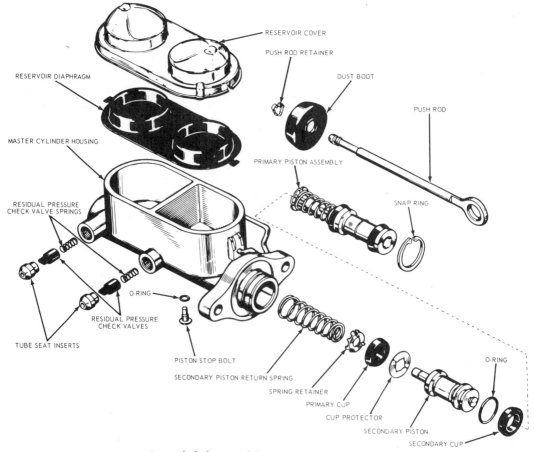

An exploded view of the 1968–74 master cylinder

gasket (diaphragm). Pour out any fluid that remains in the cylinder reservoir. Do not use any fluids other than brake fluid or alcohol to clean the master cylinder.

2. Unscrew the piston stop from the bottom of the cylinder body. Remove the O-ring seal from the piston stop. Discard the seal.

3. Remove the pushrod boot, if so equipped, from the groove at the rear of the master cylinder and slide the boot away from the rear of the master cylinder.

4. Remove the snap-ring which retains the primary and secondary piston assemblies within the cylinder body.

5. Remove the pushrod (if so equipped) and primary piston assembly from the master cylinder. Discard the piston assembly, including the boot (if so equipped).

6. Apply an air hose to the rear brake outlet port of the cylinder body and carefully blow the secondary piston out of the cylinder body.

7. Remove the return spring, spring retainer, cup protector, and cups from the secondary piston. Discard the cup protector and cups.

8. Clean all of the remaining parts in clean isopropyl alcohol and inspect the parts for chipping, excessive wear or damage. Replace them as required.

NOTE: *When using a master cylinder repair kit, install all the parts supplied in the kit.*

9. Check all recesses, openings and internal passages to be sure that they are open and free from foreign matter. Use compressed air to blow out dirt and cleaning solvent remaining after the parts have been cleaned in the alcohol. Place all the parts on a clean pan, lint-free cloth, or paper to dry.

10. Dip all the parts, except the cylinder body, in clean brake fluid.

11. Assemble the two secondary cups, back-to-back, in the grooves near the end of the secondary piston.

12. Install the secondary piston assembly in the master cylinder.

13. Install a new O-ring on the piston stop, and start the stop into the cylinder body.

14. Position the boot, snap-ring and pushrod retainer on the pushrod. Make sure that the pushrod retainer is seated securely on the ball end of the rod. Seat

the pushrod in the primary piston assembly.

15. Install the primary piston assembly in the master cylinder. Push the primary piston inward and tighten the secondary piston stop to retain the secondary piston in the bore.

16. Press the pushrod and pistons inward and install the snap-ring in the cylinder body.

17. Before the master cylinder is installed on the vehicle, the unit must be bled: support the master cylinder body in a vise, and fill both fluid reservoirs with brake fluid.

18. Loosely install plugs in the front and rear brake outlet bores. Depress the primary piston several times until air bubbles cease to appear in the brake fluid.

19. Tighten the plugs and attempt to depress the piston. The piston travel should be restricted after all air is expelled.

20. Remove the plugs. Install the cover and gasket (diaphragm) assembly, and make sure that the cover retainer is tightened securely.

21. Install the master cylinder in the vehicle and bleed the hydraulic system.

BLEEDING THE BRAKES

When any part of the hydraulic system has been disconnected for repair or replacement, air may get into the lines and cause spongy pedal action (because air can be compressed and brake fluid cannot). To correct this condition, it is necessary to bleed the hydraulic system after it has been properly connected to be sure that all air is expelled from the brake cylinders and lines.

When bleeding the brake system, bleed one brake cylinder at a time, beginning at the cylinder with the longest hydraulic line (farthest from the master cylinder) first. Keep the master cylinder reservoir filled with brake fluid during the bleeding operation. Never use brake fluid that has been drained from the hydraulic system, no matter how clean it is.

It will be necessary to centralize the pressure differential valve after a brake system failure has been corrected and the hydraulic system has been bled.

During the entire bleeding operation,

do not allow the reservoir to run dry. Keep the master cylinder reservoirs filled with brake fluid.

NOTE: *When bleeding disc brake systems, the bleeder rod of the metering valve on the end of the pressure differential/metering/proportioning valve must be held out on the E-100 and 150, and in on the E-250 and 350. This is done to allow fluid flow to the front brakes.*

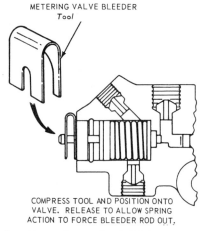

METERING VALVE BLEEDER
Tool

COMPRESS TOOL AND POSITION ONTO VALVE. RELEASE TO ALLOW SPRING ACTION TO FORCE BLEEDER ROD OUT.

A spring clip can be used to hold the pressure differential/metering/proportioning valve's bleeder valve out on E-100 and 150 disc brake systems

1. Clean all dirt from around the master cylinder fill cap, remove the cap and fill the master cylinder with brake fluid until the level is within ¼ in. of the top edge of the reservoir.

2. Clean off the bleeder screws at all 4 wheel cylinders. The bleeder screws are located on the inside of the brake backing plate or splash shield.

3. Attach a length of rubber hose over the nozzle of the bleeder screw at the wheel to be done first. Place the other end of the hose in a clean jar, submerged in brake fluid.

4. Open the bleeder screw valve ½–¾ turn.

5. Have an assistant slowly depress the brake pedal. Close the bleeder screw valve and tell your assistant to allow the brake pedal to return slowly. Continue this pumping action to force any air out of the system. When bubbles cease to appear at the end of the bleeder hose, close the bleeder valve and remove the hose.

6. Check the master cylinder fluid

level and add fluid accordingly. Do this after bleeding each wheel.

7. Repeat the bleeding operation at the remaining 3 wheels, ending with the one closest to the master cylinder. Fill the master cylinder reservoir.

Centralizing the Pressure Differential Valve

After any repair or bleeding of the primary (front brake) or secondary (rear brake) system, the dual-brake system warning light will usually remain illuminated due to the pressure differential valve remaining in the off-center position.

To centralize the pressure differential valve and turn off the warning light after the systems have been bled, follow the procedure below.

1. Turn the ignition switch to the ACC or ON position.

2. Check the fluid level in the master cylinder reservoirs and fill them to within ¼ in. of the top with brake fluid, as necessary.

3. Depress the brake pedal and the piston should center itself causing the brake warning light to go out.

4. Turn the ignition switch to the OFF position.

5. Before driving the vehicle, check the operation of the brakes and be sure that a firm pedal is obtained.

Front Disc Brakes

All 1975–77 models have front disc brakes. The E-100 and E-150 use a sliding caliper, single piston brake; the 1975 E-250 and E-350 use a floating caliper, dual piston brake; and the 1976–77 E-250 and E-350 use a rail sliding caliper, dual piston brake. Both the floating and sliding calipers are allowed to move slightly to align with the disc (rotor). The floating caliper is retained by through-bolts, and the sliding caliper by a key.

PADS

Inspection

1. Support the front end on jackstands.
2. Remove the wheel and tire.

3. Visually inspect the thickness of the pad linings through the ends and top of the caliper. Minimum acceptable pad thickness is $1/32$ in. from the rivet heads on riveted linings and $1/32$ in. lining thickness on bonded linings. Unless you want to remove the pads to measure the actual thickness from the rivet heads, you will have to make the limit for riveted lining visual inspection $1/16$ in. or more. The same applies if you don't know what kind of lining you have.

NOTE: *These manufacturer's specifications may not agree with your state inspection law.*

Removal and Installation

E-100 and E-150

1. Remove and discard some of the fluid from the master cylinder without contaminating the contents to avoid overflow later on.

2. Support the front suspension on jackstands. Remove the wheel and tire.

3. Put an 8 in. C-clamp over the caliper and use it to push the outer pad in and pull the caliper out. This bottoms the caliper piston in its bore.

4. Remove the key retaining screw. Drive the caliper support key and spring out toward the outside, using a brass drift.

5. Push the caliper down and rotate the upper end up and out. Support the caliper, so as not to damage the brake hose.

6. Remove the outer pad from the caliper. You may have to tap it to loosen it. Remove the inner pad, removing the anti-rattle clip from the lower end of the shoe.

7. Thoroughly clean the sliding contact areas on the caliper and spindle assembly.

8. Put the new anti-rattle clip on the lower end of the new inner pad. Put the pad and clip in the pad abutment with the clip tab against the abutment and the loop-type spring away from the disc. Compress the clip and slide the upper end of the pad into place.

9. If the caliper piston isn't bottomed, bottom it with a C-clamp.

10. The replacement outer pad may differ slightly from the original equipment. Put the outer pad in place and press the tabs into place with your fingers. You can press the pad in with a C-clamp, but be careful of the lining.

11. Position the caliper on the spindle assembly by pivoting it around the upper mounting surface. Be careful of the boot.

12. Use a screwdriver to hold the upper machined surface of the caliper against the support assembly. Drive a new key and spring assembly into place with a plastic mallet. Install the retaining screw and tighten to 12–20 ft lbs.

13. Replace the wheels and tires and lower the truck to the floor. Fill the master cylinder as specified in Chapter 1. Depress the brake pedal firmly several times to seat the pads on the disc. Don't drive until you get a firm pedal.

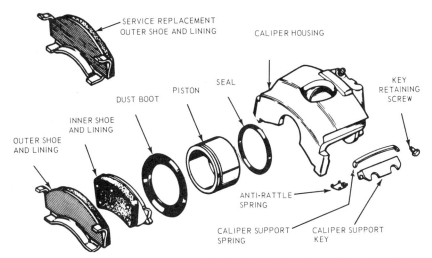

The sliding caliper, single piston, disc brake used on the E-100 and E-150

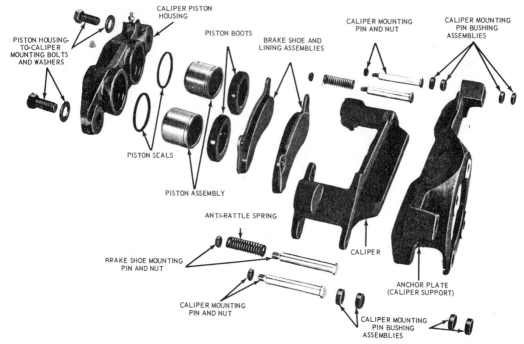

CALIPER PISTON HOUSING

PISTON BOOTS

BRAKE SHOE AND LINING ASSEMBLIES

CALIPER MOUNTING PIN AND NUT

CALIPER MOUNTING PIN BUSHING ASSEMBLIES

PISTON HOUSING-TO-CALIPER MOUNTING BOLTS AND WASHERS

PISTON SEALS

PISTON ASSEMBLY

ANTI-RATTLE SPRING

BRAKE SHOE MOUNTING PIN AND NUT

CALIPER

CALIPER MOUNTING PIN AND NUT

ANCHOR PLATE (CALIPER SUPPORT)

CALIPER MOUNTING PIN BUSHING ASSEMBLIES

The floating caliper, dual piston disc brake used on the 1975 E-250 and E-350

1975 E-250 AND E-350

1. Remove and discard some of the fluid from the master cylinder without contaminating the contents to avoid overflow later on.

2. Support the front suspension on jackstands. Remove the wheel and tire.

3. Remove the pad mounting pins, anti-rattle springs, and the pads.

4. Loosen the piston housing to caliper mounting bolts enough to put in the new pads. Do not move the pistons.

5. Install the new pads, mounting pins, and anti-rattle springs. Be sure the spring tangs engage the pad holes. Tighten the pad mounting pins to 17–23 ft lbs.

6. Tighten the piston housing bolts evenly and squarely to reset the pistons in the cylinders. Torque them to 155–185 ft lbs.

7. Replace the wheels and tires and lower the truck to the floor. Fill the master cylinder as specified in Chapter 1. Depress the brake pedal firmly several times to seat the pads on the disc. Don't drive till you get a firm pedal.

1976–77 E-250 AND E-350

1. Remove and discard some of the fluid from the master cylinder without

contaminating the contents to avoid overflow later on.

2. Support the front suspension on jackstands. Remove the wheel and tire.

3. Remove the key retaining screw. Drive the key and spring out toward the inside, using a brass drift.

4. Rotate the key end of the caliper out and away from the disc. Slide the opposite end clear and support the caliper, to prevent brake hose damage.

5. Remove the pad anti-rattle spring and both pads.

6. Thoroughly clean the sliding contact areas on the caliper and support.

7. Put the old inner pad back in place and use a C-clamp to force the pad and pistons back, until the pistons bottom. Make sure the pistons are bottomed.

8. Install the new pads and anti-rattle spring.

9. Put the caliper rail into the support slide and rotate the caliper onto the disc.

10. Put the key and spring in place and start them by hand. The spring should be between the key and caliper and the spring ends should overlap the key. If necessary, use a screwdriver to hold the caliper against the support assembly. Drive the key and spring into position, aligning the correct notch with the hole

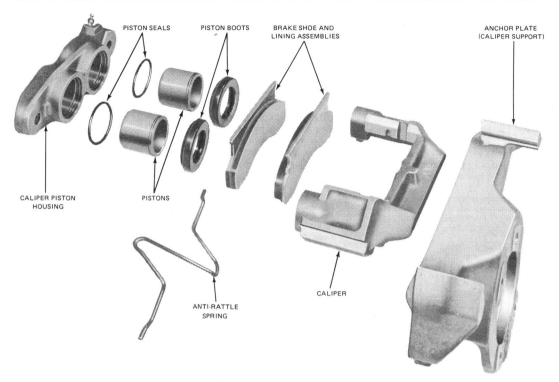

PISTON SEALS — PISTON BOOTS — BRAKE SHOE AND LINING ASSEMBLIES — ANCHOR PLATE (CALIPER SUPPORT) — CALIPER PISTON HOUSING — PISTONS — ANTI-RATTLE SPRING — CALIPER

The rail sliding caliper, dual piston disc brake used on the 1976–77 E-250 and E-350

in the support. Install the key retaining screw and tighten to 12–20 ft lbs.

11. Replace the wheels and tires and lower the truck to the floor. Fill the master cylinder as specified in Chapter 1. Depress the brake pedal firmly several times to seat the pads on the disc. Don't drive till you get a firm pedal.

CALIPER

Removal and Installation

E-100 AND E-150

1. Support the front end on jackstands. Remove the wheel and tire.

2. Disconnect the brake hose. Cap the hose and plug the caliper.

3. Remove the caliper and pads as described under Pad Removal and Installation.

4. Check for leakage. A small amount of wetness inside the boot is normal. Clean the sliding contact areas on the support and caliper.

5. Replace the pads and caliper, connect the hose with a new washer, and bleed the system of air.

6. Replace the wheel and tire.

1975 E-250 AND E-350

1. Support the front end on jackstands. Remove the wheel and tire.

2. Disconnect the brake hose. Cap the hose and plug the caliper.

3. Remove the pins and nuts holding the caliper to the anchor plate and remove the caliper.

4. Grease the pins lightly before installation. Tighten the nuts to 17–23 ft lbs. Use a new brake hose washer.

5. Bleed the system of air.

6. Replace the wheel and tire.

1976–77 E-250 AND E-350

1. Support the front end on jackstands. Remove the wheel and tire.

2. Disconnect the brake hose. Cap the hose and plug the caliper.

3. Remove the key retaining screw and drive the key out with a brass drift.

4. Rotate the key end of the caliper out and slide the other end out.

5. Thoroughly clean the sliding areas.

6. To install, position the caliper rail into the slide on the support and rotate the caliper onto the rotor. Start the key

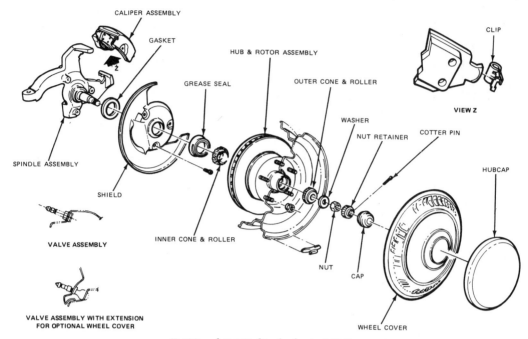

E-100 and E-150 disc brake installation

and spring by hand. The spring should be between the key and caliper and the spring ends should overlap the key. If necessary, use a screwdriver to hold the caliper against the support assembly. Drive the key and spring into position, aligning the correct notch with the hole in the support. Install the key retaining screw and tighten to 12–20 ft lbs.

7. Bleed the system of air. Replace the wheel and tire and lower the truck to the floor.

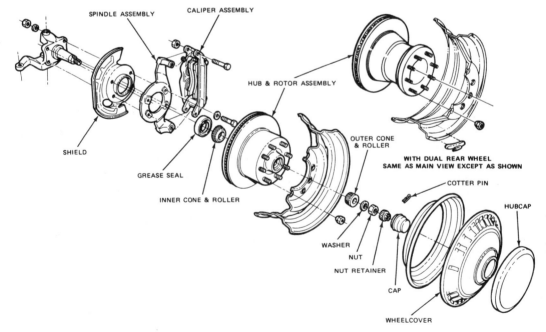

1975 E-250 and E-350 disc brake installation

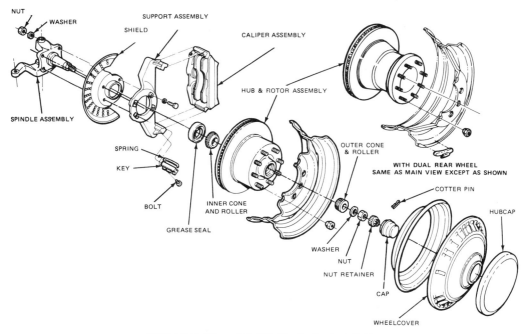

NUT
WASHER
SHIELD
SUPPORT ASSEMBLY
CALIPER ASSEMBLY
HUB & ROTOR ASSEMBLY
SPINDLE ASSEMBLY
SPRING
KEY
BOLT
INNER CONE AND ROLLER
GREASE SEAL
OUTER CONE & ROLLER
WITH DUAL REAR WHEEL
SAME AS MAIN VIEW EXCEPT AS SHOWN
COTTER PIN
HUBCAP
WASHER
NUT
NUT RETAINER
CAP
WHEELCOVER

1976–77 E-250 and E-350 disc brake installation

DISC (ROTOR)

Removal and Installation

This is covered in Chapter 1 under Front Wheel Bearing Packing and Adjustment.

Inspection

If the disc shows heavy scoring or rust, it should be refinished. The final thickness should not be less than the minimum amount marked on the disc hub. No more than .020 in. may be machined equally off each side. Runout, measured at a point 1 in. from the edge with a dial indicator, must not exceed .010 in. total within a 6 in. span.

Drum Brakes

BRAKE DRUMS

Removal and Installation

CAUTION: *Do not blow the brake dust out of the drums with an air hose. Powdered asbestos has been found to be a cancer producing agent, when inhaled.*

FRONT

1. Raise the vehicle until the tire clears the floor.

2. Remove the wheel cover or hub cap and the wheel bearing dust cap. Remove the cotter pin, nut lock, nut and washer.

3. Pull the brake drum approximately 2 in. out, then push it back into position. Remove the wheel bearing and pull off the brake drum and hub assembly. Back off on the brake adjustment if the brake drum will not slip over the brake shoes.

To install the brake drums:

4. If the hub and drum assembly are to be replaced, remove the protective coating from a new drum with carburetor degreaser. Install new bearings and a new grease seal. Pack the wheel bearings. If the original drum is being used, be sure that the hub is clean and lubricated adequately.

5. Install the drum assembly, outer wheel bearing, washer, and adjusting nut.

6. Adjust the wheel bearing, install the nut lock and cotter pin, and the grease cap.

7. Install the wheel and hub cap. Adjust the brake shoes if they were backed off to remove the drum.

Rear

E-100, E-150, and E-200

1. Raise the vehicle so that the wheel to be worked on is clear of the floor and install jackstands under the vehicle.

2. Remove the hub cap and the wheel/tire assembly. Remove the 3 retaining nuts and remove the brake drum. It may be necessary to back off the brake shoe adjustment in order to remove the brake drum. This is because the drum might be grooved or worn from being in service for an extended period of time.

3. Before installing a new brake drum, be sure to remove any protective coating with carburetor degreaser.

4. Install the brake drum in the reverse order of removal and adjust the brakes.

E-250, E-300, and E-350

This procedure is covered thoroughly in Chapter 1 under Rear Wheel Bearing Packing and Adjustment. It requires removing the axle shaft.

Inspection

After the brake drum has been removed from the vehicle, it should be inspected for run-out, severe scoring, cracks, and the proper inside diameter.

Minor scores on a brake drum can be removed with fine emery cloth, provided that all grit is removed from the drum before it is installed on the vehicle.

A badly scored, rough, or out-of-round (run-out) drums can be ground or turned on a brake drum lathe. Do not remove any more material from the drum than is necessary to provide a smooth surface for the brake shoe to contact. The maximum diameter of the braking surface is shown on the inside of each brake drum. Brake drums that exceed the maximum braking surface diameter shown on the brake drum, either through wear or refinishing, must be replaced. This is because after the outside wall of the brake drum reaches a certain thickness (thinner than the original thickness) the drum loses its ability to dissipate the heat created by the friction between the brake drum and the brake shoes, when the brakes are applied. Also, the brake drum will have more tendency to warp and/or crack.

The maximum braking surface diameter specification, which is shown on each drum, allows for a 0.060 in. machining cut over the original nominal drum diameter plus 0.030 in. additional wear before reaching the diameter where the drum must be discarded. Use a brake drum micrometer to measure the inside diameter of the brake drums.

BRAKE SHOES

Removal and Installation

E-100, E-150, and E-200

1. Raise and support the vehicle and remove the wheel and brake drum from the wheel to be worked on.

NOTE: *If you have never replaced brakes before and are not too familiar with the procedures involved, only disassemble and assemble one side at a time, leaving the other side intact as a reference during reassembly.*

2. Install a clamp over the ends of the wheel cylinder to prevent the pistons of the wheel cylinder from coming out, causing loss of fluid and much grief.

3. Contract the brake shoes by pulling the self-adjusting lever away from the starwheel adjustment screw and turn the starwheel up and back until the pivot nut is drawn onto the starwheel as far as it will come.

4. Pull the adjusting lever, cable and automatic adjuster spring down and toward the rear to unhook the pivot hook from the large hole in the secondary shoe web. Do not attempt to pry the pivot hook from the hole.

5. Remove the automatic adjuster spring and the adjusting lever.

6. Remove the secondary shoe-to-anchor spring with a brake tool. (Brake tools are very common implements and are available at auto parts stores). Remove the primary shoe-to-anchor spring and unhook the cable anchor. Remove the anchor pin plate.

7. Remove the cable guide from the secondary shoe.

8. Remove the shoe hold-down springs, shoes, adjusting screw, pivot nut, and socket. Note the color of each hold-down spring for assembly. To remove the hold-down springs, reach behind the brake backing plate and place one finger on the end of one of the brake hold-down spring mounting pins. Using a pair of

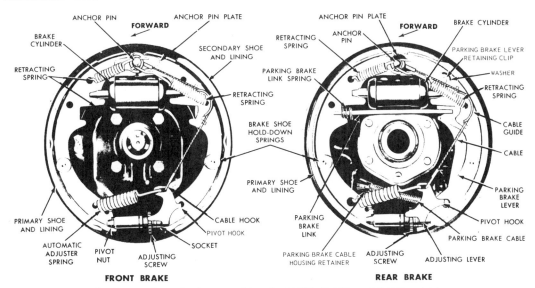

ANCHOR PIN   FORWARD   ANCHOR PIN PLATE
BRAKE CYLINDER
SECONDARY SHOE AND LINING
RETRACTING SPRING
RETRACTING SPRING
PARKING BRAKE LINK SPRING
RETRACTING SPRING
BRAKE SHOE HOLD-DOWN SPRINGS
PRIMARY SHOE AND LINING
PRIMARY SHOE AND LINING
AUTOMATIC ADJUSTER SPRING
PIVOT NUT
ADJUSTING SCREW
SOCKET
PIVOT HOOK
CABLE HOOK
PARKING BRAKE LINK

ANCHOR PIN PLATE   FORWARD   BRAKE CYLINDER
ANCHOR PIN
RETRACTING SPRING
PARKING BRAKE LEVER RETAINING CLIP
WASHER
RETRACTING SPRING
CABLE GUIDE
CABLE
PARKING BRAKE LEVER
PIVOT HOOK
PARKING BRAKE CABLE
PARKING BRAKE CABLE HOUSING RETAINER
ADJUSTING SCREW
ADJUSTING LEVER

FRONT BRAKE   **REAR BRAKE**

The front and rear brake assemblies for E-100, E-150, and E-200 vehicles

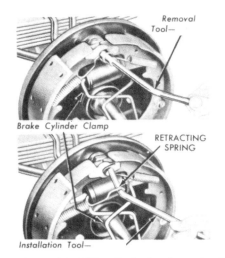

Removal Tool—

Brake Cylinder Clamp

RETRACTING SPRING

Installation Tool—

Removing and installing the brake shoe retracting springs with a brake spring tool

pliers, grasp the washer-type retainer on top of the hold-down spring that corresponds to the pin which you are holding. Push down on the pliers and turn them 90° to align the slot in the washer with the head on the spring mounting pin. Remove the spring and washer retainer and repeat this operation on the hold-down spring on the other shoe.

9. On rear brakes, remove the parking brake link and spring. Disconnect the parking brake cable from the parking brake lever.

10. After removing the rear brake secondary shoe, disassemble the parking brake lever from the shoe by removing the retaining clip and spring washer.

To assemble and install the brake shoes:

11. On rear brakes, assemble the parking brake lever to the secondary shoe and secure with it with the spring washer and retaining clip.

12. Apply a *light* coating of Lubriplate® at the points where the brake shoes contact the backing plate.

13. Position the brake shoes on the backing plate, and install the hold-down spring pins, springs, and spring washer-type retainers. On the rear brake, install the parking brake link, spring and washer. Connect the parking brake cable to the parking brake lever.

14. Install the anchor pin plate, and place the cable anchor over the anchor pin with the crimped side toward the backing plate.

15. Install the primary shoe-to-anchor spring with the brake tool.

16. Install the cable guide on the secondary shoe web with the flanged holes fitted into the hole in the secondary shoe web. Thread the cable around the cable guide groove.

17. Install the secondary shoe-to-anchor (long) spring. Be sure that the cable end is not cocked or binding on the anchor pin when installed. All of the parts should be flat on the anchor pin. Remove the wheel cylinder piston clamp.

18. Apply Lubriplate® to the threads and the socket end of the adjusting star-

wheel screw. Turn the adjusting screw into the adjusting pivot nut to the limit of the threads and then back off ½ turn.

NOTE: *Interchanging the brake shoe adjusting screw assemblies from one side of the vehicle to the other would cause the brake shoes to retract rather than expand each time the automatic adjusting mechanism operated. To prevent this, the socket end of the adjusting screw is stamped with an "R" or an "L" for RIGHT or LEFT. The adjusting pivot nuts can be distinguished by the number of lines machined around the body of the nut; one line indicates left-hand nut and two lines indicates a right-hand nut.*

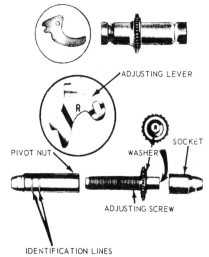

ADJUSTING LEVER

PIVOT NUT

WASHER

SOCKET

ADJUSTING SCREW

IDENTIFICATION LINES

Identification of the rear brake adjusting screws and self-adjusting lever components, the one at the top is for the E-250, E-300, and E-350.

19. Place the adjusting socket on the screw and install this assembly between the shoe ends with the adjusting screw nearest to the secondary shoe.

20. Place the cable hook into the hole in the adjusting lever from the backing plate side. The adjusting levers are stamped with an "R" (right) or an "L" (left) to indicate their installation on the right or left-hand brake assembly.

21. Position the hooked end of the adjuster spring in the primary shoe web and connect the loop end of the spring to the adjuster lever hole.

22. Pull the adjuster lever, cable and automatic adjuster spring down toward the rear to engage the pivot hook in the large hole in the secondary shoe web.

23. After installation, check the action of the adjuster by pulling the section of the cable between the cable guide and the adjusting lever toward the secondary shoe web far enough to lift the lever past a tooth on the adjusting screw starwheel. The lever should snap into position behind the next tooth, and release of the cable should cause the adjuster spring to return the lever to its original position. This return action of the lever will turn the adjusting screw starwheel one tooth. The lever should contact the adjusting screw starwheel one tooth above the centerline of the adjusting screw.

If the automatic adjusting mechanism does not perform properly, check the following:

1. Check the cable and fittings. The cable ends should fill or extend slightly beyond the crimped section of the fittings. If this is not the case, replace the cable.

2. Check the cable guide for damage. The cable groove should be parallel to the shoe web, and the body of the guide should lie flat against the web. Replace the cable guide if this is not so.

3. Check the pivot hook on the lever. The hook surfaces should be square with the body on the lever for proper pivoting. Repair or replace the hook as necessary.

4. Make sure that the adjusting screw starwheel is properly seated in the notch in the shoe web.

E-250, E-300, AND E-350

1. Raise and support the vehicle.

2. Remove the wheel and drum.

3. On a front wheel, remove the spring clip retainer fastening the adjustment cable anchor fitting to the brake anchor pin. On a rear wheel, remove the parking brake lever assembly retaining nut from behind the backing plate and remove the parking brake lever assembly.

NOTE: *From this point on, the removal of the front and rear brakes is the same.*

4. Remove the adjusting cable assembly from the anchor pin, cable guide, and adjusting lever.

5. Remove the brake shoe retracting springs.

6. Remove the brake shoe hold-down spring from each shoe.

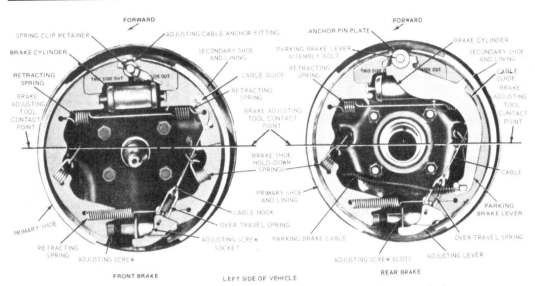

The front and rear brake assemblies for E-250, E-300 and E-350 vehicles

7. Remove the brake shoes and adjusting screw assembly.

8. Disassemble the adjusting screw assembly.

To install the brake shoes:

9. Clean the ledge pads on the backing plate. Apply a light coat of Lubriplate to the ledge pads (where the brake shoes rub the backing plate).

10. Apply Lubriplate to the adjusting screw assembly and the hold-down and retracting spring contacts on the brake shoes.

11. Install the upper retracting spring on the primary and secondary shoes and position the shoe assembly on the backing plate with the wheel cylinder pushrods in the shoe slots.

12. Install the brake shoe hold-down springs.

13. Install the brake shoe adjustment screw assembly with the slot in the head

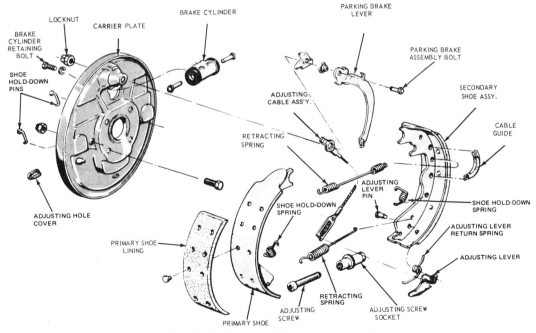

E-250, E-300, and E-350 rear brake details

of the adjusting screw toward the primary shoe, lower retracting spring, adjusting lever spring, adjusting lever assembly, and connect the adjusting cable to the adjusting lever. Position the cable in the cable guide and install the cable anchor fitting on the anchor pin.

14. Install the adjusting screw assemblies in the same locations from which they were removed. Interchanging the brake shoe adjusting screws from one side of the vehicle to the other will cause the brake shoes to retract rather than expand each time the automatic adjusting mechanism is operated. To prevent incorrect installation, the socket end of each adjusting screw is stamped with an R or an L to indicate their installation on the right or left-side of the vehicle. The adjusting pivot nuts can be distinguished by the number of lines machined around the body of the nut. Two lines indicate a right-hand nut; one line indicates a left-hand nut.

15. On a rear wheel, install the parking brake assembly in the anchor pin and secure with the retaining nut behind the backing plate.

16. Adjust the brakes before installing the brake drums and wheels. Install the brake drums and wheels.

17. Lower the vehicle and road test the brakes. New brakes may pull to one side or the other before they are seated. Continued pulling or erratic braking should not occur.

WHEEL CYLINDERS

NOTE: *Front brake lining life can be increased on 1969–74 E-200 and E-300 models by decreasing the size of the front wheel cylinders and increasing the size of the rear. Front cylinders are decreased from $1^1/8$ in. to $1^1/16$ in., E-200 rear cylinders are increased from $^{13}/_{16}$ in. to $^7/_8$ in., E-300 rear cylinders are increased from $^7/_8$ in. to $^{15}/_{16}$ in. The necessary part numbers are given in Ford Technical Service Bulletin No. 86 of March 21, 1975.*

Overhaul

Wheel cylinder rebuilding kits are available for reconditioning the wheel cylinders. The kits usually contain new cup springs, cylinder cups, and in some cases, new boots. The most important factor to keep in mind when rebuilding wheel cylinders is cleanliness. Keep all dirt away from the wheel cylinders when you are reassembling them.

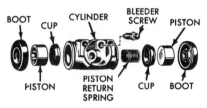

An exploded view of a wheel cylinder

1. To remove the wheel cylinder, jack up the vehicle and remove the wheel, hub, and drum.

2. Disconnect the brake line at the fitting on the brake backing plate.

3. Remove the brake assemblies.

4. Remove the screws which hold the wheel cylinder to the backing plate and remove the wheel cylinder from the vehicle.

5. Remove the rubber dust covers on the ends of the cylinder. Remove the pistons and piston cups and the spring. Remove the bleeder screw and make sure that it is not plugged.

6. Discard all of the parts which the rebuilding kit will replace.

7. Examine the inside of the cylinder. If it is severely rusted, pitted or scratched, then the cylinder must be replaced as the piston cups won't be able to seal against the walls of the cylinder.

8. Using a wheel cylinder hone or emergy cloth and crocus cloth, polish the inside of the cylinder. The purpose of this is to put a new surface on the inside of the cylinder. Keep the inside of the cylinder coated with brake fluid while honing.

9. Wash out the cylinder with clean brake fluid after honing.

10. When reassembling the cylinder, dip all of the parts in clean brake fluid. Assemble the wheel cylinder in the reverse order of removal and disassembly.

BRAKE BACKING PLATE

Removal and Installation

1. In order to remove the brake backing plate, the brake assemblies must be removed.

2. Disconnect the hydraulic line from

the wheel cylinder and submerge the end of the line in a container of brake fluid to minimize brake fluid loss and bleeding.

3. Remove the wheel cylinder.

4. On rear brakes, remove the parking brake lever from the cable. Rotate the flanged axle shaft so that the hole in the axle shaft flange aligns with the backing plate retaining nuts, then remove the nuts. Remove the axle shaft. Lift off the backing plate.

5. On the front brake assemblies, remove the capscrews which retain the backing plate to the spindle and remove the backing plate.

6. Install the backing plate in the reverse order of removal.

Parking Brake

Adjustment

1966–67

1. Make a few stops in reverse to make sure the rear drum brakes are fully adjusted.

2. Raise and support the rear axle.

3. Pull the parking brake handle up one notch from the release position.

4. Loosen the locknut on the cable equalizer (under the truck).

5. Tighten the adjusting nut until a slight drag is felt when turning the rear wheels forward.

6. Tighten the locknut to hold the adjustment.

7. Release the parking brake handle. There should be no drag at the rear wheels.

1968–77

The factory-recommended procedure is to use a tension gauge on the cables with the handle fully applied (1968–74) or with the pedal pushed down two clicks (1975–77). Tension should be 300 lbs. for 1968–74 E-100 and 200, 225 lbs for 1968–74 E-300, and 70 lbs. for 1975–77. If the tension gauge is not available, a method similar to that explained for 1966–67 models can be used. The most important point is to make sure that there is no drag when the brake is released and that the brake locks the wheel when fully applied. If there is brake shoe drag after adjustment on E-250, 300, and 350 models, remove the drums and check the clearance between the parking brake operating lever and the cam plate. It should be .015 in. with the parking brake released.

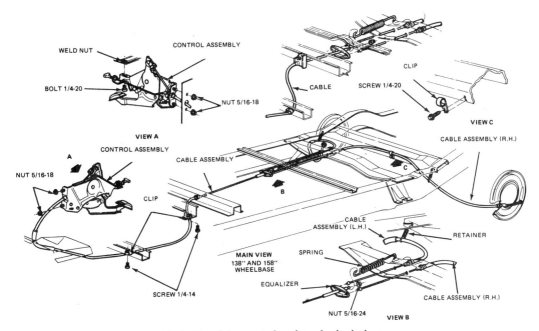

1975–77 pedal-operated parking brake linkage

Brake Specifications
(All measurements given in in.)

Year	Model	Master Cylinder Bore	Wheel Cylinder Bore		Brake Drum Diameter
			Front	Rear	
1966–69	All	1.0	1.125	0.8125	10.00
1970–74	E-100, E-200	1.0	1.125	0.8125	10.00①
	E-300	1.0	1.125	0.8750	12.00
1975	E-100, E-150	——	2.875	0.8125	10.00
	E-250	——	2.180	0.8125	11.03
	E-350	——	2.180	0.8750	12.00
1976–77	E-100, E-150	——	2.875	0.9375	11.03
	E-250	——	2.180	1.0000	12.00
	E-350	——	2.180	1.0620	12.00

① 11.03 in. on E-200
—— Not specified

Chapter 10

Body

Doors

Removal and Installation

FRONT DOORS

1. Remove the screws which hold the door to the hinge (1968–77 models) or the hinge to the door post (1966–67 models).

Remove any access panels to gain access to the retaining bolts.

2. Slide the door off the hinges (1968–77 models) or lift the door from the vehicle with the hinges attached (1966–67 models).

NOTE: *The 1966–67 models have rivets which retain the door to the hinges. In order to remove the hinges from the door, the rivets must be drilled out*

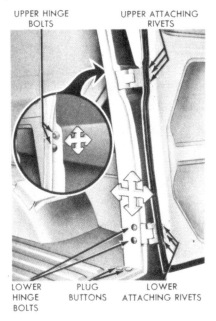

Rear cargo door hinge adjustment on 1966–67 models

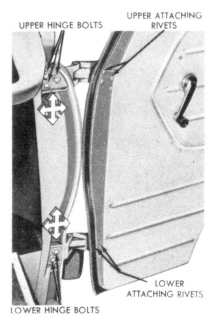

Front door hinge adjustment on 1966–67 models

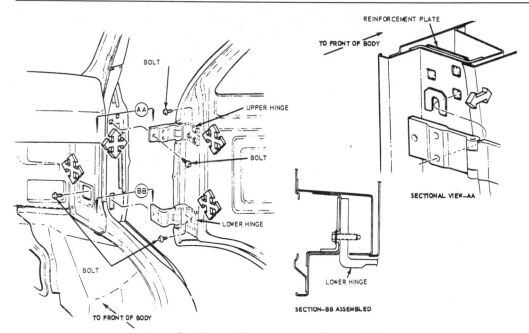

Front door hinge adjustment on 1968–74 models

with a 1 in. drill and replaced with nuts, bolts, and lockwashers.

3. Install the doors in the reverse order of removal. Do not tighten any of the attaching bolts until the door and door latch are aligned with the latch striker and the surrounding body panels. On the 1968–77 models, all of the attaching bolt holes are elongated to be adjustable in all directions. On the 1966–67 models, only the hinge-to-body attaching bolts are adjustable.

Side and Rear Hinged Cargo Doors

The rear and side cargo doors are removed, installed and adjusted in the same manner as described above for the front doors.

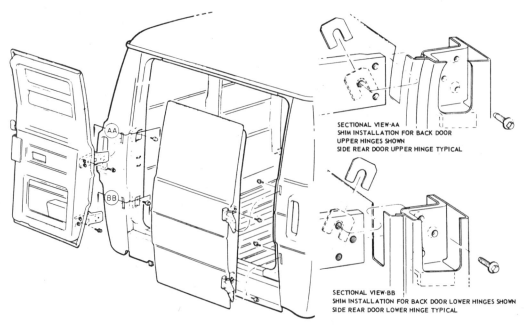

Rear cargo door hinge adjustment on 1968–74 models

Sliding Door Adjustment

1. To adjust the upper edge of the door in or out, loosen the upper roller retaining nut and move the roller in or out.

2. To adjust the lower front door edge in or out, support the door so it won't move up or down and loosen the guide assembly retaining screws. Move it forward to bring the door in and back to move it out.

3. To move the front of the door up or

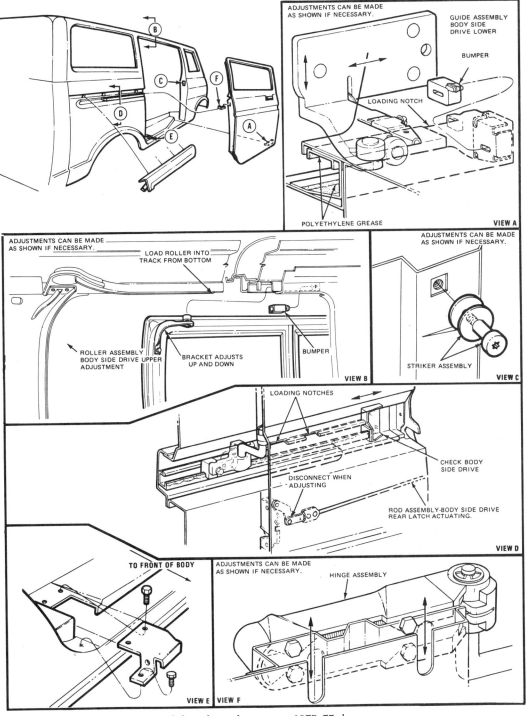

Sliding door adjustments, 1975–77 shown

down, loosen the three lower guide attaching screws and rotate the guide around the lower screw. Loosen the upper roller bracket assembly screws and adjust so that the bottom edge of the roller assembly is about $1/16$ in. from the bottom flange of the upper track.

4. To move the rear edge of the door up or down, remove the trim panel or plug buttons. With the door open, loosen the hinge assembly screws and move the hinge assembly up or down.

5. The rear latch striker assembly can be adjusted up or down and in or out.

6. To adjust the door fore and aft, remove the nuts holding the center track shield. Remove the nuts and screws from outside the truck. Remove the shield. Loosen the three hinge check bolts. Re-move the B pillar post trim panel. Loosen the two striker bolts and remove the striker. Fit the door and adjust the door check so that it is fully engaged with the upper hinge lever and the check bumper is fully depressed with the hinge casting. Install the front striker and add or remove shims to obtain proper front latch operations.

Hood

Alignment

On those vehicles equipped with a hood, the hood can be adjusted fore and

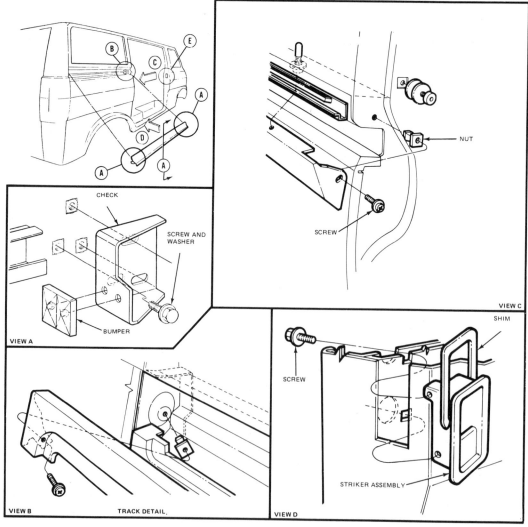

More sliding door adjustments, 1975–77 shown

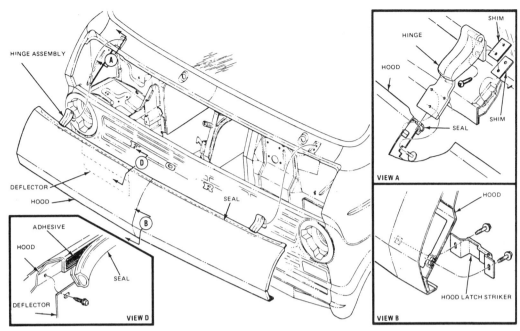

1968–74 Hood assembly installation

aft and up and down to obtain the proper clearance. To adjust the hood, loosen the hood-to-hinge attaching screws until they are just snug. Then, reposition the hood as required, and tighten the attaching screws. On 1968–74 models, the hood is adjusted up and down by placing shims between the hinge and the body. On 1975–77 models, loosen the hinge to cowl attaching screws for up and down adjustment. After the hood has been adjusted, check the hood latch and striker adjustment. Adjust the hood latch and striker as required.

Pickup Tailgate

Removal and Installation

1. Remove the 2 bolts which retain the hinges to the rear lower body panel, disconnect the support arms, and remove the tailgate and hinges from the truck.
2. Position the tailgate and hinges to the rear lower body panel and install the hinge retaining bolts.
3. Connect the support arms.

Fuel Tank

Removal and Installation

1. Raise the rear of the vehicle.
2. To avoid electrical sparking at the tank, disconnect the ground cable on the vehicle battery. Then disconnect the fuel gauge sending unit wire at the fuel tank.
3. Remove the fuel tank drain plug and drain the fuel into a suitable container. It will be necessary to siphon the fuel out of the tank on 1975–77 models.
   CAUTION: *Use some sort of siphon pump; do not start the siphon by mouth.*
4. Loosen the hose clamps, slide the clamps forward and disconnect the fuel line at the fuel gauge sending unit. Disconnect the fuel tank vapor lines, if so equipped, by removing the clamps at the emission control valve.
5. If the fuel gauge sending unit is to be removed, turn the unit retaining ring counterclockwise and remove the sending unit, retaining ring, and gasket.
6. Loosen the clamp on the fuel filler pipe hose at the tank, and disconnect the hose at the tank.

7. Remove the strap retaining nut at each tank mounting strap, swing the strap down, and lower the tank enough to gain access to the tank vent hose.

8. Disconnect the fuel tank vent hose at the top of the tank.

9. Lower the tank and remove it from under the vehicle.

10. Install the fuel tank in the reverse order of removal, using a new sealing gasket at the sending unit if it was removed from the tank.

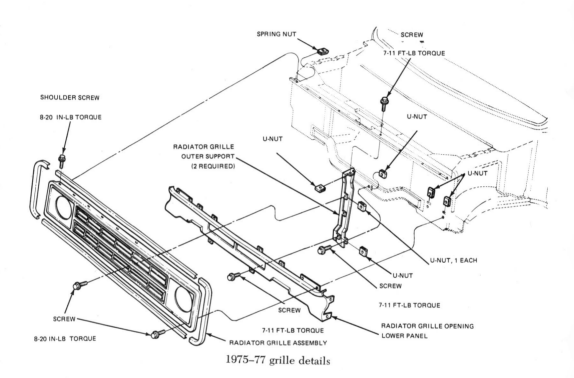

1975–77 grille details

Appendix

General Conversion Table

Multiply by	To convert	To	
2.54	Inches	Centimeters	.3937
30.48	Feet	Centimeters	.0328
.914	Yards	Meters	1.094
1.609	Miles	Kilometers	.621
.645	Square inches	Square cm.	.155
.836	Square yards	Square meters	1.196
16.39	Cubic inches	Cubic cm.	.061
28.3	Cubic feet	Liters	.0353
.4536	Pounds	Kilograms	2.2045
4.226	Gallons	Liters	.264
.068	Lbs./sq. in. (psi)	Atmospheres	14.7
.138	Foot pounds	Kg. m.	7.23
1.014	H.P. (DIN)	H.P. (SAE)	.9861
———	To obtain	From	Multiply by

Note: 1 cm. equals 10 mm.; 1 mm. equals .0394".

Conversion—Common Fractions to Decimals and Millimeters

INCHES			INCHES			INCHES		
Common Fractions	Decimal Fractions	Millimeters (approx.)	Common Fractions	Decimal Fractions	Millimeters (approx.)	Common Fractions	Decimal Fractions	Millimeters (approx.)
1/128	.008	0.20	11/32	.344	8.73	43/64	.672	17.07
1/64	.016	0.40	23/64	.359	9.13	11/16	.688	17.46
1/32	.031	0.79	3/8	.375	9.53	45/64	.703	17.86
3/64	.047	1.19	25/64	.391	9.92	23/32	.719	18.26
1/16	.063	1.59	13/32	.406	10.32	47/64	.734	18.65
5/64	.078	1.98	27/64	.422	10.72	3/4	.750	19.05
3/32	.094	2.38	7/16	.438	11.11	49/64	.766	19.45
7/64	.109	2.78	29/64	.453	11.51	25/32	.781	19.84
1/8	.125	3.18	15/32	.469	11.91	51/64	.797	20.24
9/64	.141	3.57	31/64	.484	12.30	13/16	.813	20.64
5/32	.156	3.97	1/2	.500	12.70	53/64	.828	21.03
11/64	.172	4.37	33/64	.516	13.10	27/32	.844	21.43
3/16	.188	4.76	17/32	.531	13.49	55/64	.859	21.83
13/64	.203	5.16	35/64	.547	13.89	7/8	.875	22.23
7/32	.219	5.56	9/16	.563	14.29	57/64	.891	22.62
15/64	.234	5.95	37/64	.578	14.68	29/32	.906	23.02
1/4	.250	6.35	19/32	.594	15.08	59/64	.922	23.42
17/64	.266	6.75	39/64	.609	15.48	15/16	.938	23.81
9/32	.281	7.14	5/8	.625	15.88	61/64	.953	24.21
19/64	.297	7.54	41/64	.641	16.27	31/32	.969	24.61
5/16	.313	7.94	21/32	.656	16.67	63/64	.984	25.00
21/64	.328	8.33						

Conversion—Millimeters to Decimal Inches

mm	inches	mm	inches	mm	inches	mm	inches	mm	inches
1	.039 370	31	1.220 470	61	2.401 570	91	3.582 670	210	8.267 700
2	.078 740	32	1.259 840	62	2.440 940	92	3.622 040	220	8.661 400
3	.118 110	33	1.299 210	63	2.480 310	93	3.661 410	230	9.055 100
4	.157 480	34	1.338 580	64	2.519 680	94	3.700 780	240	9.448 800
5	.196 850	35	1.377 949	65	2.559 050	95	3.740 150	250	9.842 500
6	.236 220	36	1.417 319	66	2.598 420	96	3.779 520	260	10.236 200
7	.275 590	37	1.456 689	67	2.637 790	97	3.818 890	270	10.629 900
8	.314 960	38	1.496 050	68	2.677 160	98	3.858 260	280	11.032 600
9	.354 330	39	1.535 430	69	2.716 530	99	3.897 630	290	11.417 300
10	.393 700	40	1.574 800	70	2.755 900	100	3.937 000	300	11.811 000
11	.433 070	41	1.614 170	71	2.795 270	105	4.133 848	310	12.204 700
12	.472 440	42	1.653 540	72	2.834 640	110	4.330 700	320	12.598 400
13	.511 810	43	1.692 910	73	2.874 010	115	4.527 550	330	12.992 100
14	.551 180	44	1.732 280	74	2.913 380	120	4.724 400	340	13.385 800
15	.590 550	45	1.771 650	75	2.952 750	125	4.921 250	350	13.779 500
16	.629 920	46	1.811 020	76	2.992 120	130	5.118 100	360	14.173 200
17	.669 290	47	1.850 390	77	3.031 490	135	5.314 950	370	14.566 900
18	.708 660	48	1.889 760	78	3.070 860	140	5.511 800	380	14.960 600
19	.748 030	49	1.929 130	79	3.110 230	145	5.708 650	390	15.354 300
20	.787 400	50	1.968 500	80	3.149 600	150	5.905 500	400	15.748 000
21	.826 770	51	2.007 870	81	3.188 970	155	6.102 350	500	19.685 000
22	.866 140	52	2.047 240	82	3.228 340	160	6.299 200	600	23.622 000
23	.905 510	53	2.086 610	83	3.267 710	165	6.496 050	700	27.559 000
24	.944 880	54	2.125 980	84	3.307 080	170	6.692 900	800	31.496 000
25	.984 250	55	2.165 350	85	3.346 450	175	6.889 750	900	35.433 000
26	1.023 620	56	2.204 720	86	3.385 820	180	7.086 600	1000	39.370 000
27	1.062 990	57	2.244 090	87	3.425 190	185	7.283 450	2000	78.740 000
28	1.102 360	58	2.283 460	88	3.464 560	190	7.480 300	3000	118.110 000
29	1.141 730	59	2.322 830	89	3.503 903	195	7.677 150	4000	157.480 000
30	1.181 100	60	2.362 200	90	3.543 300	200	7.874 000	5000	196.850 000

To change decimal millimeters to decimal inches, position the decimal point where desired on either side of the millimeter measurement shown and reset the inches decimal by the same number of digits in the same direction. For example, to convert 0.001 mm into decimal inches, reset the decimal behind the 1 mm (shown on the chart) to 0.001; change the decimal inch equivalent (0.039″ shown) to 0.000039″.

Tap Drill Sizes

National Fine or S.A.E.		
Screw & Tap Size	Threads Per Inch	Use Drill Number
No. 5	44	37
No. 6	40	33
No. 8	36	29
No. 10	32	21
No. 12	28	15
1/4	28	3
5/16	24	1
3/8	24	Q
7/16	20	W
1/2	20	29/64
9/16	18	33/64
5/8	18	37/64
3/4	16	11/16
7/8	14	13/16
1 1/8	12	1 3/64
1 1/4	12	1 11/64
1 1/2	12	1 27/64

National Coarse or U.S.S.		
Screw & Tap Size	Threads Per Inch	Use Drill Number
No. 5	40	39
No. 6	32	36
No. 8	32	29
No. 10	24	25
No. 12	24	17
1/4	20	8
5/16	18	F
3/8	16	5/16
7/16	14	U
1/2	13	27/64
9/16	12	31/64
5/8	11	17/32
3/4	10	21/32
7/8	9	49/64
1	8	7/8
1 1/8	7	63/64
1 1/4	7	1 7/64
1 1/2	6	1 11/32

Decimal Equivalent Size of the Number Drills

Drill No.	Decimal Equivalent	Drill No.	Decimal Equivalent	Drill No.	Decimal Equivalent
80	.0135	53	.0595	26	.1470
79	.0145	52	.0635	25	.1495
78	.0160	51	.0670	24	.1520
77	.0180	50	.0700	23	.1540
76	.0200	49	.0730	22	.1570
75	.0210	48	.0760	21	.1590
74	.0225	47	.0785	20	.1610
73	.0240	46	.0810	19	.1660
72	.0250	45	.0820	18	.1695
71	.0260	44	.0860	17	.1730
70	.0280	43	.0890	16	.1770
69	.0292	42	.0935	15	.1800
68	.0310	41	.0960	14	.1820
67	.0320	40	.0980	13	.1850
66	.0330	39	.0995	12	.1890
65	.0350	38	.1015	11	.1910
64	.0360	37	.1040	10	.1935
63	.0370	36	.1065	9	.1960
62	.0380	35	.1100	8	.1990
61	.0390	34	.1110	7	.2010
60	.0400	33	.1130	6	.2040
59	.0410	32	.1160	5	.2055
58	.0420	31	.1200	4	.2090
57	.0430	30	.1285	3	.2130
56	.0465	29	.1360	2	.2210
55	.0520	28	.1405	1	.2280
54	.0550	27	.1440		

Decimal Equivalent Size of the Letter Drills

Letter Drill	Decimal Equivalent	Letter Drill	Decimal Equivalent	Letter Drill	Decimal Equivalent
A	.234	J	.277	S	.348
B	.238	K	.281	T	.358
C	.242	L	.290	U	.368
D	.246	M	.295	V	.377
E	.250	N	.302	W	.386
F	.257	O	.316	X	.397
G	.261	P	.323	Y	.404
H	.266	Q	.332	Z	.413
I	.272	R	.339		

ANTI-FREEZE CHART

Temperatures Shown in Degrees Fahrenheit
+32 is Freezing

Cooling System Capacity Quarts	Quarts of **ETHYLENE GLYCOL** Needed for Protection to Temperatures Shown Below													
	1	2	3	4	5	6	7	8	9	10	11	12	13	14
10	+24°	+16°	+ 4°	−12°	−34°	−62°								
11	+25	+18	+ 8	− 6	−23	−47								
12	+26	+19	+10	0	−15	−34	−57°							
13	+27	+21	+13	+ 3	− 9	−25	−45							
14			+15	+ 6	− 5	−18	−34							
15			+16	+ 8	0	−12	−26							
16			+17	+10	+ 2	− 8	−19	−34	−52°					
17			+18	+12	+ 5	− 4	−14	−27	−42					
18			+19	+14	+ 7	0	−10	−21	−34	−50°				
19			+20	+15	+ 9	+ 2	− 7	−16	−28	−42				
20				+16	+10	+ 4	− 3	−12	−22	−34	−48°			
21				+17	+12	+ 6	0	− 9	−17	−28	−41			
22				+18	+13	+ 8	+ 2	− 6	−14	−23	−34	−47°		
23				+19	+14	+ 9	+ 4	− 3	−10	−19	−29	−40		
24				+19	+15	+10	+ 5	0	− 8	−15	−23	−34	−46°	
25				+20	+16	+12	+ 7	+ 1	− 5	−12	−20	−29	−40	−50°
26					+17	+13	+ 8	+ 3	− 3	− 9	−16	−25	−34	−44
27					+18	+14	+ 9	+ 5	− 1	− 7	−13	−21	−29	−39
28					+18	+15	+10	+ 6	+ 1	− 5	−11	−18	−25	−34
29					+19	+16	+12	+ 7	+ 2	− 3	− 8	−15	−22	−29
30					+20	+17	+13	+ 8	+ 4	− 1	− 6	−12	−18	−25

For capacities over 30 quarts divide true capacity by 3. Find quart Anti-Freeze for the 1/3 and multipl by 3 for quarts to add.

For capacities under 10 quarts multiply true capacity by 3. Find quarts Anti-Freeze for the tripled volume and divide by 3 for quarts to add.

To Increase the Freezing Protection of Anti-Freeze Solutions Already Installed

Cooling System Capacity Quarts	Number of Quarts of **ETHYLENE GLYCOL** Anti-Freeze Required to Increase Protection												
	From +20°F. to					From +10°F. to					From 0°F. to			
	0°	−10°	−20°	−30°	−40°	0°	−10°	−20°	−30°	−40°	−10°	−20°	−30°	−40°
10	1 3/4	2 1/4	3	3 1/2	3 3/4	3/4	1 1/2	2 1/4	2 3/4	3 1/4	3/4	1 1/2	2	2 1/2
12	2	2 3/4	3 1/2	4	4 1/2	1	1 3/4	2 1/2	3 1/4	3 3/4	1	1 3/4	2 1/2	3 1/4
14	2 1/4	3 1/4	4	4 3/4	5 1/2	1 1/4	2	3	3 3/4	4 1/2	1	2	3	3 1/2
16	2 1/2	3 1/2	4 1/2	5 1/4	6	1 1/4	2 1/2	3 1/2	4 1/4	5 1/4	1 1/4	2 1/4	3 1/4	4
18	3	4	5	6	7	1 1/2	2 3/4	4	5	5 3/4	1 1/2	2 1/2	3 3/4	4 3/4
20	3 1/4	4 1/2	5 3/4	6 3/4	7 1/2	1 3/4	3	4 1/4	5 1/2	6 1/2	1 1/2	2 3/4	4 1/4	5 1/4
22	3 1/2	5	6 1/4	7 1/4	8 1/4	1 3/4	3 1/4	4 3/4	6	7 1/4	1 3/4	3 1/4	4 1/2	5 1/2
24	4	5 1/2	7	8	9	2	3 1/2	5	6 1/2	7 1/2	1 3/4	3 1/2	5	6
26	4 1/4	6	7 1/2	8 3/4	10	2	4	5 1/2	7	8 1/4	2	3 3/4	5 1/2	6 3/4
28	4 1/2	6 1/4	8	9 1/2	10 1/2	2 1/4	4 1/4	6	7 1/2	9	2	4	5 3/4	7 1/4
30	5	6 3/4	8 1/2	10	11 1/2	2 1/2	4 1/2	6 1/2	8	9 1/2	2 1/4	4 1/4	6 1/4	7 3/4

Test radiator solution with proper hydrometer. Determine from the table the number of quarts of solution to be drawn off from a full cooling system and replace with undiluted anti-freeze, to give the desired increased protection. For example, to increase protection of a 22-quart cooling system containing Ethylene Glycol (permanent type) anti-freeze, from +20°F. to −20°F. will require the replacement of 6 1/4 quarts of solution with undiluted anti-freeze.